T0213958

IFIP Advances in Information and Communication Technology 581

Editor-in-Chief

Kai Rannenberg, Goethe University Frankfurt, Germany

Editorial Board Members

TC 1 – Foundations of Computer Science
  Luís Soares Barbosa⊚, University of Minho, Braga, Portugal
TC 2 – Software: Theory and Practice
  Michael Goedicke, University of Duisburg-Essen, Germany
TC 3 – Education
  Arthur Tatnall⊚, Victoria University, Melbourne, Australia
TC 5 – Information Technology Applications
  Erich J. Neuhold, University of Vienna, Austria
TC 6 – Communication Systems
  Burkhard Stiller, University of Zurich, Zürich, Switzerland
TC 7 – System Modeling and Optimization
  Fredi Tröltzsch, TU Berlin, Germany
TC 8 – Information Systems
  Jan Pries-Heje, Roskilde University, Denmark
TC 9 – ICT and Society
  David Kreps⊚, University of Salford, Greater Manchester, UK
TC 10 – Computer Systems Technology
  Ricardo Reis⊚, Federal University of Rio Grande do Sul, Porto Alegre, Brazil
TC 11 – Security and Privacy Protection in Information Processing Systems
  Steven Furnell⊚, Plymouth University, UK
TC 12 – Artificial Intelligence
  Eunika Mercier-Laurent⊚, University of Reims Champagne-Ardenne, Reims, France
TC 13 – Human-Computer Interaction
  Marco Winckler⊚, University of Nice Sophia Antipolis, France
TC 14 – Entertainment Computing
  Rainer Malaka, University of Bremen, Germany

IFIP – The International Federation for Information Processing

IFIP was founded in 1960 under the auspices of UNESCO, following the first World Computer Congress held in Paris the previous year. A federation for societies working in information processing, IFIP's aim is two-fold: to support information processing in the countries of its members and to encourage technology transfer to developing nations. As its mission statement clearly states:

IFIP is the global non-profit federation of societies of ICT professionals that aims at achieving a worldwide professional and socially responsible development and application of information and communication technologies.

IFIP is a non-profit-making organization, run almost solely by 2500 volunteers. It operates through a number of technical committees and working groups, which organize events and publications. IFIP's events range from large international open conferences to working conferences and local seminars.

The flagship event is the IFIP World Computer Congress, at which both invited and contributed papers are presented. Contributed papers are rigorously refereed and the rejection rate is high.

As with the Congress, participation in the open conferences is open to all and papers may be invited or submitted. Again, submitted papers are stringently refereed.

The working conferences are structured differently. They are usually run by a working group and attendance is generally smaller and occasionally by invitation only. Their purpose is to create an atmosphere conducive to innovation and development. Refereeing is also rigorous and papers are subjected to extensive group discussion.

Publications arising from IFIP events vary. The papers presented at the IFIP World Computer Congress and at open conferences are published as conference proceedings, while the results of the working conferences are often published as collections of selected and edited papers.

IFIP distinguishes three types of institutional membership: Country Representative Members, Members at Large, and Associate Members. The type of organization that can apply for membership is a wide variety and includes national or international societies of individual computer scientists/ICT professionals, associations or federations of such societies, government institutions/government related organizations, national or international research institutes or consortia, universities, academies of sciences, companies, national or international associations or federations of companies.

More information about this series at http://www.springer.com/series/6102

Zhongzhi Shi · Sunil Vadera ·
Elizabeth Chang (Eds.)

Intelligent Information Processing X

11th IFIP TC 12 International Conference, IIP 2020
Hangzhou, China, July 3–6, 2020
Proceedings

Springer

Editors
Zhongzhi Shi
Institute of Computing Technology
Chinese Academy of Sciences
Beijing, China

Sunil Vadera
University of Salford
Manchester, UK

Elizabeth Chang
Australian Defence Force Academy
UNSW Canberra
Canberra, ACT, Australia

ISSN 1868-4238   ISSN 1868-422X (electronic)
IFIP Advances in Information and Communication Technology
ISBN 978-3-030-46933-7   ISBN 978-3-030-46931-3 (eBook)
https://doi.org/10.1007/978-3-030-46931-3

© IFIP International Federation for Information Processing 2020
This work is subject to copyright. All rights are reserved by the Publisher, whether the whole or part of the material is concerned, specifically the rights of translation, reprinting, reuse of illustrations, recitation, broadcasting, reproduction on microfilms or in any other physical way, and transmission or information storage and retrieval, electronic adaptation, computer software, or by similar or dissimilar methodology now known or hereafter developed.
The use of general descriptive names, registered names, trademarks, service marks, etc. in this publication does not imply, even in the absence of a specific statement, that such names are exempt from the relevant protective laws and regulations and therefore free for general use.
The publisher, the authors and the editors are safe to assume that the advice and information in this book are believed to be true and accurate at the date of publication. Neither the publisher nor the authors or the editors give a warranty, expressed or implied, with respect to the material contained herein or for any errors or omissions that may have been made. The publisher remains neutral with regard to jurisdictional claims in published maps and institutional affiliations.

This Springer imprint is published by the registered company Springer Nature Switzerland AG
The registered company address is: Gewerbestrasse 11, 6330 Cham, Switzerland

Preface

This volume comprises of papers presented at the 11th IFIP International Conference on Intelligent Information Processing (IIP 2020). As the world proceeds quickly into the Information Age, it encounters both successes and challenges, and it is well recognized that intelligent information processing provides the key to solve many challenges in the Information Age. Intelligent information processing supports the most advanced techniques that are able to change human life and the world. However, the path to success is never a straight one. Every new technology brings with it many challenging problems, and researchers are in great demand to tackle these. This conference provides a forum for engineers and scientists from research institutes, universities, and industries to report and discuss their latest research progresses in all aspects of intelligent information processing.

We received more than 36 papers, of which 24 papers are included in this program as regular papers and 5 as short papers. All papers submitted were reviewed by three reviewers. We are grateful for the dedicated work of both authors and reviewers.

A conference such as this cannot succeed without help from many individuals who contributed their valuable time and expertise. We want to express our sincere gratitude to the Program Committee members and referees, who invested many hours into reviews and deliberations. They provided detailed and constructive review comments that significantly improved the quality of the papers included in these proceedings.

We are very grateful to have the sponsorship of the following organizations: IFIP TC12, Key Laboratory of Brain Machine Collaborative Intelligence of Zhejiang Province at Hangzhou Dianzi University and Institute of Computing Technology, Chinese Academy of Sciences. We specially thank Wanzeng Kong, Jianhai Zhang and Yang Song for organizing the conference and Xuanyu Jin, Wenfen Ling for carefully checking the proceedings.

Finally, we hope you find this volume inspiring and informative. We wish that the research results reported in these proceedings will lead to exciting new findings in the years to come.

March 2020

Zhongzhi Shi
Sunil Vadera
Elizabeth Chang

Organization

General Chairs

U. Furbach, Germany
B. Goertzel, USA
Q. Wu, China

Program Chairs

Z. Shi, China
S. Vadera, UK
E. Chang, Australia

Local Organizing Committee

Wanzeng Kong (Chair), China
Jianhai Zhang (Co-chair), China
Yang Song (General Secretary), China

Program Committee

B. An, Singapore
E. Chang, Australia
L. Chang, China
S. Ding, China
Q. Dou, China
E. Ehlers, South Africa
J. Feng, China
Y. Feng, China
Z. Feng, China
U. Furbach, Germany
Y. Gao, China
Q. He, China
Z. Huang,
  The Netherlands
S. Jiang, China
F. Kong, China
H. Leung, Hong Kong

G. Li, Australia
Q. Li, China
H. Leung, Hong Kong
H. Ma, China
J. Ma, China
S. Ma, China
X. Mao, China
L. Maglogiannis, Greece
Z. Meng, China
E. Mercier-Laurent,
  France
P. Novias, Portugal
M. Owoc, Poland
Vasile Palade, UK
G. Pan, China
L. Qin, China
A. Rafea, Egypt

Y. H. Shi, China
Z. P. Shi, China
K. Shimohara, Japan
A. Skowron, Poland
I. Timm, Germany
G. Wang, China
P. Wang, USA
Y. Xu, Australia
H. Xiong, USA
Y. Yao, Canada
B. Zhang, China
J. Zhang, China
S. Zhang, China
Z. Zhang, China
J. Zhou, China
Z. Zhou, China
F. Zhuang, China

Abstracts of Keynotes
and Invited Presentations

Tensor Networks and Their Applications in Image and Time Series Reconstruction and Prediction

Andrzej Cichocki

Skolkovo Institute of Science and Technology (SKOLTECH), Russia

Abstract. Tensor factorizations/decompositions and their extensions tensor networks have become emerging techniques in AI and machine learning methods. Tensor networks have already been successfully used over a number of applied areas in machine learning, including deep neural networks, generalized regression, classification, clustering, support tensor machines (STM), tensor canonical correlation analysis (TCCA), higher order partial least squares (HOPLS), multilinear independent component analysis (MLICA), Non-negative Tensor Factorization (NTF), multiway robust PCA (MRPCA), and Higher order SVD.

In this talk, we will start with a brief overview of these applications, and special emphasis will be given to emerging applications in image reconstructions and enhancement, and higher order time series forecasting (TSF).

Behavior Based Artificial Intelligence from the Perspective of Automatic Control

Fuchun Sun

Tsinghua University, China

Abstract. In the development of human society, the invention and use of machinery is an important sign of human beings entering into industrialization, and machinery becomes an independent actuator, which realizes the separation of executor and action instruction sender from us as humans. Furthermore, the emergence of artificial intelligence makes it possible for a machine to become a sender of instructions through interactions with the environment and humans, and as a result, the sender and executor of the instruction are unified as the machine itself. This report systematically analyzes behavior-based artificial intelligence from evolution of automatic control. Then, taking into account the topic "how to sense like a human being," the talk puts forward the framework of robot active perception, introduces the main achievements of the team in visual multi-target detection, visual tactile representation, multimodal fusion, and developmental learning, and tackles "how to operate like a human being" as a problem, providing the main achievements of the team in learning smart operation skills such as active imitation learning and preference learning achievements. Next, taking into account the topic "how to make decision like a human being," some new points are given in terms of micro-size intelligence. Finally, the development trend of robot dexterous operation skill learning under the condition of incomplete information is given.

Tensor Network Representations in Machine Learning

Qibin Zhao

RIKEN AIP, Japan

Abstract. Tensor networks are factorizations of very large tensors into networks of smaller tensors, it is shown to be a general extension of typical tensor decomposition to high dimensional case. Recently, tensor networks are also increasingly finding applications in machine learning such as model compression or acceleration of computations. In this talk, I will first present the general concept of tensor network related research in machine learning, and then introduce our studies on fundamental tensor network model, algorithm, and applications. In particular, the tensor ring decomposition model is introduced and shown to be a powerful and efficient representation. In addition, we will present recent progresses on how tensor networks can be employed to solve challenging problems in tensor completion, multi-task learning, and multi-modal learning.

Uncertainty Between Prediction and Interpretability

Junping Zhang

Fudan University, China

Abstract. The goal of artificial intelligence is to approximate human's minds, making a computer indistinguishable with human beings. In the era of deep learning, we see the prediction performance of computer program is almost superior to that of human. However, the higher the prediction performance, the farther the distance that we reach the real intelligence. In this talk, I will discuss this issue from the view of the uncertainty between prediction and interpretability, and mention some possible direction based on the uncertainty principle.

Neuromorphic Computing Approach to Auditory and Visual Perception

Huajin Tang

Zhejiang University, China

Abstract. Neuromorphic computing has become an important methodology to emulate brain style intelligence. This talk will present an overview of neuromorphic approach to auditory and visual perception and highlight the recent state of the art.

In recent years neuromorphic computing has become an important methodology to emulate brain style intelligence. There has been rapid progress in computational theory, learning algorithms, signal processing, and circuit design and implementation. By using neural spikes to represent the outputs of sensors and for communication between computing blocks, and using spike timing based learning algorithms, neuromorphic computational models and hardware have achieved promising real-time learning performance. This talk will start by introducing the computational principles and architecture found in neural systems, and present a new theme of neuromorphic approach to auditory and visual perception. In neuromorphic vision, the model extracts temporal features embedded in address-event representation (AER) data and discriminates different objects by using spiking neural networks (SNNs). We use multispike encoding to extract temporal features contained in the AER data. These temporal patterns are then learned through a spiking neural network using a supervised learning algorithm. The presented model is consistently implemented in a temporal learning framework, where the precise timing of spikes is considered in the feature-encoding and learning process. For neuromorphic auditor perception, I will introduce a robust multi-label classification model based on deep spiking neural networks to handle multi-pitch estimation tasks. In this model, we propose a novel biological spiking coding method that fits the expression of musical signals. This coding method can encode time, frequency, and intensity information into spatiotemporal spike trains. And the spatio-temporal credit assignment (STCA) algorithm is used to train deep spiking neural networks.

Neuromusicology with Machine Learning – How Human Understands Music

Toshihisa Tanaka

Tokyo University of Agriculture and Technology, Japan

Abstract. This talk addresses my recent neurophysiological studies of music cognition. I will talk about the neural entrainment to the familiarity of a listener with music using both the electroencephalogram (EEG) signals and the music. It is shown that the cross-correlation between EEG and the music when listening to unfamiliar music is significantly stronger than that when listening to familiar music. Moreover, the familiarity of music can be classified by machine learning techniques such as neural networks and support vector machines.

Intelligent Analysis of Brain Imaging for Early Diagnosis of Brain Diseases

Daoqiang Zhang

Nanjing University of Aeronautics and Astronautics, China

Abstract. In recent years, the brain research projects have received considerable public and governmental attention worldwide. Brain imaging technique is an important tool for brain science research. However, due to the high-dimensional, multi-modality, heterogenous, and time-variant characteristics of brain images, it is very challenging to develop both efficient and effective methods for brain image analysis. In this talk, I will introduce our recent works on intelligent methods of brain imaging, based on machine learning techniques. Specifically, this talk will cover the topics including multi-modal brain image fusion and classification, image genomic association analysis, functional alignment and brain network analysis, as well as their applications in early diagnosis of brain disease and brain decoding.

Data-Driven Security Analysis of Machine Learning Systems

Chao Shen

Xi'an Jiaotong University, China

Abstract. Human society is witnessing a wave of machine learning (ML) driven by deep learning techniques, bringing a technological revolution for human production and life. In some specific fields, ML has achieved or even surpassed human-level performance. However, most previous ML theories have not considered the open and even adversarial environments, and the security and privacy issues are gradually rising. Besides of insecure code implementations, biased models, adversarial examples, sensor spoofing can also lead to security risks, which are hard to be discovered by traditional security analysis tools. This talk reviews previous works on ML system security and privacy, revealing potential security and privacy risks. Firstly, we introduce a threat model of ML systems, including attack surfaces, attack capabilities, and attack goals. Secondly, we analyze security risks and countermeasures in terms of four critical components in ML systems: data input (sensor), data preprocessing, ML model, and output. Finally, we discuss future research trends on the security of ML systems. The aim is to rise the attention of the computer security society and the ML society on security and privacy of ML systems, and so that they can work together to unlock ML's potential to build a brighter future.

Contents

Pattern Recognition

Computer Vision and Image Understanding

Machine Learning

A Salient Object Detection Algorithm
Based on Region Merging and Clustering

Weiyi Wei, Yijing Yang[✉], Wanru Wang, Xiufeng Zhao,
and Huifang Ma

College of Computer Science and Engineering, Northwest Normal University,
Lanzhou, Gansu, China
2190438736@qq.com

Abstract. Salient object detection has recently drawn much attention in computer vision such as image compression and object tracking. Currently, various
heuristic computational models have been designed. However, extracting the
salient objects with a complex background in the image is still a challenging
problem. In this paper, we propose a region merging strategy to extract salient
region. Firstly, boundary super-pixels are clustered to generate the initial saliency
maps based on the prior knowledge that the image boundaries are mostly background. Next, adjacent regions are merged by sorting the multiple feature values
of each region. Finally, we get the final saliency maps by merging adjacent or non-
adjacent regions by means of the distance from the region to the image center and
the boundary length of overlapping regions. The experiments demonstrate that
our method performs favorably on three datasets than state-of-art.

Keywords: Salient object detection · Clustering · Region merging

1 Introduction

Salient object detection is an essential problem in computer vision which aims at
highlighting the visually outstanding regions/object/structures from the surrounding
background [1]. It has received substantial attention over the last decade due to its wide
range of applications in image compression [2], behavior recognition [3] and co-
segmentation [4].

According to the human visual systems, salient object detection methods can be
divided into two categories: one is a bottom-up method; the other is the top-down
methods. In the top-down approaches, the salient object obtained in a scene is always
discrepant for different people. Therefore, it is more complex to construct the top-down
salient object detection model, so there are few models for salient object detection. On
the contrary, the bottom-up approach has attracted much attention and many salient
object detection models have been proposed. In the traditional bottom-up methods, the
salient object detection based on spatial and frequency domains. In spatial domains,
Sun et al. [5] propose a salient object detection method for region merging. Shen et al.
[6] propose a unified approach via low-rank matrix recovery. Peng et al. [7] propose a
structured matrix decomposition model to increase the distance between the background and the foreground for salient object detection. Feng et al. [20] propose a salient

© IFIP International Federation for Information Processing 2020
Published by Springer Nature Switzerland AG 2020
Z. Shi et al. (Eds.): IIP 2020, IFIP AICT 581, pp. 3–13, 2020.
https://doi.org/10.1007/978-3-030-46931-3_1

detection method by fusing image color and spatial information to obtain saliency values to separate foreground and background for images. Xu et al. [21] propose a universal edge-oriented framework to get saliency maps. These salient object detection methods mentioned above could basically complete the salient object detection task, but the results are not accurate. Zhao et al. [24] obtain the saliency map by combining sparse reconstruction and energy optimization. Yu et al. [25] construct the quaternion hypercomplex and multiscale wavelet transform to detect the salient object. Guo et al. [26] obtain the saliency map by combining the boundary contrast map and the geodesics-like map. Marcon et al. [27] propose an update to the traditional pipeline, by adding a preliminary filtering stage to detect the salient object. As the demand for application scenarios continues to increase, co-saliency detection method [8] and moving salient object detection method [9] also introduced into the field of salient object detection, but there are also challenges for its application.

In order to improve the accuracy of the salient object detection results, several frequency domain methods have been developed, Hou et al. [10] argue that a salient detection model for spectral residuals. Guo et al. [11] use the spectral phase diagram of the quaternion Fourier transform to detect the spatiotemporal salient object. Achanta et al. [12] exploit color and luminance features detect the salient region by frequency tuning method. Early studies of salient object detection models are designed to predict human eye fixation. It mainly detects salient points where people look rather than salient regions [13]. In [14] for each color subband, the saliency maps are obtained by an inverse DWT over a set of scale-weighted center-surround responses, where the weights are derived from the high-pass wavelet coefficients of each level. Spectrum analysis is easy to understand, computationally efficient and effective, but the relevant interpretation of the frequency domain is unclear.

Nowadays, the deep learning based methods have been applied to saliency detection. Li et al. [22] propose a CNN based saliency detection methods by fusing deep contrast feature and handcrafted low-level features to acquire saliency maps. Li et al. [23] use optimized convolutional neural network extract the high-level features, and then the high-level features and low-level features were fused to obtain the fusion features. Finally, the fusion features were input into SVM to separate the foreground and background for images. However, these two methods have high time complexity.

This paper focuses on the incomplete salient region and unclear boundary of the salient regions in the detection results, we propose a super-pixel level salient object detection method based on clustering and region merging strategy to improve the performance of detecting the salient object in a scene. The work flow of our salient object detection framework is described in Fig. 1. Firstly, the SLIC [15] (Simple Linear Iterative Cluster) algorithm is used for super-pixel segmentation. Secondly, generate the initial saliency maps. This step involves two processes: the super-pixels lie in image boundaries are clustered and calculate the distance between the remaining super-pixels and the classes centers. Color background maps and spatial relationship background maps are calculated by calculating the distance between the super-pixels and the boundary class. Then the color background maps and the spatial relation background maps are combined linearly to produce the initial saliency map. Thirdly, the final saliency maps obtained after two steps regions merging. The first stage is based on the initial saliency map where adjacent regions are merged by taking into account color features and spatial information. The second stage is to calculate the saliency value of the regions and merge the regions according to the saliency value. The main contributions are summarized as follows:

(1) We cluster the boundary super-pixels to generate the initial saliency maps based on the prior knowledge that the image boundaries are mostly background.
(2) A two-stage optimization strategy is proposed to further optimize the saliency. In the first stage, we merge adjacent small regions with identical or similar features. In the second stage, we merge adjacent or no-adjacent regions according to the ranking of regional saliency values.

2 Construction of Initial Saliency Map

Given an image I, we represent it by N super-pixels produced by SLIC. Then M different classes are generated by clustering boundary super-pixels in the CIELab color space with K-means algorithm. We establish an initial saliency map with three steps: (i) Constructing color background maps. (ii) Constructing spatial correlation background maps. (iii) Constructing initial saliency maps. The color background maps and spatial background maps are merged to construct initial saliency maps. The specific process is as follows.

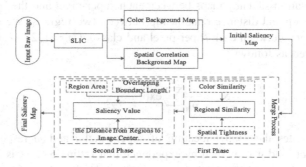

Fig. 1. The work flow of the proposed salient object detection framework.

2.1 Constructing Color Background Map

In this paper, we first use the k-means algorithm to cluster the boundary super-pixels into M classes. Next, calculate the feature gap between other super-pixels and the M different classes, this can measure the probability that the super-pixels to be the object regions. In this paper, we build M background maps C_m based on the number of M clusters. C_m is defined as the color feature difference between super-pixels $i(i = 1, 2, \cdots, N)$ and the boundary classed $m(m = 1, 2, \cdots, M)$. The class maps can be formulated as follows.

$$C_m = \frac{1}{p_m} \sum_{i=1}^{N} \frac{1}{\exp(\frac{-|c_m, c_i|}{2\alpha_1^2}) + \eta} \tag{1}$$

where c_m and c_i denotes the color features of each boundary class and super-pixel respectively. $|c_m, c_i|$ denotes the Euclidean distance between each super-pixel and boundary classes in CIELab color space, α_1, η are balance factors, $p_m(m = 1, 2, \cdots, M)$ is the number of super-pixels in different boundary classes. Through lots of experiments, the detection results are more accurate when $\alpha_1 = 0.2, \eta = 10, M = 3$. The three background maps generated in this paper are shown in Fig. 2.

Fig. 2. Color background maps. From left to right are input image; 1st class map, 2nd class map, 3rd class map, GT.

2.2   Constructing Spatial Correlation Background Map

In salient object detection, distance is always used to measure the spatial correlation between regions. The closer the distance between the two regions is, the greater the degree of influence and association in the space, and vice versa [16]. So we construct the spatial correlation saliency maps between each super-pixel and the boundary class by means of the spatial distance relationship between two regions. We defined S_m as the spatial distance between each super-pixel and class $m(m = 1, 2, \cdots, M)$, so the S_m can be formulated as follows.

$$S_m = \frac{1}{p_m} \sum_{i=1}^{N} \exp(\frac{-|s_i, s_m|}{2\alpha_2^2}) \tag{2}$$

where s_i, s_m denotes the spatial location of super-pixel i and m respectively. α_2 is control parameter, and it is learned by experience that setting $\alpha_2 = 1$ is most suitable. We calculate the distance between the super-pixels of the first class of background area and the other super-pixels to obtain the 1st class map. In the experiment, we calculated the spatial correlation background maps of three class of background areas, in which the bright part represents the salient area and the dark area represents the no-salient area. The boundary clustering results are shown in Fig. 3.

Fig. 3. Spatial correlation background maps. From left to right are input image, 1st class map, 2nd class map, 3rd class map.

2.3 Constructing Initial Saliency Map

As shown in the first map of Fig. 4, because there are two black objects, it is very difficult to distinguish their saliency by means of the color feature. But it can be seen from the map that the aircraft is closer to the center of the image than the tree, so we can use spatial distance to enhance the saliency of the aircraft and weaken the saliency of the tree. Let S_m denotes the intensity factor to restrict the C_m. The initial saliency map can be written as follows.

$$SC = \sum_{m=1}^{M} C_m \cdot S_m \tag{3}$$

The merging result as shown in the third map of Fig. 4. We can see from the result map that the brightness of the aircraft is higher than the tree. That is, the saliency of aircraft is strengthened and the saliency of the tree is weakened. Therefore, the image merging method is effective.

Fig. 4. Initial saliency map. From left to right are input image, GT, Initial saliency map.

3 Optimization of Merger Strategy

The object region can be revealed after merging, but we can see from the third map in Fig. 4, many background regions are also enhanced as the object regions are brightened. In order to optimize the rough initial saliency maps and detect salient object more accurate, a regional merging model is established in this section, which merges those adjacent background regions with similar features. In this paper, we merge the relevant regions with two stages. Firstly, we merge adjacent small regions with identical or similar features. Secondly, we merge adjacent or non-adjacent regions according to the ranking of regional saliency values.

3.1 The First Phase of the Merging

The relationship tightness of each region with its adjacent regions be calculated first and then merging them according to the degree of the relationship tightness. In this paper, the relationship tightness between regions is represented by color similarity and spatial tightness.

Color Similarity. Color similarity is defined as the difference in color feature between the super-pixel i and j, it can be formulated as follows.

$$C(i,j) = \|c_i - c_j\| \tag{4}$$

where c_i and c_j represent the average color value for super-pixels i and j respectively, $\|c_i - c_j\|$ is the Euclidean distance between the region i and adjacent region j.

Spatial Tightness. The spatial tightness between two regions can measure their degree of association in space. The closer the distance between the two regions is, the greater their spatial tightness. The correlation is measured by the boundary length of the overlapping regions. The longer the length of the boundaries that they co-own is, the greater the degree of association is. Let $ST(i,j)$, $S(i,j)$ and $T(i,j)$ as the spatial tightness, the spatial distance and spatial tightness between the super-pixel i and adjacent super-pixel j. The formula can be written respectively as follows.

$$S(i,j) = \|s_i - s_j\| \tag{5}$$

$$T(i,j) = \frac{B(i,j)}{\min(L(i), L(j))} \tag{6}$$

$$ST(i,j) = (1 - S(i,j)) \cdot T(i,j) \tag{7}$$

where s_i, s_j denote the spatial location for super-pixel i and j, $\|s_i - s_j\|$ is the Euclidean distance between region i and region j, $B(i,j)$, $L(i)$ and $L(j)$ denote the length of their overlapping boundaries, the length of the boundary of super-pixels i and j. Finally, we define $P(i,j)$ as the importance of the region j to the adjacent region i by calculating their color similarity and spatial tightness. The region i and the region j will be merged if they have higher importance. The importance $P(i,j)$ can be formulated as follows.

$$P(i,j) = \omega_1(1 - C(i,j)) + \omega_2 ST(i,j) \tag{8}$$

Some small region s_i must be merged into a large region s_j with greater relationship tightness. The merging results are shown in Fig. 5. Through experiments, the detection result is more accurate when $\omega_1 = 0.68$, $\omega_2 = 0.32$.

Fig. 5. The first phase merges maps. From left to right are input image, initial saliency map, first phase of the merging map, GT.

3.2 The Second Phase of the Merging

Based on the above first merging, it is noted that the majority of background regions are merged. However, there are some non-adjacent or adjacent background regions with greater intensity are not belong to salient regions (as shown in the third map of Fig. 5). Hence, in order to eliminate these background regions, we use Sal to denote these regional saliency value, utilize the Sal value to decide whether to merge it with background regions or not. Sal is influenced by the region area (V), the distance from regions to image center (CS) and the overlapping boundary length with image boundaries (BL). The region with a low value of Sal is merged with background regions.

Region Area. Regions with the larger area are more salient than smaller regions, so larger regions will be assigned greater saliency values. The formula can be written as

$$V = \frac{v}{\max(v)} \tag{9}$$

where v is the area of each associated object in the image, and $\max(v)$ is the area of the largest associated object region in the first merged maps.

Center Distance. In general, the center regions of the image more attractive than others, and they are more likely to be salient regions [16]. In this paper, therefore, calculates the region Sal according to the distance between the regions and the center of the scene.

$$CS = \frac{\sum_{i=1}^{nP} \|R, PC_i\|}{areaP} \tag{10}$$

Where nP is the number of super-pixel in the region P, PC is the spatial location of the super-pixels included in the region P, R is the center position of the image, and $areaP$ is the area of the region P.

Overlapping Boundary Length. The longer the overlapped boundary between a region with the image boundaries is, the greater the possibility of being background regions, so BL can be written as follows.

$$BL = \frac{PB}{RB} \tag{11}$$

where PB is the length of overlapped boundary that between each salient object and image boundaries, and RB is the total length value of the image boundaries. Hence, the saliency value Sal is defined as follows.

$$Sal = V + CS - BL \tag{12}$$

We merge the small salient objects into the large area by means of the Sal sorted. When some regions Sal value is very close, these regions can't be retained. The results are shown in Fig. 6.

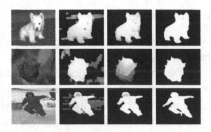

Fig. 6. Second phase merge map. From left to right are input image. The first stage merged map. The second stage merged map. GT.

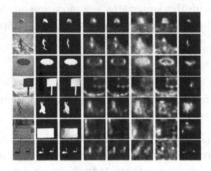

Fig. 7. Visual effect map. From left to right: input image, GT, Ours, SS, SR, SIM, SER, FES.

4   Experimental Results and Analysis

We test on ASD, ECSSD and DUT-OMRON datasets. ASD and ECSSD contain 1000 images respectively, the DUT-OMRON dataset contains 5168 images and salient object maps that artificially annotated. Moreover, we compare our method with 5 classic salient detection algorithms. They are SER [17], SS [18], SR [10], SIM [14], FES [19].

4.1   Visually Compare

In Fig. 7, we have selected some representative experimental results from our algorithm and comparison algorithm.

In the first map in Fig. 7, the salient region is very small, and the background region is uniform. Our algorithm result is very close to the GT. There are too many backgrounds are revealed in the SS, SR, SIM, and SER result maps. In the second map, the black object is in sharp contrast with the white background. It can be seen from the map that our algorithm detects more salient object than others, and only a small part is not detected successfully, because we use super-pixel to pre-process image, this small object is segmented into the background, causing it to be viewed as background. In the third and fourth maps, the salient object detected by our algorithm is complete, the boundary is clear. In the fifth map, the background is complex. The salient object detected by our algorithm is complete and the boundary is clear. In the face of complex background, the comparison algorithm will also display the background regions. Although our algorithm will show it in the first stage of the merging, it will be merged with the background in the second stage, which improves the accuracy of our algorithm. The background of the sixth map is complex, with salient background objects and high detection difficulty. Therefore, in the detection results of SS, SR, SIM, and SER, most of the background is revealed, and the salient object is displayed inaccurate. Our algorithm detection results are similar to the GT map and superior to algorithms. The last map is multi-objective images. Therefore, our algorithm is ideal in visual effects than 5 comparison algorithms.

4.2 Objective Evaluations

We evaluate the performance using Precision-recall (P-R) curve and F-measure. The comparison result diagrams are shown as Fig. 8.

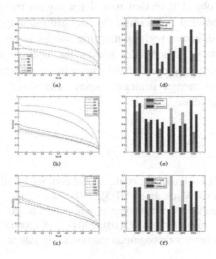

Fig. 8. Contrast data diagram. The first column denotes recall and precision curves of different methods in ASD dataset, ECSSD dataset and DUT-OMRON dataset (from top to bottom). The second column denotes recall, precision and F-measure value in ASD dataset, ECSSD dataset, DUT-OMRON dataset (from top to bottom).

From (a) and (b), we can see that the numerical line of our algorithm is above the numerical line than other algorithms. This shows that the performance of our algorithm is better than all comparison algorithms. In (d) and (e), the F-measure of our algorithm is higher. In the ECSSD dataset, although the background in the images is more complex, the accuracy and recall of algorithm are also close to 90%, which is much higher than the FES algorithm. The F-measure of the six kinds of algorithms are 0.87, 0.49, 0.20, 0.39, 0.48, and 0.60, respectively. That is, the F-measure of our algorithm is higher than other algorithms. The four data diagrams show that the detection results of our method are more accurate. The images in DUT-OMRON dataset are complex. Many salient objects are small, the background is complex, or there are more than one salient objects, so all algorithms are less effective than 70%. In (c), the curve of our algorithm is higher than other algorithms, but our algorithm curve is lower than the FES algorithm before 0.27. The main reason is that the salient objects in the image are very small and can easily be merged into the background area, which leads to the reduction of the accuracy of our algorithm. The F-measure are 0.55, 0.39, 0.38, 0.31, 0.33, and 0.49 respectively, of which the highest is 0.55 of our algorithm and higher than the FES algorithm which is 0.49. That is to say, our algorithm is superior to the FES algorithm.

In summary, our algorithm can reveal the salient object completely and showing good results.

5   Conclusion

In this paper, a salient object detection model for region merging is proposed. The initial saliency map is obtained by merging the background map, and in order to obtain the final saliency map, effective regions merging model is proposed to optimize the rough initial saliency map. This model makes the optimized saliency map more accurate. Experimental results show that our algorithm is effective and more accurate. In the future work, better merger strategies, such as Bayesian mergers, will be considered during the merge phase.

References

1. Cheng, M.M., Mitra, N.J., Huang, X., et al.: Global contrast based salient region detection. IEEE Trans. Pattern Anal. Mach. Intell. **37**(3), 569–582 (2015)
2. Itti, L.: Automatic foveation for video compression using a neurobiological model of visual attention. IEEE Trans. Image Process. **13**(10), 1304–1318 (2004)
3. Wang, X.F., Qi, C.: A behavior recognition method using salient object detection. J. Xi'an Jiaotong Univ. (2018)
4. Li, R., Li, J.P., Song, C.: Research on co-segmentation of image based on salient object detection. Modern Comput. (16), 19–23 (2017)
5. Sun, F., Qing, K.H., Sun, W., et al.: Image saliency detection based on region merging. J. Comput. Aided Des. Graph. **28**(10), 1679–1687 (2016)
6. Shen, X., Wu, Y.: A unified approach to salient object detection via low rank matrix recovery. In: Computer Vision and Pattern Recognition, pp. 853–860. IEEE (2012)
7. Peng, H., Li, B., Ling, H., et al.: Salient object detection via structured matrix decomposition. IEEE Trans. Pattern Anal. Mach. Intell. **39**(4), 818–832 (2017)
8. Zhang, D., Fu, H., Han, J., et al.: A review of co-saliency detection algorithms: fundamentals, applications, and challenges. ACM Trans. Intell. Syst. Technol. (TIST) **9**(4), 38 (2018)
9. Yazdi, M., Bouwmans, T.: New trends on moving object detection in video images captured by a moving camera: a survey. Comput. Sci. Rev. **28**, 157–177 (2018)

10. Hou, X., Zhang, L.: Saliency detection: a spectral residual approach. In: Proceedings of IEEE Conference on Computer Vision and Pattern Recognition, pp. 1–8 (2007)
11. Guo, C., Ma, Q., Zhang, L.: Spatio-temporal saliency detection using phase spectrum of quaternion Fourier transform. In: Proceedings of IEEE Conference on Computer Vision and Pattern Recognition, pp. 1–8 (2008)
12. Achanta, R., Hemami, S., Estrada, F., et al.: Frequency-tuned salient region detection. In: Proceedings of IEEE Conference on Computer Vision and Pattern Recognition, pp. 1597–1604 (2009)
13. Zhang, Q., Lin, J., Li, W., Shi, Y., Cao, G.: Salient object detection via compactness and objectness cues. Vis. Comput. **34**(4), 473–489 (2017). https://doi.org/10.1007/s00371-017-1354-0
14. Murray, N., Vanrell, M., Otazu, X., et al.: Saliency estimation using a non-parametric low-level vision model. In: IEEE Conference on Computer Vision and Pattern Recognition, pp. 433–440 (2011)
15. Achanta, R., Shaji, A., Smith, K., et al.: Slic superpixels. EPFL, Technical report 149300, November 2010
16. Rahtu, E., Kannala, J., Salo, M., Heikkilä, J.: Segmenting salient objects from images and videos. In: Daniilidis, K., Maragos, P., Paragios, N. (eds.) ECCV 2010. LNCS, vol. 6315, pp. 366–379. Springer, Heidelberg (2010). https://doi.org/10.1007/978-3-642-15555-0_27
17. Seo, H.J., Milanfar, P.: Static and space-time visual saliency detection by self-resemblance. J. Vis. **9**(12), 1–27 (2009)
18. Hou, X., Harel, J., Koch, C.: Image signature: highlighting sparse salient regions. IEEE Trans. Pattern Anal. Mach. Intell. **34**(1), 194–201 (2012)
19. Rezazadegan Tavakoli, H., Rahtu, E., Heikkilä, J.: Fast and efficient saliency detection using sparse sampling and kernel density estimation. In: Heyden, A., Kahl, F. (eds.) SCIA 2011. LNCS, vol. 6688, pp. 666–675. Springer, Heidelberg (2011). https://doi.org/10.1007/978-3-642-21227-7_62
20. Feng, L., Wen, P., Miao, Y., et al.: An image saliency detection algorithm based on color and space information. In: 2017 International Symposium on Intelligent Signal Processing and Communication Systems (ISPACS). IEEE (2017)
21. Xu, Q., Wang, F., Gong, Y., et al.: An edge-oriented framework for saliency detection. In: 2017 IEEE 17th International Conference on Bioinformatics and Bioengineering (BIBE). IEEE (2017)
22. Li, G., Yu, Y.: Visual saliency detection based on multiscale deep CNN features. IEEE Trans. Image Process. **25**, 5012–5024 (2016)
23. Li, H., Chen, J., Lu, H., et al.: CNN for saliency detection with low-level feature integration. Neurocomputing **226**, 212–220 (2017)
24. 赵恒, 安维胜, 田怀文. 结合稀疏重构与能量方程优化的显著性检测. 计算机应用研究 (6) (2019)
25. 余映, 吴青龙, 邵凯旋, et al.: 超复数域小波变换的显著性检测. 电子与信息学报 **41**(9) (2019)
26. Guo, Y., Liu, Y., Ma, R.: Image saliency detection based on geodesic-like and boundary contrast maps. ETRI J. **41**(6), 797–810 (2019)
27. Marcon, M., Spezialetti, R., Salti, S., Silva, L., Di Stefano, L.: Boosting object recognition in point clouds by saliency detection. In: Cristani, M., Prati, A., Lanz, O., Messelodi, S., Sebe, N. (eds.) ICIAP 2019. LNCS, vol. 11808, pp. 321–331. Springer, Cham (2019). https://doi.org/10.1007/978-3-030-30754-7_32

Link-Based Cluster Ensemble Method for Improved Meta-clustering Algorithm

Changlong Shao[1] and Shifei Ding[1,2(✉)]

[1] School of Computer Science and Technology,
China University of Mining and Technology, Xuzhou 221116, China
dingsf@cumt.edu.cn
[2] Mine Digitization Engineering Research Center of Ministry of Education
of the People's Republic of China, Xuzhou 221116, China

Abstract. Ensemble clustering has become a hot research field in intelligent information processing and machine learning. Although significant progress has been made in recent years, there are still two challenging issues in the current ensemble clustering research. First of all, most ensemble clustering algorithms tend to explore similarity at the level of object but lack the ability to explore information at the level of cluster. Secondly, many ensemble clustering algorithms only focus on the direct relationship, while ignoring the indirect relationship between clusters. In order to solve these two problems, a link-based meta-clustering algorithm (L-MCLA) have been proposed in this paper. A series of experiment results demonstrate that the proposed algorithm not only produces better clustering effect but is also less influenced by different ensemble sizes.

Keywords: Inter-cluster similarity · Ensemble clustering · Clustering · Connected triple · Meta-clustering algorithm (MCLA)

1 Introduction

In the field of intelligent information processing and machine learning, clustering analysis is an important learning tool for unlabeled data. Generally speaking, clustering is to classify a given dataset into clusters, so that the data objects within the cluster have larger similarity, while the data objects between clusters are quite different from each other [1]. Clustering has been used in various fields, such as image processing [2], cognitive computing [3], time series analysis [20] and medical diagnosis [17]. In the past few decades, a large number of clustering algorithms have been developed, among which the most representative ones are partitional clustering [18], hierarchical clustering [19], spectral clustering [4, 5], density clustering [6, 7], adaptive clustering [8, 9] and semi-supervised clustering [1, 21]. Nevertheless, there are still some problems in the current clustering algorithm. For instance, the clustering result largely depends on parameters and initialization without which the clustering result is not robust enough. In order to solve these problems, ensemble clustering was proposed by researchers.

Unlike the traditional method of using an algorithm to generate a single clustering result, ensemble clustering is a process of ensemble multiple different clustering results to generate better clustering result. Due to the effectiveness of ensemble clustering

© IFIP International Federation for Information Processing 2020
Published by Springer Nature Switzerland AG 2020
Z. Shi et al. (Eds.): IIP 2020, IFIP AICT 581, pp. 14–25, 2020.
https://doi.org/10.1007/978-3-030-46931-3_2

algorithm, more researchers have been attracted and proposed many related algorithms. Despite significant advances in ensemble clustering research, most algorithms only focus on direct connection, while ignoring indirect connection between clusters. As shown in Fig. 1, two objects appear in the same cluster and thus we say that they are directly connected. However, like (b) and (c), two objects are in two different clusters but we cannot conclude that there is no connection between them because they are likely to be related to each other indirectly. Such indirect connection information may affect the consensus result. In order to explore indirect connection information, we propose a link-based meta-clustering Algorithm (L-MCLA) in this paper.

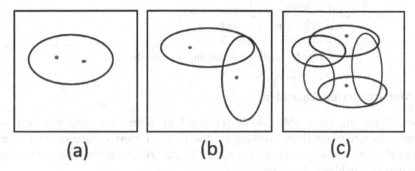

(a)   **(b)**   **(c)**

Fig. 1. Relationship between two points. (a) In the same cluster. (b) Belong to two clusters with common parts. (c) Belong to two unrelated clusters, but both of them are related to the third cluster.

The remainder of paper is organized as follows. Section 2 reviews the background of this study. Section 3 details the proposed method in this paper. Section 4 shows the experiment results. Section 5 concludes this paper.

2 Background

2.1 Ensemble Clustering

Ensemble clustering is an algorithm to improve the clustering effect by ensemble multiple base clusterings, which can be generally expressed as follows:

Let $X = \{x_1, x_2, \ldots, x_n\}$ denotes a dataset with n objects. We use clustering algorithms to obtain m clustering results $P = \{p_1, p_2, \ldots p_m\}$ and call them as base clusterings. Each base clustering contains several clusters, which is written as $p_i = \{C_i^1, C_i^2, \ldots C_i^j\}$, where j is the number of clusters in the base clustering p_i. Ensemble clustering is to merge the set P through the consensus function T to obtain the final clustering result P*. The specific process of ensemble clustering is shown in Fig. 2.

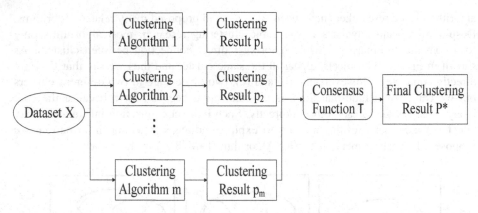

Fig. 2. Ensemble clustering process diagram

2.2   Meta-clustering Algorithm

Meta-clustering algorithm (MCLA) is proposed by Strehl and Ghosh which is an ensemble clustering algorithm working on the level of cluster. Jaccard coefficient is used to calculate similarity between clusters. The jaccard coefficient between cluster C_i and C_j can be calculated as follows:

$$J(C_i, C_j) = \frac{|C_i \cap C_j|}{|C_i \cup C_j|} \tag{1}$$

Where $\cap$ denotes the intersection of two sets, $\cup$ denotes the union of two sets, and $|*|$ denotes the number of objects in a set.

Specifically, the meta-clustering algorithm consists of the following four steps:

(1) Construct a similarity matrix by calculating jaccard coefficient between clusters contained in base clusterings.
(2) Regard the similarity matrix of the previous step as an undirected graph, which is called meta-graph.
(3) Use graph partitioning package METIS [16] to divide the meta-graph of the previous step to obtain the meta-cluster and each meta-cluster contains several clusters.
(4) Assign each object to the corresponding meta-cluster to get the final clustering result.

3   Link-Based Meta-clustering Algorithm

3.1   Construct Similarity Matrix

The meta-clustering algorithm is superior, but it still has a shortcoming. The similarity matrix constructed by Jaccard coefficient can only reflect the direct relationship between clusters while lacking capability to find the indirect relationship. In 2011, the concept of weighted connected-triple (WCT) was proposed by Iam-On et al. [12], which makes it possible to explore the hidden indirect relationship between clusters.

In this section, connected triple is used to construct a refined cluster similarity matrix. The connected triple is shown in Fig. 3.

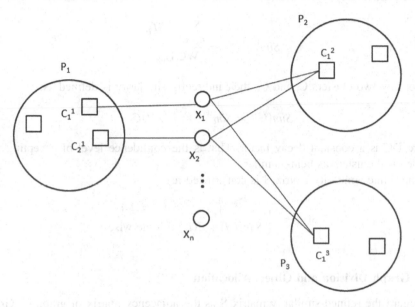

Fig. 3. Connected triple diagram

P_1, P_2, P_3 are three base clusterings. C_1^1 and C_2^1 are unrelated clusters (i.e., have no public part) and in common sense should have no similarity. C_1^1 and C_1^2 have a common point x_1, and C_2^1 and C_1^2 have a common point x_2. Therefore, C_1^1 and C_1^2 are similar and C_2^1 and C_1^2 are similar. Because both C_1^1 and C_2^1 have a similar third-cluster C_1^2, C_1^1 and C_2^1 are indirectly connected to each other. In the same way, C_1^1 and C_1^3 have a common point x_1 while C_2^1 and C_1^3 have a common point x_2. Accordingly, C_1^1 and C_2^1 have indirectly connection to each other. It can be seen that connected triple can help find more connection between clusters, which is beneficial for reaching a consensus result later.

Firstly, similarity matrix Z is constructed by jaccard coefficient.

$$Z(i,j) = \begin{cases} 1, & i = j \\ J(C_i, C_j) & \text{otherwise} \end{cases} \tag{2}$$

Let C_k have similarity with C_i and C_j, then the weighted connected triple between C_i and C_j is defined as follow:

$$WCT_{ij}^k = \min(J(C_i, C_k), J(C_j, C_k)) \tag{3}$$

Then the indirectly connection between cluster C_i and C_j is calculated as follows:

$$Sim^{WCT}(i,j) = \frac{\sum\limits_{C_k \in C} WCT_{ij}^k}{WCT_{max}} \tag{4}$$

For any two clusters C_i and C_j, their indirectly similarity is defined as:

$$Sim(i,j) = Sim^{WCT}(i,j) \times DC \tag{5}$$

Where DC is a constant decay factor. That is the confidence level of accepting two nonidentical clusters as being similar.

The refine similarity matrix S is constructed as:

$$S(i,j) = \begin{cases} 1, & i = j \\ Sim(i,j) + Z(i,j) & \text{otherwise} \end{cases} \tag{6}$$

3.2   Graph Division and Object Allocation

We regard the refined similarity matrix S as the adjacency matrix of graph G. Graph segmentation algorithm is our consensus function. In the selection of graph segmentation algorithm, since the normalized cut (Ncut) is effective and robust, we select it in this study [13]. Normalized cut is a kind of spectral clustering. The basic idea is to define a cut criterion, which considers the total dissimilarity between different clusters and the total similarity within the cluster.

By normalized cut, K meta-cluster groups can be obtained, that is:

$$MC = \{MC_1, MC_2, \ldots, MC_K\} \tag{7}$$

Here we use the voting method to assign objects. For given object x_i, x_i belong to zero or more clusters in MC_j. Specifically, the voting score of x_i for the meta-cluster MC_j can be defined as follow:

$$Score(x_i, MC_j) = \frac{1}{|MC_j|} \sum_{C_h \in MC_j} l$$

$$l = \begin{cases} 1, & \text{if } x_i \in C_h \\ 0, & \text{otherwise} \end{cases} \tag{8}$$

Where $|MC_j|$ denotes the number of clusters in MC_j.

We assign the point x_i to the meta-cluster with the highest score. The final clustering result can be obtained by this way.

For clarity, the algorithm of L-MCLA is described in Algorithm 1.

Algorithm 1: Link-Based Meta-Clustering Algorithm.

Input: Dataset X, number of clusters K

1) Using clustering algorithm to generate m base clusterings $P = \{p_1, p_2, \dots p_m\}$ for dataset X.
2) The inter-cluster similarity matrix Z is constructed by jaccard coefficients, which can be calculated by the equation (2).
3) For similarity matrix Z, equation (3)-(6) is used to obtain the refined similarity matrix S.
4) The similarity matrix S is regarded as a graph G. K meta-clusters are obtained by using Ncut algorithm to segment this graph as equation (7).
5) The clustering result Label is obtained by allocating object to corresponding meta-cluster by equation (8).

Output: Final cluster result Label

---

4   Experiments

In this section, we conduct experiments on multiple real-world datasets and compare results with several existing ensemble clustering algorithms to evaluate the performance of the algorithm proposed in this paper. Moreover, the robustness of the algorithm is evidenced by experiment on different ensemble sizes.

4.1   Datasets and Evaluation Measures

In our experiments, nine datasets in the UCI (University of California Irvine) machine learning database are used as experimental datasets [22]. Table 1 lists the detail of each dataset:

Table 1. Description of UCI datasets

Datasets	Object	Dimension	Class
Aggregation	788	2	7
Cardiotocograph (CTG)	2126	21	10
Diabetes	768	8	2
Ecoli	336	8	8
Ionosphere	351	34	2
Segmentation	2130	19	7
Soybean	47	35	4
Thyroid	215	5	3
Yeast	1484	8	10

In our experiments, adjusted Rand index (ARI) and normalized mutual information (NMI) are selected to evaluate the performance of the clustering results. The two evaluation are described as follows:

ARI is a clustering evaluation index that measures the similarity between two clustering results by calculating the number of sample point pairs in the same cluster and different clusters. The equation is as follow:

$$\text{ARI} = \frac{2(ad - bc)}{(a+b)(b+d) + (a+c)(c+d)} \tag{9}$$

Where a denotes the number of point pairs that belong to the same cluster in both real and experimental, b denotes the number of point pairs that belong to the same cluster in real label and different clusters in experimental result, and c denotes the number of point pairs that belong to the same cluster in the experimental result and different clusters in the real label, and d represents the number of point pairs that belong to different clusters in both real and experimental. Its value range $[-1, 1]$. The larger the value is, the more consistent it is with the real result, namely the better clustering effect.

NMI is a common external evaluation index of clustering. It evaluates the similarity of two clustering results from the perspective of communication theory. Let the experimental result be X and the real label be Y, then the equation is as follows:

$$\text{NMI}(X, Y) = \frac{I(X,Y)}{\sqrt{H(X)H(Y)}} \tag{10}$$

Where $I(X, Y)$ represents the mutual information between X and Y, and $H(X)$ and $H(Y)$ represent the entropy of X and Y. Its value range $[0, 1]$. The larger value indicates more shared information with the real label, that is, the better clustering result.

4.2   Comparative Methods and Experimental Settings

In our experiments, seven ensemble clustering algorithms are compared with L-MCLA algorithm. The seven comparison algorithms are as follows:

(1) Evidence accumulation clustering (EAC) [10]
(2) Hybrid bipartite graph formulation (HBGF) [14]
(3) Weighted evidence accumulation clustering (WEAC) [15]
(4) Graph partitioning with multi-granularity link analysis (GP-MGLA) [15]
(5) Cluster-based similarity partitioning algorithm (CSPA) [11]
(6) Hypergraph partitioning algorithm (HGPA) [11]
(7) Meta-clustering algorithm (MCLA) [11]

The experiments are implemented in MATLAB R2016a. The PC configuration is as follows: Windows7 64-bit, Intel i5 1.7 GHz CPU, 8G RAM.

In our experiments, k-means is used to generate base clusterings with the parameter k randomly selected in the range $[2, \sqrt{N}]$. For parameter DC, high DC values (i.e., 0.7 to 0.9) bring about a data partition of exceptionally good quality [12], so we set DC = 0.9 in our experiment. We call the number of base clusterings m as ensemble size and set ensemble size m = 50 to compare the L-MCLA algorithm with other ensemble clustering algorithms. Furthermore, we change the ensemble size to test the robustness of L-MCLA algorithm.

4.3   Comparison with Other Ensemble Clustering Methods

This section make a comparison experiment of our algorithm. Each ensemble clustering algorithm runs 20 times on each dataset and each run randomly generates base clustering according to Sect. 4.2. The average scores and standard deviation of ARI and NMI are recorded. The experimental results are shown in Table 2 and Table 3, with the highest score shown in bold.

Table 2. Average ARI scores by different ensemble clustering methods. The highest score in each comparison is in bold

	EAC	HBGF	WEAC	GP-MGLA	CSPA	HGPA	MCLA	L-MCLA
Aggregation	0.804 (±0.044)	0.805 (±0.050)	0.806 (±0.045)	0.860 (±0.082)	0.549 (±0.006)	0.621 (±0.022)	0.612 (±0.027)	**0.925** (**±0.057**)
CTG	0.133 (±0.007)	0.130 (±0.008)	0.129 (±0.008)	0.137 (±0.004)	0.115 (±0.003)	0.117 (±0.010)	0.120 (±0.004)	**0.140** (**±0.005**)
Diabetes	0.051 (±0.027)	0.044 (±0.028)	0.018 (±0.013)	0.007 (±0.011)	−0.001 (±0.001)	−0.001 (±0.001)	−0.001 (±0.001)	**0.061** (**±0.032**)
Ecoli	0.495 (±0.069)	0.416 (±0.015)	0.468 (±0.059)	0.471 (±0.049)	0.300 (±0.013)	0.333 (±0.026)	0.367 (±0.030)	**0.542** (**±0.053**)
Ionosphere	0.150 (±0.011)	0.167 (±0.010)	0.148 (±0.010)	0.162 (±0.013)	0.124 (±0.000)	0.020 (±0.023)	0.163 (±0.014)	**0.169** (**±0.004**)
Segmentation	0.347 (±0.075)	0.425 (±0.054)	0.404 (±0.059)	0.442 (±0.031)	0.384 (±0.034)	0.255 (±0.036)	0.436 (±0.074)	**0.447** (**±0.039**)
Soybean	0.551 (±0.006)	0.547 (±0.005)	0.553 (±0.009)	0.547 (±0.004)	0.483 (±0.029)	0.543 (±0.013)	0.552 (±0.008)	**0.568** (**±0.029**)
Thyroid	0.370 (±0.182)	0.378 (±0.178)	0.497 (±0.053)	0.558 (±0.031)	0.129 (±0.037)	0.104 (±0.025)	0.271 (±0.070)	**0.587** (**±0.036**)
Yeast	0.173 (±0.018)	0.148 (±0.005)	0.173 (±0.015)	0.167 (±0.004)	0.109 (±0.013)	0.093 (±0.016)	0.125 (±0.006)	**0.182** (**±0.007**)

Table 3. Average NMI scores by different ensemble clustering methods. The highest score in each comparison is in bold

	EAC	HBGF	WEAC	GP-MGLA	CSPA	HGPA	MCLA	L-MCLA
Aggregation	0.868 (±0.027)	0.867 (±0.031)	0.868 (±0.027)	0.900 (±0.047)	0.688 (±0.008)	0.748 (±0.014)	0.746 (±0.015)	**0.932** (**±0.037**)
CTG	0.267 (±0.007)	0.273 (±0.011)	0.264 (±0.008)	**0.274** (**±0.006**)	0.244 (±0.005)	0.246 (±0.013)	0.253 (±0.005)	0.274 (±0.006)
Diabetes	0.018 (±0.010)	0.017 (±0.012)	0.007 (±0.004)	0.003 (±0.004)	0.001 (±0.000)	0.001 (±0.000)	0.001 (±0.000)	**0.025** (**±0.013**)
Ecoli	0.579 (±0.027)	0.537 (±0.012)	0.568 (±0.025)	0.567 (±0.025)	0.442 (±0.010)	0.465 (±0.024)	0.504 (±0.020)	**0.608** (**±0.021**)
Ionosphere	0.115 (±0.007)	**0.126** (**±0.005**)	0.114 (±0.006)	0.123 (±0.007)	0.102 (±0.000)	0.018 (±0.018)	0.120 (±0.009)	0.123 (±0.004)
Segmentation	0.480 (±0.066)	0.529 (±0.052)	0.523 (±0.047)	**0.562** (**±0.024**)	0.502 (±0.026)	0.374 (±0.040)	0.545 (±0.055)	0.545 (±0.029)

(*continued*)

Table 3. (*continued*)

	EAC	HBGF	WEAC	GP-MGLA	CSPA	HGPA	MCLA	L-MCLA
Soybean	0.714 (±0.003)	0.712 (±0.002)	0.714 (±0.005)	0.711 (±0.002)	0.619 (±0.023)	0.706 (±0.017)	0.714 (±0.004)	**0.721** (**±0.010**)
Thyroid	0.316 (±0.075)	0.325 (±0.104)	0.369 (±0.026)	0.411 (±0.036)	0.164 (±0.022)	0.153 (±0.011)	0.213 (±0.031)	**0.484** (**±0.035**)
Yeast	0.264 (±0.012)	0.257 (±0.006)	0.267 (±0.011)	0.273 (±0.005)	0.206 (±0.015)	0.191 (±0.020)	0.226 (±0.005)	**0.290** (**±0.007**)

As shown in Table 2, the ARI score of L-MCLA algorithm on 9 datasets are all the highest. As can be seen from Table 3, L-MCLA algorithm on six datasets has the highest NMI value, which is only slightly inferior on the CTG, Ionosphere and Segmentation, but the difference is not significant. To summarize, the L-MCLA method exhibits overall better performance (with respect to ARI, NMI) than the other methods.

4.4 Robustness to Ensemble Size

In this section, we evaluate the performance of L-MCLA algorithm under different ensemble size on nine datasets. Ensemble size is in the range of [10, 100], increasing by 10. The generation settings for base clustering are same as Sect. 4.2. Then we record the average score of ARI and NMI. The change of score is shown in Fig. 4 and Fig. 5.

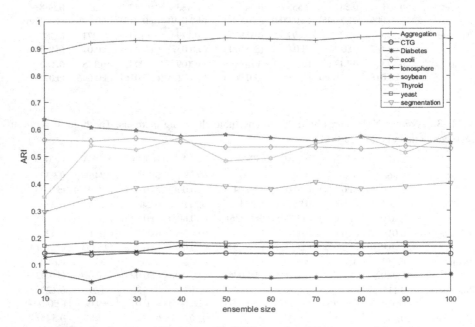

Fig. 4. Average ARI scores of L-MCLA under different ensemble size

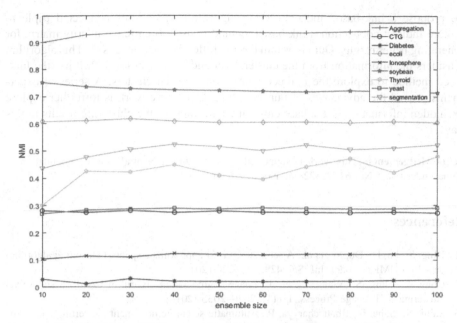

Fig. 5. Average NMI scores of L-MCLA under different ensemble size

Figure 4 shows the ARI index values of the L-MCLA algorithm in 9 datasets under different ensemble sizes. It can be seen from the observation that there is only a slight fluctuation in the L-MCLA algorithm on most datasets and the fluctuation gradually decreases after the integration scale reaches 40. In addition to the Thyroid dataset and the Soybean dataset, the ARI value of the Thyroid data set increases sharply from 10 to 20, and then shows a state of fluctuating increase with the increase of ensemble sizes. With the increase of base clusterings, the ARI value of the Soybean dataset shows a slow decline but the range is small.

Figure 5 shows the NMI index values of the L-MCLA algorithm on 9 datasets under different ensemble sizes. It can be seen from observation that the NMI values of most datasets tend to be stable except for the Thyroid datasets. However, the NMI value of the Thyroid dataset shows a significant upward trend when the base clusterings are about 10–40, but slightly decreases when the base clusterings is 40–50, and then shows an upward trend and gradually stabilizes.

According to the above experimental analysis, the ensemble size has little influence on L-MCLA algorithm. On most datasets, L-MCLA algorithm relys on fewer base clusterings to obtain more robust results.

5   Conclusion

Ensemble clustering is the use of multiple clustering results to generate better clustering results. However, the existing ensemble clustering algorithms often only pay attention to the direct inter-cluster connection and ignore the indirect connection. In this paper, we propose a link-based meta-clustering algorithm which uses connected triple to explore indirect connection. Link-based method is used to enrich similarity matrix for generating better results. Our algorithm has the following advantages: 1. This algorithm considers the information from the cluster level and the object level. 2. It use the link-based method to explore the indirect connection between clusters. A series of experiments proved the advantages of our algorithm. Our future work is to further explore the hidden information in the base clustering and improve the clustering results in this way.

Acknowledgements. This work is supported by the National Natural Science Foundation of China under Grant No. 61672522 and No. 61976216.

References

1. Ding, S., Jia, H., Du, M., et al.: A semi-supervised approximate spectral clustering algorithm based on HMRF model. Inf. Sci. **429**, 215–228 (2018)
2. Cong, L., Ding, S., Wang, L., et al.: Image segmentation algorithm based on superpixel clustering. IET Image Process. **12**(11), 2030–2035 (2018)
3. Saini, N., Saha, S., Bhattacharyya, P.: Automatic scientific document clustering using self-organized multi-objective differential evolution. Cogn. Comput. **11**(2), 271–293 (2018). https://doi.org/10.1007/s12559-018-9611-8
4. Ding, S., Cong, L., Hu, Q., et al.: A multiway p-spectral clustering algorithm. Knowl. Based Syst. **164**, 371–377 (2019)
5. Løkse, S., Bianchi, F.M., Salberg, A.-B., Jenssen, R.: Spectral clustering using *PCKID* – a probabilistic cluster kernel for incomplete data. In: Sharma, P., Bianchi, F.M. (eds.) SCIA 2017. LNCS, vol. 10269, pp. 431–442. Springer, Cham (2017). https://doi.org/10.1007/978-3-319-59126-1_36
6. Liu, R., Wang, H., Yu, X.: Shared-nearest-neighbor-based clustering by fast search and find of density peaks. Inf. Sci. (2018). https://doi.org/10.1016/j.ins.2018.03.031
7. Du, M., Ding, S., Xue, Yu., Shi, Z.: A novel density peaks clustering with sensitivity of local density and density-adaptive metric. Knowl. Inf. Syst. **59**(2), 285–309 (2018). https://doi.org/10.1007/s10115-018-1189-7
8. Fan, S., Ding, S., Xue, Y.: Self-adaptive kernel K-means algorithm based on the shuffled frog leaping algorithm. Soft Comput. **22**(3), 861–872 (2018)
9. Ding, S., Xu, X., Fan, S., et al.: Locally adaptive multiple kernel k-means algorithm based on shared nearest neighbors. Soft Comput. **22**(14), 4573–4583 (2018)
10. Fred, A.L.N., Jain, A.K.: Combining multiple clusterings using evidence accumulation. IEEE Trans. Pattern Anal. Mach. Intell. **27**(6), 835–850 (2005)
11. Strehl, A., Ghosh, J.: Cluster ensembles—a knowledge reuse framework for combining multiple partitions. J. Mach. Learn. Res. **3**, 583–617 (2003)
12. Iam-On, N., Boongoen, T., Garrett, S.M., et al.: A link-based approach to the cluster ensemble problem. IEEE Trans. Softw. Eng. **33**(12), 2396–2409 (2011)
13. Shi, J., Malik, J.: Normalized cuts and image segmentation. IEEE Trans. Pattern Anal. Mach. Intell. **22**(8), 888–905 (2000)
14. Fern, X.Z., Brodley, C.E.: Solving cluster ensemble problems by bipartite graph partitioning. In: Proceedings of the Twenty-First International Conference on Machine Learning, p. 36. ACM (2004). https://doi.org/10.1145/1015330.1015414

15. Huang, D., Lai, J.H., Wang, C.D.: Combining multiple clusterings via crowd agreement estimation and multi-granularity link analysis. Neurocomputing **170**, 240–250 (2015)
16. Karypis, G., Kumar, V.: A fast and high quality multilevel scheme for partitioning irregular graphs. SIAM J. Sci. Comput **20**(1), 359–392 (1998)
17. Thanh, N.D., Ali, M.: A novel clustering algorithm in a neutrosophic recommender system for medical diagnosis. Cogn. Comput. **9**(4), 526–544 (2017)
18. Nguyen, B., De Baets, B.: Kernel-based distance metric learning for supervised k-means clustering. IEEE Trans. Neural Netw. Learn. Syst. 1–12 (2019). https://doi.org/10.1109/tnnls.2018.2890021
19. Cohen-Addad, V., Kanade, V., Mallmann-Trenn, F., et al.: Hierarchical clustering: objective functions and algorithms. J. ACM (JACM) **66**(4), 26 (2019)
20. Mikalsen, K.Ø., Bianchi, F.M., Soguero-Ruiz, C., et al.: Time series cluster kernel for learning similarities between multivariate time series with missing data. Pattern Recogn. **76**, 569–581 (2018)
21. Zhang, H., Lu, J.: SCTWC: an online semi-supervised clustering approach to topical web crawlers. Appl. Soft Comput. **10**(2), 490–495 (2010)
22. Asuncion, A., Newman, D.J.: UCI Machine Learning Repository (2007). http://www.ics.uci.edu/mlearn/MLRepository.html

Large-Scale Spectral Clustering
with Stochastic Nyström Approximation

Hongjie Jia[✉], Liangjun Wang, and Heping Song

Jiangsu University, Zhenjiang 212013, Jiangsu, China
jiahj@ujs.edu.cn

Abstract. In spectral clustering, Nyström approximation is a powerful technique to reduce the time and space cost of matrix decomposition. However, in order to ensure the accurate approximation, a sufficient number of samples are needed. In very large datasets, the internal singular value decomposition (SVD) of Nyström will also spend a large amount of calculation and almost impossible. To solve this problem, this paper proposes a large-scale spectral clustering algorithm with stochastic Nyström approximation. This algorithm uses the stochastic low rank matrix approximation technique to decompose the sampled sub-matrix within the Nyström procedure, losing a slight of accuracy in exchange for a significant improvement of the algorithm efficiency. The performance of the proposed algorithm is tested on benchmark data sets and the clustering results demonstrate its effectiveness.

Keywords: Spectral clustering · Nyström approximation · Stochastic SVD · Large dataset

1 Introduction

Spectral clustering algorithms can well deal with the datasets of non-convex structures, and they have been successfully applied in many fields. But the traditional spectral clustering algorithms only suit for small-scale datasets, because they need to store an $n \times n$ affinity matrix and make eigen-decomposition on it. The required space complexity and time complexity are respectively $O(n^2)$ and $O(n^3)$. The high complexity problems limit the application of spectral clustering methods in large data [1]. Therefore it is needed to develop a new data processing strategy to adapt to the continuous growth of the data size while maintaining the quality and speed of the clustering.

Fortunately, the spectral clustering method only needs a small part of the head (or tail) of the eigenvalues/eigenvectors, then we can use the Arnoldi method to do partial SVD [2]. However, experience shows that only when the matrix is sparse or very few eigenvectors are extracted, the running time will be significantly reduced. Another method to reduce the computational complexity is using low rank matrix approximation, such as the commonly used Nyström method [3]. It selects a subset of $m \ll n$ columns from the kernel matrix, and then constructs the low rank approximation of the kernel matrix by using the correlation between the samples and the remaining columns. In computation, the Nyström method only requires the decomposition of a small

© IFIP International Federation for Information Processing 2020
Published by Springer Nature Switzerland AG 2020
Z. Shi et al. (Eds.): IIP 2020, IFIP AICT 581, pp. 26–34, 2020.
https://doi.org/10.1007/978-3-030-46931-3_3

$m \times m$ sub-matrix and the time complexity can be significantly reduced; in the occupied space, it is only need to store the sampled m columns, and other matrix involved in the computation can be calculated by the m columns, so its space complexity is small. This makes the Nyström method has high scalability. Fowlkes et al. [4] successfully apply it to spectral clustering for image segmentation. In order to improve the accuracy of Nyström approximation, we need to select a lot of samples, but the large sampled sub-matrix is also very difficult to decompose [5].

Halko et al. [6] propose a stochastic SVD method to construct approximate low rank matrix factorization. This method extends the Monte Carlo algorithm in literature [7]. Similar to the standard Nyström method, this method only need the eigen-decomposition on part of matrix. But this method does not simply select a subset of columns, it first construct a low dimensional subspace that captures the activity of the input matrix. Then, compress the matrix into the subspace, and make the standard factorization on the reduced matrix. Although the method is a stochastic algorithm, experiments show that it has great potential to produce accurate approximations. However, this algorithm needs to traverse at least once the input matrix, so it is more time-consuming than the Nyström method which is only based on sampled columns. On large data sets, the performance difference between these algorithms will be significant.

In this paper, we combine the advantages of standard Nyström method and stochastic SVD algorithm. Standard Nyström is very efficient, but need to collect a large number of columns; stochastic SVD algorithm has high accuracy, but the efficiency is relatively low. Inspired by this, when using the Nyström method for large scale spectral clustering, we can use stochastic SVD to replace the original standard SVD on the sampled sub-matrix to cope with efficiency decrease caused by the increasing sample number m, and accelerate the process of calculating approximate eigenvectors. The main contributions of this paper are:

- We propose a large-scale spectral clustering algorithm with stochastic Nyström approximation, which can achieve a good balance between the clustering accuracy and the operating efficiency.
- The approximation error of stochastic SVD process in the proposed method can be compensated by selecting more sample columns.
- Experimental results show that the proposed method can further reduce the calculation complexity of Nyström spectral clustering.

The rest of this paper is organized as follows. Section 2 briefly reviews the related research background. Section 3 introduces the proposed large-scale spectral clustering algorithm with stochastic Nyström approximation. The experimental results are given in Sect. 4, and the last section is conclusion.

2 Research Background

2.1 Nyström Approximation

The spectral methods such as Ratio Cut and Normalized Cut are based on the eigenvectors of Laplacian matrix to do clustering [8]. Suppose the Laplacian matrix is $L = D^{-1/2}WD^{-1/2}$, where D is the degree matrix and W is the weight matrix. The eigenvector matrix U can be calculated by the eigen-decomposition of Laplacian matrix L, namely $LU = U\Lambda_L$. The eigenvectors in matrix U are orthogonal and these eigenvectors embed the data objects into a low dimensional subspace. Then we may use k-means algorithm to cluster U, and obtain the final partition results. When the amount of data n is very large, it becomes very difficult to decompose the Laplacian matrix. The Nyström method use a subset of matrix columns (or rows) to do approximate spectral decomposition for a large matrix, which can significantly reduce the computational complexity [9].

Given the $n \times n$ weight matrix W, we randomly select $m \ll n$ data points from data set and rearrange matrix W as follows:

$$W = \begin{bmatrix} A & B \\ B^T & C \end{bmatrix} \tag{1}$$

where $A \in \mathbb{R}^{m \times m}$ contains the similarities among the data samples, $B \in \mathbb{R}^{m \times (n-m)}$ contains the similarities among the samples and the rest points, and $C \in \mathbb{R}^{(n-m) \times (n-m)}$ contains the similarities among the rest points.

Nyström approximation gets the approximate eigenvectors of Laplacian matrix using the eigenvectors of a small sub-matrix. Let matrix $H = [A \quad B]^T$, matrix W can be approximated as:

$$\tilde{W} = HA^{-1}H^T \tag{2}$$

To get the orthogonal approximate eigenvectors of $\tilde{W}$, Fowlkes et al. [4] define a matrix $M = A + A^{-1/2}BB^TA^{-1/2}$. We decompose M as $M = U_M\Lambda_M U_M^T$. The eigenvector matrix of $\tilde{W}$ are:

$$U_W = HA^{-1/2}U_M\Lambda_M^{-1/2} \tag{3}$$

where $\tilde{W} = U_W\Lambda_M U_W^T$. It can be proved that U_W and its transpose matrix are orthogonal, namely $U_W^T U_W = I$.

In order to compute the first k approximate eigenvectors and eigenvalues of W, the total time complexity of this algorithm is $O(m^3 + kmn)$, where $O(m^3)$ is the eigen-decomposition time of M, and $O(kmn)$ is corresponding to the multiply operations about matrix H. Because $m \ll n$, its complexity is much lower than the $O(n^3)$ complexity that directly SVD on W. Although the efficiency of Nyström method is high, it needs to select a sufficient number of samples to better approximate the original eigen-space. Then we consider use stochastic SVD to further reduce the complexity of Nyström method.

2.2 Stochastic SVD

Halko et al. [6] propose a simple and efficient stochastic SVD algorithm, which is used to solve the approximate eigenvalues and eigenvectors of the low rank matrix. Given a real symmetric matrix $M \in \mathbb{R}^{m \times m}$, this stochastic SVD algorithm includes two stages: first, it uses random sampling to construct a low dimensional subspace to approximate the range of M; then, it limits M in the obtained sub-space, and makes standard QR or SVD decomposition based on the reduced matrix. The following Algorithm 1 gives the concrete steps of the stochastic SVD, through which we can quickly obtain a low rank approximation of a real symmetric matrix M.

Algorithm 1. Stochastic SVD.

   Input: symmetric matrix $M \in \mathbb{R}^{m \times m}$, matrix rank k, over sampling parameter p, power parameter q.
   Output: the eigenvector matrix U_M, the eigenvalue matrix Λ_F.
   Step 1. Construct an $m \times (k + p)$ standard Gaussian random matrix Ω.
   Step 2. Calculate matrix $Z = M\Omega$ and $Y = M^{q-1}Z$.
   Step 3. Find an orthogonal matrix Q through the QR decomposition, so that $Y = QQ^TY$.
   Step 4. According to $F(Q^T\Omega) = Q^TZ$, compute the matrix F.
   Step 5. Conduct SVD on F and get $F = U_F\Lambda_F U_F^T$.
   Step 6. Compute matrix $U_M = QU_F$.

Specifically, the first stage of Algorithm 1 includes Step 1–Step 3. It first produces an $m \times (k + p)$ standard Gaussian random matrix Ω, each element of Ω is independent Gaussian random variables, the mean is 0, the variance is 1. Among them, p is an over sampling parameter, so that the column number of Ω is slightly higher than the required rank k. Then calculate the matrix $Y = M\Omega$, and construct the matrix $Q \in \mathbb{R}^{m \times (k+p)}$ through the QR decomposition. Q is an orthogonal matrix, and its column constitutes the orthogonal basis of Y. In order to make $Y = M\Omega$ have a larger range to extend to the k dimensional subspace of M, the value of p is generally a small number, such as 5 or 10.

The second stage of Algorithm 1 includes Step 4–Step 6. M is restricted to the subspace generated by Y, we can further obtain the reduced matrix $F = Q^TMQ$. And then conduct the standard SVD on F, that is $F = U_F\Lambda_F U_F^T$. The SVD of M can be approximated as:

$$M \simeq QFQ^T = (QU_F)\Lambda_F(QU_F)^T \tag{4}$$

Finally, let $U_M = QU_F$, we can obtain the low rank approximation of M as $M \approx U_M\Lambda_F U_M^T$. The time complexity of Algorithm 1 is $O(m^2k + k^3)$, which is proportional to the square of m. Algorithm 1 is easy to implement, and can be applied to large scale clustering problem. Therefore, we introduce the stochastic SVD into

Nyström approximation to deal with the complex eigen-decomposition problem when the sampled sub-matrix is too large.

3 Large-Scale Spectral Clustering with Stochastic Nyström Approximation

The Nyström approximation technology uses the sample points to compute the approximate eigenvectors. It can effectively reduce the computational complexity of traditional spectral clustering algorithm. The performance of Nyström approximation is closely related to sample number. Although improving the sampling proportion can improve the clustering results, the complexity of the algorithm is also significantly increased. Careful observation can be found that when the sample number m is large, the most time-consuming operation of the algorithm is the eigen-decomposition of the $m \times m$ sub-matrix M. In order to solve this problem, we develop the stochastic Nyström approximation method to solve the approximate eigenvalue and eigenvector of M. We try to improve the efficiency of the algorithm as far as possible in the premise of ensuring the clustering accuracy. Therefore we propose a large-scale spectral clustering algorithm with stochastic Nyström approximation. The details of the proposed algorithm is shown in Algorithm 2.

Algorithm 2. Large-scale spectral clustering with stochastic Nyström approximation (SNA-SC).

Input: data set X of n data points, number of sample points m, number of classes k.
Output: clustering results of k clusters.
Step 1. According to Eq. (1), form matrix $A \in \mathbb{R}^{m \times m}$ and matrix $B \in \mathbb{R}^{m \times (n-m)}$ with the m sample points.
Step 2. Calculate the diagonal degree matrix $D = \text{diag}\left(\begin{bmatrix} A\mathbf{1}_m + B\mathbf{1}_{n-m} \\ B^T\mathbf{1}_m + B^T A^{-1} B\mathbf{1}_{n-m} \end{bmatrix} \right)$
with matrix A and B.
Step 3. Calculate the normalized matrix A and B as $\bar{A} = D_{1:m,1:m}^{-1/2} A D_{1:m,1:m}^{-1/2}$, $\bar{B} = D_{1:m,1:m}^{-1/2} B D_{m+1:n,m+1:n}^{-1/2}$, and form matrix $H = \begin{bmatrix} \bar{A} & \bar{B} \end{bmatrix}^T$.
Step 4. Construct matrix $M = \bar{A} + \bar{A}^{-1/2} \bar{B} \bar{B}^T \bar{A}^{-1/2}$ with matrix $\bar{A}$ and $\bar{B}$.
Step 5. Make the eigen-decomposition of M by Algorithm 1, namely $M \approx U_M \Lambda_F U_M^T$, and ensure the descending order of the eigenvalues in Λ_F.
Step 6. Calculate the top k orthogonal eigenvectors of the Laplacian matrix using Eq. (3): $\tilde{V} = H\bar{A}^{-1/2}(U_M)_{:,1:k}(\Lambda_F^{-1/2})_{1:k,1:k}$.
Step 7. Normalize matrix $\tilde{V}$ by Eq. (5) and get matrix $\tilde{U}$.

$$\tilde{U}_{ij} = \frac{\tilde{V}_{ij}}{\sqrt{\sum_{r=1}^{k} \tilde{V}_{ir}^2}}, \quad i = 1, \cdots, n, \quad j = 1, \cdots, k \tag{5}$$

Step 8. The rows of $\tilde{U}$ can be seen as new data points and we can divide them into k clusters by traditional clustering algorithms, such as k-means.

The proposed Algorithm 2 combines the advantages of Nyström approximation and the stochastic SVD, and has a good performance in the clustering efficiency and accuracy. In essence, the low rank approximation of the original $n \times n$ affinity matrix W can be expressed as $\tilde{W} = HA^{-1}H^T = U_W \Lambda_M U_W^T = U_W U_M^T M U_M U_W^T$ according to Eq. (3). Through Algorithm 1 and Eq. (4), we can obtain the approximate M as $M \simeq QFQ^T$. So the more accurate approximation form of W in Algorithm 2 is as follows:

$$\tilde{W} \simeq U_W U_M^T QFQ^T U_M U_W^T \tag{6}$$

Different with the Nyström method, Algorithm 2 adopts stochastic SVD method for solving the approximate eigenvalues and eigenvectors of matrix M. Its time complexity is $O(m^2k + k^3)$. In addition, the matrix H related multiplication operations need to spend $O(kmn)$ time. Usually $n \gg m \geq k$, so the total time complexity of Algorithm 2 is $O(k^3 + kmn)$. Compared to the $O(m^3 + kmn)$ complexity of Nyström method, the complexity of Algorithm 2 is lower. This means that, for the same size of problem, Algorithm 2 can finish the task in a shorter time.

4   Experimental Analysis

To validate the performance of the proposed SNA-SC algorithm, our experiments are done on the four real world data sets from UCI machine learning repository. These data sets are listed in Table 1.

Table 1. Basic properties of the data sets.

Data set	Data points' number	Attributes' number	Clusters' number
Corel	2074	144	18
Seismic	98528	50	3
RCV1	193844	47236	103

Based on the data sets in Table 1, we compare three different clustering algorithms in the experiments. In addition to the proposed SNA-SC algorithm, there are approximate kernel k-means algorithm (AKK-means) [10], the spectral clustering algorithm based on Nyström extension (Nyström-SC) [11]. The performance of each algorithm are evaluated by the clustering accuracy and running time. All algorithms are implemented by MATLAB, running on a high-performance workstation with 3.20 GHz CPU. In the experiments, the affinities of data points are measured by radial basis function. The max iterations of AKK-means algorithm is 1000. The sample points in Nyström-SC and SNA-SC algorithm are obtained by random sampling.

Table 2 is the clustering accuracy of these algorithms on each data set, in which the bold value is the best clustering result. AKK-means, Nyström-SC and SNA-SC use part of the kernel matrix for approximate computation, so they need to sample some data points. From Table 2, we know that the clustering accuracy of each algorithm is different in different sampling proportion. Overall, the increase in the proportion of sampling is helpful to improve the quality of clustering. However, sometimes more samples will also make the clustering quality slightly worse, because it contains more noise data. AKK-means algorithm constructs the approximate kernel matrix by random sampling, and based on this, it can reduce the space complexity of the original kernel k-means by computing the class center of kernel k-means in a smaller subspace. AKK-means clustering can get the highest accuracy on Corel data set. However, on other data sets, AKK-means is not as good as Nyström-SC and SNA-SC algorithm. Nyström-SC is suitable for processing RCV1 data set. SNA-SC has good performance on Seismic data set.

Table 2. Clustering accuracy of algorithms (%).

Data set	Sampling ratio (m/n)	Algorithm		
		AKK-means	Nyström-SC	SNA-SC
Corel	2%	31.62 (±1.51)	30.42 (±0.76)	31.21 (±1.63)
	4%	34.16 (±1.07)	30.92 (±0.85)	33.64 (±1.41)
	6%	37.27 (±0.54)	32.46 (±0.72)	36.86 (±1.25)
	8%	**38.58** (±0.76)	33.27 (±0.57)	37.16 (±1.08)
Seismic	2%	62.46 (±1.24)	60.48 (±1.56)	64.13 (±1.29)
	4%	64.14 (±0.43)	62.57 (±1.12)	67.23 (±0.42)
	6%	64.81 (±0.62)	63.44 (±1.81)	67.75 (±0.83)
	8%	65.27 (±0.53)	64.91 (±0.34)	**68.34** (±0.37)
RCV1	2%	12.55 (±0.76)	11.27 (±0.65)	12.43 (±0.84)
	4%	13.82 (±0.53)	14.24 (±0.46)	14.67 (±0.39)
	6%	15.42 (±0.72)	16.73 (±0.67)	15.94 (±0.65)
	8%	16.26 (±0.51)	**18.12** (±0.34)	16.63 (±0.41)

The clustering time of different algorithms are compared in Table 3. Table 3 shows that SNA-SC has the highest running efficiency on each data set. On RCV1 data set, SNA-SC only takes 44 s to do the clustering under 8% sampling rate, while Nyström-SC takes 162 s. Because with the sampling rate increase, the decomposition of the internal sub-matrix in Nyström-SC will cost a lot of time. AKK-means is a k-means-like algorithm. It repeatedly relocate the cluster center to optimize the lose function. The clustering time of AKK-means is mainly related to the iteration times. Although more samples will help increase the approximation accuracy, but it also increases the clustering time. For AKK-means and SNA-SC, their clustering time increase linearly with the sampling ratio increasing. But the clustering time of Nyström-SC has violent changes because of the cubic time complexity of the eigen-decomposition of the internal sub-matrix.

Table 3. Clustering time of algorithms (s).

Data set	Sampling ratio (m/n)	Algorithm		
		AKK-means	Nyström-SC	SNA-SC
Corel	2%	0.11	0.06	0.05
	4%	0.14	0.09	0.05
	6%	0.16	0.10	0.07
	8%	0.18	0.36	0.08
Seismic	2%	6.10	0.82	0.72
	4%	7.69	3.03	1.75
	6%	11.68	6.15	2.68
	8%	19.38	26.75	5.86
RCV1	2%	40.44	21.36	20.66
	4%	56.01	27.33	25.02
	6%	73.94	64.29	31.25
	8%	110.96	162.32	44.12

5 Conclusion

Nyström approximation will help reduce the complexity of spectral clustering using approximate eigenvectors. However, when the sample number is too large, internal SVD of Nyström will take a very long time. This paper applies the stochastic SVD algorithm to improve the performance of large-scale Nyström spectral clustering. Unlike standard Nyström method, we use the stochastic low rank matrix approximation strategy to do the eigen-decomposition of the internal sub-matrix, and propose a large-scale spectral clustering called SNA-SC. Experimental results show that SNA-SC is more efficient than standard Nyström spectral clustering, and it can well balance the clustering accuracy and efficiency.

Acknowledgement. This work was supported by the National Natural Science Foundations of China (grant numbers 61906077, 61601202), the Natural Science Foundation of Jiangsu Province (grant numbers BK20190838, BK20170558), and the Natural Science Foundation of the Jiangsu Higher Education Institutions of China (grant number 18KJB520009, 16KJB520008).

References

1. Kang, Z., et al.: Multi-graph fusion for multi-view spectral clustering. Knowl.-Based Syst. **189** (2020). https://doi.org/10.1016/j.knosys.2019.105102
2. Tang, M., Marin, D., Ayed, I.B., Boykov, Y.: Kernel cuts: kernel and spectral clustering meet regularization. Int. J. Comput. Vis. **127**(5), 477–511 (2019). https://doi.org/10.1007/s11263-018-1115-1
3. Jia, H., Ding, S., Du, M.: A Nyström spectral clustering algorithm based on probability incremental sampling. Soft Comput. **21**(19), 5815–5827 (2016). https://doi.org/10.1007/s00500-016-2160-8

4. Fowlkes, C., Belongie, S., Chung, F., Malik, J.: Spectral grouping using the Nystrom method. IEEE Trans. Pattern Anal. Mach. Intell. **26**(2), 214–225 (2004)
5. Li, M., Bi, W., Kwok, J.T., Lu, B.L.: Large-scale Nyström kernel matrix approximation using randomized SVD. IEEE Trans. Neural Netw. Learn. Syst. **26**(1), 152–164 (2014)
6. Halko, N., Martinsson, P.G., Tropp, J.A.: Finding structure with randomness: Probabilistic algorithms for constructing approximate matrix decompositions. SIAM Rev. **53**(2), 217–288 (2011)
7. Drineas, P., Kannan, R., Mahoney, M.W.: Fast Monte Carlo algorithms for matrices II: computing a low-rank approximation to a matrix. SIAM J. Comput. **36**(1), 158–183 (2006)
8. Jia, H., Ding, S., Du, M., Xue, Y.: Approximate normalized cuts without Eigen-decomposition. Inf. Sci. **374**, 135–150 (2016)
9. Wang, S., Gittens, A., Mahoney, M.W.: Scalable kernel K-means clustering with Nyström approximation: relative-error bounds. J. Mach. Learn. Res. **20**(1), 431–479 (2019)
10. Chitta, R., Jin, R., Havens, T.C., Jain, A.K.: Approximate kernel k-means: solution to large scale kernel clustering. In: Proceedings of the 17th ACM SIGKDD International Conference on Knowledge Discovery and Data Mining, pp. 895–903. ACM, San Diego (2011)
11. Chen, W.Y., Song, Y., Bai, H., Lin, C.J., Chang, E.Y.: Parallel spectral clustering in distributed systems. IEEE Trans. Pattern Anal. Mach. Intell. **33**(3), 568–586 (2011)

Feature Selection Algorithm Based on Multi Strategy Grey Wolf Optimizer

Guangyue Zhou[1], Kewen Li[1(✉)], Guoqiang Wan[2], and Hongtu Ji[2]

[1] College of Computer Science and Technology, China University of Petroleum,
Qingdao 266580, China
guangyuezhou@qq.com, likw@upc.edu.cn
[2] Shengli Oilfield Company, SINOPEC, Dongying 257015, China
{wanguoqiang.slyt,jihongtu.slyt}@sinopec.com

Abstract. Feature selection is an important part of data mining, image recognition and other fields. The efficiency and accuracy of classification algorithm can be improved by selecting the best feature subset. The classical feature selection technology has some limitations, and heuristic optimization algorithm for feature selection is an alternative method to solve these limitations and find the optimal solution. In this paper, we proposed a Multi Strategy Grey Wolf Optimizer algorithm (MSGWO) based on random guidance, local search and subgroup cooperation strategies for feature selection, which solves the problem that the traditional grey wolf optimizer algorithm (GWO) is easy to fall into local optimization with a single search strategy. Among them, the random guidance strategy can make full use of the random characteristics to enhance the global search ability of the population, and the local search strategy makes grey wolf individuals make full use of the search space around the current best solution, and the subgroup cooperation strategy is very important to balance the global search and local search of the algorithm in the iterative process. MSGWO algorithm cooperates with each other in three strategies to update the location of grey wolf individuals, and enhances the global and local search ability of grey wolf individuals. Experimental results show that MSGWO can quickly find the optimal feature combination and effectively improve the performance of the classification model.

Keywords: Feature selection · Heuristic optimization algorithm · Multi Strategy Grey Wolf Optimizer algorithm

1 Introduction

Feature selection plays an important role in machine learning, data mining and other classification applications. Its goal is to remove the noise in the original

Supported by organization from the National Natural Science Foundation of China (No. 61673396), and the Natural Science Foundation of Shandong Province, China (No. ZR2017MF032).

© IFIP International Federation for Information Processing 2020
Published by Springer Nature Switzerland AG 2020
Z. Shi et al. (Eds.): IIP 2020, IFIP AICT 581, pp. 35–45, 2020.
https://doi.org/10.1007/978-3-030-46931-3_4

data and select the best identification feature. In addition, feature selection can improve the efficiency of classification by reducing the dimension of the original data. In recent years, more and more heuristic search algorithms are used for feature selection. Heuristic search algorithm can get a group of solutions at a time, which can get good results with less time and calculation cost. Many experts and scholars have done a lot of research on heuristic search algorithm: Genetic Algorithm (GA) is an evolutionary algorithm, which can search randomly and find the optimal solution based the evolution law of nature [1]. Particle Swarm Optimization (PSO) is a classical swarm intelligence optimization algorithm, which is based on the research of birds' predatory behavior. Each solution is regarded as a particle with a specific position, fitness and speed vector, and its motion direction and speed are adjusted according to the global optimal solution and the optimal solution found by the particle itself, and gradually approach the optimal solution [2]. The Whale Optimization Algorithm (WOA) is a heuristic optimization algorithm, which simulates the predatory behavior of humpback whales in nature. Compared with other swarm optimization algorithms, the main difference is that WOA simulates the bubble net attack of whales by following the best or random individuals and using the spiral mechanisms [3]. The Grey Wolf Optimizer (GWO) is a new evolutionary algorithm, which mainly simulates the predatory behavior of grey wolf group, through the process of wolves tracking, encircling, chasing and attacking to achieve the purpose of optimized search [4]. As GWO has the advantages of simple principle, few parameters to be adjusted, easy to realize and strong global search ability, its research has made remarkable progress. Emary and others first applied GWO to feature selection in 2015, and proposed two binary GWO feature selection methods based on different update mechanisms [5].

GWO algorithm can not effectively find the global optimal feature combination due to its single search strategy and insufficient global search ability [6]. Therefore, in order to improve the effectiveness of GWO for feature selection, this paper proposes a Multi Strategy Grey Wolf Optimizer algorithm (MSGWO), which solves the problem caused by a single search strategy and improves the accuracy of the original GWO. MSGWO includes three different search strategies—Random guidance strategy, local search strategy and sub group cooperation strategy. The grey wolf optimizer algorithm with three strategies can further improve the search efficiency and find the optimal feature combination.

2   Grey Wolf Optimizer (GWO)

GWO is an intelligent optimization algorithm proposed by Mirjalili [4] in 2014. Due to its simple principle, fewer parameters to be adjusted, simple implementation and strong global search ability, the method is becoming more and more popular. Many research have been carried out using GWO [7–11]. GWO algorithm is inspired by the predatory behavior of grey wolves, and it optimizes search through hunting, searching for prey, encircling prey, and attacking prey.

There is a strict hierarchy between them. α, β, δ and ω represent different grades of grey wolves, and the dominance rate decreases from top to bottom. In order to model the grey wolf's social system mathematically, α is regarded as the optimal solution, β and δ are regarded as the suboptimal solution and the third optimal solution, respectively. They lead other wolves toward the possible position of prey. ω is regarded as the rest of the solutions, which is updated according to the positions of α, β and δ. Three definitions of the algorithm [4] are given below.

Definition 1. Distance between Grey Wolf and Prey

$$\vec{D} = |\vec{C} \cdot \vec{X_p}(t) - \vec{X}(t)| \tag{1}$$

where t indicates the current iteration, $\vec{X_p}$ represents position vector of prey, $\vec{X}(t)$ represents current position vector of grey wolf.

$$\vec{C} = 2 \cdot \vec{r_1} \tag{2}$$

where r_1 is random vector in $[0, 1]$, $\vec{C}$ is coefficient vector. We can explore and exploit search space by randomly enhancing $(C > 1)$ or weakening $(C < 1)$ the distance between prey and grey wolf.

Definition 2. Update position of Grey Wolf

$$\vec{X}(t+1) = \vec{X_p}(t) - \vec{A} \cdot \vec{D} \tag{3}$$

$$\vec{A} = 2\vec{a} \cdot \vec{r_2} - \vec{a} \tag{4}$$

where components of $\vec{a}$ are linearly decreased from 2 to 0, r_2 is random vector in $[0,1]$. As A decreases, half of the iterations are used for exploring $(|A| > 1)$, and the rest for exploiting $(|A| < 1)$.

Definition 3. Determine position of prey

In the abstract search space, the exact position of the prey (optimal solution) is not known. According to the hierarchy of grey wolves, hunting is usually guided by α, β and δ. Therefore, it is assumed that α (optimal candidate solution), β (suboptimal candidate solution), and δ (third optimal candidate solution) have a better acquaintance of the position of prey. It is known that grey wolves α, β and δ are closest to prey. By preserving the obtained three optimal solutions during each iteration, the orientation of prey can be determined according to the positions of the three optimal solutions, and other grey wolf individuals are forced to update their positions according to the three optimal solutions. The mathematical descriptions of grey wolf individuals tracking prey orientation are as follows:

$$\vec{D_\alpha} = |\vec{C_1} \cdot \vec{X_\alpha} - \vec{X}|, \vec{D_\beta} = |\vec{C_2} \cdot \vec{X_\beta} - \vec{X}|, \vec{D_\delta} = |\vec{C_3} \cdot \vec{X_\delta} - \vec{X}| \tag{5}$$

$$\vec{X_1} = \vec{X_\alpha} - \vec{A_1} \cdot \vec{D_\alpha}, \vec{X_2} = \vec{X_\beta} - \vec{A_2} \cdot \vec{D_\beta}, \vec{X_3} = \vec{X_\delta} - \vec{A_3} \cdot \vec{D_\delta} \tag{6}$$

$$\vec{X}(t+1) = 1/3(\vec{X_1} + \vec{X_2} + \vec{X_3}) \tag{7}$$

The distances between grey wolf individuals and α, β and δ are calculated in terms of formulas (5) and (6). Then the direction of grey wolf individuals moving towards prey are judged in terms of formula (7). Where $\overrightarrow{X_\alpha}, \overrightarrow{X_\beta}, \overrightarrow{X_\delta}$ represent the positions of α, β, δ respectively, $\overrightarrow{C_1}, \overrightarrow{C_2}, \overrightarrow{C_3}$ are random vectors and $\overrightarrow{X}$ is the position of the current solution.

3   Multi Strategy Grey Wolf Optimizer Algorithm

3.1   Random Guidance Strategy

In GWO, α, β and δ lead ω to the promising region to search for the optimal solution, but only following the optimal solution to update is easy to lead to premature convergence in the current optimal position, making GWO fall into the local optimum. In this paper, we randomly select a grey wolf position $\overrightarrow{X_{rand}}$, and make other individuals update the position according to $\overrightarrow{X_{rand}}$. The mathematical description is as follows:

$$\overrightarrow{D_{rand}} = |\overrightarrow{C_g} \cdot \overrightarrow{X_{rand}} - \overrightarrow{X}| \tag{8}$$

$$\overrightarrow{X_g} = \overrightarrow{X_{rand}} - \overrightarrow{A_g} \cdot \overrightarrow{D_{rand}} \tag{9}$$

$$\overrightarrow{X}(t+1) = \overrightarrow{X_g} \tag{10}$$

where $\overrightarrow{D_{rand}}$ is the distance between grey wolf individual and $\overrightarrow{X_{rand}}$, $\overrightarrow{X}(t+1)$ is the updated position, and $\overrightarrow{C_g}$ is the random vector.

This strategy can make the gray wolf individuals that converge too early jump out of the local optimum, expand the global search range of the population, and increase the possibility of finding the global optimum solution.

3.2   Local Search Strategy

Because the whale optimization algorithm approaches the prey according to the shrinking encirclement mechanism, and moves along the spiral path according to the spiral renewal mechanism, it can expand the local search range of whales. Inspired by the whale optimization algorithm, this paper improves the single update mechanism of grey wolf position, which makes the grey wolf individuals explore the surrounding solutions while moving towards the optimal solution, greatly expanding the range of local search. The mathematical description of the strategy is as follows:

$$\overrightarrow{X_{loc}} = \overrightarrow{D'} * e^{bl} * cos(2\pi l) + \overrightarrow{X} \tag{11}$$

$$\overrightarrow{D'} = 1/3(\overrightarrow{D_\alpha} + \overrightarrow{D_\beta} + \overrightarrow{D_\delta}) \tag{12}$$

Where $\overrightarrow{D'}$ is the mean distance between grey wolf individual and α, β, δ, b is constant defining the shape of a logarithmic spiral, and l is the random number between $[-1, 1]$.

The local search strategy is to make the grey wolf move along the spiral path as well as within the shrinking circle. In order to simulate the two simultaneous behaviors, we assume that there is a 0.5 probability of the contraction encirclement mechanism or spiral update mechanism to choose to update the location of the grey wolves. The mathematical description of the strategy is as follows:

$$\overrightarrow{X}(t+1) = \begin{cases} 1/3(\overrightarrow{X_1} + \overrightarrow{X_2} + \overrightarrow{X_3}) & p < 0.5 \\ \overrightarrow{X_{loc}} & p >= 0.5 \end{cases} \tag{13}$$

where p is the random number between $[0, 1]$.

3.3 Sub Group Cooperation Strategy

In order to give full play to the advantages of random guidance strategy and local search strategy, expand the search space of the algorithm as much as possible, and guide algorithm jump out of the local optimum, this paper proposes a sub group cooperation strategy, the basic idea is as follows:

In the evolutionary process, the population is divided into three subgroups A, B and C according to the fitness values. A represents the subgroup with large fitness value, B represents the subgroup with medium fitness value, and C represents the subgroup with poor fitness value. The fitness value of grey wolf individuals in subgroup A is large, which indicates that the convergence degree is high and it is easy to fall into local optimum. In this case, grey wolf individuals update their positions according to formula (13), so that the individual can search around the extreme point more finely, find the position with better fitness than before, enhance the local search ability. The fitness value of grey wolf individuals in subgroup B is medium, which is updated according to the formulas (5)–(7) in the standard grey wolf algorithm. The fitness value of grey wolf individuals in subgroup C is poor, which is updated according to the formulas (8)–(10), and this subgroup can cover all possible solutions as much as possible by the random guidance strategy, so as to enhance the global search ability. The grey wolf individuals in subgroups A, B and C evolve according to their own update strategies, and each grey wolf individual migrates to the corresponding subgroup according to the new fitness value after every iteration until the termination condition is satisfied.

3.4 Multi Strategy Grey Wolf Optimizer Algorithm (MSGWO)

In this paper, we combine the random guidance strategy, local search strategy, sub group cooperation strategy and the standard grey wolf algorithm to propose a Multi Strategy Grey Wolf Optimizer algorithm. In the continuous MSGWO, each individual can change its position to any point in the space. The purpose of this paper is to use MSGWO for feature selection, so the value of each dimension in the individual position is limited to 0 or 1. 0 means that the feature in the corresponding position is not selected, and 1 means that the feature in the corresponding position is selected. Thus, the updating formula of MSGWO for feature selection is as follows:

$$x_{in}^{k+1} = \begin{cases} 1 & if \quad sigmoid(x_{in}^{k+1}) >= 0.5 \\ 0 & otherwise \end{cases} \tag{14}$$

sigmoid is defined as follows:

$$sigmoid(a) = 1/(1 + e^{-10(a-5)}) \tag{15}$$

In order to provide the more intuitive description of the MSGWO algorithm, we draw an algorithm flowchart of it. It is shown in Fig. 1.

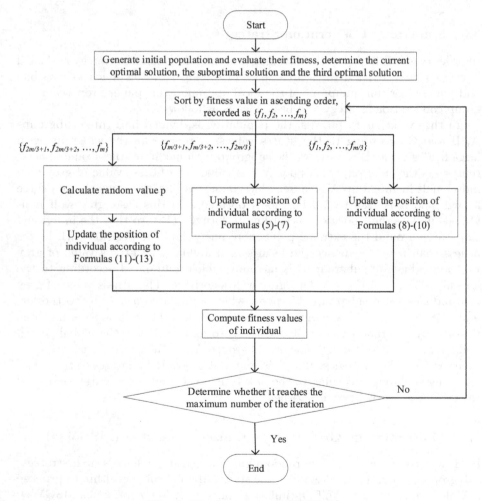

Fig. 1. The flow chart of MSGWO

As can be seen from Fig. 1, the local search strategy enables grey wolf individuals to make full use of the search space around the current best solution, which has good local search ability and helps to find more accurate solutions. For the random guidance strategy, we make full use of the random characteristics to improve the diversity of the population, thus enhancing the global search ability. In addition to the above two strategies, the sub group cooperation strategy is very important to balance the global search and local search in the iterative process. It not only guarantees the convergence speed of the algorithm, but also expands the search range of the population, and prevents the algorithm from falling into local stagnation in the later stage of the iteration. Due to the slow convergence speed in the early stage and the fast convergence speed in the later stage, the time complexity of the MSGWO is the same as that of the GWO.

4 Experiment

In order to prove the effectiveness of MSGWO proposed for feature selection in this paper, we evaluated the proposed algorithm using the Vehicle, Wine, Glass, Zoo, Landsat and Segment public datasets from UCI repository. Table 1 lists the details of the six datasets used in the evaluation. In order to prove the superiority of MSGWO in feature selection, we used the classical K-Nearest-Neighbor (KNN) classifier and Support Vector Machine (SVM) as the benchmark classifier, and compared the performance on six public datasets of our proposed MSGWO method and several classical feature selection methods including analysis of variance (ANOVA) [12], principal component analysis (PCA) [13], PSO [2], WOA [3] and GWO, in which no feature selection is recorded as NFS. In the experiment, KNN and SVM adopt default parameters. For KNN, k-value is set to 5. For SVM, penalty parameter c is set to 1 and the gauss kernel is set to the kernel function. We carried on experiments by using five-folds cross validation for 5 times, and set the number of grey wolves in GWO, particles in PSO and killer whales in WOA were all set to 15. Table 2 and Table 3 list the comparison of the average values of accuracy and F1 of five-folds cross validation on SVM and KNN, respectively.

Table 1. Details of the six datasets used in the evaluation

No	Dataset	Number of samples	Dimension of samples	Number of categories
1	Vehicle	946	18	4
2	Wine	178	13	3
3	Glass	214	9	6
4	Zoo	101	16	7
5	Landsat	2000	36	6
6	Segment	2100	18	7

Table 2. Comparison of classification performance between various feature selection algorithms on SVM

Datasets	Metrics	NFS	ANOVA	PCA	PSO	WOA	GWO	MSGWO
Vehicle	Accuracy	0.633	0.709	0.639	0.825	0.819	0.825	0.846
	F1	0.584	0.695	0.592	0.822	0.827	0.836	0.849
Wine	Accuracy	0.613	0.894	0.736	0.993	0.992	0.992	1
	F1	0.554	0.892	0.711	0.994	0.996	0.997	1
Glass	Accuracy	0.784	0.846	0.776	0.921	0.927	0.920	0.940
	F1	0.747	0.829	0.738	0.915	0.918	0.924	0.943
Zoo	Accuracy	0.733	0.940	0.733	0.978	0.984	0.974	0.988
	F1	0.685	0.923	0.685	0.974	0.985	0.993	0.997
Landsat	Accuracy	0.696	0.822	0.710	0.868	0.870	0.874	0.885
	F1	0.673	0.819	0.689	0.863	0.868	0.877	0.893
Segment	Accuracy	0.885	0.926	0.879	0.950	0.953	0.955	0.970
	F1	0.889	0.926	0.881	0.949	0.951	0.956	0.964

Table 3. Comparison of classification performance between various feature selection algorithms on KNN

Datasets	Metrics	NFS	ANOVA	PCA	PSO	WOA	GWO	MSGWO
Vehicle	Accuracy	0.697	0.675	0.697	0.813	0.810	0.805	0.826
	F1	0.670	0.635	0.667	0.802	0.798	0.816	0.833
Wine	Accuracy	0.955	0.961	0.949	0.994	0.994	0.992	0.996
	F1	0.960	0.960	0.949	0.992	0.993	0.992	0.996
Glass	Accuracy	0.841	0.856	0.808	0.945	0.951	0.940	0.962
	F1	0.826	0.846	0.781	0.938	0.960	0.952	0.963
Zoo	Accuracy	0.928	0.962	0.919	0.987	0.997	0.991	1
	F1	0.915	0.953	0.906	0.993	1	0.996	1
Landsat	Accuracy	0.825	0.833	0.826	0.861	0.863	0.869	0.875
	F1	0.820	0.829	0.821	0.861	0.861	0.867	0.876
Segment	Accuracy	0.914	0.922	0.903	0.945	0.949	0.951	0.964
	F1	0.911	0.921	0.900	0.944	0.949	0.951	0.964

From Table 2 and Table 3, we can see that the classification effect of NFS is very poor, which shows the necessity of feature selection. The performance of ANOVA and PCA is not high, because the filter selection method needs to manually specify the number of selected features, and the most appropriate number of features is difficult to determine. The results of feature selection by heuristic method are ideal. The performance of standard GWO algorithm for different datasets is sometimes better than PSO and WOA, and sometimes lower than PSO and WOA. The MSGWO proposed in this paper is not only better than GWO, but also better than PSO and WOA for all the datasets listed in this paper in terms of accuracy and F1 value, which proves the effectiveness of MSGWO.

Because the heuristic method is a random search method, the results of each search may be different. In order to verify that the MSGWO method proposed in this paper can not only select the optimal feature combination, but also has good stability. In this paper, only the accuracy is analyzed. Figure 2 and Figure 3 show the box diagram of the accuracy of five times random experiments among four feature selection algorithms on SVM and KNN classifiers. From Fig. 2 and Fig. 3, it can be concluded that whether SVM or KNN is used as the base classifier, the maximum, minimum and average accuracy of MSGWO algorithm is superior to the other three heuristic methods, which further proves that MSGWO can effectively improve the performance of the classifier. In addition, by introducing the standard deviation to further analyze the stability of the algorithm, the standard deviations of the accuracy of five times random experiments are recorded in Table 4. According to Table 4, it can be seen that accuracy of MSGWO is relatively stable and the standard deviation is the smallest in almost all datasets, which proves that MSGWO is stable.

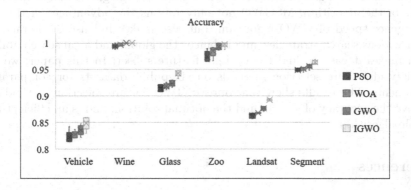

Fig. 2. Comparison of the accuracy of heuristic feature selection methods on SVM

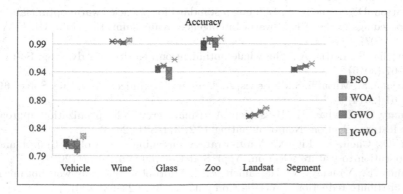

Fig. 3. Comparison of the accuracy of heuristic feature selection methods on KNN

Table 4. Comparison of classification performance between various feature selection algorithms on SVM and KNN

Datasets	SVM				KNN			
	PSO	WOA	GWO	MSGWO	PSO	WOA	GWO	MSGWO
Vehicle	1.03E−2	5.84E−3	8.51E−3	4.40E−3	6.41E−3	6.24E−3	9.88E−3	4.17E−3
Wine	3.93E−3	2.99E−3	0	0	0	0	2.44E−3	2.44E−3
Glass	6.07E−3	6.11E−3	5.17E−3	4.26E−3	5.53E−3	2.00E−3	1.03E−2	0
Zoo	8.90E−3	9.48E−3	6.31E−3	5.11E−3	7.80E−3	4.40E−3	7.91E−3	0
Landsat	4.13E−3	5.85E−3	3.30E−3	1.61E−3	1.73E−3	1.73E−3	2.19E−3	1.16E−3
Segment	3.87E−3	3.28E−3	3.80E−3	2.74E−3	3.40E−3	2.65E−3	1.78E−3	9.80E−4

5   Conclusion

In this paper, we propose a Multi Strategy Grey Wolf Optimizer algorithm based on random guidance, local search and sub group cooperation strategies for feature selection. In MSGWO, the search agent updates its position through the cooperation of three search strategies, which improves the global and local search ability of the algorithm. MSGWO not only retains the advantages of the fast convergence speed of GWO algorithm, but also makes full use of characteristics of various search strategies, and balances the global and local search ability, which makes it easy to find the optimal feature subset. In this paper, we use a variety of feature selection methods on six public datasets for comparative experiments. The results show that our MSGWO feature selection method can improve the accuracy of search, find the optimal solution, and is an efficient and reliable algorithm.

References

1. Holland, J.: Adaptation in Natural and Artificial Systems. University of Michigan Press, Ann Arbor (1975)
2. Bratton, D., Kennedy, J.: Defining a standard for particle swarm optimization. In: Proceedings of the IEEE Swarm Intelligence Symposium, Honolulu, HI, USA, pp. 1–5 (2007)
3. Mirjalili, S., Lewis, A.: The whale optimization algorithm. Adv. Eng. Softw. **95**, 51–67 (2016)
4. Mirjalili, S., Mirjalili, S.M., Lewis, A.: Grey wolf optimizer. Adv. Eng. Softw. **69**(3), 46–61 (2014)
5. Emary, E., Zawbaa, H., Hassanien, A.: Binary grey wolf optimization approaches for feature selection. Neurocomputing **172**, 371–381 (2016)
6. Tu, Q., Chen, X., Liu, X.: Multi-strategy ensemble grey wolf optimizer and its application to feature selection. Appl. Soft Comput. **76**, 16–30 (2019)
7. Emary, E., Yamany, W., Hassanien, A.E.: Multi-objective gray-wolf optimization for attribute reduction. Procedia Comput. Sci. **65**, 623–632 (2015)

8. Elhariri, E., El-Bendary, N., Hassanien, A.E.: Grey wolf optimization for one-against-one multi-class support vector machines. In: 7th International Conference of Soft Computing and Pattern Recognition (SoCPaR), pp. 7–12. Kyushu University, Fukuoka (2015)
9. Heidari, A.A., Pahlavani, P.: An efficient modified grey wolf optimizer with levy flight for optimization tasks. Appl. Soft Comput. **60**, 115–134 (2017)
10. Zhu, A., Xu, C., Li, Z.: Hybridizing grey wolf optimization with differential evolution for global optimization and test scheduling for 3D stacked SoC. J. Syst. Eng. Electron. **26**(2), 317–328 (2015)
11. Wei, Z., Zhao, H., Han, B.: Grey wolf optimization algorithm with self-adaptive searching strategy. Comput. Sci. **44**(3), 259–263 (2017)
12. Dai, J., Yuan, J.: The comparison of test methods between single factor analysis of variance and multiple linear regression analysis. Stat. Decis. **09**, 23–26 (2016)
13. Li, J.: Combination of feature extraction in text classification algorithm based on PCA. Appl. Res. Comput. **30**(08), 2398–2401 (2013)

A Novel Fuzzy C-means Clustering Algorithm Based on Local Density

Jian-jun Liu[1] and Jian-cong Fan[1,2,3(✉)]

[1] College of Computer Science and Engineering,
Shandong University of Science and Technology, Qingdao, China
fanjiancong@sdust.edu.cn
[2] Provincial Key Laboratory for Information Technology of Wisdom Mining
of Shandong Province, Shandong University of Science and Technology,
Qingdao, China
[3] Provincial Experimental Teaching Demonstration Center of Computer,
Shandong University of Science and Technology, Qingdao, China

Abstract. Fuzzy C-means (FCM) clustering algorithm is a fuzzy clustering algorithm based on objective function. FCM is the most perfect and widely used algorithm in the theory of fuzzy clustering. However, in the process of clustering, FCM algorithm needs to randomly select the initial cluster center. It is easy to generate problems such as multiple clustering iterations, low convergence speed and unstable clustering. In order to solve the above problems, a novel fuzzy C-means clustering algorithm based on local density is proposed in this paper. Firstly, we calculate the local density of all sample points. Then we select the sample points with the local maximum density as the initial cluster center at each iteration. Finally, the selected initial cluster center are combined with the traditional FCM clustering algorithm to achieve clustering. This method improved the selection of the initial cluster center. The comparative experiment shows that the improved FCM algorithm reduces the number of iterations and improves the convergence speed.

Keywords: Fuzzy C-means algorithm · Local density · Clustering

1 Introduction

Cluster analysis [1–5] is an important function of data mining, and the clustering algorithm is the core of current research. Clustering is to divide the data set into multiple clusters or classes based on the similarity between a set of unlabeled data objects. A good clustering algorithm should be able to produce high-quality clustering results: clusters. These clusters must have two characteristics: (1) high intra-cluster similarity; (2) low inter-cluster similarity. The quality of the clustering results depends not only on the similarity evaluation method and its specific implementation, but also on whether the method can find some hidden patterns or all hidden patterns [6].

Fuzzy C-means (FCM) clustering algorithm [7–10] is one of the widely used fuzzy clustering algorithms. FCM algorithm belongs to the category of fuzzy clustering algorithms based on objective functions. However, the traditional FCM algorithm has

© IFIP International Federation for Information Processing 2020
Published by Springer Nature Switzerland AG 2020
Z. Shi et al. (Eds.): IIP 2020, IFIP AICT 581, pp. 46–58, 2020.
https://doi.org/10.1007/978-3-030-46931-3_5

some disadvantages. One of the issues is that the number of clusters needs to be determined manually, and the algorithm is sensitive to the initial cluster center. In addition, the FCM algorithm is prone to problems such as multiple clustering iterations, low convergence speed and local optimal solution. Many algorithms have been proposed to improve the FCM algorithm. Wang et al. [11] systematically improved the traditional fuzzy clustering algorithm. They proposed a new method by combining PSO (particle swarm optimization) and fuzzy C-means algorithm. By a simple and effective particle encoding method, the best initial cluster center and fuzzy weighting exponent were both searched in the process of PSO. Li et al. [12] proposed a scheduling algorithm based on fuzzy clustering and two-level scheduling mode. Geweniger et al. [13] combined the median c-means algorithm with the fuzzy c-means method to improve the accuracy of the algorithm. Median clustering is a powerful methodology for prototype based clustering of similarity/dissimilarity data. The approach is only applicable for vector (metric) data in its original variant. Wang et al. [14] presented a rough-set [15, 16] based measurement for the membership degree of fuzzy C-means algorithm, and take the advantage of the positive region set and the boundary region set of rough set. Lai et al. [17] presented a rough k-means clustering algorithm by minimizing the dissimilarity to solve the divergence problem of the original approaches that the cluster centers may not be converged to their final positions. Cai et al. [18] proposed a novel initial cluster centroids selection algorithm, called WLV-K-means (weighted local variance K-means). The WLV-K-means algorithm employs the weighted local variance to measure the density of each sample, which can find samples with higher density. This algorithm also uses the improved max-min method to select cluster centroid heuristically. Liu et al. [19] proposed to combine the FCM algorithm and DPC (Clustering by fast search and find of density peaks) algorithm. Firstly, DPC algorithm is used to automatically select the center and number of clusters, and then FCM algorithm is used to realize clustering. The comparison experiments show that the improved FCM algorithm has a faster convergence speed and higher accuracy. Khan and Ahmad [20] proposed a new cluster center initialization algorithm (CCIA). By clustering the samples in each dimension, we find that the K' ($K' > K$) clusters have the same pattern points, and get the center points of the K' clusters. Then we use the data compression method in reference [21] to merge the neighborhood of high-density samples, and finally get the K initial center points. In this paper, we fully consider the constraints of cluster centers in the process of cluster center selection and optimization. Firstly, the initial cluster center is selected by calculating the local density of each sample point. Then the selected initial cluster center is combined with the traditional FCM algorithm to cluster the data. Therefore, we propose a novel fuzzy C-means clustering algorithm based on local density (LD-FCM).

The rest of this paper are organized as follows. In Sect. 2, the concept of fuzzy clustering and Fuzzy C-means clustering algorithms are briefly reviewed. Some important preliminary knowledge used in our proposed approaches are stated. In Sect. 3, we present the algorithms proposed in this paper, and some theories and analysis necessary in it. In Sect. 4, experimental studies are conducted to verify the effectiveness of our proposed algorithm. Section 5 concludes the paper.

2 Preliminaries

2.1 Fuzzy Cluster Analysis

The concept of fuzzy clustering was firstly proposed by Professor Ruspiniv [22]. Fuzzy clustering is an algorithm combining fuzzy mathematics with clustering methods. Fuzzy clustering determines the fuzzy relationship between the samples by method of fuzzy mathematics. In other words, the clustering results are blurred, so that the problem of data attribution in the real world can be described objectively from multiple angles. Therefore, fuzzy clustering analysis has become one of the mainstream directions of clustering research.

Fuzzy clustering [23] calculates the similarity between different data samples by using some distance measurement method. Each data sample is divided into different clusters according to the similarity between data samples. For any number of data sample subsets k $(1 \leq k \leq C)$, where C is the number of clusters, the data sample $X_i (1 \leq i \leq N)$ (N is the number of samples) will belong to this cluster with a fuzzy membership degree, which is similar to a probability value. The fuzzy clustering will obtain membership matrix $[u_{ik}]$ $(1 \leq k \leq C, 1 \leq i \leq N)$ and cluster center $V = \{v_1, v_2, \cdots v_c\}$. And then the membership matrix is judged by hardening matrix technology to determine the final attribution result of data samples. The membership matrix is composed of the fuzzy degree that each data sample belongs to a subset. The value range of each element in the membership matrix is [0, 1]. In other words, if the membership degree of data sample to a subset is greater than that of other subsets, it means that the sample is more likely to belong to the subset. When $u_{ik} = 1$, it means that x_i belongs completely to the k-th cluster, while when $u_{ik} = 0$, it means that x_i does not belong to the k-th cluster at all.

2.2 Fuzzy C-means Clustering Algorithm

Fuzzy C-means (FCM) clustering algorithm [8] is an improvement of the common C-means algorithm. The common C-means algorithm is hard for data classification, while FCM is a soft fuzzy division. Many of the discussions in this paper are based on the FCM algorithm. Therefore, the FCM algorithm is described in detail.

Supposed that the data sample set $X = \{x_1, x_2, \ldots, x_n\} \subset R^s$ is an s-dimensional data set in Euclidean space, n is the number of samples. Where x_i contains the s dimensions, which is expressed as $x_i = \{x_i^1, \ldots, x_i^d, \ldots, x_i^s\}$. FCM algorithm divides X into C classes $(2 \leq C \leq n)$, and has C cluster centers $V = \{v_1, v_2, \ldots, v_c\}$. Thus, FCM algorithm can be expressed as the following mathematical programming matters:

$$Minimize\, J(X, U, V) = \sum\nolimits_{j=1}^{n} \sum\nolimits_{i=1}^{c} \left(u_{ij}\right)^m \left\| x_j - v_i \right\|^2 \tag{1}$$

And satisfied

$$\sum\nolimits_{i=1}^{c} u_{ij} = 1 \, (j = 1, 2, \cdots, n) \tag{2}$$

Where u_{ij} is the membership degree of data sample x_j belonging to a certain class i. $U = (u_{ij})_{c \times n}$ is the fuzzy partition matrix. The value of membership degree of each data sample relative to each cluster can be found from the fuzzy partition matrix. The similarity between the data sample x_j and the class center of the class i is calculated by Euclidean distance, which is recorded as $d_{ij} = \|x_j - v_i\|$. m is the fuzzy weight index, also known as the fuzzy factor. m is mainly used to adjust the fuzzy degree of the fuzzy partition matrix.

The specific steps of the algorithm are as follows.

Step 1: We set the number of clusters C and the fuzzy factor m (usually 1.5 to 2.5), We initialize the membership matrix $U^{(\gamma)}(\gamma = 0)$, and make it satisfy the Eq. (2);

Step 2: The cluster center $V^{(\gamma + 1)} = \{v_1, v_2, \ldots, v_c\}$ is updated according to Eq. (3);

$$v_i^{(\gamma+1)} = \frac{\sum_{j=1}^{n} (u_{ij}^{(\gamma)})^m \cdot x_j}{\sum_{j=1}^{n} (u_{ij}^{(\gamma)})^m}, i = 1, 2, \ldots, c \tag{3}$$

Step 3: The membership matrix $U^{(\gamma + 1)} = (u_{ij})_{c \times n}$ is updated according to Eq. (4);

$$u_{ij}^{(\gamma+1)} = [\sum_{k=1}^{c} \left(\frac{\|x_j - v_i\|^{2(\gamma)}}{\|x_j - v_k\|^{2(\gamma)}}\right)^{\frac{2}{m-1}}]^{-1}, i = 1, 2, \ldots, c; j = 1, 2, \ldots, n \tag{4}$$

Step 4: We calculate $e = \|U^{(\gamma + 1)} - U^{(\gamma)}\|$. If $e \leq \eta$ (η is the threshold, generally 0.001 to 0.01), then the algorithm stops; Otherwise, $\gamma = \gamma + 1$, go to Step 2.

Step 5: The samples are classified and output according to the final membership matrix U. If the sample x_j satisfies $u_{ij} > u_{kj}$, then x_j is classified into the i-th cluster, where u_{ij} represents the membership degree of the sample x_j to the cluster center v_i.

The FCM algorithm [24] is a point-by-point iterative clustering algorithm based on the sum of squared errors as a criterion function. This iterative process starts from a random cluster center. In order to find the minimum value of the objective function $J(X, U, V)$, the cluster center V and the membership matrix U are iteratively calculated by Eq. (3) and Eq. (4). Therefore, the value of the objective function $J(X, U, V)$ is continuously reduced until the value is minimized. Generally, the convergence condition of the algorithm is that the difference between the objective functions of two iterations is less than the threshold η, or the specified number of iterations is reached. When the objective function is minimized, the final clustering result of the data samples is obtained, that is, the cluster center V and the membership matrix U after the fuzzy division. Then the purpose of determining the sample category is achieved.

3 Fuzzy C-means Clustering Algorithm Based on Local Density (LD-FCM)

3.1 Selection of Initial Cluster Center

The traditional FCM clustering algorithm is a sort of local optimal search algorithm. FCM algorithm has some imperfections, such as being sensitive to the initial cluster center and tending to be trapped in the local optimal solution. The random selection of the initial cluster center of the FCM algorithm will lead to the unstable clustering results that are different each time. Therefore, the effect of the clustering may not be best every time, which limits the application of the algorithm. In order to solve the above problems, the paper improve the selection of initial cluster centers in the FCM algorithm. We propose a novel fuzzy C-means clustering algorithm based on local density (LD-FCM). LD-FCM algorithm calculates the local density ρ_i of all sample points in the algorithm and select the sample point with the local maximum density as the initial cluster center by using the distance matrix D and the distance threshold α in each iteration. In this way, the selection of the initial cluster center not only ensures the compactness of the objects in the same cluster, but also ensures the separation of the cluster centers [25]. The specific improvements on the selection of the initial cluster center are as follows:

Supposed that the data sample set $X = \{x_1, x_2, \ldots, x_n\} \subset R^s$ is an s-dimensional data set in Euclidean space, n is the number of samples. Where x_i contains the s dimensions, which is expressed as $x_i = \{x_i^1, \ldots, x_i^d, \ldots, x_i^s\}$. LD-FCM algorithm divides X into C classes ($2 \leq C \leq n$), and has C cluster centers $V = \{v_1, v_2, \ldots, v_c\}$.

Step 1: Calculate the distance between any two samples according to Euclidean Distance Eq. (5), and generate a distance matrix D

$$d_{ij} = \sqrt{\sum_{d=1}^{s} \left(x_i^d - x_j^d \right)^2} \tag{5}$$

Step 2: Calculate the local density ρ_i of the data object x_i according to Eq. (6)

$$\rho_i = \sum_{x_j \in X} \chi\left(d_{ij} - d_c \right) \tag{6}$$

Where d_c represents the truncation distance. $\chi(x) = \begin{cases} 1, & x \leq 0 \\ 0, & x > 0 \end{cases}$, the meaning of this equation is to count the number of data points whose distance to the i-th data point is less than the truncation distance d_c, and use it as the local density of the i-th data point.

Step 3: Arrange the local density of each sample point from large to small: $\rho_i > \rho_j > \rho_k > \cdots > \rho_n$, and take the sample point with the local maximum density ρ_i as the first cluster center v_1.

Step 4: Select the distance threshold α, then find all samples whose distance from the first cluster center v_1 is greater than α by using the distance matrix D. And select the sample point with the highest local density among these samples as the second cluster center v_2.

Step 5: Similarly, find all samples whose distance from the found sample points is greater than α in the remaining samples, and select the sample point with the highest local density among these samples as the third cluster center v_3.

Step 6: Repeat Step 5 until C clusters are found. In this way, C initial cluster centers will be obtained.

3.2   The LD-FCM Algorithm

LD-FCM clustering algorithm is divided into two stages. In the first stage, the method of local maximum density and the distance threshold α are used to select the initial cluster center. In the second stage, the FCM algorithm is performed with the initial cluster center that obtained in the first stage. The specific steps of the LD-FCM algorithm are as follows.

Step 1: Calculate the distance between any two samples according to Euclidean Distance Eq. (5), and generate a distance matrix D;

Step 2: Calculate the local density ρ_i of the data object x_i according to Eq. (6). Arrange the local density of each sample point from large to small: $\rho_i > \rho_j > \rho_k > \cdots > \rho_n$, and take the sample point with the highest local density ρ_i as the first cluster center v_1;

Step 3: Select the distance threshold α ($\alpha > 0$), then find all samples whose distance from the first cluster center v_1 is greater than α by using the distance matrix D. And select the sample point with the highest local density among these samples as the second cluster center v_2;

Step 4: Similarly, find all samples whose distance from the found sample points is greater than α in the remaining samples, and select the sample point with the highest local density among these samples as the third cluster center v_3;

Step 5: Repeat Step 4 until C clusters are found. In this way, C initial cluster centers $v_i(k)$, $(i = 1, 2, \ldots, C)$ iterations will be obtained;

Step 6: Set the number of iterations $k = 1$, and use the result of Step 5 as the initial cluster center $v_i(k)$, $(i = 1, 2, \ldots, C)$;

Step 7: The membership matrix $U^{(\gamma+1)} = (u_{ij})_{c \times n}$ ($i = 1, \ldots, c$, $j = 1, \ldots, n$) is updated according to initial cluster center $v_i(k)$ and Eq. (4);

Step 8: The cluster center $V^{(\gamma+1)} = \{v_1, v_2, \ldots, v_c\}$ is updated according to Eq. (3);

Step 9: We calculate $e = \|U^{(\gamma+1)} - U^{(\gamma)}\|$. If $e \leq \eta$ (η is the threshold, generally 0.001 to 0.01), then the algorithm stops; Otherwise, $\gamma = \gamma + 1$, go to Step 7.

Step 10: The samples are classified and output according to the final membership matrix U. If the sample x_j satisfies $u_{ij} > u_{kj}$, then x_j is classified into the i-th cluster, where u_{ij} represents the membership degree of the sample x_j to the cluster center v_i.

4 Results

In order to test the effect of the LD-FCM algorithm, we have used several artificial datasets and real datasets in UCI for experiments. We also compared the LD-FCM algorithm proposed in this paper with FCM algorithm, K-means algorithm, DBSCAN (Density-Based Spatial Clustering of Applications with Noise) algorithm and DP-FCM (Density peak-based FCM) algorithm. The K-means algorithm and the DBSCAN algorithm are classic algorithms in the partition-based clustering algorithm and the density-based clustering algorithm, respectively. In the K-means [26] algorithm, each cluster is represented by the mean of the objects in the corresponding cluster. However, K-means algorithm can only obtain local optimal solution by adopting iterative algorithms. In addition, K-means algorithm work well when analyzing small and medium-sized data sets to find circular or spherical clusters. But K-means algorithm perform poorly when analyzing large-scale data sets or complex data types, so they need to be extended [27–29]. DBSCAN [30] algorithm derives the maximum density connected set according to the density reachability relationship, which is a category or cluster for our final clustering. DBSCAN algorithm can divide areas with enough density into clusters, and find clusters of arbitrary shape in the spatial database with noise [31]. The DP-FCM algorithm is proposed by Liu et al. [19]. Firstly, DPC algorithm is used to automatically select the center and number of clusters, and then FCM algorithm is used to realize clustering.

4.1 The Datasets and Evaluation Indexes of Experiment

The information of the experimental datasets is shown in Table 1 and Table 2, where Table 1 is artificial datasets and Table 2 is a real datasets in UCI [32]. These datasets have some discrimination in the number of attributes and the number of clusters.

Table 1. Description of the artificial datasets.

Dataset	Size	Attribute	Number of class
Set	5000	2	15
R15	600	2	15
Shape	1000	2	4
Sizes	1000	2	4
Twenty	1000	2	20
Target	770	2	6

Table 2. Description of the real datasets in UCI.

Dataset	Size	Attribute	Number of class
Iris	150	4	3
Aggregation	788	2	7
Wine	178	13	3
Pima	768	8	2
Compound	399	2	6
Seeds	210	7	3
Wingnut	1016	2	2
Glass	214	10	7

The evaluation indexes of the experimental results are Accuracy, NMI (Normalized Mutual Information) and ARI (Adjusted Rand index) [33, 34]. Accuracy is the number of right samples divided by the total number of samples. NMI is an information measure in information theory, and its value range is [0, 1]. ARI is the goodness of fit which measures the distribution of two data, and its value range is [−1, 1]. The larger the values of the three evaluation indexes are, the better the clustering result is. Their definitions are as follows.

$$ACC = \frac{\sum_{i=1}^{k} a_i}{|U|} \tag{7}$$

Where K is the number of clusters, a_i is the number of samples correctly classified into C_i, and U is the all samples.

$$I(X, Y) = \sum_{h=1}^{k(a)} \sum_{l=1}^{k(b)} n_{h \cdot l} log \left(\frac{n \cdot n_{h \cdot l}}{n_h^{(a)} n_l^b} \right) \tag{8}$$

$$H(X) = \sum_{h=1}^{k(a)} n_h^{(a)} log \frac{n_h^{(a)}}{n} \tag{9}$$

$$H(Y) = \sum_{l=1}^{k(b)} n_l^{(b)} log \frac{n_l^{(b)}}{n} \tag{10}$$

$$NMI(X, Y) = \frac{I(X, Y)}{\sqrt{H(X)H(Y)}} \tag{11}$$

Where X and Y are the random variables, $I(X; Y)$ represents the mutual information of two variables, and $H(X)$ is the entropy of X.

$$RI = \frac{a + b}{C_2^{n_{samples}}} \tag{12}$$

$$ARI = \frac{RI - E|RI|}{max(RI) - E|RI|} \tag{13}$$

Where C is the actual category information. K is the clustering result. a represents the logarithms of elements of the same categories in both C and K. b represents the logarithms of elements of the different categories in both C and K. $C_2^{n_{samples}}$ represents the logarithm that can be formed in the datasets. RI represents the Rand index. E is the expectation. $max()$ is the function to find the maximum value.

4.2   Results on the Artificial Datasets

As shown in Fig. 1(a)–(f), it shows the clustering results of the LD-FCM algorithm on six different artificial datasets. The datasets including Set, R15, Shape, Sizes, Twenty and Target. Figure 1 shows that the LD-FCM algorithm can correctly cluster the datasets with spherical or elliptical shapes. The experimental results show that the LD-FCM algorithm is very effective in seeking clusters with any shape, density, distribution and number. LD-FCM algorithm solves the disadvantages of the original algorithm. LD-FCM algorithm can reasonably select the initial cluster center, then correctly calculate the membership of each sample, and each clustering result is relatively stable.

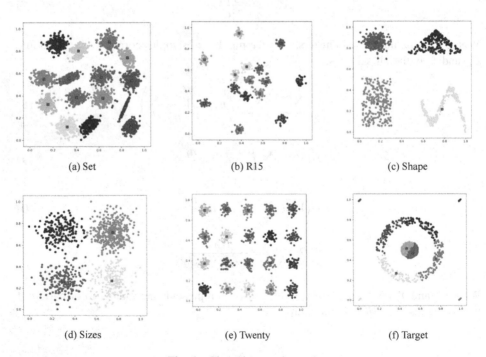

(a) Set   (b) R15   (c) Shape

(d) Sizes   (e) Twenty   (f) Target

Fig. 1. Clustering result graph.

4.3   Results on the Real Datasets in UCI

The experimental results of the real datasets in UCI are shown in Table 3, Table 4 and Table 5. These tables show the Accuracy, NMI and ARI of each clustering result in every algorithm. The experimental results are showed by the way of percentages. The numbers highlighted in bold in the three tables indicate the best performance in the evaluation aspect.

Table 3. Comparison of accuracy of clustering algorithms.

Dataset	K-means (%)	DBSCAN (%)	FCM (%)	DP-FCM (%)	LD-FCM (%)
Iris	74.56	63.45	89.33	91.33	**91.69**
Aggregation	69.25	77.23	64.34	**92.21**	80.25
Wine	67.93	75.74	70.79	70.79	**95.50**
Pima	65.84	65.21	66.66	65.12	**69.34**
Compound	65.77	63.34	61.74	65.91	**66.79**
Seeds	**90.56**	62.85	87.22	87.27	90.47
Wingnut	93.24	92.58	92.08	**98.43**	95.29
Glass	83.42	80.33	79.85	85.49	**85.83**

Table 4. Comparison of NMI of clustering algorithms.

Dataset	K-means (%)	DBSCAN (%)	FCM (%)	DP-FCM (%)	LD-FCM (%)
Iris	70.93	72.19	70.21	**74.96**	73.03
Aggregation	76.22	79.69	73.35	82.99	**83.15**
Wine	79.04	80.31	71.20	38.33	**84.35**
Pima	1.84	2.06	1.29	**4.05**	3.97
Compound	69.22	66.15	67.23	70.03	**70.12**
Seeds	**70.03**	56.83	60.52	61.51	67.35
Wingnut	81.92	**86.22**	67.88	85.73	73.92
Glass	63.22	**65.83**	29.14	40.27	47.32

Table 5. Comparison of ARI of clustering algorithms.

Dataset	K-means (%)	DBSCAN (%)	FCM (%)	DP-FCM (%)	LD-FCM (%)
Iris	70.83	62.32	70.02	**74.64**	72.49
Aggregation	70.04	76.21	57.15	**83.62**	71.34
Wine	76.35	60.06	79.22	37.21	**84.97**
Pima	3.97	3.22	5.93	9.32	**10.69**
Compound	50.94	32.72	50.01	51.99	**52.72**
Seeds	70.65	48.67	70.40	64.29	**71.62**
Wingnut	**92.29**	81.03	73.21	90.87	77.01
Glass	37.76	**42.22**	16.67	33.73	34.11

Based on the three evaluation indicators, it can be found that the clustering results of the LD-FCM algorithm are generally better than the other four algorithms. LD-FCM algorithm can effectively cluster the data set and produces improved clustering results. For datasets with a large number of clusters and high dimensions, the LD-FCM algorithm can still effectively cluster the datasets. In addition, when there are many noise samples in the data set and the boundaries between clusters are not clear, the LD-FCM algorithm is more suitable, which also proves the effectiveness of the LD-FCM algorithm.

Table 6. Comparison of running time of clustering algorithms (seconds/s).

Dataset	K-means (%)	DBSCAN (%)	FCM (%)	DP-FCM (%)	LD-FCM (%)
Iris	0.059	0.565	0.148	0.884	0.032
Aggregation	0.309	1.016	2.602	3.068	0.059
Wine	0.098	0.832	0.168	1.203	0.032
Pima	0.223	1.457	0.372	1.776	0.099
Compound	0.984	5.223	0.564	4.251	0.090
Seeds	0.122	0.973	0.164	0.932	0.074
Wingnut	0.159	1.006	0.439	2.041	0.197
Glass	8.722	10.021	0.313	0.806	0.912

Table 6 shows the time performance of each algorithm on different datasets. From the experimental results, we can see that the algorithm in this paper inherits the time advantage of FCM algorithm, and running time takes less time than other algorithms, so it has some advantages in both running time and memory consumption.

5   Conclusion

Firstly, this paper introduces the concepts of fuzzy clustering. The principle of fuzzy C-means clustering algorithm is explained. Considering that the selection of the initial cluster center of the traditional FCM clustering algorithm is random, which will lead to the unstable clustering results and the clustering effect may not be the best each time. In order to solve the above problems, a novel fuzzy C-means clustering algorithm based on local density is proposed in this paper. This algorithm uses the local maximum density of sample points to improve the selection of the initial cluster center, which reduces the number of iterations and avoids falling into a local optimal solution. Through specific experiments, better clustering results are obtained by using artificial datasets. The real datasets in UCI were used to analyze the algorithm from three evaluation indexes about Accuracy, NMI, ARI and running time of real datasets. The experimental results show that the LD-FCM algorithm is better than FCM algorithm, K-means algorithm, DBSCAN algorithm and DP-FCM algorithm. Running time of LD-FCM algorithm takes less time than other algorithms. Therefore, it can be concluded that the LD-FCM algorithm has good effectiveness and robustness.

Acknowledgements. We would like to thank the anonymous reviewers for their valuable comments and suggestions. This work is supported by Shandong Provincial Natural Science Foundation of China under Grant ZR2018MF009, ZR2019MF003, The State Key Research Development Program of China under Grant 2017YFC0804406, National Natural Science Foundation of China under Grant 91746104, 61976126, the Special Funds of Taishan Scholars Construction Project, and Leading Talent Project of Shandong University of Science and Technology.

References

1. He, Z.H., Lei, Y.J.: Research on intuitionistic fuzzy C-means clustering algorithm. Control Decis. **26**(6), 847–856 (2011)
2. Zhang, Y., Li, Z.M., Zhang, H., Yu, Z., Lu, T.T.: Fuzzy C-means clustering-based mating restriction for multiobjective optimization. Int. J. Mach. Learn. Cybernet. **9**, 1609–1621 (2018)
3. Wang, X.Z., Xing, H.J., Li, Y.: A study on relationship between generalization abilities and fuzziness of base classifiers in ensemble learning. IEEE Trans. Fuzzy Syst. **23**(5), 1638–1654 (2015)
4. Wang, R., Wang, X.Z., Sam, K., Chen, X.: Incorporating diversity and informativeness in multiple-instance active learning. IEEE Trans. Fuzzy Syst. **25**(6), 1460–1475 (2017)
5. Liu, C.S., Xu, Q.L.: A fuzzy C-means clustering algorithm based on density peak algorithm optimization. Comput. Eng. Appl. **54**(14), 153–157 (2018)
6. Fan, J.C., Niu, Z.H., Liang, Y.Q., Zhao, Z.Y.: Probability model selection and parameter evolutionary estimation for clustering imbalanced data without sampling. Neurocomputing **211**, 172–181 (2016)
7. Xie, X.L., Beni, G.: A validity measure for fuzzy clustering. IEEE Trans. PAMI **13**(13), 841–847 (1991)
8. Bezdek, J.C.: Pattern recognition with fuzzy objective function algorithms. Adv. Appl. Pattern Recogn. **22**(1171), 203–239 (1981)
9. Kosko, B.: Fuzzy systems as universal approximators. IEEE Trans. Comput. **43**(11), 1329–1333 (1994)
10. Fan, J.C.: OPE-HCA: an optimal probabilistic estimation approach for hierarchical clustering algorithm. Neural Comput. Appl. **31**(7), 2095–2105 (2019)
11. Wang, Z.H., Liu, Z.J., Chen, D.H.: Research of PSO-based fuzzy C-means clustering algorithm. Comput. Sci. **39**(9), 166–169 (2012)
12. Li, W.J., Zhang, Q.F., Ping, L.D., Pan, X.Z.: Cloud scheduling algorithm based on fuzzy clustering. J. Commun. **33**(3), 147–154 (2012)
13. Geweniger, T., Zülke, D., Hammer, B., Villmann, T.: Median fuzzy C-means for clustering dissimilarity data. Neurocomputing **73**, 1109–1116 (2010)
14. Wang, Z.H., Fan, J.C.: A rough-set based measurement for the membership degree of fuzzy C-means algorithm. In: Proceedings of SPIE the International Society for Optical Engineering, 3rd International Workshop on Pattern Recognition (2018)
15. Pawlak, Z.: Rough sets. Int. J. Comput. Inf. Sci. **11**(5), 341–356 (1982)
16. Fan, J.C., Li, Y., Tang, L.Y., Wu, G.K.: RoughPSO: rough set-based particle swarm optimisation. Int. J. Bio-inspired Comput. **12**, 245–253 (2018)
17. Lai, J.Z.C., Juan, E.Y.T., Lai, F.J.C.: Rough clustering using generalized fuzzy clustering algorithm. Pattern Recogn. **46**, 2538–2547 (2013)

18. Cai, Y.H., Liang, Y.Q., Fan, J.C., Li, X., Liu, W.H.: Optimizing initial cluster centroids by weighted local variance in K-means algorithm. J. Front. Comput. Sci. Technol. **10**(5), 732–741 (2016)
19. Liu, X.Y., Fan, J.C., Chen, Z.W.: Improved fuzzy C-means algorithm based on density peak. Int. J. Mach. Learn. Cybern. **11**, 545–552 (2020)
20. Khan, S.S., Ahmad, A.: Cluster center initialization algorithm for K-means clustering. Pattern Recogn. Lett. **25**(11), 1293–1302 (2004)
21. Mitra, P., Murthy, C.A., Pal, S.K.: Density-based multiscale data condensation. IEEE Trans. Pattern Anal. Mach. Intell. **24**(6), 734–747 (2002)
22. Ruspini, E.H.: A new approach to clustering. Inf. Control **15**(1), 22–32 (1969)
23. Li, Y., Fan, J., Pan, J.-S., Mao, G., Wu, G.: A novel rough fuzzy clustering algorithm with a new similarity measurement. J. Internet Technol. **20**(4), 1145–1156 (2019)
24. Xue, Z., Shang, Y., Feng, A.: Semi-supervised outlier detection based on fuzzy rough C-means clustering. Math. Comput. Simul. **80**(9), 1911–1921 (2010)
25. Xia, Y.Y., Liu, Y., Huang, Y.D.: Community discovery based on improved clustering algorithm with central constraints. Comput. Eng. Appl. **54**(8), 265–270 (2018)
26. Kanungo, T., Mount, D.M., Netanyahu, N.S., Piatko, C.D., Silverman, R., Wu, A.Y.: An efficient K-means clustering algorithm: analysis and implementation. IEEE Trans. Pattern Anal. Mach. Intell. **24**(7), 881–892 (2002)
27. Yang, S.L., Li, Y.S., Hu, X.X., Pan, R.Y.: Optimization study on K value of K-means algorithm. Syst. Eng. Theory Pract. **2**, 97–101 (2006)
28. Zhang, Y.F., Mao, J.L., Xiong, Z.Y.: An improved K-means algorithm. Comput. Appl. **23**(8), 31–60 (2003)
29. Wang, Z., Liu, G.J., Chen, E.H.: A K-means algorithm based on optimized initial center points. Pattern Recog. Artif. Intell. **22**(2), 299–304 (2009)
30. Sander, J., Ester, M., Kriegel, H.P., Xu, X.W.: Density-based clustering in spatial databases: the algorithm GDBSCAN and its applications. Data Min. Knowl. Discov. **2**(2), 169–194 (1998)
31. Wang, G., Lin, G.Y.: Improved adaptive parameter DBSCAN clustering algorithm. Comput. Eng. Appl. 1–8 (2019). https://doi.org/10.3778/j.issn.1002-8331.1908-0501
32. UCI. http://archive.ics.uci.edu/ml/index.php. Accessed 17 Sept 2019
33. Fahad, A., Alshatri, N., Tari, Z.: A survey of clustering algorithms for big data: taxonomy and empirical analysis. IEEE Trans. Emerg. Top. Comput. **2**(3), 267–279 (2014)
34. Bie, R., Mehmood, R., Ruan, S.: Adaptive fuzzy clustering by fast search and find of density peaks. Pers. Ubiquit. Comput. **20**(5), 785–793 (2016)

A Novel Method to Solve the Separation Problem of LDA

Meng Zhang[1], Wei Li[1], and Bo Zhang[1,2(✉)]

[1] School of Mechatronic Engineering, China University of Mining and Technology,
Xuzhou 221116, People's Republic of China
zhangmeng@163.com, liwei_cmee@163.com, zbcumt@163.com
[2] School of Computer Science and Technology,
China University of Mining and Technology,
Xuzhou 221116, People's Republic of China

Abstract. Linear discriminant analysis (LDA) is one of the most classical linear projection techniques for feature extraction, widely used in kinds of fields. Classical LDA is contributed to finding an optimal projection subspace that can maximize the between-class scatter and minimize the average within-class scatter of each class. However, the class separation problem always exists and classical LDA can not guarantee that the within-class scatter of each class get its minimum. In this paper, we proposed the *k-classifiers* method, which can reduce every within-class scatter of classes respectively and alleviate the class separation problem. This method will be applied in LDA and Norm LDA and achieve significant improvement. Extensive experiments performed on MNIST data sets demonstrate the effectiveness of *k-classifiers*.

Keywords: Linear discriminant analysis · Class separation problem · Within-class scatter

1 Introduction

Linear discriminant analysis (LDA) is one of the most popular linear dimension reduction (LDR) and feature extraction methods, which has been widely used in kinds of fields, such as face recognition, cancer classification and text document classification [9]. It is a supervised learning technique that finds an orientation W to project the feature vectors from the original sample space to a lower space in such a way that maximizes the between-class scatter and minimizes the within-class scatter simultaneously.

LDA was first proposed by Fisher (FLDA) [2] to solve the binary classification problem and then was generalized by Rao [6] to multiple classes. Although LDA is a classical LDR method, it still suffers from the class separation problem, close class pairs tend to mix up in the subspace. For a K-class problem, the Fisher criterion is actually decomposed into pairwise Fisher criteria under certain assumptions [5]. Conventional LDA seeks to maximize the average pairwise

© IFIP International Federation for Information Processing 2020
Published by Springer Nature Switzerland AG 2020
Z. Shi et al. (Eds.): IIP 2020, IFIP AICT 581, pp. 59–66, 2020.
https://doi.org/10.1007/978-3-030-46931-3_6

distance between class means and minimize the average within-class pairwise distance over all classes. It is, in fact, desirable for every pairwise distance between two class means to be as large as possible and every within-class pairwise distance to be as small as possible. There are three main kinds of methods used to relieve the class separation problem. First, it is the optimal choice to design a Bayes optimal criterion for general multi-class discriminative dimension reduction [3,7,12]. However, this kind of method is quite difficult, as the Bayes error cannot be expressed analytically [3]. Second, many weighting methods have been proposed. In these methods, approximate weights are introduced into FLDA [1,5,10]. Whereas, the above weights methods cannot address the problem thoroughly. Lastly, the max-min methods have also been applied to solve the Class separation problem. These methods focus on maximizing the minimum pairwise between-class distance of all classes in the projected subspace [1,8,13].

The methods above almost all focus on how to make the pairwise distance larger and larger, and they all ignore reducing each within-class pairwise distance except WLDA [13]. However, for WLDA, only the maximum within-class scatter is minimized. We propose a novel method called *k-classifiers* to reduce every within-class scatter respectively and the method is applied in LDA and Norm LDA to improve their corresponding classification performance in this paper. For LDA, *k-classifiers* method can make every within-class of each class smaller as far as possible. For Norm LDA, *k-classifiers* method can make the scatter of orientation in maximum scatter smaller as far as possible. The difference of *k-classifiers* method in LDA and Norm LDA depends on its own geometric meaning. Norm LDA is an LDA method which based on different criterion refer to Sect. 2.2.

The rest of the paper is organized as follows: Sect. 2 introduces briefly FLDA and Norm LDA. The idea of *k-classifiers* and the corresponding classification strategy are presented in Sect. 3. The experiments are presented in Sect. 4. Finally, we give conclusions and future work in Sect. 5.

2 Related Work

In this section, we briefly review two supervised dimensionality reduction methods, i.e., LDA and Norm LDA, which is the basis of the proposed method.

2.1 Classical LDA

Given a set of data containing C classes $\{Z_i\}_{i=1}^{C}$, with each class consisting of a number of samples: $Z_i = \{z_{ij}\}_{j=1}^{C_i}$, a total of $N = \sum_{i=1}^{C} N_i$ samples are available in the set. Each sample is represented as a column vector of length n, i.e. $z_{ij} \in R^n$, where R^n denotes the n-dimensional real space. We can define the within-class scatter S_w and between-class scatter S_b as follow:

$$S_w = \frac{1}{N} \sum_{i=1}^{C} \sum_{x \in Z_i} (x - m_i)(x - m_i)^T, \tag{1}$$

$$S_b = \frac{1}{N} \sum_{i=1}^{C} (m_i - m)(m_i - m)^T, \tag{2}$$

where $m_i = \frac{1}{N_i} \sum_{x \in Z_i} x$ is the mean of the samples in class Z_i, and $m = \frac{1}{N} \sum_{x \in Z} x$ is the mean of all the samples.

For multi-class problem, based on maximizing the between-class scatter and minimizing the within-class scatter simultaneously, the trace ratio criterion is proposed naturally:

$$W = \arg\max_W \frac{trace(W^T S_b W)}{trace(W^T S_w W)}. \tag{3}$$

In fact, there does not exist a closed-form solution for the trace ratio criterion [11]. For easy to solve, a suboptimal substitute of the trace ratio criterion has been proposed, which called determinant ratio (ratio trace):

$$W = \arg\max_W \frac{|W^T S_b W|}{|W^T S_w W|}. \tag{4}$$

Solving the above criterion with the Lagrange equation, we can find that the basis vectors W correspond to the first M eigenvectors with the largest eigenvalues of $(S_w^{-1} S_b)$, when S_w is non-singular.

2.2 Norm LDA

As we all know, the conventional criterion or the criterion having the similar geometric meaning with conventional criterion can't always get the optimal performance in all database. Since S_w and S_b are positive semi-definite, we can always find Q and R such that $S_w = QQ^T$ and $S_b = RR^T$. A series of objective functions can be represented as:

$$J(W) = \arg\max_W \frac{\| (W^T R)^T \|}{\| (W^T Q)^T \|}, \tag{5}$$

where $\| \cdot \|$ is a sub-multiplicative and unitary invariant matrix norm, i.e. $\| AB \| \leq \| A \| \| B \|$ with A and B being any compatible matrix, and $\| AB \| = \| B \|$ with B being any unitary matrix.

By using the F-norm, the objective (5) is equivalent to:

$$\frac{trace(W^T S_b W)}{trace(W^T S_w W)} = \frac{\| (W^T R)^T \|}{\| (W^T Q)^T \|}, \tag{6}$$

Which is the trace ratio of $W S_b W^T$ and $W S_w W^T$.

By using the 2-norm, the objective (5) becomes:

$$J(W) = \arg\max_W \frac{\| (W^T R)^T \|_2}{\| (W^T Q)^T \|_2}, \tag{7}$$

Which is the ratio between the largest eigenvalue of $W S_b W^T$ and $W S_w W^T$.

We can also define the objective function by using mixed norms, i.e.

$$J(W) = \arg\max_{W} \frac{\| (W^T R)^T \|_F}{\| (W^T Q)^T \|_2}. \tag{8}$$

Q can be decomposed by singular value decomposition (SVD) as:

$$Q = U\Sigma V^T, \tag{9}$$

where $UU^T = I_n \times n$, $VV^T = I_n \times n$.

Without loss of generality, we set $W = U\Sigma^- \tilde{W}$. Then we can get the unified analytical solution to the objective function (7) and (8), $W = U\Sigma^-$. However, it is not the solution to the objective function (6). We should emphasize that this unified analytical solution is only a projection and will not reduce the dimension of the feature space, and thus, we should conduct PCA to reduce dimensionality before using this method when the SSS problem occurs. According to the geometric meanings of SVD and eigenvalue, the distribution of discriminant information in each feature generated by Norm LDA is more uniform than in LDA. i.e. $W \in R^n \times n$, and any $W \neq U\Sigma^-$ results in

$$J(W) \leq J(U\Sigma^-). \tag{10}$$

As we know many LDA methods reduce the dimension of the feature space through the linear projection. Nevertheless, it is apparent that any W with $m < n$ cannot deliver a better result than $W = U\Sigma^-$ in sense of Eqs. (7) and (8).

3   Method

As formulated in Eq. (3), LDA simultaneously seeks to maximize the average of between-class scatter of each two classes and minimize the average within-class scatter of each all classes. However, the Fisher criterion cannot guarantee class separation since within-class scatter matrixes of each class are different. In this section, *k-classifiers* method is proposed to ensure the every within-class scatter as smaller as possible by designing k criterion according to k classes.

3.1   k-Classifiers Method

Methods about LDA proposed in the above literatures all contain just one projection orientation. They cannot diminish every within-class scatter matrix as far as possible. When the *k-classifiers* method is applied into LDA, the k criterions can be got corresponding to k within-class scatter matrixes as follow:

$$F(W_i) = \arg\max_{W_i} \frac{|W_i^T S_b W_i|}{|W_i^T S_{wi} W_i|}, \tag{11}$$

where $i = 1, 2, ..., k$. Inspired by the solution in Sect. 2.1, i-th $(1 \leq i \leq k)$ criterion can be solved and we can find that when $S_w i$ is non-singular, the basis vectors W_i correspond to the first M eigenvectors with the largest eigenvalues of $(S_w^{-1} S_b)$. According to the geometric meaning of the above criterion, we can find that for LDA, *k-classifiers* method can make the every within-class of each class smaller as far as possible.

When the *k-classifiers* is applied into Norm LDA, we can obtain k criterions as follow:

$$J(W_i) = \arg \max_{W_i} \frac{\| (W_i^T R)^T \|}{\| (W_i^T Q)^T \|}, \tag{12}$$

where $i = 1, 2, ..., k$. By the method proposed in Sect. 2.2, we can solve the above k criterions. The i-th optimal projection matrixes can be calculated and $W_i = \Sigma_i^- U_i$.

By the prove in the Sect. 2.2, we can work out that any $W_i \neq \Sigma_i^- U_i$ results in $J(W_i) \leq J(U_i \Sigma_1^-)$. We can define k classifiers by the k optimal projection matrixes according to the geometric meaning of 2-Norm and the above criterion, it's obvious that for Norm LDA, *k-classifiers* method can make the scatter of orientation in maximum scatter smaller as far as possible.

Similarly, this method also can be applied to many other methods proposed in the literature.

3.2   Classification Strategy

Assuming normal distribution for each class with the common covariance matrix, classification based on maximum likelihood estimation results in a nearest class centroid rule. Assuming equal prior for all classes for simplicity, a test point y is classified as class j if

$$\| W_j^T (y - c^j) \|_F^2 \tag{13}$$

is minimized over j = 1,...,k. It can be shown as:

$$\arg \max_j \{\| W_j^T (y - c^j) \|_F^2\}, \tag{14}$$

where W_j is the optimal projection matrix corresponding to LDA and Norm LDA and c^j is described as follows, $i = 1, 2, ..., k$:

$$c^j = \frac{1}{N_i} \sum_{x \in z_i} W_i^T x. \tag{15}$$

Classifier can be built based on Eq. (14). The applications of *k-classifiers* method in LDA and Norm LDA are described as follows:

1. Calculate the k optimal projection places of LDA and Norm LDA from train data by the $(S_{wi}^- S_b)$ and $\Sigma_i^- U_i$ respectively.
2. Project i-th class into i-th place and the center of i-th class in i-th place is achieved, $i = 1, 2, ..., k$.
3. For a test point y, the j-th distance between y and the each j-th class in the corresponding place can be calculated by Eq. (13).
4. Classifiers can be built by the Eq. (14). If the j-th distance is the minimum of k distances, then the point y belongs to j-th class.

4   Experiment

In order to demonstrate the effectiveness of the proposed fault diagnosis method, the MNIST database is used.

4.1   Experiments on the MNIST Database

The MNIST database [4] of handwritten digits is a widely known benchmark that consists of a training set of 60,000 examples, and a test set of 10,000 examples.

In this experiment, we conduct PCA firstly to reduce the dimension. Then we select the training set to calculate the optimal projection matrixes corresponding to four methods. The dimensionality of the subspace generated by LDA is at most $k-1$, which depends on the rank of the between-class scatter matrix. When the dimension reduced by PCA is less than nine-dimensional, LDA will not be used as a dimension reduction method, and it just as a projection method. Otherwise, the subspace generated by LDA will be a nine-dimensional space. Lastly, classifiers corresponding to four methods will be designed based on the methods proposed in Sect. 2. We repeat the experiment 20 times, and the average classification accuracy rates have been shown in Fig. 1.

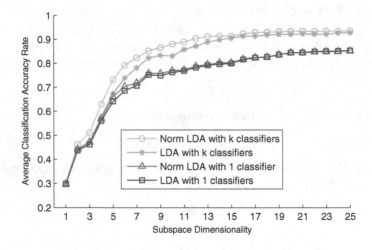

Fig. 1. Average classification accuracy rates on the MNIST database

Figure 1 shows that on the whole, the methods with *k-classifiers* obtain better classification results than the methods with 1 classifier. So, the application of *k-classifiers* is very successful and *k-classifiers* can actually alleviate the Class separation problem. We can conclude that decreasing the within-class scatter of each class by the *k-classifiers* method can actually improve the classification performance. It is also obvious that Norm LDA is a little better than LDA in both low and high dimension, under this kind of data distribution.

4.2 Experimental Result Analysis

We summarize the observations from the above experiments and then make the analysis as follows:

(1) On the whole, the method of Norm LDA with *k-classifiers* outperforms the other three methods in the high dimension, and sometimes in the low dimension. LDA emphasizes the increase of determinant ratio between-class scatter and average within-class scatter of each class. Norm LDA devotes to increasing the ratio between the largest eigenvalue of between-class scatter and average within-class scatter of each class. For some datasets, Norm LDA is more suitable than LDA.

(2) The application of *k-classifiers* in Norm LDA is very successful. When the method of *k-classifiers* is applied in LDA, the method of LDA with *k-classifiers* is better than LDA with 1 classifier in both low and high dimensions. Norm LDA and LDA emphasize the equal decrease of within-class scatter of each class. The combination of *k-classifiers* and LDA, Norm LDA is devoting to the reduction of the within-class scatter of each class. As a result, on the whole, methods with *k-classifiers* can have a better performance.

5 Conclusions and Future Work

The class separation problem occurring in LDA has been continuously studied in recent years. Many ideas have been applied in LDA to improve its performance, including weights schemes, max-min, and Bayes optimal criterion. The application of weights schemes and max-min methods all ignored the importance of decreasing every within-class scatter. In this paper, we present a *k-classifiers* method to reduce every within-class pairwise. We also apply *k-classifiers* method into LDA and Norm LDA. Based on the MNIST handwriting database, we have demonstrated that the applications of *k-classifiers* method in LDA and Norm LDA are very successful.

There is still room to improve the classification performance. We can put the max-min ideas and weights schemes into our method to make every pairwise distance between two classes as larger as possible, and make within-class scatter of every class as smaller as possible.

Acknowledgments. The work was supported by China Postdoctoral Science Foundation (No. 2017M621862) and Jiangsu Planned Projects for Postdoctoral Research Funds (No. 1701193B).

References

1. Bian, W., Tao, D.: Max-min distance analysis by using sequential SDP relaxation for dimension reduction. IEEE Trans. Pattern Anal. Mach. Intell. **33**(5), 1037–1050 (2010)

2. Fisher, R.A.: The use of multiple measurements in taxonomic problems. Ann. Eugenics **7**(2), 179–188 (1936)
3. Hamsici, O.C., Martinez, A.M.: Bayes optimality in linear discriminant analysis. IEEE Trans. Pattern Anal. Mach. Intell. **30**(4), 647–657 (2008)
4. LeCun, Y., Cortes, C., Burges, C.: MNIST handwritten digit database (2010)
5. Loog, M., Duin, R.P.W., Haeb-Umbach, R.: Multiclass linear dimension reduction by weighted pairwise fisher criteria. IEEE Trans. Pattern Anal. Mach. Intell. **23**(7), 762–766 (2001)
6. Rao, C.R.: The utilization of multiple measurements in problems of biological classification. J. Roy. Stat. Soc. Ser. B (Methodol.) **10**(2), 159–203 (1948)
7. Schervish, M.J.: Linear discrimination for three known normal populations. J. Stat. Plan. Infer. **10**(2), 167–175 (1984)
8. Shao, G., Sang, N.: Max-min distance analysis by making a uniform distribution of class centers for dimensionality reduction. Neurocomputing **143**, 208–221 (2014)
9. Sharma, A., Paliwal, K.K.: Linear discriminant analysis for the small sample size problem: an overview. Int. J. Mach. Learn. Cybern. **6**(3), 443–454 (2014). https://doi.org/10.1007/s13042-013-0226-9
10. Tao, D., Li, X., Wu, X., Maybank, S.J.: Geometric mean for subspace selection. IEEE Trans. Pattern Anal. Mach. Intell. **31**(2), 260–274 (2008)
11. Wang, H., Yan, S., Xu, D., Tang, X., Huang, T.: Trace ratio vs. ratio trace for dimensionality reduction. In: 2007 IEEE Conference on Computer Vision and Pattern Recognition, pp. 1–8. IEEE (2007)
12. Yao, C., Cheng, G.: Approximative bayes optimality linear discriminant analysis for Chinese handwriting character recognition. Neurocomputing **207**, 346–353 (2016)
13. Zhang, Y., Yeung, D.Y.: Worst-case linear discriminant analysis. In: Advances in Neural Information Processing Systems, pp. 2568–2576 (2010)

Multi-label Classification of Short Text Based on Similarity Graph and Restart Random Walk Model

Xiaohong Li[✉], Fanyi Yang, Yuyin Ma, and Huifang Ma

College of Computer Science and Engineering, Northwest Normal University,
Lanzhou, China
xiaohongli@nwnu.edu.cn, 1521497745@qq.com,
mahuifang@yeah.net

Abstract. A multi-label classification method of short text based on similarity graph and restart random walk model is proposed. Firstly, the similarity graph is created by using data and labels as the node, and the weights on the edges are calculated through an external knowledge, so the initial matching degree of between the sample and the label set is obtained. After that, we build a label dependency graph with labels as vertices, and using the previous matching degree as the initial prediction value to calculate the relationship between the sample and each node until the probability distribution becomes stable. Finally, the obtained relationship vector is the label probability distribution vector of the sample predicted by the method in this paper. Experimental results show that we provides a more efficient and reliable multi-label short-text classification algorithm.

Keywords: Multi-label classification · Short text · Similarity graph · Restart random walk · WordNet

1 Introduction

Traditional single-label classification learning means that each sample has a unique category label, where each label belongs to a mutually exclusive label set L(|L| > 1). However, In practical applications, usually a sample belong to multiple categories at the same time, we call such data as multi-label data [1]. For example, a news report can could be classified into "entertainment" and "technologies", simultaneously. A movie can be both an "action movie" and a "thriller". The multi-label classification is significantly different from the traditional single-label classification. The correlation and co-occurrence between categories lead to those existed single-label classification method cannot be directly applied to the multi-label classification problem. But also multi-label classification is gradually becoming the current research hotspot and difficulty, especially in the fields of text classification, gene function classification, image semantic annotation, etc.

Researchers is finding the optimal classification algorithm to improve the classification accuracy of multi-label data. There are two most common ideas for multi-label classification [2]. One is to convert multi-label dataset into single-label dataset, and

© IFIP International Federation for Information Processing 2020
Published by Springer Nature Switzerland AG 2020
Z. Shi et al. (Eds.): IIP 2020, IFIP AICT 581, pp. 67–77, 2020.
https://doi.org/10.1007/978-3-030-46931-3_7

then apply traditional data classification algorithm to them (abbreviated as PT). Binary Relevance (BR) [3] is a typical PT method. BR considers the prediction of each label as an independent single classification problem, and designs an independent classifier for each label, and trains each classifier using all training data. However, it ignores the interrelationships between tags, and often fails to achieve satisfying classification performance. Guo [4] propose a improved binary relevance algorithm, it sets two layers to decompose the multi-label classification problem into L-independent binary classification problems respectively. Liu [5] propose a classifier chain algorithm based on dynamic programming and greedy classifier chain algorithm to search for global optimal labels, which compensated for the Classifier Chain algorithm (CC) defects sensitive to label selection [6]. Label Powerset (LP) [7] encodes every label permutation as a binary number and obtains new labels. Another idea is to modify existing single-label learning algorithm to solve multi-label learning problem. For example, the MLkNN algorithm calculates the prior probability of each label through statistics in the label set, and the probability of the sample with labeled and no label, and then predicts whether the sample has label [8]. Tsoumakas [9] proposed the Random k-Labelsets method to decompose the initial label set into several small random subsets, and use the Label Powerset algorithm to train the classifier. In addition, other researchers have also used various methods for multi-label classification research [10–13]. In the data prediction training process, the existing multi-label classification algorithms either ignore the interdependence between category labels, or ignore the important influence of initial features on the predicted value, and even add these tags to the original features as an additional function. It makes the feature set that has a very high dimension more complicated. Even if the dependency relationship between category labels is fully utilized, the multi-label classification algorithm ignores the initial prediction value between the label set and the training set, it maks the multi-label classification inaccurate.

We propose a multi-label short-text classification algorithm which combines the similarity graph and the restart random walk model (abbreviated as *SGaRW*). On the one hand, the similarity graph is used to calculate the original relationship between the text and the labels, and on the other hand, we utilize the restarted random walk model to calculate the potential semantic relationships between the labels and the labels. Finally, reasonable fusion is performed to make multi-label classification result more accurate.

2   Preliminary and Background

We review the existing basic concepts and define the problem of multi-label classification in this section.

2.1   Multi-label Classification

Fundamentally, multi-label classification can be considered as a label ranking problem [14, 15]. This correlation is scored based on the correlation between the test sample and each category label, and then the label to which the sample belongs is determined based on the score value. Assume that $X = \{x_1, x_2, \ldots, x_n\}$ indicates the sample set, $Y = \{y_1, y_2, \ldots, y_m\}$ is label set, and $D = \{(x_i, Y_i)|1 \leq i \leq n\}$ is dataset, $Y_i \subseteq Y$ is label set of the sample x_i. Thus prediction of the label for sample x could be expressed as following vector H(x).

$$H(x) = (h_1(x), \cdots, h_i(x), \cdots, h_m(x)) \tag{1}$$

In the vector, $h_i(x) \in [0,1]$ describes relevancy between sample x and label y_i. Multi-label classification is to achieve a classifier h: $X \rightarrow 2^Y$ using training data. Given new sample x, the classifier can predict label set of the sample x subsumes. Therefore, multi-label classification is to seek an optimal classification algorithm to construct a high-precision score vector H(x) to achieve the purpose of accurate classification.

2.2 Similarity Graph

Similarity graph [16, 17] built based on WordNet is a directed weighted graph G = (V, E) is used to calculate semantic similarity among nodes in the graph, V = {*itemsset*, *senseset*}, *itemsset* is a collection of nodes (*item*) that represent words, *senseset* is a set composed of nodes (*sense*) that represent senses. According to the corresponding relationship between them, a directed edges $<v_i, v_j>$ is added between two sense nodes, or between an *item* and a *sense*, or between two *items*. weight on the edge is signed as w_{ij}, w_{ij} represents the probability of thinking of the node v_j definitely when seeing the current node v_i, therefore, the weight w_{ij} reflects a conditional probability. So the similarity graph can be called a probability graph.

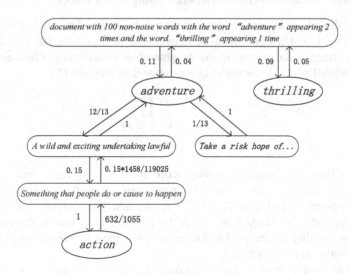

Fig. 1. Similarity graph

Such as the similarity graph shown in Fig. 1, *itemsset* = {adventure, thrilling, action}, *senseset* = {"a wild and exciting undertaking lawful", "take a risk in the hope of ...", "something that people do or cause to happen"}. In WordNet, the word "adventure" has two meanings in total, the using frequency of the first meaning is 0.92, and using frequency of the second meaning is 0.08, so the weight from the *item* node "adventure" to the first *sense* node "a wild and exciting undertaking lawful" is 0.92, which means that the probability that someone is interested in the first meaning after seeing the word "adventure" is 0.92. In turn, The weight from *sense* node "a wild and exciting undertaking lawful" to *item* node "adventure" is 1, which means that someone must think of the word "adventure" when they see either "a wild and exciting undertaking lawful" or "take a risk in the hope of ...".

3   Implement Multi-label Classification of Short Text

Implementing multi-label classification of text is divided into two stages in this paper. At the first step, we create a similarity graph based on the text content, and calculates the original relationship between the text and the label set, which is the initial predicted value $H(x)$. In the second phase, a label dependency graph is constructed and the restart random walk algorithm is performed on this graph to mine the potential semantic relationships between the labels. When the algorithm converges, we can obtain a vector consisting of the probability that the text belongs to each label, so we get labels which belong to the text.

3.1   Calculate Initial Association Between Sample and Labels

We consider short texts as *sense* nodes, map labels to *item* nodes, and create similarity graph $G_1 = (V_1, E_1)$. Then affinity score between the text and the label on a directed path can be defined as the product of the weights of all adjacent edges between the text node and the label node on the path [18], as shown in formula (2):

$$affinity_{pt}(v_{doc}|v_{label}) = \prod_{\substack{v_i, v_j \in pt \\ (v_i, v_j) \in E1}} P_{pt}(v_i|v_j) \tag{2}$$

Where, $affinity_{pt}(v_{doc}|v_{label})$ is affinity score from v_{doc} to v_{label}, nodes sequence $pt = <v_{doc}, \ldots v_i, v_j, \ldots v_{label}>$ is a directed path from v_{doc} to v_{label}, $p_{pt}(v_i|v_j)$ is weight on the edge between v_i and v_j in G_1, which support calculating affinity scores between two nodes. According to Markov model, as the path length increases, the value of the conditional probability decreases. The longer the path, the less evidence of an intimate relationship between the two nodes.

We also know that there is more than one directed path from v_{doc} to v_{label} in the similarity graph G_1. So affinity scores of the text-to-label on the entire graph G_1 can be expressed as the sum of the affinity score on all directed paths between these two nodes. $Aff'(v_{doc}, v_{label})$ denote affinity scores in formula (3)

$$Aff'(v_{doc}, v_{label}) = \sum affinity_{pt}(v_{doc}|v_{label}) \tag{3}$$

Due to the asymmetric nature of the affinity scores, the final affinity scores between two nodes can be obtained by formula (4).

$$Aff(v_{doc}, v_{label}) = \frac{Aff'(v_{doc}, v_{label}) + Aff'(v_{label}, v_{doc})}{2} \tag{4}$$

Treat the affinity scores between v_{doc} and v_{label} as the correlation score $h_i(x)$ between sample x and label y_i, That is:

$$h_i(x) = Aff(x, y_i) \tag{5}$$

Taking all the labels into account, we can get the correlation scores of the sample x and all labels in label set Y, as shown in formula (6)

$$H(x) = [Aff(x, y_1), \ldots Aff(x, y_i) \ldots Aff(x, y_m)]^T \tag{6}$$

3.2   Random Walk on Label Dependency Graph

3.2.1   Obtain Dependency Among Labels

We construct graph $G_2 = (V_2, E_2)$ to encode dependency among labels. Vertices in the graph G_2 represent labels in Y. If the label y_i and y_j mark the text x at the same time, add an edge between y_i and y_j, and the weight w_{ij} is defined as the number of samples labeled by labels y_i and y_j commonly:

$$w_{ij} = \left|\{x_k | y_i \in x_k \land y_j \in x_k\}\right| \quad if\ i \neq j \tag{7}$$

The adjacency matrix is used to store graph G_2 and m × m dimensional symmetric matrix is obtained. Therefore, the obtained matrix after utilizing Eq. (8) to make it asymmetric is represented as S, and its element s_{ij} is used to represent the jump probability from label y_i to label y_j, m_j is number of non-zero elements in the j-th column.

$$s_{ij} = \frac{w_{ij}}{m_j} \tag{8}$$

3.2.2   Restart Random Walk

Random walk with restart [19] is defined as Eq. (9), it starts from a random node to retrieve graph. The retriever iteratively transmits to its neighborhood with the probability that is proportional to their edge weights, or it has some probability α to return to the starting point, until the steady-state is reached.

$$P_i = aSP_i + (1 - a)H \tag{9}$$

Since prediction of every label can be delivered to other labels to some extent, label prediction related to samples not only is determined by samples, but also could be strengthened by other labels. We uses random walk model to predict multiple labels of a sample. Additionally, initial probability between sample x and each label is defined as $1/m$.

$$\begin{cases} P(Y)_x(0) = [\frac{1}{m}, \ldots, \frac{1}{m}]_m^T \\ P(Y)_x^{(t+1)} = aSP(Y)_x^{(t)} + (1 - a)H(x) \end{cases} \tag{10}$$

$P(Y)_x^{(t)}$ is probability distribution vector which represent the relationship between the sample and each label at time t. S is probability transformation matrix. $H(x)$ is aforementioned initial prediction value vector of labels of sample x. The process continues until $P(Y)_x$ converges. Prediction of the label is updated repeatedly, dependency among labels could be utilized sufficiently.

4   Experimental Result and Analysis

In this section, we explain the means by which similarity graph and restart random walk model are evaluated, whilst providing a description of the multi-label dataset and other settings used in the experimental study. Finally, the experimental results on the dataset and the statistical analysis are discussed.

4.1   Dataset

The data used in the experiment is English movie titles and overviews collected manually, it is called Movies dataset. Dataset statistics is shown as Table 1, in which label density equals to size of label set q divided by potential of the label set c, indicating probability that a label appears.

Table 1. Several statistical value

Dataset name	Size	Size of label set (q)	Label density	Size of elements in Y(c)
Movies	2000	14	0.212	2.972

4.2   Evaluation Metrics

Traditional single classification performance evaluation metrics, such as recall and accuracy, cannot be used directly to evaluate the multiple-label classification performance. Therefore, we use the following three metrics to measure the performance of our method.

4.2.1 Hamming Loss

Hamming Loss [20] measures classification error based on single-label classification, that is, labels that belong to the sample do not appear in the labels set, but labels that the sample do not have appear. Smaller value means better performance of a classification model. The best is when it is 0. It is defined as:

$$Hamming-loss(x_i, y_i) = \frac{1}{|D|} \sum_{i=1}^{D} \frac{xor(x_i, y_i)}{|L|} \tag{11}$$

$|D|$ represents total number of samples. $|L|$ represents total number of labels. x_i and y_j represent prediction result and true label respectively.

4.2.2 Jaccard Index

Jaccard Index [21] measures how similar two sets are. It is defined as size of intersection divided by size of union. Bigger value means better performance of a classification model. It is defined as:

$$Jaccard(A, B) = \frac{|A \cap B|}{|A \cup B|} \tag{12}$$

4.2.3 Accuracy-Score

Accuracy-score [22] is used to compute accuracy of prediction. In multi-label classification, the function returns accuracy of subsets. The accuracy is 1 if entire prediction labels are consistent with real labels, meaning it reaches the best performance, otherwise is 0. It is defined as following:

$$accuracy(y, \hat{y}) = \frac{1}{|L|} \sum_{i=1}^{|L|} 1(\hat{y}_i = y_i) \tag{13}$$

$\hat{y}_i$ is prediction value of the i-th sample and y_i is corresponding real value.

4.3 Experimental Result and Analysis

Three experiments are designed to evaluate performance of algorithm of this paper on multi-label text classification. (1) Analyze influence of different α on algorithm, (2) Compare and analyze results by change the size of training set and test set v, (3) Compare our algorithm with other algorithms.

Experiment 1. Analyze influence of different α on our method. Let $\alpha = 0.0001$, 0.00007, 0.00004, 0.00001 to operate experiment respectively. From Table 2 we see that three metrics reach all the largest when $\alpha = 0.00007$, and the result is optimal at this point. When α is larger than 0.00007 or smaller than 0.00007, the performance of the algorithm tend to be poor. Generally speaking, influence of α on performance is limited (not exceeds $\pm 0.36\%$).

Table 2. Experimental results when s values are different

α	Hamming-loss	Jaccard	Accuracy-score
0.00010	0.1073	0.6588	0.8957
0.00007	**0.1043**	**0.6610**	**0.8959**
0.00004	0.1032	0.6609	0.8958
0.00001	0.1050	0.6573	0.8950

Experiment 2. Use training set t and test set v of different sizes and analyze experimental results. Use training set whose size is 300, 600, 900, 1200, 1500 and test set whose size is 100, 300, 500. As Table 3 shows, when the size of test set $|t| = 100$ and the size of training set $|v|$ is 300, the performance outperforms the others. When $|t| = 300$ and $|v| = 1200$, the result is wonderful. In summary, the performance obtained by our method is optimal when $|t| = 500$ and $|v| = 1500$.

Next, we select a group of data with the best classification performance for further comparative analysis. Specifically, $|t| = 500$, and the size of training set v has different scales. It can be observed from Fig. 2 that Hamming's Loss gradually decreases and Accuracy-score continues to increase as the size of the training set increasing, it means that classification performance of the algorithm tend to get better when the ratio between training data and test data increases. When $|v| = 1500$, the classification score both reaches the optimal.

Table 3. Experimental results when the training set v is different from the test set t scale

Test (t)	Training (v)	Hamming-loss	Jaccard	Accuracy-score
$|t| = 100$	$|v| = 300$	**0.1097**	**0.5609**	**0.8359**
	$|v| = 600$	0.1171	0.6512	0.8929
	$|v| = 900$	0.1246	0.6017	0.8731
	$|v| = 1200$	0.1464	0.5524	0.8536
$|t| = 300$	$|v| = 900$	0.1219	0.5803	0.8781
	$|v| = 1200$	**0.1117**	**0.6088**	**0.8583**
	$|v| = 1500$	0.1245	0.5734	0.8754
$|t| = 500$	$|v| = 1000$	0.1403	0.5219	0.8613
	$|v| = 1500$	**0.1073**	**0.6657**	**0.8786**

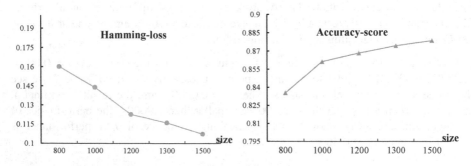

Fig. 2. When $|t| = 500$, changes in Hamming loss and accuracy-score with different $|v|$

Experiment 3. To demonstrate how our method improves multi-label text classification performance, we compare our method with other methods in comparison to those existed similar methods, they are *BR*, *LP*, *CC* and *MLkNN* and so on. It should be noted that the parameter value of the *MLkNN* algorithm is set to k = 20, and parameters in other algorithms use the default value. The classifiers for the *BR*, *LP* and *CC* use the Naive Bayes classification.

Figure 3 show that *SGaRW* algorithm has a larger Accuracy-score value compared with *MLkNN*, it indicates that the accuracy of the labels of the text predicted by our method is higher. The Jaccard index of our method is greater than *MLkNN*, while the Hamming loss is less than *MLkNN*. In other words, using the *SGaRW* algorithm will make the labels that do not belong to the text appear in the predicted label set as little as possible, which reduce the error rate a lot. Comparison with *BR*, *LP*, *CC* and *MLkNN* algorithms shows that *SGaRW* algorithm has great advantage over other algorithms.

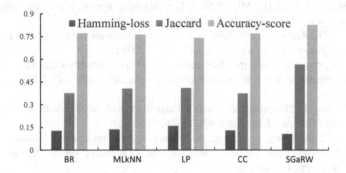

Fig. 3. Comparison of the different algorithms

5 Conclusion

We introduces a novel method *SGaRW* algorithm combining similarity graph and random walk model, which can resolve multi-label text classification problems efficiently. Utilizing prior information from WordNet to build similarity graph, and computing initial match value between labels and texts on it. Then a label dependency graph is constructed, and random walk with restart is been run on it. Finally labels of the text are determined. Core of the future work is to consider expanding dataset, introduce short text semantic understanding to improve performance of short text multi-label classification and optimize effectiveness of the algorithm furtherly.

Acknowledgments. This work was supported in part by National Natural Science Foundation of China (No. 61762078, 61862058, 61967013), Youth Teacher Scientific Capability Promoting Project of NWNU (No. NWNU-LKQN-16-20).

References

1. Tsoumakas, G., Katakis, I., Vlahavas, I.: Mining multi-label data. In: Maimon, O., Rokach, L. (eds.) Data Mining and Knowledge Discovery Handbook, pp. 667–685. Springer, Boston (2009). https://doi.org/10.1007/978-0-387-09823-4_34
2. Zhang, M.L., Zhou, Z.H.: Multi-label neural networks with applications to functional genomics and text categorization. IEEE Trans. Knowl. Data Eng. **18**(10), 1338–1351 (2006)
3. Trohidis, K., Tsoumakas, G., Kalliris, G.: Multi-label classification of music by emotion. EURASIP J. Audio Speech Music. Process. **2011**(1), 4 (2011)
4. Guo, T., Li, G.Y.: An improved binary relevance algorithm for multi-label classification. Appl. Mech. Mater. **536–537**, 394–398 (2014)
5. Liu, W., Tsang, I.W.: On the optimality of classifier chain for multi-label classification. In: International Conference on Neural Information Processing Systems. MIT Press (2015)
6. Read, J., Pfahringer, B., Holmes, G., et al.: Classifier chains for multi-label classification. Mach. Learn. **85**(3), 333 (2011). https://doi.org/10.1007/s10994-011-5256-5
7. Zhang, M.L., Zhou, Z.H.: ML-KNN: a lazy learning approach to multi-label learning. Pattern Recognit. **40**(7), 2038–2048 (2007)
8. Tsoumakas, G., Katakis, I., Vlahavas, I.: Random k-labelsets for multi-label classification. IEEE Trans. Knowl. Data Eng. **23**(7), 1079–1089 (2011)
9. Read, J.: A pruned problem transformation method for multi-label classification. In: New Zealand Computer Science Research Student Conference (NZCSRS 2008), vol. 143150, p. 41 (2008)
10. Jizhao, Q., Hua, J.I., Huaxiang, Z.: Modified algorithm with label-specific features for multi-label learning. Comput. Eng. Appl. **49**(22), 163–166 (2013)
11. Huang, J., Li, G., Wang, S., Zhang, W., Huang, Q.: Group sensitive classifier chains for multi-label classification. In: IEEE International Conference on Multimedia and Expo (ICME), Turin, pp. 1–6 (2015)
12. Huang, J., Li, G., Huang, Q., et al.: Learning label-specific features and class-dependent labels for multi-label classification. IEEE Trans. Knowl. Data Eng. **28**(12), 3309–3323 (2016)
13. Qiao, L., Zhang, L., Sun, Z., et al.: Selecting label-dependent features for multi-label classification. Neurocomputing **259**, 112–118 (2017)
14. Li, X., Ouyang, J., Zhou, X.: Supervised Topic Models for Multi-Label Classification. Elsevier Science Publishers B.V., Amsterdam (2015)
15. Soleimani, H., Miller, D.J.: Semi-supervised multi-label topic models for document classification and sentence labeling. In: ACM International on Conference on Information & Knowledge Management. ACM (2016)
16. Stanchev, L.: Creating a similarity graph from WordNet. In: 4th International Conference on Web Intelligence, Mining and Semantics (WIMS14), pp. 1–11. Association for Computing Machinery, New York (2014). Article no. 36
17. Stanchev, L.: Semantic document clustering using a similarity graph. In: IEEE Tenth International Conference on Semantic Computing, pp. 1–8. IEEE (2016)
18. Stanchev, L.: Creating a probabilistic graph for WordNet using markov logic network. In: 6th International Conference on Web Intelligence, Mining and Semantics, pp. 1–12 (2016)
19. Tong, H., Faloutsos, C., Pan, J.Y.: Fast random walk with restart and its applications. In: 6th International Conference on Data Mining (ICDM 2006), pp. 613–622. IEEE (2006)
20. Díez, J., Luaces, O., del Coz, J.J., et al.: Optimizing different loss functions in multi-label classifications. Prog. Artif. Intell. **3**(2), 107–118 (2015). https://doi.org/10.1007/s13748-014-0060-7

21. Hamers, L., Hemeryck, Y., Herweyers, G., et al.: Similarity measures in scientometric research: the Jaccard index versus Salton's cosine formula. Inf. Process. Manag. **25**(3), 315–318 (1989)
22. Hubley, A.M.: Using the Rey-Osterrieth and modified Taylor complex figures with older adults: a preliminary examination of accuracy score comparability. Arch. Clin. Neuropsychol. Off. J. Natl. Acad. Neuropsychol. **25**(3), 197 (2010)

Environmental Parameters Analysis and Power Prediction for Photovoltaic Power Generation Based on Ensembles of Decision Trees

Shuai Zhang[1,2,3(✉)], Hongwei Dai[1], Aizhou Yang[1],
and Zhongzhi Shi[2]

[1] Dongfang Electronics Co. Ltd., Yantai 264000, China
82234841@qq.com
[2] Chinese Academy of Sciences, Beijing 110010, China
[3] Shandong Technology and Business University, Yantai 264005, China

Abstract. Due to the influence of solar irradiation, temperature and other environmental factors, the output power of photovoltaic power generation has great randomness and randomness discontinuity. In this paper, a method for analyzing environment data related photovoltaic power generation based on ensembles of decision trees algorithm is studied. Firstly, the characteristics of environmental factors of photovoltaic power generation are analyzed by K-means clustering. And then the corresponding cluster label is assigned. Furthermore, the Radom Forests is combined to build a model. Finally, the method is validated by given data above from a real project. The results show that the proposed method can provide reference for the forecasting of photovoltaic power.

Keywords: K-means clustering · Ensembles of decision trees · Photovoltaic power generation · Environmental data · Feature analysis and prediction

1 Introduction

With the replace old growth drivers with new ones strategy being implemented [1, 2], new energy industry has become a strategic and pioneering one in the world. Photovoltaic power generation has been developing rapidly due to its advantages in safety, reliability, less geographic restrictions and short construction period [3]. At present, photovoltaic generation related technology have matured, but the output power has great randomness and randomness discontinuity by the influence of solar irradiation, temperature and other environmental factors [4, 5]. Therefore, it is difficult to integrate into the power grid, and which is also disadvantage to rational planning for using of local energy. How to applying environmental data to analysis and predict solar power generation will become a major energy in the future [6, 7].

The development of artificial intelligence, big data, data mining and other new generation of information technology have provided a good solution for solving the problem [8, 9]. The reference [10] applied the K-means clustering to the actual operation data processing of a PV station in the city of Foshan, Guangdong Province, and

© IFIP International Federation for Information Processing 2020
Published by Springer Nature Switzerland AG 2020
Z. Shi et al. (Eds.): IIP 2020, IFIP AICT 581, pp. 78–85, 2020.
https://doi.org/10.1007/978-3-030-46931-3_8

achieved the operation state pattern recognition. A short-term forecasting method for photovoltaic (PV) power is proposed in the reference [11], which established an SVM forecasting model and uses leave-one-out algorithm to optimize the Kernel parameter and penalty parameter to achieve the forecasting of PV power. The reference [12] proposed a novel model called forest for photovoltaic power generation (FPPG), which is an assembly predict model composed by multi regression tree and can perform better generated in power forecasting. However, photovoltaic power generation is influenced by environmental factors greatly, such as temperature, humidity, irradiation and so on, which are varies dramatically from one region to another. So how to make better those data and improve data quality a still a hot topic.

In this paper, an approach which combined K-means clustering with random forests, an ensemble of decision trees method, are researched and analyzed by some measured data from a photovoltaic power station in Shandong province. Firstly, some environmental data related photovoltaic power generation are analyzed. At the same time, measured data from a photovoltaic power station are given. And then, the algorithm principle of K-means clustering and random forests are introduced briefly. Moreover, an algorithm which combined K-means clustering with random forests and its flow chart are proposed. Finally, the method is validated by given data above from a real project. The results show that the proposed method can provide reference for the forecasting of PV power.

2 Some Environmental Data Related Photovoltaic Power Generation

The operating state of the photovoltaic power generation system is not only related to the working state of the system internal components, but also related to the changes of environmental parameters. There are many factors influencing the output power of

	SDATE	TIME	QX000	QX001	...	QX003	QX004	QX005	SYCG_SUMP
0	17532	15	2.5100	112	...	0.0919	1021.679993	5.4794	0.0
1	17532	30	1.5599	126	...	0.0929	1021.679993	6.3926	0.0
2	17532	45	1.6400	113	...	0.0919	1021.690002	5.4794	0.0
3	17532	60	1.5200	96	...	0.0909	1021.570007	6.3926	0.0
4	17532	75	1.6200	114	...	0.0889	1021.479980	6.3926	0.0
...	...	...	...	...	...	...	...	...	...
7483	17614	1380	1.1699	178	...	0.1509	1018.219971	0.9132	0.0
7484	17614	1395	2.0999	168	...	0.1500	1018.210022	0.0000	0.0
7485	17614	1410	2.2999	159	...	0.1489	1018.219971	0.0000	0.0
7486	17614	1425	2.0499	175	...	0.1489	1018.200012	0.0000	0.0
7487	17614	1440	2.2199	183	...	0.1469	1018.099976	0.0000	0.0

[7488 rows x 9 columns]

Fig. 1. Part of the samples

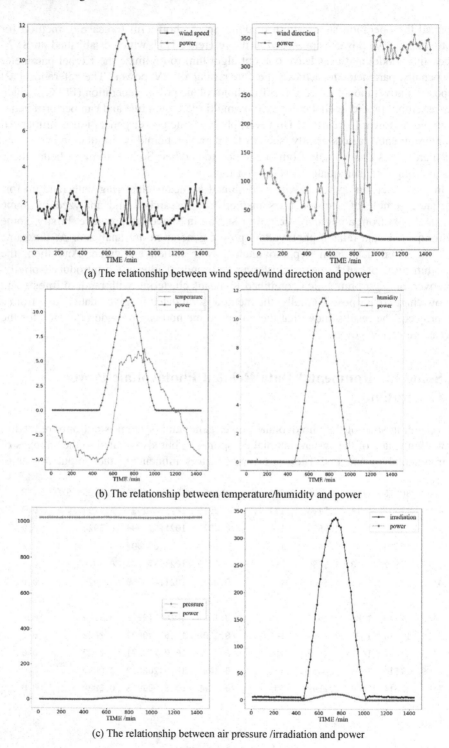

(a) The relationship between wind speed/wind direction and power

(b) The relationship between temperature/humidity and power

(c) The relationship between air pressure /irradiation and power

Fig. 2. (a)–(c) Various environmental factors and power line chart/day

photovoltaic system. Furthermore, these factors also have a complex relationship with the output power of photovoltaic power generation, especially the environmental data, mainly including temperature, humidity, wind speed, air pressure, irradiation and so on, which are the objective factors beyond human controlling but the key. Therefore, this method has an experimental application and a research meaning to analyze the environmental characteristics and find out the relationship between each factor and actual power output for further prediction.

In this paper, the measured data samples of a 40 MW photovoltaic power station system in Shandong province are given. The samples including the wind speed, wind direction, temperature, humidity, air pressure, irradiation factor and power at the same sampling time. The sampling data are sampled at a 15-min interval, 96 sampling points per day. A total of 7,488 samples were collected from 78 consecutive days. Part of the samples are shown in Fig. 1.

Where 'SDATE' stands for date marking, 'TIME' stands for sampling time, 'SYCG_SUMP' stands for power and 'QX000'–'QX005' stands for: wind speed, wind direction, temperature, humidity, air pressure and irradiation, respectively.

The relationship between environmental factors and power are visualized by using line graphs. For the clarity of the data presentation, take only diurnal variation as an example, which are shown in Fig. 2(a)–(c).

From Fig. 2, we can see that power output has obvious correlation with temperature, irradiation and humidity, but poor correlation with wind speed, wind direction and air pressure, which can apply to preprocessed for subsequent cluster analysis to accurately cluster data ranges.

3 The Algorithm Principle of K-means Clustering and Random Forests

3.1 K-means Clustering [14]

The goal of cluster analysis is to partition the observations into groups ("clusters") so that the pairwise dissimilarities between those assigned to the same cluster tend to be smaller than those in different clusters. The K-means algorithm is one of the most popular iterative descent clustering methods. It is intended for situations in which all variables are of the quantitative type, and squared Euclidean distance Eq. (1) is chosen as the dissimilarity measure.

$$d(x_i, xi') = \sum\nolimits_{j=1}^{p} (x_{ij} - x_{i'j}) = \|x_i - x_{x'}\| \tag{1}$$

Note that weighted Euclidean distance can be used by redefining the x_{ij} values.

The within-point scatter can be written as

$$W(C) = \frac{1}{2} \sum\nolimits_{k=1}^{K} \sum\nolimits_{C(i)=k} \sum\nolimits_{C(i')=k} \|x_i - x_{i'}\|^2 = \sum\nolimits_{k=1}^{K} N_k \sum\nolimits_{C(i)=k} \|x_i - \bar{x}_k\|^2 \tag{2}$$

Where $\bar{x}_k = (\bar{x}_{1k}, \cdots, \bar{x}_{pk})$ is the mean vector associated with the kth cluster, and $N_k = \sum_{i=1}^{N} I(C(i) = k)$. Thus, the criterion is minimized by assigning the N observations to the K clusters in such a way that within each cluster the average dissimilarity of the observations from the cluster mean, as defined by the points in that cluster, is minimized.

3.2 Ensembles of Decision Trees– Random Forests [13, 14]

Decision trees are a widely used models for some machine learning tasks. But a main drawback of decision trees is that they tend to overfit the training data. Although there are some measures for prevent it, such as pre-pruning and post-pruning, even with the use of pre-pruning, decision trees tend to overfit, and provide poor generalization performance.

Ensembles are methods that combine multiple machine learning models to create more powerful models, which are one way to address this problem. Random Forests are the model that belong to this category. Random forests are essentially a collection of decision trees, where each tree is slightly different from the others. To implement this strategy, we need to build many decision tree. The specific algorithm is as follow Table 1:

Table 1. The algorithm of random forests [14]

Random Forest
1. For b = 1 to B:
(a) Draw a bootstrap sample Z^* of size N from the training data.
(b) Grow a random-forest tree T_b to the bootstrapped data, by recursively repeating the following steps for each terminal node of the tree, until the minimum node size nmin is reached.
i. Select m variables at random from the p variables.
ii. Pick the best variable/split-point among the m.
iii. Split the node into two daughter nodes.
2. Output the ensemble of trees $\{T_b\}_1^B$.
To make a prediction at a new point x:
Regression: $\hat{f}_{rf}^B(x) = \frac{1}{B} \sum_{b=1}^{B} T_b(x)$
Classification: Let $\hat{C}_b(x)$ be the class prediction of the bth random-forest tree. Then $\hat{C}_{rf}^B(x)$ = majority vote $\{\hat{C}_b(x)\}_1^B$

Firstly, we first take what is called a bootstrap sample of our data. A bootstrap sample means from our n_samples data points, we repeatedly draw an example randomly with replacement (i.e. the same sample can be picked multiple times), n_samples times. This will create a dataset that is as big as the original dataset, but some data points will be missing from it, and some will be repeated.

Next, a decision tree is built based on this newly created dataset. The bootstrap sampling leads to each decision tree in the random forest being built on a slightly different dataset. Because of the selection of features in each node, each split in each tree operates on a different subset of features. Together these two mechanisms ensure that all the trees in the random forests are different.

4 The Algorithm Combined K-means Clustering with Random Forests and Engineering Testing

4.1 The Algorithm Combined K-means Clustering with Random Forests

In Random Forests Algorithm, critical parameter in this process is max_features. If we set max_features to n_features, that means that each split can look at all features in the dataset, and no randomness will be injected. If we set max_features to one, that means that the splits have no choice at all on which feature to test, and can only search over different thresholds for the feature that was selected randomly [13]. So, we applied K-means Clustering to preprocessing the data, thus, we can obtain a cluster label for every sampling point. Next, we let this label as the target function to establish a random forest to achieve forecast. The specific algorithm flow is shown in Fig. 3.

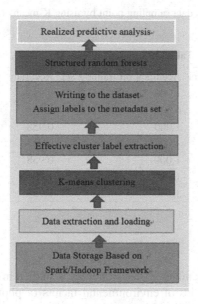

Fig. 3. Algorithm flow

4.2 Engineering Testing

Based on Spark/Hadoop framework and python language, the data of the second part above are applied and analyzed. Due to limited space, only 1 day's data sampling point is taken as a legend and 7 days' data analysis is taken as a table example in Fig. 4 and Table 2. It can be seen that K-means clustering has well realized self-analysis of data, and given cluster labels. In the last, a stable prediction accuracy is obtained.

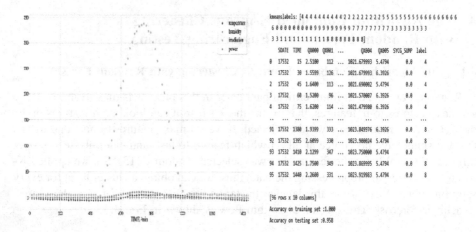

Fig. 4. The result of 1 day's data sampling point by using K-means Clustering-Random Forests

Table 2. Forecast results for 7 days

Sdate	n_clusters	Accuracy on training set	Accuracy on testing set
17532	10	1.000	0.958
17533	10	0.986	0.917
17534	10	1.000	0.958
17535	10	1.000	0.917
17536	10	1.000	0.958
17537	10	1.000	1.000
17538	10	1.000	0.958

5   Conclusions

One method based on ensembles of decision trees is studied in this paper. By K-means clustering, the characteristics of environmental factors of photovoltaic power generation are analyzed, and data related to the power output through visualization are found out, and simultaneously, the corresponding cluster label is assigned. After that, the Radom Forests is combined to build a model, and then power generation environment data and predict the power are analyzed. The results show that this method has stable prediction accuracy and certain reference value for the environment data analysis and power prediction of photovoltaic power generation.

References

1. The Approval about the Overall Plan of Shandong the Replace Old Growth Drivers with New One Comprehensive Reform Pilot Area by the State Council. http://www.gov.cn/zhengce/content/2018-01/10/content_5255214.htm

2. People's Government of Shandong Province: Implementation Planning for the Key Projects of the Replace Old Growth Drivers with New Ones in Shandong Province. http://www.shandong.gov.cn/art/2018/3/16/art_2522_11096.html

3. China Electricity Council: China Electric Power Industry Annual Development Report. China Electric Power Press, Beijing (2018)

4. Bird, L., Lew, D., Milligan, M.: Wind and solar energy curtailment: a review of international experience. Renew. Sustain. Energy Rev. **65**, 577–586 (2016)

5. Zhang, C.Q., Zheng, Q.: SKBA-LSSVM short-term forecasting model for PV power generation. Proc. CSU-EPSA **31**(8), 86–93 (2019)

6. Wu, J.Z.: Drivers and state-of-the-art of integrated energy systems in Europe. Autom. Electr. Power Syst. **40**(5), 1–7 (2016)

7. Ai, X., Han, X.N., Sun, Y.Y.: The development status and prospect of grid-connected photovoltaic generation and its related technologies. Mod. Electr. Power **30**(1), 1–7 (2013)

8. He, Q., Li, N., Luo, W.J., Shi, Z.Z.: A survey of machine learning algorithms for big data. Pattern Recog. Artif. Intell. **27**(4), 327–335 (2014)

9. Hu, K.Y., Li, Y.L., Jiang, X., Li, J., Hu, Z.H.: Application of improved neural network model in photovoltaic power generation prediction. Comput. Syst. Appl. **28**(12), 37–46 (2019)

10. Yang, D.Y., Ge, Q., Dong, Y.C., Tang, Y.L., He, C.X.: Research on operation state pattern recognition of PV station based on the principle of K-means clustering. Power Syst. Prot. Control **44**(14), 25–30 (2016)

11. Yu, Q.L., Xu, C.Q., Li, S., Liu, H., Song, Y., Liu, X.O.: Application of fuzzy clustering algorithm and support vector machine to short-term forecasting of PV power. Proc. CSU-EPSA **28**(12), 115–129 (2016)

12. Song, X.H., Guo, Z.Z., Guo, H.P., Wu, S.H., Wang, Z.Q., Wu, C.A.: A new forecasting model based on forest for photovoltaic power generation. Power Syst. Prot. Control **43**(2), 13–18 (2015)

13. Müller, A.C., Sarah, G.: Introduction to Machine Learning with Python. O'Reilly Media, Inc., Sebastopol (2016)

14. Hastic, T., Tibshirani, R., Friedman, J.: The Elements of Statistical Learning: Data Mining, Inference, and Prediction, 2nd edn. Springer, New York (2009). https://doi.org/10.1007/978-0-387-84858-7

The Conjugate Entangled Manifold of Space–Time Induced by the Law of Unity of Contradiction

Jiali Feng[1(✉)] and Jingjuan Feng[2]

[1] Information Engineering College, Shanghai Maritime University,
Shanghai 201306, China
jlfeng@shmtu.edu.cn
[2] TRC Solutions, Inc., Oakland, CA 94612, USA
DoveFeng@gmail.com

Abstract. The mechanism of the contradiction between two different objects u and v is attributed to a mechanism that their opposite position information "x_u" and "x_v" of u and v are transmitted, respectively, from the initial time t_0 , at different speeds $\dot{x}_u(t)$ and $\dot{x}_v(t)$ ($\dot{x}_v = -\varsigma \dot{x}_u(t)$), and is meeting at the contradiction point $t = t_\lambda$ and $x = x_\lambda$. Because the coordinate of contradiction point can be noted by $z_\lambda(t_\lambda, x_\lambda)$ and $z_\lambda^*(x_\lambda, t_\lambda)$ in two space time Complex Coordinates Systems which origins are $z_o(0_t, 0_x)$ and $z_o^*(1_t, 1_t)$, respectively, such that the time t_λ and the position x_λ of the contradictory points can be expressed as the sum of the complex numbers $z_\lambda(t_\lambda, x_\lambda)$ and its conjugate $\bar{z}_\lambda(t_\lambda, x_\lambda) : t_\lambda = z_\lambda(t_\lambda, x_\lambda) + \bar{z}_\lambda(t_\lambda, x_\lambda) = w_\lambda(z_\lambda, \bar{z}_\lambda)$, and the difference of $z_\lambda^*(x_\lambda, t_\lambda)$ and its conjugate: $\bar{z}_\lambda^*(x_\lambda, t_\lambda) : x_\lambda = z_\lambda^*(x_\lambda, t_\lambda) - \bar{z}_\lambda^*(x_\lambda, t_\lambda) = w_\lambda^*(z_\lambda^*, \bar{z}_\lambda^*)$. By synthesizing the time-space coordinate and the space-me coordinate, such their time axis $[0_t, 1_t]$ and the space axis $[1_x, 0_x]$ of the two complex coordinate systems are coincide with the intervals $[u, v]$, respectively, then the contradiction point can be expressed in the synthesis Coordinate System to be a wave function: $\psi(w_\lambda, w_\lambda^*) = t_\lambda - ix_\lambda = w_\lambda - iw_\lambda^*$. Because of the varying direction of two information "x_u" and "x_v" and their increments $\Delta x_u(\Delta_u t) = \dot{x}_u(\Delta_u t)\Delta_u t$ and $\Delta x_v(\Delta_v t) = \dot{x}_v(\Delta_v t)\Delta_v t$ with time t and increment $\Delta t = t - 0_t$ are opposite each other, so the t_λ of the wave function ψ is on the time axis $[0_t, 1_t]$ and the x_λ on the space axis $[1_x, 0_x]$, constructed a pair of information transmission streams entangled in opposite directions appear, such that the interval [u, v] constitutes a space-time conjugate entangled manifold. The invariance of the contradiction point or wave function $\psi(w_\lambda, w_\lambda^*)$, under the unit scale transformation of time and distance measurement, not only make all points $z(t, x) \in [u, v]$ is contradiction point, and makes $\lambda = \frac{1}{2}$ and $\zeta = \frac{4}{1} - \lambda$ It is also shown that since λ changes from 0 to $\frac{1}{2}$ is equivalent to the integral for the on t_λ and x_λ in wave function ψ from 0 to $\frac{1}{2}$, respectively, by it not only the inner product ψ of the ψ and the time component t_λ, respectively $\psi(w, w^*).t_\lambda$, and the outer product of ψ and the spatial component $\psi(w, w^*) \wedge x_\lambda$ can be get, but also their sum: $\psi(w, w^*) \cdot \psi_t + \psi(w, w^*) \wedge \psi_x$ can be gotten too.

© IFIP International Federation for Information Processing 2020
Published by Springer Nature Switzerland AG 2020
Z. Shi et al. (Eds.): IIP 2020, IFIP AICT 581, pp. 86–98, 2020.
https://doi.org/10.1007/978-3-030-46931-3_9

Keywords: Location Information Oppositely Transmission ·
Conjugate-Entangled Manifold · Entanglement of Clifford Geometric Product ·
Qualitative Grid Computer

1 Introduction

According to Formal logic and Mathematical logic, there is no contradiction among the most basic laws of the world. On the contrary, dialectical logic believes that the world is full of contradictions, and regards "unity of opposites, mutual change between quality and quantity and negation of negation" as "The basic law of universal application".

Can the law of non-contradiction and the law of contradiction be reconciled? How to reconcile? These questions has long broken through the scope of philosophy, epistemology and logic, and has become a basic subject that must be studied in almost all fields involving mathematics, physics, chemistry, biology, psychology, intelligence, thinking, as well as sociology, economics, political science, military science, etc. The core question about how contradictions arise is the entrance to the study of contradictions.

The source of contradiction between two oppositions u and $v(v \neq u)$ has been attributed to whether there exist a non-zero distance $d(x_u, x_v) \neq 0$ or not? The contradiction of u and v is varying with time t has been conversed into the function of the distance $d(x_u, x_v)(\neq 0)$ vary with time t, $f(t) = f(d(x_u(t), x_v(t)))$.

In mathematics, the distance of $x_u(t)$ and $x_v(t)$ can be represented by complex number $z_u(t, x)$ and $z_v(t, x)$ in Complex Coordinate, respectively, and the distance $d(x_u, x_v)$ is defined as the root of inner product of a pair of vectors $z_u(t, x)$ and $z_v(t, x)$: $d(x_u(t), x_v(t)) = \sqrt{z_u(t, x) \cdot z_v(t, x)}$. Since an inner product is not only a core concept throughout mathematics, physics and neural network, but also a polarization invariant quantity under coordinate translation, by it an Entangled Vector and Clifford Geometric Product can be induced too, as well as a category and a topos, such that Artificial Neural Network defined by Inner Product can be converted into computing of tensor follow.

The emergence of the contradiction between two different objects u and v is attributed to a mechanism that their opposite position information is transmitted and is meeting at a contradiction point. To describe this mechanism, the paper constructed the a coordinate system in which the invariances of the contradiction points can perform certain transformations, such as the phase switching of time and space, the scale transformation of the measurement unit, and the invariances of the contradiction point position transfers from 0 to 1 as the relative velocity ratio information of the two opposite objects changes.

It is shown that the time-space (or spatial-time) complex coordinate system can be obtained by shifting of the time (or space) axis to $t = -\frac{1}{2}$, and rotating the spatial (or time) axis by $\theta = \frac{\pi}{2}$, in which the mechanism of contradiction emerging and meeting at the contradiction point can be expressed as a function of the position component of a pair of conjugate complex numbers vary with time component (or on contrary) and meeting at the contradiction points, and by the transformation of plane-polar coordinates, even to expressed as a wave function.

It is also shown that, by a synthesizing of the time-space coordinate and the space-me coordinate, a Conjugate-Entangled Coordinate System can be constructed, in which the Inner Product induced by the invariance of contradiction point transfer as the relative velocity ratio information of the two opposite objects changes from 0 to 1. This induces not only an integral for all contradiction points in interval $[0_x, 1_x]$, but also a Conjugate-Entangled Manifold, in which the invariance of Inner Product under the transformation and rotating of coordinate system can be represented. It is known that inner product is a key concept across philosophy, mathematics and physics, and artificial neural networks, and can be defined by inner product. However, we propose that a qualitative mapping can be induced by inner product too such that a qualitative grid computer can be proposed in this way.

2　The Representation for the Mechanism of Contradiction Emerging

The mechanism of the emerging of the contradiction between two objects u and v, which are separated by a unit distance, is attributed to that the location information of u and v is transmitted to each other at unit velocities $\dot{x}_u(t)\left(|\dot{x}_u(t)| = \frac{1_x}{1_t}\right)$ and $\dot{x}_v(t)\left(= \dot{x}_u(t) = -\frac{1_x}{1_t}\right)$, respectively, from time $t = 0_t$, and meets at the midpoint of the line segment connecting u and v in a half of unit time $\frac{1_t}{2}$, or the contradiction point (Fig. 1).

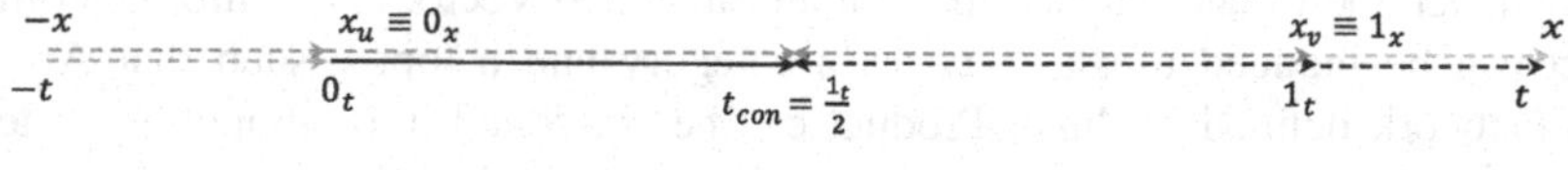

Fig. 1. Contradiction point $\left(t_{con}, x_u\left(\frac{1_t}{2}\right)\right) = \left(\frac{1_t}{2}, \frac{1_x}{2}\right)$ (or $x_v\left(\frac{1_t}{2}\right) = -\frac{1_x}{2}x_v\left(\frac{1_t}{2}\right) = -\frac{1_x}{2}x_v\left(\frac{1_t}{2}\right) = -\frac{1_x}{2}x_v\left(\frac{1_t}{2}\right) = -\frac{1_x}{2}x_v\left(\frac{1_t}{2}\right) = -\frac{1_x}{2}$) position information $x_u \equiv 0_x$ and $x_v \equiv 1_x$ respectively are moving at unit of velocity $\dot{x}_u(t) = 1_{\frac{x}{t}}$ and $\dot{x}_v(t) = -1_{\frac{x}{t}}$ forward to oppositions

Because the objects u and v themselves do not move, the problem of the mechanism of the contradiction in philosophy not only is translated into the relative transmission of position information between u and v, but also such that the three major laws of two contradiction u and v, i.e, t, the unity of contradiction, the mutual change of quality and the negation of negation, are converted into the physical-mathematical-logical mechanism and structural problems at the contradiction point, which are the caused by encounter and collision. This paper not only analyzes the relations and differences between they and the related mechanisms and structures in physics, mathematics, logic, and artificial intelligence, but also provides a possible philosophical framework for their unification.

For the convenience of mathematical discussion, let "$x_u \equiv 0_x$" and "$x_v \equiv 1_x$" be the located positions of two opposite objects u and $v (v \neq u)$, their distance is $\Delta(u, v) = \Delta(x_u, x_v) = \Delta x = x_v - x_u = 1_x - 0_x$, here, $|1_x - 0_x|$ is the unit of distance. (Since there are not physical move of u and v, here x_u and x_v are only noted the position of u and v, respectively.)

Let "$t_0 \equiv 0_t$" and "$t_1 \equiv 1_t$" be the starting point and the end point of the unit time $|1_t - 0_t|$, respectively, $\dot{x}_u \left(|\dot{x}_u| = \frac{1_x}{1_t} \right)$ and $\dot{x}_v (\dot{x}_v = -\dot{x}_u)$ the transmission velocity of position information "x_u" and "x_v", then it takes the unit time for information "x_u" from the point "$x_u \equiv 0_x$" to "$x_v \equiv 1_x$", as well as the information "x_v" from the point "$x_v \equiv 1_x$" to "$x_u \equiv 0_x$".

Let $\Delta_u t = t - 0_t$ and $\Delta_v t = t - 1_t$ the time increments, then the increment distance of information x_u and x_v is varied respectively with the time increment $\Delta_u t$ and $\Delta_v t$ can be written as: $\Delta x_u(\Delta_u t) = \dot{x}_u(\Delta_u t)\Delta_u t$ and $\Delta x_v(\Delta_v t) = \dot{x}_v(\Delta_v t)\Delta_v t$.

Suppose $t = t_\lambda$ is the meeting time between the two increment distances of $\Delta x_u(\Delta_u t)$ and $\Delta x_v(\Delta_v t)$, since the direction of time increment $\Delta_u t$ opposite to the direction of $\Delta_v t$, then we have that:

$$\Delta_u t - \Delta_v t = t_\lambda - 0_t - (t_\lambda - 1_t) = 1_t - 0_t \tag{2.1}$$

(2.1) shows us that when the two information "x_u" and "x_v" are meeting at the contradiction point, the sum of the time increments of the two is exactly equal to the unit time. On the contrary, since $\Delta_u t$ and $\Delta_v t$ have opposite time directions, their sum is equal to 0:

$$\Delta_u t + \Delta_v t = t_\lambda - 0_t + t_\lambda - 1_t = 2t_\lambda - (1_t + 0_t) = 0 \tag{2.2}$$

Then we get that

$$t_\lambda = \frac{1_t + 0_t}{2} \tag{2.3}$$

In fact, when the information "x_u" and "x_v" meet at the contradiction point, the transmission time of the two information "x_u" and "x_v" is exactly half of the unit time, namely: $t_\lambda = \frac{1_t + 0_t}{2} = \frac{1_t}{2}$, so:

$$t_\lambda = \frac{1}{2}0_t + \frac{1}{2}1_t \tag{2.4}$$

This is mean that the time subscript of the contradiction point $\lambda = \frac{1}{2}$ is valid. The transmission increments of information "x_u" and "x_v" are respectively:

$$\Delta x_u(\Delta_u t) = \dot{x}_u(\Delta_u t)\Delta_u t = \frac{x_\lambda - 0_x}{t_{\frac{1}{2}} - 0_t} \left(t_{\frac{1}{2}} - 0_t \right) = x_\lambda - 0_x \tag{2.5}$$

And

$$\Delta x_v(\Delta_v t) = \dot{x}_v(\Delta_v t)\Delta_v t = \frac{x_\lambda - 1_x}{t_{\frac{1}{2}} - 1_t}\left(t_{\frac{1}{2}} - 1_t\right) = x_\lambda - 1_x \tag{2.6}$$

$(2.5) - (2.6)$ we get:

$$\Delta x_u(\Delta_u t) - \Delta x_v(\Delta_v t) = 2x_\lambda + 1_x - 0_x = 0 \tag{2.7}$$

The (2.7) shows us that because $\Delta x_u(\Delta_u t)$ and $\Delta x_v(\Delta_v t)$ are opposite each other, when $\Delta x_u(\Delta_u t)$ transmits from 0_x to x_λ, and $\Delta x_v(\Delta_v t)$ also transmits from 1_x to x_λ, the whole interval from 0_x to 1_x is just covered by the sum of $\Delta x_u(\Delta_u t)$ and $\Delta x_v(\Delta_v t)$.

From the perspective of information transmission, the two statements are equivalent: (1) the two location information "$x_u \equiv 0_x$" and "$x_v \equiv 1_x$" are meeting at the contradiction point x_λ. (2) the information "$x_v \equiv 1_x$" has being transmitted to the location of u "$x_u \equiv 0_x$", as well as the location information of u "$x_u \equiv 0_x$". In information term, the $(2.5) - (2.6)$ such that $\Delta x_u(\Delta_u t) - \Delta x_v(\Delta_v t) = 0$ is mean that information transmission had being completed. It also can be interpreted as follows: know the contradiction point x_λ, equivalent to know opposite. Therefore, the right side of (2.7) is equal to 0, that is mean:

$$x_\lambda = \frac{0_x - 1_x}{2} = -\frac{1_x}{2} \tag{2.8}$$

So we get that $\lambda_x = -\frac{1}{2}$ is valid.

However, if the transmission velocity $\dot{x}_v(\Delta_v t)$ and $\dot{x}_u(\Delta_u t)$ are not equal each other, and suppose $\dot{x}_v(\Delta_v t) = -\varsigma\dot{x}_u(\Delta_u t)$, then we get

$$\Delta x_v(\Delta_v t) = \dot{x}_v(\Delta_v t)\Delta_v t = \frac{x_\lambda - 1_x}{-t_{\frac{1}{2}} - 1_t}\left(-t_{\frac{1}{2}} - 1_t\right) = -\varsigma\dot{x}_u(\Delta_u t) = -\varsigma\frac{x_\lambda - 0_x}{t_{\frac{1}{2}} - 0_t}\left(t_{\frac{1}{2}} - 0_t\right) \tag{2.9}$$

Substituting (2.9) into (2.8), we have:

$$\Delta x_u(\Delta_u t) - \Delta x_v(\Delta_v t) = \frac{x_\lambda - 0_x}{t_\lambda - 0_t}(t_\lambda - 0_t) + \varsigma\frac{x_\lambda - 0_x}{t_\lambda - 0_t}(t_\lambda - 0_t)$$
$$= \frac{x_\lambda - 0_x}{t_\lambda - 0_t}(t_\lambda - 0_t)[1 + \varsigma] = 1_x - 0_x \tag{2.10}$$

$$x_\lambda - 0_x = \frac{1_x - 0_x}{(1 + \varsigma)} \tag{2.11}$$

$$x_\lambda - 0_x = (\lambda - 1)0_x + (1 - \lambda)1_x = (1 - \lambda)(1_x - 0_x) = \frac{1_x - 0_x}{(1 + \varsigma)} \tag{2.12}$$

$$(1 - \lambda)(1 + \varsigma) = 1 \tag{2.13}$$

$$\lambda(1 + \varsigma) = \varsigma \tag{2.14}$$

$$\begin{cases} \lambda = \frac{\varsigma}{(1+\varsigma)} \\ \varsigma = \frac{\lambda}{(1-\lambda)} \end{cases} \tag{2.15}$$

Together (2.4), (2.8) and (2.15) we have

$$\begin{cases} \lambda_t = \left(\frac{1}{2}, \frac{1}{2}\right) & \left(t_\lambda = \frac{1}{2}0_t + \frac{1}{2}1_t\right) \\ \lambda_t = \left(\frac{1}{2}, \frac{1}{2}\right) & \left(t_\lambda = \frac{1}{2}0_t + \frac{1}{2}1_t\right) \\ \varsigma_x = \frac{\lambda_x}{(1-\lambda_x)} \end{cases} \tag{2.16}$$

3 The Topologic Space Induced by the Opposite Increment of $\Delta x_u(\Delta t_u)$ and $\Delta x_v(\Delta t_v)$ and Calculus on It

$$\Delta x_u(\Delta t_u) = \dot{x}_u(\Delta t_u)\Delta t_u = \dot{x}_u\left(\frac{1_t}{2}\right)\frac{1_t}{2} = \frac{1_x}{2} \tag{3.1}$$

and

$$\Delta x_v(\Delta t_v) = \dot{x}_v(t)\Delta t_v = \dot{x}_v(\Delta t)\frac{1_t}{2} = -\frac{1_x}{2} \tag{3.2}$$

In other hand, since $\Delta t_v = (1_t - 0_t)$, $\dot{x}_u = \lim\limits_{(1_t - 0_t) \to 0} \frac{x_1 - x_0}{1_t - 0_t}$ and $\Delta x_u(\Delta t_u) = \sqrt{(\Delta t_u)^2 + (\dot{x}_u)^2}$, such that the triangle $\Delta z_{(0,0_x)} z_{(1_t, 0_x)} z_{(1_t, 1_x)}$ can be constructed by three points of $z_0(0_t, 0_x)$, $z_{(0,1)}(1_t, 0_x)$ and $z_{(0,1)}(1_t, 1_x)$.

But

$$\Delta t_u = 1_t - 0_t = \left(1_t - \frac{1_t}{2}\right) + \left(\frac{1_t}{2} - 0_t\right) \tag{3.3}$$

So we get that

$$\begin{aligned} \Delta x_u(\Delta t_u) = \dot{x}_u\Delta t_u = \dot{x}_u(1_t - 0_t) &= \dot{x}_u\left(\left(1_t - \frac{1_t}{2}\right) + \left(\frac{1_t}{2} - 0_t\right)\right) \\ &= \dot{x}_u^{\frac{1_t}{2}}\left(1_t - \frac{1_t}{2}\right) + \dot{x}_u^{0_t}\left(\frac{1_t}{2} - 0_t\right) \end{aligned} \tag{3.4}$$

Here

$$\dot{x}_u = \lim\limits_{(1_t - 0_t) \to 0} \frac{x_1 - x_0}{1_t - 0_t} = \frac{dx}{dt}\Big|_{0_t} \tag{3.5}$$

$$\begin{cases} \dot{x}_u^{\frac{1_t}{2}} = \lim_{(1_t-\frac{1_t}{2})\to 0} \frac{x_1-x_{\frac{1}{2}}}{1_t-\frac{1_t}{2}} = \frac{dx}{dt}\big|_{\frac{1_t}{2}} = \frac{dx}{dt}\big|_{\frac{1_t}{2}} & (3.6-1) \\ \dot{x}_u^{0_t} = \lim_{(\frac{1_t}{2}-0_t)\to 0} \frac{x_{\frac{1}{2}}-x_0}{\frac{1_t}{2}-0_t} = \frac{dx}{dt}\big|_{0_t} & (3.6-2) \end{cases}$$

$$\dot{x}_u^{\frac{1_t}{2}}\left(1_t-\frac{1_t}{2}\right) = \lim_{(1_t-\frac{1_t}{2})\to 0} \frac{x_1-x_{\frac{1}{2}}}{1_t-\frac{1_t}{2}}\left(1_t-\frac{1_t}{2}\right) = \left(\frac{dx}{dt}\big|_{\frac{1_t}{2}}\right)\left(1_t-\frac{1_t}{2}\right) + (x_1-x_{\frac{1}{2}}) \qquad (3.7)$$

$$\dot{x}_u^{0_t}\left(\frac{1_t}{2}-0_t\right) = \lim_{(\frac{1_t}{2}-0_t)\to 0} \frac{x_{\frac{1}{2}}-x_0}{\frac{1_t}{2}-0_t}\left(\frac{1_t}{2}-0_t\right) = \frac{dx}{dt}\big|_{0_t}\left(\frac{1_t}{2}-0_t\right) + \left(x_{\frac{1}{2}}-x_0\right) \qquad (3.8)$$

$(3.7) + (3.8)$

$$\left(\frac{dx}{dt}\big|_{\frac{1_t}{2}}\right)\left(1_t-\frac{1_t}{2}\right) + (x_1-x_{\frac{1}{2}}) + \frac{dx}{dt}\big|_{0_t}\left(\frac{1_t}{2}-0_t\right) + \left(x_{\frac{1}{2}}-x_0\right) \qquad (3.9)$$

since $\Delta t_v = (0_t - 1_t)$, $\dot{x}_v = \lim_{(0_t-1_t)\to 0} \frac{x_0-x_1}{0_t-1_t}$ and $\Delta x_v(\Delta t) = \sqrt{(\Delta t)^2 + (\dot{x}_v)^2}$, such that the triangle $\Delta z_{(1_t,1_x)} z_{(0,1_x)} z_{(0,0_x)}$ can be constructed by three points of $z_0(1_t, 1_x)$, $z_{(0,1)}(0_t, 1_x)$ and $z_{(0,1)}(0_t, 0_x)$.

Since

$$\Delta t_v = 0_t - 1_t = \left(0_t - \frac{1_t}{2}\right) + \left(\frac{1_t}{2} - 1_t\right) \qquad (3.10)$$

$$\Delta x_v(\Delta t_v) = \dot{x}_v \Delta t_v = \dot{x}_v(0_t - 1_t) = \dot{x}_v\left(\left(0_t - \frac{1_t}{2}\right) + \left(\frac{1_t}{2} - 1_t\right)\right) = \dot{x}_v^{\frac{1_t}{2}}\left(0_t - \frac{1_t}{2}\right) + \dot{x}_v^{1_t}\left(\frac{1_t}{2} - 1_t\right)$$

$$(3.11)$$

Here

$$\dot{x}_v = \lim_{(0_t-1_t)\to 0} \frac{x_0-x_1}{0_t-1_t} = \frac{dx}{dt}\big|_{1_t} \qquad (3.12)$$

$$\begin{cases} \dot{x}_v^{\frac{1_t}{2}} = \lim_{(0_t-\frac{1_t}{2})\to 0} \frac{x_0-x_{\frac{1}{2}}}{0_t-\frac{1_t}{2}} = \frac{dx}{dt}\big|_{\frac{1_t}{2}} = \frac{dx}{dt}\big|_{\frac{1_t}{2}} & (3.13-1) \\ \dot{x}_v^{1_t} = \lim_{(\frac{1_t}{2}-1_t)\to 0} \frac{x_{\frac{1}{2}}-x_1}{\frac{1_t}{2}-1_t} = \frac{dx}{dt}\big|_{1_t} & (3.13-2) \end{cases}$$

$$\dot{x}_v^{\frac{1_t}{2}}\left(0_t - \frac{1_t}{2}\right) = \lim_{(0_t-\frac{1_t}{2})\to 0} \frac{x_0-x_{\frac{1}{2}}}{0_t-\frac{1_t}{2}}\left(0_t - \frac{1_t}{2}\right) = \left(\frac{dx}{dt}\big|_{\frac{1_t}{2}}\right)\left(0_t - \frac{1_t}{2}\right) + \left(x_0-x_{\frac{1}{2}}\right) \qquad (3.14)$$

$$\dot{x}_v^{1_t}\left(\frac{1_t}{2} - 1_t\right) = \lim_{(0_t-\frac{1_t}{2})\to 0} \frac{x_{\frac{1}{2}}-x_1}{\frac{1_t}{2}-1_t}\left(\frac{1_t}{2} - 1_t\right) = \frac{dx}{dt}\big|_{1_t}\left(\frac{1_t}{2} - 1_t\right) + \left(x_{\frac{1}{2}}-x_1\right) \qquad (3.15)$$

$(3.14) + (3.15)$

$$\left(\frac{dx}{dt}_{|\frac{1}{2}}\right)\left(0_t - \frac{1_t}{2}\right) + \left(x_0 - x_{\frac{1}{2}}\right) + \left(\frac{dx}{dt}_{|1_t}\right)\left(\frac{1_t}{2} - 1_t\right) + \left(x_{\frac{1}{2}} - x_1\right) \qquad (3.16)$$

(3.8) + (3.16)

$$\left(\frac{dx}{dt}_{|\frac{1}{2}}\right)\left(1_t - \frac{1_t}{2}\right) + \left(x_1 - x_{\frac{1}{2}}\right) + \left(\frac{dx}{dt}_{|0_t}\right)\left(\frac{1_t}{2} - 0_t\right) + \left(x_{\frac{1}{2}} - x_0\right) + \left(\frac{dx}{dt}_{|\frac{1}{2}}\right)\left(0_t - \frac{1_t}{2}\right)$$

$$+ \left(x_0 - x_{\frac{1}{2}}\right) + \left(\frac{dx}{dt}_{|1_t}\right)\left(\frac{1_t}{2} - 1_t\right) + \left(x_{\frac{1}{2}} - x_1\right) = \left[\left(\frac{dx}{dt}_{|1_t}\right) - \left(\frac{dx}{dt}_{|\frac{1}{2}}\right)\right]\left(\frac{1_t}{2} - 1_t\right)$$

$$+ \left[\left(\frac{dx}{dt}_{|0_t}\right) - \left(\frac{dx}{dt}_{|\frac{1}{2}}\right)\right]\left(\frac{1_t}{2} - 0_t\right) = -\left[\left(\frac{dx}{dt}_{|1_t}\right) - \left(\frac{dx}{dt}_{|\frac{1}{2}}\right)\right]\left(1_t - \frac{1_t}{2}\right) - \left[\left(\frac{dx}{dt}_{|0_t}\right) - \left(\frac{dx}{dt}_{|\frac{1}{2}}\right)\right]\left(0_t - \frac{1_t}{2}\right)$$

$$(3.17)$$

Here $\left(\frac{dx}{dt}_{|1_t}\right) - \left(\frac{dx}{dt}_{|\frac{1}{2}}\right)$ is the increment of the differential $\frac{dx}{dt}$ from $t = \frac{1}{2}$ to $t = 1_t$, and

$\left(\frac{dx}{dt}_{|0_t}\right) - \left(\frac{dx}{dt}_{|\frac{1}{2}}\right)$ is the increment of the differential $\frac{dx}{dt}$ from $t = 0_t$ to $t = \frac{1}{2}$.

This is mean that the triangle $\Delta z_{(\frac{1}{2},\frac{1}{2})} z_{(\frac{1}{2},1_x)} z_{(1_t,1_x)}$ can be constructed by the product

of the integration $\int_{\frac{1_t}{2}}^{1_t} \dot{x}_u^2 dt$ and $\left(1_t - \frac{1}{2}\right)$. Similarly, the triangle $\Delta z_{(0_t,0_x)} z_{(\frac{1}{2},\frac{1}{2})} z_{(\frac{1}{2},0_x)}$ can

be constructed by the product of the integration $\int_{0_t}^{\frac{1_t}{2}} \dot{x}_v^2 dt$ and $\left(1_t - \frac{1}{2}\right)$. Therefore, sum of

$\left[\dot{x}_u^2\left(1_t - \frac{1}{2}\right) + \dot{x}_u^{0_t}\left(\frac{1}{2} - 0_t\right)\right] + \left[\dot{x}_v^2\left(0_t - \frac{1}{2}\right) + \dot{x}_v^{1_t}\left(\frac{1}{2} - 1_t\right)\right]$ is the area of two reangle,

one equals to the sum of a pair of triangles: $\Delta z_{(0_t,0_x)} z_{(\frac{1}{2},\frac{1}{2})} z_{(\frac{1}{2},0_x)} + \Delta z_{(\frac{1}{2},\frac{1}{2})} z_{(0_t,\frac{1}{2})} z_{(0_t,0_x)}$,

other equal to the sum of triangles $\Delta z_{(\frac{1}{2},\frac{1}{2})} z_{(\frac{1}{2},1_x)} z_{(1_t,1_x)} + \Delta z_{(\frac{1}{2},\frac{1}{2})} z_{(1_t,\frac{1}{2})} z_{(1_t,1_x)}$ (Fig. 2).

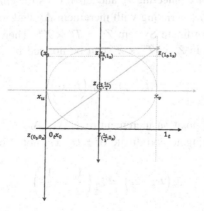

Fig. 2. Two triangles constructed by the product of the integration $\int_{\frac{1_t}{2}}^{1_t} \dot{x}_u^2 dt$ and $\left(1_t - \frac{1}{2}\right)$

Since there is a right hand spiral can be produced by the pair of triangles, by which a Clifford Geometric Product [1] can be induced too. In adding, because $\Delta t_u = 1_t - 0_t$ as the measurement unit of time is very arbitrary, this is mean that there is not only the invariances of the Contradiction Point under the scale transformation of unit, but also an Entanglement between the pair of triangles, by which the opposite and unifying of contradiction between the u and v can be represented, can be induced.

By the comparison and analysis of (3.1), (3.2), (3.3), (3.4), (3.5), (3.6-1), (3.6-2), (3.12), (3.13-1), (3.13-2) and (3.17). It is found that the (3.17) is just a half of (3.5) + (3.12), this means that by subdividing of $[0_t, 1_t] = [0_t, \frac{1}{2}) \cup [\frac{1}{2}, 1_t]$, some of interesting of mathematical construction, such as the Clifford Geometric Product, Complex Analysis Function, and so on, could be produced by the position increment $\Delta x_u(\Delta t)$ and $\Delta x_v(\Delta t)$ varies with time increment Δt, if adding matters m_u and m_v then some of physical construction can be discussed in it.

It is need special to be point out that the scale of unit $|\Delta t_u| = |1_t - 0_t|$ is reduced by right spiral, but is expanded by left spiral, in the extreme, the entanglement between a pair of triangles could be changed to be the quantum entanglement, but the expanding of they could be conversed in to relative expanding.

Since Artificial Neural Unit is defined as a Inner Product, and an Attribute Grid Computer Based Qualitative Mapping [2], such that a Qualitative Grid Computer based Conjugate Entangled Manifold can be build in this Frame.

It is natural to ask what coordinate system is for expressing some invariant of contradiction point under the transformation of time-spatial component? and how to achieve it?

4   The Conjugate Entangled Coordinate System for Contradiction Point

Let the line from 0_t to 1_t be the time axis T^u for the time increment Δt, and translate it by $\frac{1}{2}$, then take the line of connecting x_u and x_v, $\overline{x_u x_v}$ as the space axis X^u, that for the position increment $\Delta x_u(\Delta t)$ variating with increment Δt, and rotate it by $\frac{\pi}{2}$, and get the time space Cartesian Coordinate System $Z^u = T^u \times X^u$. Then the coordinate of contradiction point $z_\lambda(t_\lambda, x_\lambda)$ in $Z^u = T^u \times X^u$ can be noticed by following:

$$z_\lambda(t_\lambda, x_\lambda) = z_{t_{\frac{1}{2}}}\left(t_{\frac{1}{2}}, x_{\frac{1}{2}}\right) \tag{4.1}$$

Since the function of position increment of v, $\Delta x_v(\Delta t) = -\frac{1_x}{2}$ can be described in $Z^u = T^u \times X^u$ as the conjugate coordinate of $z_\lambda(t_\lambda, x_\lambda)$ noted by following:

$$\bar{z}_\lambda\left(t_{\frac{1}{2}}, -x_{\frac{1}{2}}\right) = \bar{z}_{t_{\frac{1}{2}}}\left(\frac{1_t}{2}, -\frac{1_x}{2}\right) \tag{4.2}$$

The formula (3.1) makes people believe that there is not necessary to set up a special coordinate system for describing the function of position increment of v.

However, due to the reverse transmission of information "x_u" and "x_v", such that not only a reciprocal convection between the two functions of position increment of u and v, $\Delta x_u(\Delta t)$ and $\Delta x_v(\Delta t)$ can be arisen at the contradiction point $z_{\frac{1}{2}}\left(t_{\frac{1}{2}}, x_{\frac{1}{2}}\right)$, by which but also a series of oppositions, conflicts and struggles could be produced. Therefore, it is necessary to provide a Coordinate System for representing the transmission increment function of x_v, $\Delta x_v(\Delta t)$ variating with time increment Δt.

Let the line from x_v to x_u be the space axis X^v, that for the position increment $\Delta x_v(\Delta t_v)$ variating with increment Δt, and rotate it by $-\frac{\pi}{2}$, then take the segment from 1_t to 0_t be the time axis T^v for the time increment Δt, and translate it by $\frac{1}{2}$, then take the segment of connecting x_v and x_u, $\overline{x_v x_u}$ as, and get the space time Cartesian Coordinate System $Z^v = X^v \times T^v$.

They are integrated to be a coordinate system: $W = Z^u \otimes Z^v = X^u \times (T^u \otimes X^v) \times T^v$, where $(T^u \otimes X^v)$ is the integration of T^u and X^v, in which the direction of T^u and X^v are opposites each other, and they are entangled each other in one, so it is called entanglement axis.

Let T be the time axis, and X the spatial axis, and $Z = T \times X$ the complex coordinate system of time-spatial components, for $(t, x) \in T \times X$, let $x_u \equiv 0_x$ and $x_v \equiv 1_x$ be the spatial positions of two opposite objects u and v, such that the distance $\Delta(u, v) \equiv 1_x$, then "$x_u(\equiv 0_x)$" and "$x_v(\equiv 1_x)$" in $Z = T \times X$, can be noted by $z_u(t, x_u) \equiv z_u(0_t, 0_x)$ and $z_v(t, x_v) \equiv z_v(1_t, 1_x)$, respectively, and $\dot{x}_u(t) = 1_{x/t}$ and $\dot{x}_v(t) = -1_{x/t}$ the transmitting velocity of position information "$x_u \equiv 0_x$" and "$x_v \equiv 1_x$", respectively, and the function of position information of "$x_u \equiv 0_x$" and "$x_v \equiv 1_x$" varying with t can be noted by $x_u(t)$ and $x_v(t)$ as following:

$$\begin{cases} x_u(t) = \dot{x}_u t \\ x_v(t) = \dot{x}_v t \end{cases} \tag{4.3}$$

It is shown a conjugate complex coordinate system can be got by two transformations as following: (1) Take time as first axis of the systems, and translates it by $t = -\frac{1}{2}$; (2) Take space as the second axis of the system, and rotates it by $\theta = \frac{\pi}{2}$, (or (1') Take space as first axis of the systems, and translates it by $x = -\frac{1}{2}$; (2') Take time as the second axis of the system, and rotates it by $t = \frac{\pi}{2}$,) can be noted by following:

$$\begin{cases} t^u = t - \frac{1}{2} \\ x^u = ix \end{cases} \tag{4.4}$$

It is obvious that a new Coordinate System can be got by (4.4), noted by $Z = T \times X$, and the position $x_u(t)$ and $x_v(t)$ at $t \in T$ and $x \in X$ in the coordinate $Z = T \times X$ can be represented by a pair of conjugate complex numbers as follow: $z_u(t, x_u) = t + ix_u(t)$ and $\bar{z}_v(t, -x_u) = t - ix_v(t)$. When time t equal to the meeting time equql to $t_\lambda = \frac{1}{2}$, and two transmitted distances of the position information $x_\lambda^u(\frac{1}{2}) = \frac{1_x}{2}$ and $x_\lambda^v(\frac{1}{2}) = -\frac{1_x}{2}$ as shown in Fig. 3.

Because the two couple of time and position $z_\lambda(t_\lambda, x_u^\lambda(\frac{1}{2})) = z_\lambda(\frac{1}{2}, \frac{1_x}{2})$ and $\bar{z}_\lambda(t_\lambda, x_v^\lambda(\frac{1}{2})) = \bar{z}_\lambda(\frac{1}{2}, -\frac{1_x}{2})$ can be represented, by a pair of conjugate complex $z_\lambda(\frac{1}{2}, \frac{1_x}{2})$ and $\bar{z}_\lambda(\frac{1}{2}, -\frac{1_x}{2})$, in Time-Spatial Complex Coordinate System $Z = T \times X$, and the time and space coordinates of the contradiction point are equal to the sum and difference of a pair of conjugate complex $z_\lambda(\frac{1}{2}, \frac{1_x}{2})$ and $\bar{z}_\lambda(\frac{1}{2}, -\frac{1_x}{2})$, respectively, as well as in space-time coordinate, $z_\lambda^*(\frac{1}{2}, \frac{1_x}{2})$, $\bar{z}_\lambda^*(\frac{1}{2}, -\frac{1_x}{2}) \in Z^*$, here $Z^* = X^* \times T^*$ is the space-time coordinate system, as shown in Fig. 3.

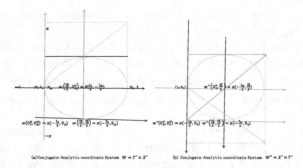

(a) Conjugate-Analytic coordinate System $W = T' \times X'$ (b) Conjugate-Analytic coordinate System $W^* = X' \times T'$

Fig. 3. The conjugate coordinate system. (1) Translatting $t = -\frac{1}{2}$ for the time axis of systems; (1') Translatting $t = -\frac{1}{2}$ for the spatial axis of systems; (2) Spining of $\theta = \frac{\pi}{2}$ for the spatial axis; (2') Spining of $\theta = \frac{\pi}{2}$ for the time axis

Let w be the transformation from $Z = T \times X$ to $W(|W|, \Xi)$, $w : Z \rightarrow W = T^u \times X^u$, such that for $w(t^u, x^u) = z\left(t - \frac{1}{2}, x\right) \in Z = T \times X$, we have:

$$w(t^u, x^u) = z\left(t - \frac{1_t}{2}, x\right) \tag{4.5}$$

Then the Coordinate of the origin point in $W = T^u \times X^u$ is

$$w(0^u_t, 0^u_x) = z\left(-\frac{1_t}{2}, 0_x\right) \tag{4.6}$$

The coordinate of the contradiction point in $W = T^u \times X^u$ is

$$w_{\frac{1}{2}}\left(t^u_{\frac{1}{2}}, x^u_{\frac{1}{2}}\right) = z_{\frac{1}{2}}\left(0_t, \frac{1_x}{2}\right) \tag{4.7}$$

Let $W(|W|, \Xi)$ be the polar coordinate of contradiction point in the polar coordinate system $W(|W|, \Xi)$ can be written as a wave function formal as follow: as shown in Fig. 4(a).

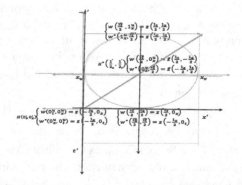

Fig. 4. Conjugate entangled coordinate system of contradiction point

$$W(t^u, x^u) = |W|e^{i\theta} = |W|(\cos\theta + i\sin\theta) \tag{4.8}$$

Let the interval $[x_u, x_v]$ be the segment connected the two objects u and v, $x_u(t) = \dot{x}_u t$ and $x_v(t) = \dot{x}_v t$ the position of informations x_u and x_v at t, then for the two velocities $\dot{x}_u$ and $\dot{x}_v$, there is a rate $\lambda = \frac{\dot{x}_u}{\dot{x}_v + \dot{x}_u}$, such that for $\forall \lambda = \frac{\dot{x}_u}{\dot{x}_v + \dot{x}_u} \in [0, 1]$, $\exists z_\lambda(t_\lambda, x_\lambda) \in [x_u, x_v]$. When $\dot{x}_u = \dot{x}_v$, $\lambda = \frac{1}{2}$, $z_{\frac{1}{2}}\left(t_{\frac{1}{2}}, x_{\frac{1}{2}}\right)$ is here contradiction point, so its coordinate in $W = T^u \times X^u$ can be noticed by

$$w_{\lambda=\frac{1}{2}}\left(t^u_{\frac{1}{2}}, x^u_{\frac{1}{2}}\right) = z_{\lambda=\frac{1}{2}}\left(0_t, \frac{1_x}{2}\right) \tag{4.9}$$

Let w^* be the transforposition from $Z = T \times X$ to $W^* = T^v \times X^v = W^*(|W^*|, \Xi^*)$ $W = T^u \times X^u$ to, $w^* : W \to W^*$ such that for

$$z^*(x^v, t^v) \in X^v \times T^v, \quad \begin{cases} x^v = x - \frac{1_x}{2} \\ t^v = it \end{cases} \tag{4.10}$$

we have:

$$w^*(x^v, t^v) = z^*\left(x - \frac{1_x}{2}, t\right) \tag{4.11}$$

$$\begin{cases} \lambda^x = \left(\frac{1}{2}, \frac{1}{2}\right) \left(x^\lambda = \frac{1}{2}0^x + \frac{1}{2}1^x\right) \\ \lambda^t = \left(\frac{1}{2}, -\frac{1}{2}\right) \left(t^\lambda = \frac{1}{2}0^t - \frac{1}{2}1^t\right) \\ \varsigma^t = \frac{\lambda^t}{(1 - \lambda^t)} \end{cases} \tag{4.12}$$

Since the sum of $z_\lambda(t_\lambda, x_\lambda)$ and its conjugate $\bar{z}_\lambda(t_\lambda, x_\lambda)$ and the difference of and the difference of $z^*_\lambda(x_\lambda, t_\lambda)$ and its conjugate equal to the time component and space component of contradictory point $z_\lambda(t_\lambda, x_\lambda) + \bar{z}_\lambda(t_\lambda, x_\lambda) = t_\lambda$ and $z^*_\lambda(x_\lambda, t_\lambda) - \bar{z}^*_\lambda(x_\lambda, t_\lambda) = x_\lambda$, respectively. If let $w(z_\lambda, \bar{z}_\lambda) = z_\lambda(t_\lambda, x_\lambda) + \bar{z}_\lambda(t_\lambda, x_\lambda) = t_\lambda$ and $w^*\left(z^*_\lambda, \bar{z}^*_\lambda\right) = z^*_\lambda(x_\lambda, t_\lambda) - \bar{z}^*_\lambda(x_\lambda, t_\lambda) = x_\lambda$, and $\psi(w, w^*) = \frac{1}{2}(w - iw^*) = \frac{1}{2}(t_\lambda - ix_\lambda)$, then the integration for $\psi(w, w^*)$ from $\lambda = 0$ to $\lambda = \frac{1}{2}$, and the inner product of $\psi(w, w^*)$ and its time component ψ_t, $\psi(w, w^*).\psi_t$ can be gotten an out product of $\psi(w, w^*)$ and its space component ψ_x, $\psi(w, w^*) \wedge \psi_x$, and a Geometric Product can be induced by the sum of $\psi(w, w^*).\psi_t + \psi(w, w^*) \wedge \psi_x$.

$$w\left(t_\lambda, x^\lambda\right) + iw^*\left(t^\lambda, x_\lambda\right) = \frac{1}{2}[(0_t, 1_t) + (0^x, 1^x)] - \frac{1}{2}i[(0^t, 1^t) - (0_x, 1_x)] \tag{4.13}$$

And

$$w\left(t_\lambda, x^\lambda\right) \cdot w^*\left(t^\lambda, x_\lambda\right) = \frac{1}{4}\left[(0_t, 1_t)^2 + (0^x, 1^x)^2\right] - \frac{1}{4}i\left[(0^t, 1^t)^2 - (0_x, 1_x)^2\right] \tag{4.14}$$

$$w(z_\lambda, \bar{z}_\lambda) = \frac{1}{2}[z_\lambda(t_\lambda, x_\lambda) + \bar{z}_\lambda(t_\lambda, x_\lambda)] = \frac{t_\lambda}{2}$$

Formule show us this is a Conjugate Coordinate in which the coordinate of contradiction point is

$$w^*_{\lambda=\frac{1}{2}}\left(\frac{1_x}{2},\frac{1_t}{2}\right) = z^*_{\frac{1}{2}}\left(0_x,\frac{1_t}{2}\right) \tag{4.15}$$

It is shown from the above discussion that the time and space positions of the contradiction point $z_{\frac{1}{2}}$ can be coordinated by two coordinate (4.9) and (4.15) in two complex coordinate system, respectively (Fig. 5).

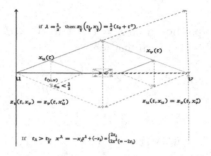

Fig. 5. Conjugate-Entangled invariant of contradiction point in synthesis of complex coordinate $H = Z \otimes Z^* = (T \times X) \otimes (X \times T)$

Acknowledgement. The authors specially thank Professor Pei-zhuang Wang for his introduction of the Factor Space Theory [3], Dr. He. Ouyang for the discussion in category and Topos and Prof. Zhongzhi Shi for his help in many time.

References

1. Feng, J.: Entanglement of inner product, topos induced by opposition and transformation of contradiction, and tensor flow. In: Shi, Z., Goertzel, B., Feng, J. (eds.) ICIS 2017. IAICT, vol. 510, pp. 22–36. Springer, Cham (2017). https://doi.org/10.1007/978-3-319-68121-4_3
2. Feng, J.: Attribute grid computer based on qualitative mapping for artificial intelligence. In: Shi, Z., Mercier-Laurent, E., Li, J. (eds.) IIP 2018. IAICT, vol. 538, pp. 129–139. Springer, Cham (2018). https://doi.org/10.1007/978-3-030-00828-4_14
3. Wang, P.Z.: Fuzzy Set and Random Set Fall Shadow. Beijing Normal University Publishing, Beijing (1984)

Similarity Evaluation with Wikipedia Features

Shahbaz Wasti[1,2], Jawad Hussain[1], Guangjiang Huang[1],
and Yuncheng Jiang[1(✉)]

[1] South China Normal University, Guangzhou 510631, Guangdong, China
shahbazwasti@gmail.com, ycjiang@scnu.edu.cn
[2] University of Education, Lahore 54000, Pakistan

Abstract. Wikipedia provides rich semantic features e.g., text, link, and category structure. These features can be used to compute semantic similarity (SS) between words or concepts. However, some existing Wikipedia-based SS methods either rely on a single feature or do not incorporate the underlying statistics of different features. We propose novel vector representations of Wikipedia concepts by integrating their multiple semantic features. We utilize the available statistics of these features in Wikipedia to compute their weights. These weights signify the contribution of each feature in similarity evaluation according to its level of importance. The experimental evaluation shows that our new methods obtain better results on SS datasets in comparison with state-of-the-art SS methods.

Keywords: Semantic similarity · IC · *tfidf* · Vector representation

1 Introduction

Semantic similarity (SS) assessment between words or concepts is a critical issue in natural language processing. The semantic features of Wikipedia concepts (e.g., article title, text, hyperlinks, and categories) have encouraged several researchers to develop word similarity methods. These different features complement each other in expressing a particular Wikipedia concept, e.g., the title represents a single concept, the article text narrates the subject matter, the hyperlinks give the related articles, and categories categorize the article. Moreover, the underlying statistics of these features can be also be exploited for weight computation. But some of the Wikipedia-based methods [4–6] either rely on a single feature or ignore the important statistical details of these features. In this paper, we propose a novel vector representation of a Wikipedia concept by combining multiple features. The entries of a vector are the assigned weights of the features computed using information content (IC) [11] and *tfidf* weighting schemes. The weights of the features will reflect their level of importance in similarity evaluation while multiple features will enhance the semantics of a concept. The rest of the paper is organized as: In Sect. 2, we present our methods.

© IFIP International Federation for Information Processing 2020
Published by Springer Nature Switzerland AG 2020
Z. Shi et al. (Eds.): IIP 2020, IFIP AICT 581, pp. 99–104, 2020.
https://doi.org/10.1007/978-3-030-46931-3_10

In Sect. 3, the detail about the experiment and evaluation criteria is provided. In Sect. 4, we present the result of our methods. Section 5 provides the related work on Wikipedia-based similarity measures. Section 6 concludes the paper.

2   Proposed Methods

Wikipedia is the largest freely available encyclopedic knowledge resource. It covers more than five million articles in various domains of life. Each of these articles describes its corresponding concept. In this paper we will refer a Wikipedia article as "concept", which comprises on multiple features such as title, text (or words), hyperlinks (or links) and categories etc. In order to represent a Wikipedia concept as a concept vector, we propose following weighting methods to compute the weights of the features.

2.1   Measurement of the Weights of the Features

The IC-based method to compute the weights of the links and categories in Wikipedia is defined as:

Definition 1 (IC of features). *Let f_i be a feature (link or category) of a Wikipedia concept, $Fr(f_i)$ be its frequency and N is the total number of Wikipedia concepts. Then, the IC of the feature f_i is computed as:*

$$IC(f_i) = \log\left(\frac{1}{P(f_i)}\right) = -log(P(f_i)) = -log(\frac{Fr(f_i)}{N}), \tag{1}$$

where $P(f_i) = \frac{Fr(f_i)}{N}$ is the probability of the feature f_i.

The *tfidf* (term frequency (tf) and inverse document frequency (idf)) is widely used to compute the weights of words in a corpus. These weights quantify the strength of association between words and concepts [2]. We use *tfidf* weighting metric to compute the weights of the words appearing in the gloss of a Wikipedia concept. We first convert a gloss into a set of individual words (we remove all the stop words, special characters and numbers). The weights of the words can be computed as:

Definition 2 (*tfidf* weight of gloss words). *Let w_i be a word in a gloss G of a Wikipedia concept. The tfidf weight of w_i is computed as:*

$$tfidf(w_i, G) = tf(w_i, G) \times log(\frac{N}{G_{w_i} + 1}), \tag{2}$$

where $tf(w_i, G)$ is the term frequency of ith word in gloss G, G_{w_i} is the number of glosses (document frequency) in Wikipedia that contain the word w_i and N is the total number of Wikipedia concepts.

Wikipedia Category Graph (WCG) is considered as a very large semantic network, where categories are organized via semantic relationships (hypernymy (hypers) and hyponymy) (hypos). These semantic relationships can be used in similarity computation [4,5]. In Wikipedia some similar concepts don't have common categories but some of their categories do have common hypers in WCG. The intuitive idea is that two concepts will be more similar if their categories have common hypers as well. However, the huge size of WCG poses two challenges, i.e., large search space and strongly connected upper regions [5]. Therefore, instead of traversing whole WCG, researchers preferred to restrict the search space to a limited depth [4,5]. In this paper, we also extract the hypers of a category c in its limited search space ($k - neighborhood$ of c). Intuitively, the $k - neighborhood$ is a subgraph, i.e., it is the set of all the categories that can be traversed from hypers and hypos of the category c via at most k edges [5]. The weight of hypers is computed with Eq. 1.

2.2   Vector Construction

Definition 3 (Features vector). *Let con be a Wikipedia concept and w_p, l_q, c_r and h_s be its gloss words, links, categories and hypers respectively. Let $tfidf_{weight}$ (Eq. 2) be the weight of words and IC_{weight} (Eq. 1) be the weights of links, categories and hypers. The features vectors are defined as:*

$$
\begin{aligned}
v_w &= (tfidf_{weight}(w_1), tfidf_{weight}(w_2), ..., tfidf_{weight}(w_p)), \\
v_l &= (IC_{weight}(l_1), IC_{weight}(l_2), ..., IC_{weight}(l_q)), \\
v_c &= (IC_{weight}(c_1), IC_{weight}(c_2), ..., IC_{weight}(c_r)), \\
v_h &= (IC_{weight}(h_1), IC_{weight}(h_2), ..., IC_{weight}(h_s)).
\end{aligned}
\tag{3}
$$

we propose three novel representations of the Wikipedia concept as a concept vector, e.g., (1) GLC_{con}, (2) GLH_{con}, and (3) $hypers_{con}$.

Definition 4 (Concept vector). *Let con be a Wikipedia concept and v_w, v_l, v_c, and v_h be its features vectors. The concept vectors of con are:*

$$
\begin{aligned}
GLC_{con} &= v_{w_i} \oplus v_{l_i} \oplus v_{c_i}, \\
GLH_{con} &= v_{w_i} \oplus v_{l_i} \oplus v_{h_i}, \\
hyper_{con} &= v_{h_i},
\end{aligned}
\tag{4}
$$

where $\oplus$ represents the concatenation of different features vectors.

2.3   Semantic Similarity Computation

Definition 5 (Semantic similarity). *Let con_i be a pair of Wikipedia concepts, and GLC_{con_i}, GLH_{con_i}, and $hyper_{con_i}$ be its concept vectors respectively. The similarity between two vectors is defined as:*

$$
\begin{aligned}
Sim_1(con_1, con_2) &= cosine(GLC_{con_1}, GLC_{con_2}), \\
Sim_2(con_1, con_2) &= cosine(GLH_{con_1}, GLH_{con_2}), \\
Sim_3(con_1, con_2) &= cosine(hyper_{con_1}, hyper_{con_2}).
\end{aligned}
\tag{5}
$$

Figure 1 illustrates the similarity computation between con_1 and con_2 using GLC_{con} concept vector. The elements of each vector are the weights of the features of corresponding concepts. To give more importance to the common words between two concept vectors, we will use the maximum $tfidf_{weight}$ for that particular word in both the concept vectors [12].

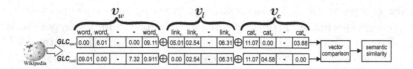

Fig. 1. GLC_{con} concept vector of Wikipedia concept pair.

3   Evaluation

We implement our approach using a Wikipedia snapshot as of December, 2018. We use Java Wikipedia Library to extract Wikipedia features, e.g., articles, categories and link structure. We remove the stop words, rare words and hyperlinks. To improve the efficiency of our approach, we compute the weights of the features offline. For $k - neighborhood$ we get the optimal results with $k = 4$.

3.1   Datasets and Evaluation Metric

We use the Pearson correlation coefficient metric to analyze the accuracy of our SS approaches on RG65 [10], MC30 [8], WS203 [1], and SimLex [3] benchmarks. We normalize the similarity judgment scales of different datasets in the range of [0,1]. Some of the terms in above benchmarks are ambiguous in Wikipedia, i.e., Wikipedia may have more than one articles for a term, e.g., minister, agony, journey, or crane etc. We adopted a simple strategy to disambiguate such concepts, i.e., we compute SS between all the associated ambiguous concepts using SS method Sim_2 and select the concept pair with highest SS score [9].

3.2   Comparison Systems

We compare our approaches with following well-known SS methods: the first system is $wpath$, it has two methods $wpath_{graph}$ and $wpath_{corpus}$ [13]. The methods measure the semantic similarity between the concepts in Knowledge Graphs (KGs) such as WordNet and DBpedia. However, in this paper we implemented $wpath$ methods in WCG. The second system is Word2Vec [7], where a neural network is used to learn continuous representations of word embedding. The third system is ESA [2] that represents the meaning of texts as high-dimensional weighted vectors of Wikipedia-based concepts. Finally, we select three methods from our previous works, $SimFou_{con}$ [6] and $SimSec_{con}$ and $SimSec_{cat}$ [9]. We implement all the comparison systems on the same Wikipedia version.

4   Results and Discussion

Table 1 shows the Pearson correlation performance of our methods and comparison systems on gold standard SS benchmarks. As we can see, both Sim_1 and Sim_2 achieve good results on all the benchmarks. Sim_2 performs better than

Table 1. Pearson correlation coefficient of proposed and comparison methods

Methods	MC30	RG65	WS203	SimLex
Sim_1	0.874	0.852	0.719	0.514
Sim_2	**0.885**	**0.868**	0.749	**0.515**
Sim_3	0.793	0.829	0.651	0.416
$wpath(corpus)$	0.514	0.781	0.482	0.356
$wpath(graph)$	0.582	0.824	0.508	0.381
$SimFou_{con}$	0.824	0.811	0.647	0.449
$SimSec_{con}$	0.845	0.827	0.712	–
$SimSec_{cat}$	0.842	0.836	0.686	–
$Word2Vec$	0.833	0.853	**0.763**	0.458
ESA	0.577	0.563	0.423	0.159

Sim_1. The reason is that combining hypers of the categories with other features (gloss words and links) yields a better semantic representation of a Wikipedia concept. It is because the concept pair will be more similar if their categories have common hypers even though they don't have a set of common categories. Our best method Sim_2 outperforms all the comparison methods on all MC30, RG65, SimLex. On benchmark WS203, Word2vec obtains the best correlation while Sim_2 shows the second best performance. All of our methods and other comparison methods relatively under-perform on SimLex as compared to other benchmarks. It is because in SimLex dataset the antonym pairs are rated dissimilar. While in KRs antonyms have a high degree of similarity.

5   Related Work

Jiang et al. [5] proposed IC-based measures by treating WCG as a large semantic ontology. However, in these methods other Wikipedia features like text and hyperlinks are not considered. Moreover, due to multiple inheritance in WCG, it is difficult to identify a single least common subsumer of two comparing categories [4]. Hussain et al. [4] proposed SS methods using multiple inheritance feature in WCG. However, the limitation of their methods is that they also do not consider the semantic details of other Wikipedia features. Qu et al. [9] proposed a series of hybrid SS methods, they combine text and categories to compute SS of Wikipedia concepts. Their methods require fine tuning of five weighting parameters to balance the contribution of each feature w.r.t Wikipedia versions and benchmarks. This hampers their applicability as a general-purpose solution in Wikipedia. In contrast, our approaches combines different Wikipedia features to construct a concept vector. Our approaches do not require any parameter tuning. Finally the results of our methods show better performance in term of correlation with human judgment.

6   Conclusion

We represent Wikipedia concept as a concept vector by integrating multiple Wikipedia features and their statistics. We use IC and $tfidf$ weights for the features. Our methods obtain show better performance on gold standard benchmarks in comparison with other SS methods. Especially the method Sim_2 proved to be more robust on all the benchmarks. The empirical evaluation shows that the integration of multiple weighted features improves the similarity assessment between concepts.

Acknowledgments. This work is supported by The National Natural Science Foundation of China under Grant Nos. 61772210 and U1911201; Guangdong Province Universities Pearl River Scholar Funded Scheme (2018); The Project of Science and Technology in Guangzhou in China under Grant No. 201807010043.

References

1. Agirre, E., Alfonseca, E., Hall, K., Kravalova, J., Paşca, M., Soroa, A.: A study on similarity and relatedness using distributional and wordnet-based approaches. In: Proceedings of Human Language Technologies, pp. 19–27 (2009)
2. Gabrilovich, E., Markovitch, S.: Computing semantic relatedness using Wikipedia-based explicit semantic analysis. In: IJcAI, vol. 7, pp. 1606–1611 (2007)
3. Hill, F., Reichart, R., Korhonen, A.: SimLex-999: evaluating semantic models with (genuine) similarity estimation. Comput. Linguist. **41**(4), 665–695 (2015)
4. Hussain, M.J., Wasti, S.H., Huang, G., Wei, L., Jiang, Y., Tang, Y.: An approach for measuring semantic similarity between Wikipedia concepts using multiple inheritances. Inf. Process. Manag. **57**(3), 102188 (2020)
5. Jiang, Y., Bai, W., Zhang, X., Hu, J.: Wikipedia-based information content and semantic similarity computation. Inf. Process. Manag. **53**(1), 248–265 (2017)
6. Jiang, Y., Zhang, X., Tang, Y., Nie, R.: Feature-based approaches to semantic similarity assessment of concepts using Wikipedia. Inf. Process. Manag. **51**(3), 215–234 (2015)
7. Mikolov, T., Chen, K., Corrado, G., Dean, J.: Efficient estimation of word representations in vector space. Comput. Sci. (2013)
8. Miller, G.A., Charles, W.G.: Contextual correlates of semantic similarity. Lang. Cogn. Processes **6**(1), 1–28 (1991)
9. Qu, R., Fang, Y., Bai, W., Jiang, Y.: Computing semantic similarity based on novel models of semantic representation using Wikipedia. Inf. Process. Manag. **54**(6), 1002–1021 (2018)
10. Rubenstein, H., Goodenough, J.B.: Contextual correlates of synonymy. Commun. ACM **8**(10), 627–633 (1965)
11. Shannon, C.E.: A mathematical theory of communication. Bell Syst. Tech. J. **27**(3), 379–423 (1948)
12. Wasti, S.H., Hussain, M.J., Huang, G., Akram, A., Jiang, Y., Tang, Y.: Assessing semantic similarity between concepts: a weighted-feature-based approach. Concurr. Comput.: Pract. Exp. **32**(7), e5594 (2020)
13. Zhu, G., Iglesias, C.A.: Computing semantic similarity of concepts in knowledge graphs. IEEE Trans. Knowl. Data Eng. **29**(1), 72–85 (2017)

Multi-Agent System

Adaptive Game AI-Based Dynamic Difficulty Scaling via the Symbiotic Game Agent

Siphesihle Philezwini Sithungu and Elizabeth Marie Ehlers[✉]

Academy of Computer Science and Software Engineering,
University of Johannesburg, Johannesburg, South Africa
{siphesihles, emehlers}@uj.ac.za

Abstract. This work presents AdaptiveSGA, a model for implementing Dynamic Difficulty Scaling through Adaptive Game AI via the Symbiotic Game Agent framework. The use of Dynamic Difficulty Balancing in modern computer games is useful when looking to improve the entertainment value of a game. Moreover, the Symbiotic Game Agent, as a framework, provides flexibility and robustness as a design principle for game agents. The work presented here leverages both the advantages of Adaptive Game AI and Symbiotic Game Agents to implement a robust, efficient and testable model for game difficulty scaling. The model is discussed in detail and is compared to the original Symbiotic Game Agent architecture. Finally, the paper describes how it was applied in simulated soccer. Finally, experimental results, which show that Dynamic Difficulty Balancing was achieved, are briefly analyzed.

Keywords: Dynamic Difficulty Balancing · Adaptive Game AI · Intelligent Agent Design · Symbiotic Game Agents

1 Introduction

Players interact with computer games uniquely and are, therefore, most likely to pursue unique strategies in order to win. This means that non-player characters (NPC) experience each player differently [1]. This phenomenon is foundational to the realisation of Adaptive Game Artificial Intelligence (AGAI): game AI that can change its behaviour based on the player's behaviour [2]. AGAI has a chance of providing entertainment to players. This adds more value to a game than static game AI since the value of a computer game is directly related to its level of entertainment [3, 4].

Dynamic Difficulty Balancing (DDB), on the other hand, refers to the act of automatically adapting the challenge the game presents to the player depending on the player's proficiency [5, 6]. This technique may help accommodate players with different playing abilities [7]. In addition, DDB aims to achieve an *even game* between the game AI and the human player. An even game is one where the difference between the number of wins and losses for each agent is relatively small [2, 4]. Furthermore, research done by Hagelback and Johansson [8] has shown that players First Person Shooter games enjoyed an even game more than one static difficulty.

In order to achieve successful DDB, the following three requirements must be met [9]: (1) the game should be quick in classifying and adapting itself to the player's

© IFIP International Federation for Information Processing 2020
Published by Springer Nature Switzerland AG 2020
Z. Shi et al. (Eds.): IIP 2020, IFIP AICT 581, pp. 107–117, 2020.
https://doi.org/10.1007/978-3-030-46931-3_11

proficiency, (2) efficient in identifying improvements and lapses in the player's performance and (3) adapting itself in a believable way.

Game AI may be implemented in various ways as an NPC controller. A natural approach to implementing an AI-based NPC controller is the use of an intelligent agent [10]. An agent typically has three main components: (1) perception, (2) decision-making and (3) action. A game agent architecture essentially follows the same convention. Therefore, the choice of the intelligent agent architecture to be used is critical to the success of a game. This work proposes the use of the Symbiotic Game Agent (SGA) architecture to achieve DDB.

SGA is a special kind of multi-agent system based on biological symbiosis [11], which is the formation of persistent relationships among candidates of different species. Symbiosis can be observed across a broad spectrum of animal and plant life on earth and is more potent than *lateral gene transfer* – a transferal of traits that may occur between different species. This is because symbiotic relationships between two entities may result in a more genetically, biochemically and behaviorally complex organism [12].

The rest of the paper is organized as follows: Sect. 2 is the problem background. Section 3 provides a literature review of similar works. Section 4 presents the model - AdaptiveSGA. Section 5 presents the experiment setup. Finally, Sect. 6 discusses experimental results, and Sect. 7 concludes the paper.

2 Problem Background

The problem this works aims to solve is designing an SGA-based model for efficiently performing AGAI-based DDB. Game AI that is adaptive alleviates the shortcomings of traditional game AI by allowing for the creation of NPCs that can effectively react to changing situations in unpredictable ways [3]. An essential part of DDB is measuring how challenging the player is finding a game to be at a given moment. This can be done by defining a *challenge function* [9] that maps the player's performance to a suitable difficulty level.

It is important to note that AGAI is not a requirement for DDB. DDB can be achieved in various ways and has been implemented in games without the use of AGAI. One common approach is to continuously modify game parameters (e.g. opponent health, the time provided to complete a task, game speed, etc.) to change the difficulty of a game. Although this approach may work, it does not solve the problem of making game AI adaptive in terms of behaviour [2]. The work presented here aims to achieve DDB through AGAI.

DDB is a worthwhile goal to achieve because it supports the concept of designing *weak AI* (i.e. AI that behaves reasonably intelligent to players) for games, as opposed to *strong AI* (i.e. AI that always makes the correct, desirable or optimal decisions and potentially surpassing human cognition).

3 Literature Review

3.1 Dynamic Difficulty Scaling Through Adaptive Game AI

Tan et al. [1] proposed two algorithms to achieve DDB through adaptive, behaviour-based AI: Adaptive Uni-Chromosome Controller (AUC) and Adaptive Duo-Chromosome Controller (ADC). Both AUC and ADC were behaviour-based controllers and were defined in terms of 7 possible behaviour states which were encoded as a chromosome vector. Each element of the vector stored a real number indicating the probability of that behaviour being activated.

Experimental results showed that the AUC and ADC controllers both achieved DDB by maintaining an even game against static controllers through 5000 game instances for each experiment. Moreover, both algorithms were able to achieve a score difference of 4 or lower for 70.22% of the time [1].

Spronck et al. [4] also proposed the use of AGAI to achieve DDB. Their method utilized dynamic scripting [3] to generate new opponent strategies (AGAI) while also scaling the difficulty level of game AI (DDB). Three approaches were used to achieve this: (1) high fitness penalizing, (2) weight clipping and (3) top culling, which was the highest performing approach.

3.2 Dynamic Difficulty Balancing Through Symbiotic Game Agents

Obodoekwe et al. [13] proposed the use of SGA to perform DDB in a serious game in order to maintain player immersion. Facial expression analysis was used to classify the expression on the player's face, and this information determined how the difficulty of the game would be adjusted.

The task of the facial expression recogniser was to continuously analyse the player's facial expression and compare it to the following basic expressions: anger, sadness, surprise, disgust, happiness and fear. The information on the player's emotion and duration was then passed to the play classifier, which modified the game's difficulty accordingly.

After a given time interval, the player's emotion and difficulty level were matched up with the player's score. A fitness value was then assigned to the emotion, difficulty and score combination, and a genetic algorithm was used to optimise the choice of difficulty for a given facial expression. This method performed well as it resulted in the overall increase in player scores over long periods of time [13].

4 AdaptiveSGA

The work presented here aims to achieve AGAI-based DDB through the SGA model. Although DDB has been implemented by Obodoekwe et al. through SGA [13], the paper did not mention the use of AGAI to achieve it. DDB was achieved by modifying two parameters: game speed and question difficulty. This does not necessarily change the game AI's behaviour. Moreover, the use of computer vision involves recording the player's face and surroundings. Some players might not be comfortable with this approach from a privacy perspective.

The discussed approaches proposed by Spronck et al. and Tan et al. used AGAI to achieve DDB through dynamic scripting and adaptive controllers (AUC and ADC), respectively. However, the work presented here seeks to achieve DDB using SGA (Please refer to Fig. 1) due to the flexibility offered by this architecture.

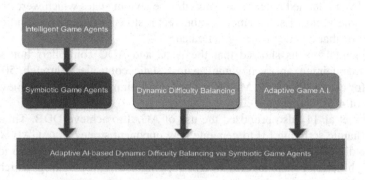

Fig. 1. A flow diagram indicating how the different concepts discussed thus far are used to realise the proposed model.

By using SGA, for example, one can swap symbiont agents without having to take their architecture into consideration. In addition, the swapping of agents may happen in real-time, without having to suspend gameplay. Cotterrell et al. performed this using a control symbiont agent. Please refer to Fig. 2 for the original SGA model by Cotterrell et al. [11].

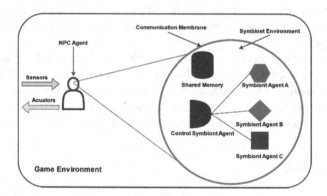

Fig. 2. The initial SGA model. Proposed by Cotterrell et al. Image adapted from [11].

The control symbiont agent is essentially an added agent with the purpose of facilitating communication among the various symbiont agents. In order to alleviate this issue, this work proposes an SGA model that does not make use of a control symbiont agent. This is achieved by placing more responsibility on the communication membrane. Figure 3 illustrates the proposed SGA model without a control symbiont agent.

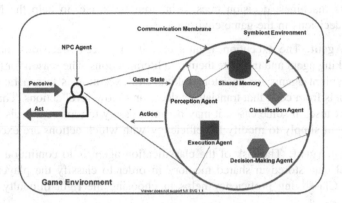

Fig. 3. The AdaptiveSGA model for achieving DDB through AGAI.

Game Environment. This is where the NPC agent interacts with the game's elements and other NPCs. Every action that the NPC performs affects the game environment accordingly. For games with dynamic environments, the environment, as well as the entities inside it, have the potential of changing the state of the NPC even if the NPC is idle.

Symbiont Environment. This environment is separated from the game environment by the communication membrane. Events that occur in the game environment cannot directly affect the symbiont environment. Symbiont agents interact with the communication membrane the shared memory within the symbiont environment.

Communication Membrane. Information about the game state is sent to the symbiont environment via the communication membrane. Furthermore, the communication membrane acts as a filter which allows only certain information to flow from the game environment into the symbiont environment and vice-versa.

4.1 NPC Agent and Symbiont Agents

The NPC Agent is the symbiotic agent and serves as the NPC controller. The NPC agent's internal workings are enabled by a multi-agent system of symbiont agents. The symbiont agents only interact with the communication membrane and shared memory.

Perception Agent. The role of the perception agent is to maintain a percept history in the shared memory for later use by the classification agent. This agent has the autonomy to decide in what format the data should be stored.

Decision-Making Agent. The decision-making agent is only responsible for decisions that the NPC makes in the game environment. Decisions relating to the symbiont environment are made by the communication membrane in conjunction with the classification agent. The decision-making agent typically makes use of algorithms such as finite-state machines, decision trees, behaviour trees, etc. to help the NPC make appropriate decisions in the game environment.

Execution Agent. The execution agent's task is to process decisions made by the decision-making agent and translate them into literal actions. The reason for having two separate symbiont agents for decision-making and execution is to separate decision-making models from code that translates a decision to low-level actions. This provides flexibility because, in some cases, it may be unnecessary to replace a decision-making symbiont agent simply to modify the efficiency with which actions are executed.

Classification Agent. The task of the classification agent is to continuously analyse the historical data stored in shared memory in order to classify the player's current proficiency. Classifying proficiency helps in choosing the right difficulty for future game instances.

5   Experimental Setup

5.1   Prototype

In order to test the applicability and feasibility of the model, we applied it to the problem of achieving DDB in simulated soccer. The soccer game application was designed using the Java programming language, and a screenshot of it is shown in Fig. 4. The team in yellow is controlled by a static game AI while the team in blue is controlled by AGAI-based SGA. Some of the rules of real-world soccer were excluded in this prototype because they do not significantly contribute to the aim of this research.

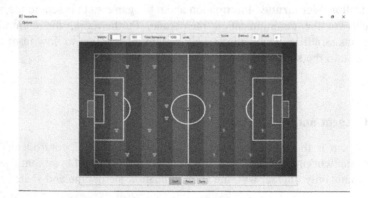

Fig. 4. Simulated soccer. The team in yellow is controlled by a static game AI while the team in blue is controlled by AGAI-based SGA. (Color figure online)

As such, goalkeepers were excluded from the game. The offside rule does not apply. When the ball leaves the pitch, it is placed at the centre of the pitch, and the game continues. Each match (game instance) was 1 min 20 s with each update cycle occurring every 80 ms. This resulted in each match lasting 1000 time steps. It should be noted that all real-world soccer rules can be incorporated into the prototype, although the problem that is being addressed by this work does not depend on their presence.

There were 8 available conditions an NPC could evaluate at any point during the game: (1) *Opponent's goals close?* (2) *Own goals close?* (3) *Teammate has the ball?* (4) *Opponent has the ball?* (5) *Do I have the ball?* (6) *Am I close to a teammate?* (7) *Teammate ahead?* (8) *Am I close to the ball?*

There were 7 available states for an NPC to transition to at any point during the game: (1) *Shoot*, (2) *Pass the ball to a teammate ahead*, (3) *Pass the ball to the closest teammate*, (4) *Make an attacking run*, (5) *Make a defensive run*, (6) *Chase the ball*, or (7) *Dribble*.

5.2 Achieving DDB Through AGAI

Static Game AI Implementation. As mention in Subsect. 5.1, the yellow team was controlled by a static game AI which did not use SGA to control the NPCs. The static game AI object made use of a finite-state machine (FSM) to make decisions and it executed the decisions itself. The FSM used by the static game AI followed the design depicted in Fig. 5.

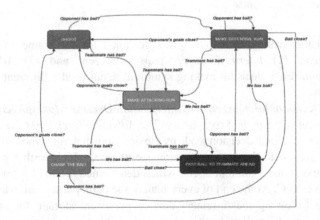

Fig. 5. FSM used by the static game AI to control the yellow team. (Color figure online)

Adaptive Game AI Implementation. The blue team was controlled by the AGAI-based SGA controller. In order to achieve AGAI, we leveraged the flexibility that SGA brings as an agent design principle: the ability to swap in and out symbiont agents during the execution of the game without interruption. Three difficulty settings were implemented: *EASY, MEDIUM* and *HARD*. The classification symbiont agent was responsible for predicting an appropriate difficulty setting.

The rules for choosing a difficulty setting were inspired by the concept of achieving an even game with the static game AI. The even-game approach is the same approach that was followed by Spronck et al. [4] and Tan et al. [1]. Therefore, the primary goal of the classification symbiont agent was to ensure that the adaptive team achieved an even game with the static team.

At the end of every match, the communication membrane provided the classification symbiont agent with the match result and the current difficulty setting. Upon predicting the next appropriate difficulty setting, the classification agent provided the new difficulty setting to the communication membrane. The communication membrane would then swap decision-making agents accordingly in order to scale the difficulty of the game (Please refer to Fig. 6).

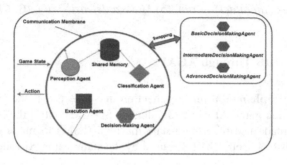

Fig. 6. An illustration of how the swapping of decision-making symbiont agents is performed by the communication membrane.

Three decision-making symbiont agents designed for this game: (1) *BasicDecisionMakingAgent*, (2) *IntermediateDecisionMakingAgent* and (3) *AdvancedDecisionMakingAgent*. Each decision-making symbiont agent used a different algorithm to reach decisions.

The *BasicDecisionMakingAgent* and *IntermediateDecisionMakingAgent* used FSMs of different logical structure and complexity. The *AdvancedDecisionMakingAgent* made use of a decision tree. Each decision made by the decision-making symbiont agent during the game was passed to the communication membrane, which further passed it as a percept to the execution symbiont agent, which determined the final action to be taken by the respective NPC. At the end of every match, the perception agent was responsible for storing the following match-related data in persistent storage for later analysis: (1) difficulty setting, (2) yellow team's score and (3) blue team's score.

6   Experimental Results

In order to test the ability of the SGA model to achieve AGAI-based DDB, we simulated 100 matches between the static game AI (yellow team) and the adaptive game AI (blue team). The aim of collecting this data was to determine if the blue team could achieve an even game with the yellow team over 100 matches. We used Eq. (1) [1] to measure how evenly matched the two teams were based on the results of each of the 100 matches.

$$W = L = \frac{(n - D)}{2} \qquad (1)$$

where W is the number of wins by the blue team, L is the number of losses by the blue team and n is the number of matches, and D is the number of draws. According to a survey performed by Tan et al., players deem a large number of draws as more frustrating than. Therefore, having achieved an even game, it is also desirable to achieve a small number of draws. Moreover, a relatively high score difference between the two teams signifies an entertaining game [1].

6.1 Achieving an Even Game

Please refer to Fig. 7 for the trend in difficulty adjustment throughout the 100 matches. For most of the matches, the difficulty transitioned between *EASY* and *MEDIUM*. It was only in match 12 and 24 that the *AdvancedDecisionMakingAgent* (i.e. *HARD* difficulty) had to be swapped in order to maintain an even game.

With regards to achieving an even game, we defined the threshold for an uneven game as $|W - L| = 0.1 * n$. Therefore, if the difference between wins and losses exceeds 10% of the total games, we declared the encounter as uneven. The number of wins for the blue team was 35 ($W = 35$) while the number of losses was also 35 ($L = 35$), which means that $|W - L| = 0$. This means that the adaptive game AI was able to achieve an even game against the static game AI.

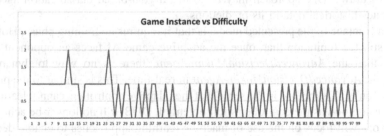

Fig. 7. A line graph depicting how the difficulty was adjusted at each game instance (match).

6.2 Achieving Entertainment Value

With regards to the number of draws, we defined the requirement for a non-frustrating game as $D < 0.1 * n$, which is 10% of the total games. The total number of draws was 30 ($D = 30$), which amounts to 30% of the total number of games. The adaptive game AI can be improved, in this aspect, so that the encounter causes the least amount of frustration for the opponent.

When looking at the score-difference history (Please see Fig. 8), we can see that 87% of all drawn matches took place within the first 50 matches. This means that the game was less frustrating in the final 50 matches. Therefore, there is definitely room for improvement. Finally, in terms of score difference - which we translated into goal difference for a soccer game - the adaptive game AI achieved a fairly entertaining game with the goal difference between the two teams being 47. This is a promising result.

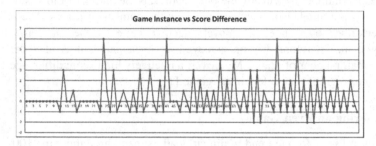

Fig. 8. A line graph depicting the score difference for each match (game instance) for all 100 matches.

7 Conclusion

The aim of this work was to achieve DDB through AGAI by making use of SGA architecture. According to experimental results, DDB was indeed achieved when using the even-game approach as a performance measure. However, there is still room for improvement with regards to reducing the level of frustration by further minimizing the number of draws. One approach may be to use a goal-based classification agent that incorporates historical data in its predictions.

The advantage of the presented model is that it requires no training phase. However, there is still the limitation that, once the adaptive game AI faces an opponent that is stronger than the *AdvancedDecisionMakingAgent,* there is no way to dynamically improve the *AdvancedDecisionMakingAgent* in real-time. This is similar to the problem faced by Tan et al.'s method in the sense that the adaptive controllers cannot learn. Once a player is as good as the controller's full potential, DDB will no longer be achievable. Future work will focus on the use of machine learning approaches to enable decision-making symbiont agents that can learn useful behavioural traits from opponents.

References

1. Tan, C.H., Tan, K.C., Tay, A.: Dynamic game difficulty scaling using adaptive behavior-based AI. IEEE Trans. Comput. Intell. AI Games **3**, 289–301 (2011)
2. Cunha, E.M.C.A.M.: An Adaptive Game AI Architecture
3. Spronck, P., Ponsen, M., Sprinkhuizen-Kuyper, I., Postma, E.: Adaptive game AI with dynamic scripting. Mach. Learn. **63**, 217–248 (2006). https://doi.org/10.1007/s10994-006-6205-6

4. Spronck, P., Sprinkhuizen-Kuyper, I., Postma, E.: Difficulty scaling of game AI. In: Proceedings of the 5th International Conference on Intelligent Games and Simulation (GAME-ON 2004) (2004)
5. Gomez-Hicks, G., Kauchak, D.: Dynamic game difficulty balancing for backgammon. In: Proceedings of the 49th Annual Southeast Regional Conference (2011)
6. Andrade, G., Ramalho, G., Gomes, A.S., Corruble, V.: Dynamic game balancing: an evaluation of user satisfaction. AIIDE 6, 3–8 (2006)
7. Hawkins, G., Nesbitt, K., Brown, S.: Dynamic difficulty balancing for cautious players and risk takers. Int. J. Comput. Games Technol. 2012, 3 (2012)
8. Hagelback, J., Johansson, S.J.: Measuring player experience on runtime dynamic difficulty scaling in an RTS game (2009). https://doi.org/10.1109/CIG.2009.5286494
9. Andrade, G., Ramalho, G., Santana, H., Corruble, V.: Extending reinforcement learning to provide dynamic game balancing. In: Proceedings of the Workshop on Reasoning, Representation, and Learning in Computer Games, 19th International Joint Conference on Artificial Intelligence (IJCAI) (2005)
10. Nareyek, A.: Intelligent agents for computer games. In: International Conference on Computers and Games (2000)
11. Cotterrell, D., Ehlers, E.: Symbiosis, game agents and the cloud (2015). https://doi.org/10.5176/2251-1679_CGAT15.35
12. Douglas, A.E.: The Symbiotic Habit. Princeton University Press, Princeton (2010)
13. Obodoekwe, C., Coulter, D.A., Ehlers, E.M.: A model for improving serious game player immersion via symbiotic agents, natural language processing, and facial expression analysis. In: International Conference on Computer Games, Multimedia & Allied Technology (CGAT) (2017)

Recommendation System

Scientific Paper Recommendation Using Author's Dual Role Citation Relationship

Donglin Hu[1], Huifang Ma[1,2(✉)], Yuhang Liu[1], and Xiangchun He[1]

[1] Northwest Normal University, Lanzhou 730070, Gansu, China
mahuifang@yeah.net
[2] Guangxi Key Lab of Multi-Source Information Mining and Security,
Guangxi Normal University, Guilin 541004, China

Abstract. Vector representations learning (also known as embeddings) for users (items) are at the core of modern recommendation systems. Existing works usually map users and items to low-dimensional space to predict user preferences for items and describe pre-existing features (such as ID) of users (or items) to obtain the embedding of the user (or item). However, we argue that such methods neglect the dual role of users, side information of users and items (e.g., dual citation relationship of authors, authoritativeness of authors and papers) when recommendation is performed for scientific paper. As such, the resulting representations may be insufficient to predict optimal author citations.

In this paper, we contribute a new model named scientific paper recommendation using Author's Dual Role Citation Relationship (ADRCR) to capture authors' citation relationship. Our model incorporates the reference relation between author and author, the citation relationship between author and paper, and the authoritativeness of authors and papers into a unified framework. In particular, our model predicts author citation relationship in each specific class. Experiments on the DBLP dataset demonstrate that ADRCR outperforms state-of-the-art recommendation methods. Further analysis shows that modeling the author's dual role is particularly helpful for providing recommendation for sparse users that have very few interactions.

Keywords: Matrix factorization · Dual role · Citation relationship · Authoritativeness · Clustering

1 Introduction

With the continuous development of information technology, scientific social networks have become the fastest and most suitable way for researchers to communicate with each other. However, as a growing numbers of scientific papers are shared in scientific social networks, which makes it difficult for researchers to locate the papers they are interested in from a large number of scientific papers. Therefore, how to recommend scientific papers of interest to researchers in social networks has become a hot research topic. Essentially, recommender system [1] provides suggestions of items that may interest to users. At present, scientific paper recommendation methods can be divided into two categories: content-based recommendation [2] and collaborative filtering [3].

© IFIP International Federation for Information Processing 2020
Published by Springer Nature Switzerland AG 2020
Z. Shi et al. (Eds.): IIP 2020, IFIP AICT 581, pp. 121–132, 2020.
https://doi.org/10.1007/978-3-030-46931-3_12

In the content-based recommendation method, researchers usually apply the title, abstract and keywords of scientific papers to generate the recommendation. Collaborative Filtering is a technique widely adapted in recommendation systems which assesses items (in this case papers) according to the former users-items interactions [4]. In this recommendation method, the researchers obtain the prediction score for the scientific papers by the researchers' scoring information on the scientific papers, and finally get a recommended list of scientific papers. Hybrid recommendation method usually combines the content-based recommendation method with the collaborative filtering recommendation method. It usually generates better recommendation results than that of recommendation methods only using one strategy, but it still has the disadvantages of data sparsity and low recommendation accuracy. To effectively improve the accuracy of scientific papers recommendation, we propose a new model named scientific paper recommendation using Author's Dual Role Citation Relationship (ADRCR), which incorporates information on both authors and papers. The contributions are summarized as follows.

- We emphasize the importance of clustering scientific papers by topic to improve the performance of recommendation.
- We develop a novel ADRCR method to learn authors' preferences for dual role by building models of explicit interactions (e.g., citation and reference) and implicit connections.
- We perform experiments on the DBLP dataset and demonstrate that the ADRCR method can improve the accuracy of scientific papers more effectively than other baseline methods.

2 Related Work

We review existing work on common latent space approach for recommendation and methods based on user feature matrix shared representation, which are related to our work, together with the emphasize of differences from ADRCR.

2.1 Common Latent Space Approach for Recommendation

The matrix decomposition method is a factual method of collaborative filtering using explicit feedback. The basic idea is to embed users and items into shared potential spaces [5]. By merging reference relationships into matrix factorization techniques, several methods have been considered from the perspective of users and items, such as item-based methods [6], user-based methods [7] and combinations of these two methods [8]. The hybrid model [8] associates the user with the paper through the label information of the paper to build a user model and a paper model. This recommendation model effectively alleviates the cold start problem. The previously proposed cross-domain model does not consider the two-way potential relationship between users and items, nor does it explicitly model user information and project characteristics. The [9] method extracts multiple user preferences in the domain while retaining the relationship between users in different potential spaces to provide recommendations in each domain [10]. This method is based on the perspective of deep learning, taking users and items characteristics as the original input, using the proposed model to learn the potential factors of users and items, and then combining the obtained potential factors to make fast and accurate predictions. However, these methods only consider the single role of the user.

2.2   Method Based on User Feature Matrix Shared Representation

There are many recommendation models based on the shared representation of user feature matrices. User feature matrix shared representation refers to the simultaneous decomposition of the rating matrix and the social relationship matrix. The recommendation model assumes that the user feature matrix is hidden in both the rating information and the social information. Several remarkable works in the field [11, 12] take user rating and social information into account, but they do not consider additional information about users and items. In fact, ratings and reviews are complementary and can be viewed as two different aspects of users and items. Therefore, [13] merging the scoring model and text reviews can effectively learn more accurate representations of users and recommended items [14]. This method considers the correlation between users. It use three independent autoencoders to learn user functions with roles of rater, truster and trustee, respectively. The method [12] is most similar to our method, but it only reflects the information of the user, not the information of the item. Our proposed method considers not only the user and item perspectives, but also the different roles assigned to the user.

3   Matrix Decomposition: A Model-Based Method

3.1   Notation and Problem Statement

Notation. We first introduce some frequent notations utilized in the following sections. We use bold capital with subscripted letters to represent column vectors (e.g., M_p), and apply bold capital letters and subscripts with transpose superscript T to represent row vectors (e.g., $(L_a)^T$), respectively. We indicate all matrices by bold upper case letters (e.g., Q), and q_{ap} denotes the entry of matrix Q corresponding to the row a and column p. We denote a predicted value, by having a $\wedge$ over it (e.g., $\hat{q}$).

Problem Statement. Given a recommendation system with n authors and m papers, $Q = [q_{ap}]_{n \times m}$ represents the author-paper citation matrix, where q_{ap} is the number of times that the author a cites the paper p. Authors and papers are usually mapped to the low-dimensional feature space. After the Q decomposition, the author a vector L_a of k-dimensional and the paper p vector M_p are obtained, respectively. Finally, we learn the feature matrices L and M by minimizing the sum of squares loss function:

$$\min_{L,M} \frac{1}{2} \sum_{(a,p)\in\gamma} \left(\left((L_a)^T M_p\right) - q_{ap}\right)^2 + \frac{\lambda_1}{2} \|L\|_F^2 + \frac{\lambda_2}{2} \|M\|_F^2 \tag{1}$$

where, γ is the set of observable (author, paper) pairs in $\mathbf{Q}$, $\| \cdot \|_F^2$ Frobenius paradigm; Regularization terms $\|L\|_F^2$ and $\|M\|_F^2$ are used to avoid over-fitting. The stochastic gradient descent algorithm is used to solve the local optimal solution of the function defined by Eq. (1), and the product of L and M is adopted to approximate the citation matrix $\mathbf{Q}$. For the missing items $\hat{q}_{ap}$ in the citation matrix $\mathbf{Q}$, we apply the inner product of L_a and M_p to predict:

$$\hat{q}_{ap} = (L_a)^T M_p \tag{2}$$

3.2 Matrix Decomposition in Scientific Research Reference Network

Let $G = (A, E, T, W)$ denote a directed social reference relation network with n nodes, where A represents a set of authors and E represents the edge set. $T = [t_{ae}]_{n\times n}$ denotes the transfer matrix of influence propagation, and t_{ae} indicates the propagation probability from author a to author e; If there is an edge from e to a in the social citation network (i.e., e trusts a), then $t_{ae} > 0$, and otherwise, $t_{ae} = 0$. The structure of G is described using the reference relation asymmetric matrix $W = [w_{ea}]_{n\times n}$ between authors, and w_{ea} expresses the strength of the reference relation between author e and author a, that is, the weight of the edge. Due to dissymmetrical property of citation, we map each author a of reference network as two distinct latent feature vectors, depicted by reference-specific feature vector L_a and referenced-specific feature vector U_a, respectively. L_a and U_a characterize the behaviors of 'to reference others' and 'to be referenced by others', respectively. After giving two vectors, the strength w_{ea} of the reference relationship is modeled as the inner product of L_a and U_e, and the feature matrix $L \in \mathbb{R}^{k\times n}$ and $U \in \mathbb{R}^{k\times n}$ can be learned by minimizing the following objective function:

$$\min_{L,U} \frac{1}{2} \sum_{(e,a)\in\delta} \left(\left((L_a)^T U_e\right) - w_{ea}\right)^2 + \frac{\lambda_1}{2} \|L\|_F^2 + \frac{\lambda_2}{2} \|U\|_F^2 \tag{3}$$

Where δ is an observable (author, author) pair sets in W, the specific calculations of t_{ae} and w_{ea} in the T and W matrices will be introduced below. The superscript c mentioned below represents a specific class.

Please note that both objective function (1) and objective function (3) use the idea of matrix factorization. The difference is that the objective function (1) learns the author's citations to the paper, while the objective function (3) learns authors' and authors' citations. The two objective functions are fused into the final objective function, reflecting the main purpose of this article, that is, the author's dual-citation role.

4 The Propose Method

4.1 Basic Framework

We now represent the proposed ADRCR model, the framework of which is illustrated in Fig. 1.

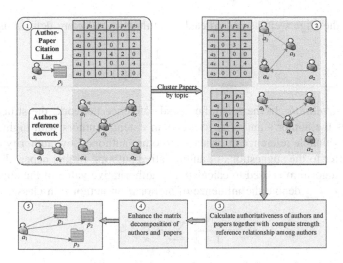

Fig. 1. The framework of ADRCR

There are five components in the framework: (1) Dividing author-paper citation matrix and reference network between authors; (2) Clustering papers by topic and deriving social reference networks for authors (excluding authors who have not cited any papers) in a specific class; (3) Calculating the strength of citation relationships between authors and the authority of authors and papers; (4) Enhancing the matrix decomposition for authors and papers; and (5) Predicting the author's citation to the paper.

4.2 Citation Relationship Strength and Authoritative Calculation

Citation Relationship Strength Calculation. In a specific scientific social reference relation network, if author e and author a have a reference relationship in class c, the number of times that author e cites author a's paper will be used to measure the strength of the reference relation between them, that is, the weight on the edge is x_{ea}^c [15].

The author's research interests may also change over time. According to the number of papers published in the six research fields on the DBLP dataset, we construct the attribute vector of each author a, and the attribute value of each dimension corresponds to the author a. The number of papers published in these fields can be adopted to calculate the similarity of author's research interest using cosine similarity, which is defined as follows:

$$s_{ea}^c = \begin{cases} 1, & a = e \\ \frac{b_a \cdot b_e}{|b_a| \times |b_e|}, & a \neq e \wedge (a, e) \in E \\ 0, & others \end{cases} \qquad (4)$$

Finally, the edge weights constructed by authors a and e are defined as follows:

$$w_{ea}^c = \frac{1}{1 + \lg(x_{ea}^c \times s_{ea}^c)} \qquad (5)$$

Influence Calculation. In the scientific social reference network, the structure of the node reflects the author's authority to a certain extent. Authors with higher authority can provide valuable reference information to other authors; Low authority authors are willing to refer to the suggestions of authoritative authors. In this paper, the influence propagation algorithm is used to calculate the authoritative value of the author in each class [16]. Let $f_{a \to e}^c$ denote the influence of author a on author e in class c as follows:

$$f_{a \to e}^c = \frac{1}{1 + \lambda} \left(\sum_{k \in N_e^c} t_{ke}^c f_{a \to k}^c + v_{a \to e}^c \right) \qquad (6)$$

$$s.t. \ f_{a \to a}^c = \alpha_a^c, \ e = a \text{ , and } \alpha_a^c > 0 \qquad (7)$$

Where $N_e^c = \{e_1, e_2, \cdots, e_n\}$ denotes a set of trusted friends of author e in class c (i.e., author e refers to a class of other authors). t_{ke}^c represents the propagation probability from author k to author e, and $\sum_{k=1}^n t_{ke}^c \leq 1$. The parameter λ is the damping coefficient, and $\alpha_a^c \in [0, 1]$ is the domain knowledge of the author a. In particular, f_a^c and $v_{a,a}^c$ are set as default in reference [16].

Centrality Calculation. We utilize three centralities to evaluate the status of nodes in the network. The central node can be regarded important because it has a favorable and influential position in the network. When a given node has more neighbors, it will occupy an important position. For a given node a, the final status of the node in the network is obtained by calculating the average of the three centralities [17], which is defined as follows:

$$AC_a^c = \frac{\sum_{k=1}^z C_k^c}{z} \qquad (8)$$

where z is the number of centralities, and C_k^c is the centrality value of node a measured according to the centrality. In our example, the value of k is 3, since we adopt three centralities.

If author a has a greater influence on author e and a very important status, then author a is more authoritative. We sort the influence and centrality of n^c authors, then let author a rank as $s_a^c = f_{a \to e}^c \times AC_a^c$ and $s_a^c \in [1, n^c]$, where n^c denotes the number of authors in W^c. The authoritative value of author a is defined as:

$$O_a^c = \frac{1}{1 + \lg(s_a^c)} \tag{9}$$

It can be seen from the above formula that when the author's influence value ranks first in class c, then $O_a^c = 1$, and O_a^c decreases as the author's ranking decreasing, that is, the author's influence value ranks lower, and the corresponding authoritative value is lower. Therefore, the authoritative values of all authors can be calculated using Eq. (9).

Authoritative Calculation of the Paper. Generally, the higher the authority, the more important the paper is on the scientific research platform, and the higher the citation rate of the paper by authors in related fields. On the contrary, the lower the authority, the lower the citation rate is. We then calculate the weight $H_{(p)}^c$ as follows:

$$H_{(p)}^c = \beta \begin{cases} 1, & p^c \in A \\ 2/3, & p^c \in B + (1 - \beta)e^{\frac{-(t - y_p) + 1}{g_p + 1}} \\ 1/3, & p^c \in C \end{cases} \tag{10}$$

where β is a parameter. (A, B, C) respectively represents the collection of A, B and C category papers recommended by the CCF Association, and $p^c \in A$ indicates that the paper p in category c belongs to A category. t represents the current time. y_p represents the publication time of the paper p, and g_p indicates the number of times the paper p has been cited. The authoritative value I_p^c of the paper p is normalized using the Sigmoid function.

4.3 Recommendation Model

In the scientific social reference network, if an author is more authoritative, it means that he has more citation times to high-quality papers; If the authoritativeness of a paper is higher, it demonstrates that it will be cited by many authors in the field. Therefore, this article also uses the authority of the author and the paper to measure the author's citations of the paper, namely:

$$\min_{L^c M^c} \frac{1}{2} \sum_{(a,p) \in \gamma^c} O_a^c I_p^c (g((L_a^c)^T M_p^c) - q_{ap}^c)^2 + \frac{\lambda_1}{2} \| L^c \|_F^2 + \frac{\lambda_2}{2} \| M^c \|_F^2 \tag{11}$$

γ^c is a set of pairs (authors, papers) in Q^c. In formula (11), if author a has higher authority in class c and the authority of the paper is also high, it means that author a has cited the paper multiple times. That is, the error between the predicted number of citation and the actual number of citation is small; In contrast, there is a large error between the predicted citation times and the actual citation times.

In order to more conveniently learn the parameters, the author's authorization value should be set between 0 and 1, thus the time of citation is mapped to the [0,1] interval by using the function $f(x) = x/Q_{max}$, where Q_{max} is the maximum citation time. The Logistic function $g(x) = 1/(1 + \exp(-x))$ fixes the inner product of the predicted citation case $(\mathbf{L}_a^c)^T \mathbf{M}_p^c$ to the interval [0,1]. Therefore, the optimization objective function in the citation model is defined as follows:

$$Z = \frac{1}{2} \sum_{(a,p) \in \gamma^c} O_a^c I_P^c (g((\mathbf{L}_a^c)^T \mathbf{M}_p^c) - q_{ap}^c)^2 +$$
$$\frac{1}{2} \lambda_c \sum_{(e,a) \in \delta^c} w_{ea}^c (g((\mathbf{U}_e^c)^T \mathbf{L}_a^c) - w_{ea}^c)^2 + \alpha(L, M, U) \qquad (12)$$

$$\alpha(L, M, U) = \frac{\lambda_1}{2} \| L^c \|_F^2 + \frac{\lambda_2}{2} \| M^c \|_F^2 + \frac{\lambda_3}{2} \| U^c \|_F^2 \qquad (13)$$

The above objective function can be minimized by performing the following gradient descent for all authors and papers M_p^c, L_a^c, U_e^c. Parameter λ_c controls the influence proportion between the times of citations and the reference relationship in the training model.

5 Experiments

All experiments are performed on a computer with an Intel (R) Core (TM) i5-6402P CPU, 2.80 GHz, and 8 GB RAM. The Operation System is Windows 10 Professional, using MATLAB2017 data processing. We perform experiments on DBLP dataset to answer the following research questions:

• **RQ1**: How does the performance of our proposed ADRCR compare with state-of-the-art recommended methods designed to learn from a large number of recommended scientific papers?
• **RQ2**: Can ADRCR help to solve data sparsity problem?

In what follows, we will first describe the experimental settings and then answer the above two questions.

5.1 Experimental Settings

In order to verify the effectiveness of the proposed method, the experiment is designed and verified.

Dataset. In order to verify the effectiveness of the proposed method, 8,301 papers published by journalists in the field of data mining (DM) in journals (DMKD, TKDE) or conferences (KDD, ICDM, SDM) are selected.

Evaluation Metrics. Two of the most classic evaluation metrics [18] are used in our experiments: mean absolute error (MAE) and root mean square error (RMSE). We perform 10-fold cross-validation. In each fold, 20% of the data set is randomly selected as the test set, and the remaining 80% is used as the training set.

Comparison Methods and Parameter Setting. To compare and evaluate the performance of our proposed methods, we chose the following three representative methods as competitors. We set the best parameters according to the corresponding references or based on our experiments.

• IBCF [6] and UBCF [7]: These methods are chosen to consider only unilateral item or user information.

• TrustMF [12]: It considers the dual role of users and the social trust network between the same users to improve the performance of the recommendation system, but it does not think over the information of the item.

The parameters β, λ_c, λ, λ_1, λ_2, λ_3 and the dimension k of the implicit feature vector will affect the recommended performance. By performing many experiments, it is found that the performance of this method is the best when the parameters $\beta = 1/2$, $\lambda_c = 1$, $\lambda = 0.176$, $\lambda_1 = \lambda_2 = \lambda_3 = 0.001$, and $k = 10$.

5.2 Experimental Results and Analysis

Performance Analysis (RQ1). We first compare our method with the collaborative filtering recommendation performance of state-of-the-art methods. Then, we study performance when the recommended number N is set to [10, 20, 50, 80]. Please note that for a author, our evaluation measure will rank all the unobserved papers in the training set. In this case, a smaller value of N will make the result more unstable. Therefore, we report relatively large results. The experimental results are recorded in Table 1, where k is the dimension of the feature space. The main observations of this experimental study are summarized in Table 1.

Table 1. Performance comparisons on DBLP dataset

N		10		20		50		80	
	Methods	MAE	RMSE	MAE	RMSE	MAE	RMSE	MAE	RMSE
$k = 10$	IBCF	0.951	1.235	0.942	1.223	0.922	1.211	0.904	1.205
	UBCF	0.942	1.217	0.933	1.215	0.917	1.205	0.902	1.203
	TrustMF	0.832	1.072	0.821	1.079	**0.817**	1.062	0.806	1.059
	ADRCR	**0.815**	**1.051**	**0.811**	**1.047**	0.818	**1.034**	**0.798**	**1.023**

We can observe that in terms of MAE and RMSE, the proposed ADRCR method always outperforms other state-of-the-art methods. In particular, compared with the best method TrustMF, When the recommended number N is 20, 50, 80, and $k = 10$, on RMSE, the performance of the ADRCR method is improved by 2.1%, 2.8% and 3.6%, respectively. In addition, as the number of recommended papers increases, so does the recommendation efficiency. This shows that an accurate dual role and an approach that takes into account both users and items information modeling can improve recommendation performance.

Impact of Data Sparsity (RQ2). The problem of sparsity usually limits the expression of recommendation systems, since some papers are rarely cited by authors. Therefore, we investigate how our proposed ADRCR model can improve the recommendation performance of the paper with few citations. Specifically, we divide all authors into groups based on the number of citation records: [0–5, 6–10, 11–15, 16–20, >20]. In each group, the number of authors ranges from 100 to 200, which can eliminate the randomness of the experimental results. For every group, we compare the performance of our method with the benchmark methods. The results are shown in Fig. 2.

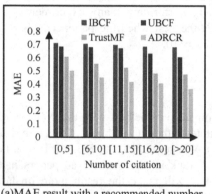
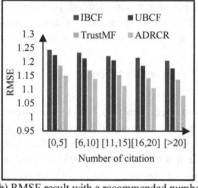

(a)MAE result with a recommended number of 50

(b) RMSE result with a recommended number of 50

Fig. 2. Performance of IBCF, UBCF, TrustMF and ADRCR on authors with different number of citation records

It can be seen from the results that when the author cites becomes sparse, the proposed ADRCR performance is better than other methods. Especially for RMSE, the performance of ADRCR is improved by 7.07% from the fifth group to the first group, while the performance of UBCF and TrustMF is improved by 4.70% and 5.06%, respectively. It is found that as the data becomes sparse, the performance gap between ADRCR and other methods becomes more apparent. Because the ADRCR model considers both authors and papers information, it can achieve good recommendation performance for authors with sparse citations.

6 Conclusions

The traditional method of recommending scientific papers does not think over the information of authors and papers simultaneously. To this end, we propose a recommendation method that considers the authority of authors and papers concurrently. Through the author's citations of scientific papers, find the scientific papers that the author is interested in, and recommend them to a large number of scientific papers. The experimental results show that compares with other traditional recommendation methods, the proposed method has achieved good recommendation results on both evaluation indicators. Especially in the topic of scientific papers, clustering is divided into different class by offline clustering. This not only enhances the recommendation speed, but also improves the recommendation efficiency.

Acknowledgement. This work is supported by the National Natural Science Foundation of China (61762078, 61363058, 61966004), Major project of young teachers' scientific research ability promotion plan (NWNU-LKQN2019-2) and Research Fund of Guangxi Key Lab of Multi-source Information Mining and Security (MIMS18-08).

References

1. Li, Z., Zhao, H., Liu, Q., Huang, Z., Mei, T., Chen, E.: Learning from history and present: next-item recommendation via discriminatively exploiting user behaviors. In: 24th International Conference on SIGKDD, pp. 1734–1743. ACM, London (2018)
2. Joseph, K., Jiang, H.: Content based news recommendation via shortest entity distance over knowledge graphs. In: The World Wide Web Conference, pp. 690–699. ACM, San Francisco (2019)
3. Huang, L., Ma, H., Li, N., Yu, L.: Collaborative filtering recommendation algorithm based on bipartite graph and joint clustering. Comput. Eng. Sci. **41**(11), 2040–2047 (2019)
4. Jannach, D., Zanker, M., Felfernig, A., Friedrich, G.: Recommender Systems: An Introduction. Cambridge University Press, Cambridge (2010)
5. Li, H., Ma, X.P., Shi, J.: Incorporating trust relation with PMF to enhance social network recommendation performance. Int. J. Pattern Recognit. Artif Intell. **30**(06), 1659016 (2016)
6. West, J.D., Wesley, S.I., Bergstrom, C.T.: A recommendation system based on hierarchical clustering of an article-level citation network. IEEE Trans. Big Data **2**(2), 113–123 (2017)
7. Dai, T., Li, Z., Cai, X., Pan, S., Yuan, S.: Explore semantic topics and author communities for citation recommendation in bipartite bibliographic network. J. Ambient Intell. Hum. Comput. **9**(9), 1–19 (2017)
8. Wang, H., Shi, X., Yeung, D.Y.: Relational stacked denoising autoencoder for tag recommendation. In: Twenty-ninth AAAI Conference on Artificial Intelligence, pp. 3052–3058. AAAI Press, Texas (2015)
9. Li, P., Tuzhilin, A.: DDTCDR: deep dual transfer cross domain recommendation. In: Proceedings of the 13th International Conference on Web Search and Data Mining, pp. 331–339. ACM, Houston (2020)
10. Nassar, N., Jafar, A., Rahhal, Y.: A novel deep multi-criteria collaborative filtering model for recommendation system. Knowl. Based Syst. **187**, 104811 (2020)

11. Tang, J., Hu, X., Gao, H., Liu, H.: Exploiting local and global social context for recommendation. In: Twenty-Third international Joint Conference on Artificial Intelligence, pp. 2712–2718. AAAI Press, Beijing (2013)
12. Yang, B., Lei, Y., Liu, J., Li, W.: Social collaborative filtering by trust. IEEE Trans. Pattern Anal. Mach. Intell. **39**(8), 1633–1647 (2017)
13. Liu, H., et al.: Hybrid neural recommendation with joint deep representation learning of ratings and reviews. Neurocomputing **374**, 77–85 (2020)
14. Pan, Y., He, F., Yu, H.: A correlative denoising autoencoder to model social influence for top-N recommender system. Front. Comput. Sci. **14**(3), 143301 (2020). https://doi.org/10. 1007/s11704-019-8123-3
15. Ma, F., Wu, Y.S.: Citation identity—a noticeable concept. Libr. Inf. Work **53**(16), 27–115 (2009)
16. Liu, Q., et al.: An influence propagation view of PageRank. ACM Trans. Knowl. Disc. Data **11**(3), 1–30 (2017)
17. Shao, Z., Liu, S., Zhao, Y.: Correction to: identifying influential nodes in complex networks based on neighbours and edges. Peer-to-Peer Netw. Appl. **12**(6), 1538 (2019)
18. Ma, H., Zhou, D., Liu, C., Lyu, M.R., King, L.: Recommender systems with social regularization. In: The Forth International Conference on Web Search and Web Data Mining, pp. 287–296. ACM, Hong Kong (2011)

A Genetic Algorithm for Travel Itinerary Recommendation with Mandatory Points-of-Interest

Phatpicha Yochum, Liang Chang$^{(\boxtimes)}$, Tianlong Gu, Manli Zhu, and Hongliang Chen

Guangxi Key Laboratory of Trusted Software,
Guilin University of Electronic Technology, Guilin 541004, China
changl@guet.edu.cn

Abstract. Traveling as a very popular leisure activity enjoyed by many people all over the world. Typically, people would visit the POIs that are popular or special in a city and also have desired starting POIs (e.g., POIs that are close to their hotels) and destination POIs (e.g., POIs that are near train stations or airports). However, travelers often have limited travel time and are also unfamiliar with the wide range of Points-of-Interest (POIs) in a city, so that the itinerary planning is time-consuming and challenging. In this paper, we view this kind of itinerary planning as MandatoryTour problem, which is tourists have to construct an itinerary comprising a series of POIs of a city and including as many popular or special POIs as possible within their travel time budget. We term the most popular and special POIs as mandatory POIs in our paper. For solving the presented MandatoryTour problem, we propose a genetic algorithm GAM. We compare our approach against several baselines GA, MaxM, and GreedyM by using real-world datasets from the Yahoo Flickr Creative Commons 100 Million Dataset (YFCC100M), which include POI visits of seven touristic cities. The experimental results show that GAM achieves better recommendation performance in terms of the mandatory POIs, POIs visited, time budget (travel time and visit duration), and profit (POI popularity).

Keywords: Travel recommendations · Itinerary recommendations · Recommendation systems · Location recommendations

1 Introduction

Traveling is entirely considered as a pleasure activity and it does not take long for travelers to travel. People have high travel expectations and enjoy their journeys and experiences. Travel itinerary or tour planning is one of the most important tasks for people to travel to unfamiliar cities and places. It mainly focuses on a plan with a sequence of visits of a given number of Points-of-Interest (POIs),

© IFIP International Federation for Information Processing 2020
Published by Springer Nature Switzerland AG 2020
Z. Shi et al. (Eds.): IIP 2020, IFIP AICT 581, pp. 133–145, 2020.
https://doi.org/10.1007/978-3-030-46931-3_13

which must be visited within a limited time. Additional information is also considered such as the number of POIs visited, travel time, and POI visit duration of the trip. Especially, in order to maximize the number of POIs and/or the visit duration, the travel time or the distance between POIs should be cut down. It is intuitive to include mandatory POIs, which are everywhere on the user's trip as they are often very popular or special POIs where tourists should visit in a city.

The existing works adapt a simple measure based on user interest and POI popularity for itinerary recommendations. In our work, we view this kind of itinerary planning as MandatoryTour problem, which is tourists have to construct an itinerary comprising a series of POIs of a city and including as many popular or special POIs as possible within their travel time budget. Hence, mandatory POIs are the term of the most popular and special POIs. We propose a travel itinerary recommendation approach, named GAM, to solve the MandatoryTour problem by using a genetic algorithm. Besides, we use real-world datasets which are derived from the Yahoo Flickr Creative Commons 100 Million Dataset (YFCC100M) provided by [1] to evaluate our approach. We make contributions to the field of itinerary recommendation as follows:

1. We introduce and formulate the MandatoryTour problem, which is the term the most popular and special POIs.
2. We propose the GAM algorithm for recommending an itinerary comprising a series of POIs of a city and including as many mandatory POIs as possible within travel time budget.
3. The results show that GAM outperforms better than several baseline methods and achieves good recommendation performance in terms of the mandatory POIs, POIs visited, time budget (travel time and visit duration), and profit (POI popularity).

The remainder of this paper is organized as follows. Section 2 introduces related work. Section 3 describes the problem definition and genetic algorithm model. In Sect. 4, our experiments are presented. The results and discussion are discussing in Sect. 5. The last section summarizes conclusions.

2   Related Work

In this section, we present state-of-the-art methods in related areas of genetic algorithm, itinerary recommendation, POI recommendation, and the differences in our research with existing works.

2.1   Genetic Algorithm in Tourism

Genetic Algorithm (GA) has its origins from the imitations of natural evolution and genetics. It uses multistage processing, such as initialization, selection, crossover, and mutation to optimize the solution. In recent years, researchers have been applied the GA to recommendations in the tourism area [2–5]. The main objectives of these works are to find the optimal travel route comprising a set of POIs, while the GA uses the fitness function to select the best route. More formally, [3] studied the problem of user preferences to recommend a travel route. They estimated popular POIs where user has visited in the past by mining from the GPS trajectories. Then, the GA was used to model the interest of user for an unvisited place and improved the accuracy of the recommendation.

2.2 Itinerary Recommendation

Itinerary recommendation is a well-studied field that typically focuses on suggesting a sequence of POIs to visit. Most existing studies on itinerary recommendations focus on user interests within the given trip constraints towards the POIs [6,7]. Several research works apply itinerary recommendations in the field of Operations Research [8–10]. Most of these works are formulated as an Integer Linear Program based on the Orienteering problem and the traveling salesman problem variants using social media datasets. [9] studied the travel recommendation problem based on the Orienteering problem by proposing the PersTour model. First, user travel histories based on geo-tagged photos were extracted. Next, they used the first and last photos taken at each POI to sort POI visiting time and construct user travel sequence. At last, the PersTour algorithm with the characteristic of POIs, users' interest preferences and trip constraints were used to recommend personalized trip itinerary to users. There are also several real-life constraints like POI popularity [11], visit duration [12], travel time [13], queuing time [8], and photo frequency [9] to recommend itinerary recommendation systems.

2.3 POI Recommendation

In POI recommendation, the problem is to provide users with the suggestion of a set of popular and interesting places to users. The common recommendation techniques have been extensively studied such as content-based [14,15], collaborative [16,17], and hybrid approach [18,19]. One example in [18], the hybrid recommendation was proposed by merging content-based, collaborative, and knowledge-based techniques into a recommendation process for travel destinations to individuals and groups. The algorithm was based on the users' ratings, personal interests, and specific demands for the next destination.

2.4 Differences with Existing Works

We focus on interesting insights into the itinerary recommendation problems. Our proposed approach differs from the above existing works in several aspects. The current state-of-the-art itinerary recommendation approaches consider POIs with various trip constraints. These approaches do not consider mandatory POIs which are the actual place covering attractions, buildings, shopping malls, universities, transports, etc. In contrast, we propose an enhance itinerary recommendation system that considers mandatory POIs through these POIs with a specific starting and ending POI and additional constraints. So, the itinerary planning can be composed of a series of POIs including mandatory POIs within a certain time. We improve an itinerary recommendation by considering several aspects with the GA method to achieve better performance.

3   Problem Definition and Genetic Algorithm Model

In this section, we give the definitions used in our work and formulate the MandatoryTour problem, and a genetic algorithm is presented for dealing with this problem.

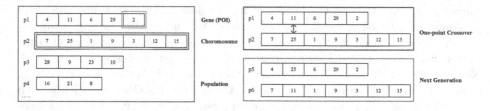

Fig. 1. An example of POI code and one-point crossover

3.1   Problem Definition

Our proposed MandatoryTour problem which recommend an itinerary with mandatory POIs is NP-hard. A shortcoming of traditional methods that use a brute-force approach is that the complexity of MandatoryTour is exponential, which is caused by the increasing of the number of POIs. The objective of this problem is to maximize the number of mandatory POIs, while keeping travel time between POIs and visit duration under a fixed time budget. The recommended itinerary includes a specified starting POI and ending POI.

This problem can be viewed as a directed graph $G = <N, E>$, where N is the set of nodes (or POIs) and E represents the set of edges. Each edge connecting node i to j has a profit, a travel time, and a visit duration, and can be represented as $f_{i,j}$, $t_{i,j}$, and $v_{i,j}$ respectively. The total time cost that includes travel time and visit duration between visited POIs for a tour is no more than the time budget T_{MAX} which limits how many POIs can be visited on the tour.

In this paper, an itinerary is defined as a path between specified starting POI and ending POI, and at least one other POI is contained. Note that all POIs in the itinerary can be visited only once, so sub-tours are excluded. Let $C = \{c_1, ..., c_L\}$ be the set of POIs, and $M = \{m_1, ..., m_K\}$ where $K < L$ be the set of mandatory POIs, ideally an itinerary with mandatory POIs can be described as $I = \{c_s, ..., m_1, ..., m_K, ...c_d\}$, where c_s is the starting POI and c_d is the destination POI and $c_s, c_d \notin M$.

Algorithm 1. GAM algorithm

Input: time budget σ,
        population size α,
        crossover rate β,
        mutation rate γ,
        iteration number δ
Output: best tour t
1: generate α individuals randomly as initially population set P
      TotalTimeCost$(p) \leq \sigma$ for each $p \in P$
2: **for** $i = 1$ **to** δ **do**
3:     **for** $j = 1$ **to** α **do**
4:         randomly select two individuals p_a and p_b from P
5:         generate p_c and p_d by one-point crossover to p_a and p_b under the crossover
    rate β
6:         save p_c and p_d to P_1
7:     **end for**
8:     **for** $j = 1$ **to** α **do**
9:         randomly select an individuals p_a from P_1
10:        randomly select a gene position from p_a and mutate it to generate a new
    individual p_a' under the mutation rate γ
11:        **if** TotalTimeCost$(p_a')> \sigma$ **then**
12:           update p_a' with a feasible tour by repairing p_a'
13:        **end if**
14:        update p_a with p_a' in P_1
15:     **end for**
16:     update $P = P_1$
17: **end for**
18: return the best tour t in P

3.2 Genetic Algorithm Model

In our genetic algorithm, P is the set of population, the set of genes of each individual p_i is represented using POIs directly, in terms of the IDs of POIs, and we encode them as shown in the left part of Fig. 1. An example of one-point crossover process is simply stated in the right part of Fig. 1.

In fact, MandatoryTour problem is a multi-objective optimize problem, and as it is difficult to design a fixed fitness score for every tour. Therefore, we optimize the objective function directly instead. By giving different priorities to the metrics used in Sect. 4, the objective function is defined as follows:

if the number of mandatory POIs in p_i has not been maximized

$$MaxF(p_x) = Max \sum_{i=1}^{|p_x|} \chi_{M(p_{x_i})}$$

where

$$\chi_{M(p_{x_i})} = \begin{cases} 1 & \text{if } p_{x_i} \in p_x \\ 0 & \text{otherwise} \end{cases}$$

if the above one has been maximized and the visit duration of p_i has not been maximized

$$MaxF(p_x) = Max \sum_{i=1}^{|p_x|-1} \sum_{j=2}^{|p_x|} v_{p_{x_i}, p_{x_j}}$$

if the above two have been maximized and the total profit of p_i has not been maximized

$$MaxF(p_x) = Max \sum_{i=1}^{|p_x|-1} \sum_{j=2}^{|p_x|} f_{p_{x_i}, p_{x_j}}$$

We use the one-point crossover in our proposed approach because of the relatively small data sets, and the probability $\beta = 0.8$. For other parameters, mutation rate $\gamma = 0.2$, time budget $\sigma \in \{300, 250, 600, 450, 350\}$ as it is different for each city, the population size $\alpha = 60$, the iteration number $\delta = 100$, and finally the best tour t is returned. The detailed optimization procedure is described in Algorithm 1.

4   Experiments

In this section, we describe our experiments, which include our datasets, baseline algorithms, evaluation metrics, and results and discussion.

4.1   Datasets

For our experiment and analysis, we use datasets from the Yahoo! Flickr Creative Commons 100M [1], which contains 100 million photos and videos. POIs with other details were collected from [10]. These geo-tagged photos were then mapped to a list of POIs based on their respective entries on cities in which the details refer to [9]. There are seven cities: Budapest, Edinburgh, Toronto, Vienna, Glasgow, Perth, and Osaka.

4.2   Baseline Algorithms

We compare our proposed GAM with several baseline algorithm to evaluate its recommendation performance.

1. **GA.** Generates an itinerary without mandatory POIs. The generated itinerary comprises a path starting at a specified POI and ending at another specified one where the total profit and visit duration are maximized, the cost is minimized, and the total travel time is limited by a given time budget. Note that mandatory POIs may be included in the itinerary, and we will show its result in the next section.

2. **GAM (our proposed model).** Generates an itinerary with mandatory POIs. This model is built upon the GA model using a similar objective function but adds mandatory POIs and the objective of maximizing the inclusion of the mandatory POIs. This model considers a general tour which generally includes popular or special POIs where tourists often want to visit.
3. **MaxM.** Generates an itinerary with a relatively large profit with mandatory POIs. Mandatory POIs are added first then the other POIs by allocating a large profit value to each POI using the greedy strategy. This approach provides a profit baseline for the Mandatory problem.
4. **GreedyM.** Generates an itinerary by adding the mandatory POIs first, then the remaining POIs. This is the simplest practical method to generate itineraries based on visiting mandatory POIs. As the tour focus on the mandatory POIs, a tour that has the most mandatory POIs within the time budget is preferred.

The algorithms used for this work were implemented using the C++ programming language.

4.3   Evaluation Metrics

We evaluate the performance of our algorithm and the baselines, which involves evaluating a specific starting and ending POI and additional constraints. The recommended itinerary contains the set of mandatory POIs or at least one of the mandatory POIs within a certain time based on travel cost budget and profit. Our algorithm utilizes evaluation metrics for the itinerary recommendation as follows:

1. **Mandatory POIs.** The set of mandatory POIs that are popular or special POIs in the recommended itinerary.
2. **POIs Visited.** The number of unique POIs that can be visited in the recommended itinerary.
3. **Time Budget.** The total time budgets both travel time and visit duration in the recommended itinerary. Hence, travel time is the time traveled from one POI to another POI while visit duration is the time visited in each POI.
4. **Profit.** The total profits of all POIs in the recommended itinerary.

4.4   Results and Discussion

In this section, we present and discuss the experimental results in term of mandatory POIs, POIs visited, time budget (travel time and visit duration), and profit (POI popularity). In addition, we considered four mandatory POI sets including one POI, two POIs, three POIs, and four POIs respectively, and they are randomly selected from the whole POI set.

Number of Mandatory POIs of Recommended Tours. The GA algorithm without mandatory POIs is the basis for comparisons with other algorithms, and

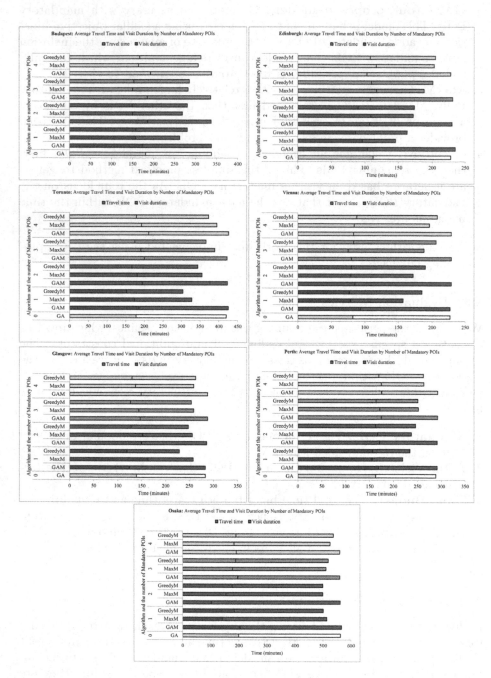

Fig. 2. Average travel time and visit duration by number of mandatory POIs for each city.

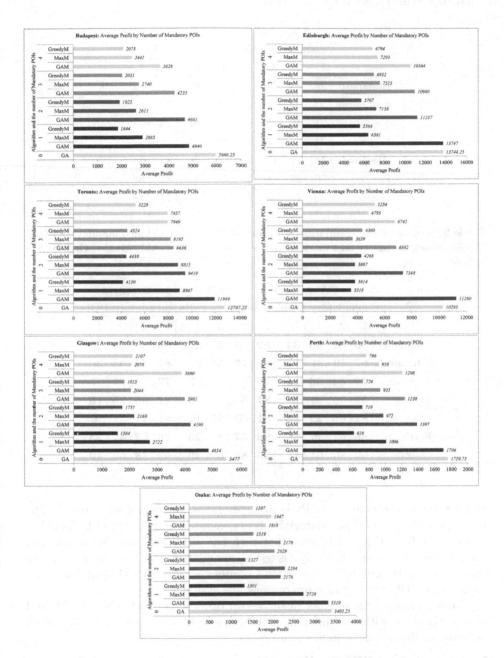

Fig. 3. Average profit by number of mandatory POIs for each city.

Table 1. Number of GA itineraries (out of 100) which visited all or at least one mandatory POIs. Higher values are better.

City	Visited all mandatory POIs				Visited at least one mandatory POIs			
	1	2	3	4	1	2	3	4
Budapest	28	13	1	1	28	65	77	82
Edinburgh	53	22	8	3	53	69	78	86
Toronto	31	18	7	1	31	67	73	88
Vienna	34	5	5	1	34	53	68	77
Glasgow	43	22	12	5	43	68	82	89
Perth	50	20	8	5	50	67	81	88
Osaka	48	15	5	1	48	65	78	88

Table 2. Number of successful itineraries (out of 100) which included mandatory POIs. Higher values are better and the best performance among GAM, MaxM, GreedyM is in bold.

City	GAM mandatory POIs				MaxM mandatory POIs				GreedyM mandatory POIs			
	1	2	3	4	1	2	3	4	1	2	3	4
Budapest	**89**	**81**	**49**	**34**	**89**	78	45	27	**89**	78	45	27
Edinburgh	**87**	50	31	15	**87**	**75**	**58**	**36**	**87**	**75**	**58**	**36**
Toronto	**77**	**54**	**36**	**14**	**77**	50	29	7	**77**	50	29	7
Vienna	**87**	56	23	10	**87**	**65**	**39**	**18**	**87**	**65**	**39**	**18**
Glasgow	**81**	**66**	**42**	**22**	**81**	60	37	16	**81**	60	37	16
Perth	**86**	63	46	21	**86**	**67**	**47**	**23**	**86**	**67**	**47**	**23**
Osaka	**99**	86	64	31	**99**	**88**	**69**	**49**	**99**	**88**	**69**	**49**

visiting any of the mandatory POIs in a generated tour is not guaranteed. The result of the inclusion of mandatory POIs of generated tours by the GA algorithm is shown in Table 1. It can be seen that with the increase of mandatory set size, the number of tours successfully visited all mandatory POIs in the mandatory sets is decreased rapidly, however, the number of tours visiting at least one mandatory POI move up as more options are available.

Table 2 presents the number of successful tours found by GAM, MaxM, and GreedyM, along with the different mandatory POI sets. The GAM algorithm achieves moderate performance in all cities.

Number of Total POIs Visited of Recommended Tours. Table 3 presents the average number of total POIs visited every algorithm's generated tours. Overall, GAM has the best performance among all algorithms over all the cities. Specifically, for the GAM algorithm, the mandatory POI set of four including

Table 3. Average number of POIs visited including failed itineraries by algorithm, mandatory POIs set size and city. Higher values are better and the best performance among GAM, MaxM, GreedyM is in bold.

City	GA	GAM mandatory POIs				MaxM mandatory POIs				GreedyM mandatory POIs			
		1	2	3	4	1	2	3	4	1	2	3	4
Budapest	12.82	**10.3**	**10.1**	**9.4**	**8.4**	4.3	4.6	5.1	5.3	4.6	4.8	5.2	5.4
Edinburgh	12.57	**12.7**	**10.4**	**10.2**	**9.8**	3.8	4.5	5.1	5.5	5.3	5.6	5.9	6.2
Toronto	12.02	**9.8**	**10.1**	**9.2**	**8.4**	4.5	4.9	5.2	5.3	4.1	4.3	4.6	4.9
Vienna	10.62	**10.4**	**7.9**	**7.6**	**7.2**	3.1	3.8	4.3	4.7	4.2	4.7	5.0	5.2
Glasgow	12.42	**10.4**	**10.0**	**9.5**	**9.1**	4.3	4.3	4.6	4.8	4.3	4.6	4.8	5.1
Perth	10.82	**10.2**	**8.9**	**8.3**	**8.2**	4.5	4.8	5.1	5.4	4.6	4.9	5.1	5.5
Osaka	10.75	**11.2**	**7.8**	**7.3**	**7.0**	5.2	5.3	5.6	5.9	5.7	5.5	5.8	6.0

more POIs than smaller mandatory sets, but for MaxM and GreedyM, they see a decline along with the increase of the mandatory POI set size. This is reasonable because of the mandatory POIs may limit the MaxM and Greedy algorithms' performance in the metric of average number POIs visited.

Travel Time and Visit Duration of Recommended Tours. From Fig. 2, we can see that the total travel time for the itineraries generated by all methods was never exceeded, and the GAM uses the time budget efficiently in all seven cities, in the meanwhile, the visit duration also utilized better, and GA has the similar results with GAM. In contrast, the GreedyM often comes the last about allocating the time budget, and MaxM's performance just above GreedyM.

Total Profit of Recommended Tours. The results of the average profit of recommended tours are shown in Fig. 3. It is clear that the GA algorithm gets the highest profit in almost every city as there are no extra constraints except the time budget, and the GAM comes the second. In addition, the reason why the MaxM algorithm does not achieve the best performance is that the greedy strategy limits it to generate a tour with the optimal solution.

5   Conclusions

In this paper, we formulated the kind of itinerary planning as MandatoryTour problem, which comprised a series of POIs of a city and including mandatory POIs within travel time budget. The mandatory POIs can be termed as the most popular and special POIs. We then solved this MandatoryTour problem by a generic algorithm and we proposed this approach as the GAM algorithm. We also used real-world datasets which are derived from the Yahoo Flickr Creative Commons 100 Million Dataset (YFCC100M), which include POI visits of seven touristic cities. Compared with several baselines GA, MaxM, and GreedyM,

GAM achieved better recommendation performance in terms of the mandatory POIs, POIs visited, time budget (travel time and visit duration), and profit (POI popularity).

Acknowledgements. This work was supported in part by the Natural Science Foundation of China (Nos. U1711263, U1811264, 61966009), and in part by the Natural Science Foundation of Guangxi Province (No. 2018GXNSFDA281045).

References

1. Thomee, B., et al.: YFCC100M: the new data in multimedia research. Commun. ACM **59**(2), 64–73 (2016)
2. Hang, L., Kang, S., Jin, W., Kim, D.: Design and implementation of an optimal travel route recommender system on big data for tourists in Jeju. Processes **6**(8), 133 (2018)
3. Ke, C., Wu, M., Ho, W., Lai, S., Huang, L.: Intelligent point-of-interest recommendation for tourism planning via density based clustering and genetic algorithm. In: PACIS (2018)
4. Sun, X., Wang, J., Wu, W., Liu, W.: Genetic algorithm for optimizing routing design and fleet allocation of freeway service overlapping patrol. Sustainability **10**(11), 4120 (2018)
5. Tiwari, S., Kaushik, S.: Modeling personalized recommendations of unvisited tourist places using genetic algorithms. In: Chu, W., Kikuchi, S., Bhalla, S. (eds.) DNIS 2015. LNCS, vol. 8999, pp. 264–276. Springer, Cham (2015). https://doi.org/10.1007/978-3-319-16313-0_20
6. Corsar, D., Edwards, P., Nelson, J., Baillie, C., Papangelis, K., Velaga, N.: Linking open data and the crowd for real-time passenger information. J. Web Semant. **43**, 18–24 (2017)
7. Sylejmani, K., Dorn, J., Musliu, N.: Planning the trip itinerary for tourist groups. Inf. Technol. Tourism **17**(3), 275–314 (2017). https://doi.org/10.1007/s40558-017-0080-9
8. Lim, K., Chan, J., Karunasekera, S., Leckie, C.: Personalized itinerary recommendation with queuing time awareness. In: Proceedings of the 40th International ACM SIGIR Conference on Research and Development in Information Retrieval. Association for Computing Machinery, pp. 325–334 (2017)
9. Lim, K.H., Chan, J., Leckie, C., Karunasekera, S.: Personalized trip recommendation for tourists based on user interests, points of interest visit durations and visit recency. Knowl. Inf. Syst. **54**(2), 375–406 (2017). https://doi.org/10.1007/s10115-017-1056-y
10. Taylor, K., Lim, K., Chan, J.: Travel itinerary recommendations with must-see points-of-interest. In: Companion Proceedings of the The Web Conference 2018. International World Wide Web Conferences Steering Committee, Republic and Canton of Geneva, CHE, pp. 1198–1205 (2019)
11. Wang, X., Leckie, C., Chan, J., Lim, K., Vaithianathan, T.: Improving personalized trip recommendation by avoiding crowds. In: Proceedings of the 25th ACM International on Conference on Information and Knowledge Management. Association for Computing Machinery, pp. 25–34 (2016)
12. Cai, G., Lee, K., Lee, I.: Itinerary recommender system with semantic trajectory pattern mining from geo-tagged photos. Expert Syst. Appl. **94**, 32–40 (2018)

13. Zhang, Y., Tang, J.: Itinerary planning with time budget for risk-averse travelers. Eur. J. Oper. Res. **267**(1), 288–303 (2018)
14. Binucci, C., Luca, F., Giacomo, E., Liotta, G., Montecchiani, F.: Designing the content analyzer of a travel recommender system. Expert Syst. Appl. **87**, 199–208 (2017)
15. Laß, C., Herzog, D., Wörndl, W.: Context-aware tourist trip recommendations. In: RecTour@RecSys (2017)
16. Wang, H., Wang, N., Yeung, D.: Collaborative deep learning for recommender systems. In: Proceedings of the 21th ACM SIGKDD International Conference on Knowledge Discovery and Data Mining, pp. 1235–1244 (2015)
17. Yang, C., Bai, L., Zhang, C., Yuan, Q., Han, J.: Bridging collaborative filtering and semi-supervised learning: a neural approach for POI recommendation. In: Proceedings of the 23rd ACM SIGKDD International Conference on Knowledge Discovery and Data Mining, pp. 1245–1254 (2017)
18. Al-hassan, M., Lu, H., Lu, J.: A semantic enhanced hybrid recommendation approach: a case study of e-government tourism service recommendation system. Decis. Support Syst. **72**, 97–109 (2015)
19. Kefalas, P., Symeonidis, P., Manolopoulos, Y.: Recommendations based on a heterogeneous spatio-temporal social network. World Wide Web **21**(2), 345–371 (2017). https://doi.org/10.1007/s11280-017-0454-0

Social Computing

Stochastic Blockmodels Meets Overlapping Community Detection

Qiqi Zhao[1], Huifang Ma[1,2(✉)], Zhixin Li[2], and Lijun Guo[3]

[1] Northwest Normal University, Lanzhou 730070, Gansu, China
zhaoqiqi@nwnu.edu.cn
[2] Guangxi Key Lab of Multi-Source Information Mining and Security,
Guangxi Normal University, Guilin 541004, Guangxi, China
mahuifang@yeah.net, lizx@gxnu.edu.cn
[3] College of Information Science and Engineering, Ningbo University,
Ningbo 315000, Zhejiang, China
guolijun@nbu.edu.cn

Abstract. It turns out that the Stochastic Blockmodel (SBM) and its variants can successfully accomplish a variety of tasks, such as discovering community structures. Note that the main limitations are inferencing high time complexity and poor scalability. Our effort is motivated by the goal of harnessing their complementary strengths to develop a scalability SBM for graphs, that also enjoys an efficient inference process and discovery interpretable communities. Unlike traditional SBM that each node is assumed to belong to just one block, we wish to use the node importance to also infer the community membership(s) of each node (as it is one of the goals of SBMs). To this end, we propose a multi-stage maximum likelihood strategy for inferring the latent parameters of adapting the Stochastic Blockmodels to Overlapping Community Detection (OCD-SBM). The intuitive properties to build the model, is more in line with the real-world network to reveal the hidden community structural characteristics. Particularly, this enables inference of not just the node's membership into communities, but the strength of the membership in each of the communities the node belongs to. Experiments conducted on various datasets verify the effectiveness of our model.

Keywords: Overlapping community detection · Stochastic Blockmodels · Maximum likelihood

1 Introduction

Studies show that classical network modeling statistical models have been explored for decades. Such real-world networks contain omnipresent features to reflect small world phenomena, overlapping clusters or community structures [1, 2]. Additionally, a crowd of the recent works have focused on recomposing classical statistical models to boost the performance of model statistical inference [3–5].

In order to partition the graph such that nodes within each group are structurally equivalent and/or tightly connected, statistical and/or probabilistic methods are typically used to partition the graph structure. Among them, stochastic blockmodel

© IFIP International Federation for Information Processing 2020
Published by Springer Nature Switzerland AG 2020
Z. Shi et al. (Eds.): IIP 2020, IFIP AICT 581, pp. 149–159, 2020.
https://doi.org/10.1007/978-3-030-46931-3_14

(SBM) is one prominent model for such purposes. Suppose that each node belongs to only one of the K groups is the simplest form of SBMs. Then the goal of the statistical learning is to infer the probability of connection between these unobserved groups and groups based on the observable edges of the entire graph [6–8]. Due to its computational flexibility and structural interpretation, SBM and its extensions have been popularizing in a variety of network analysis tasks.

Non-overlapping. Recent years have seen work on SBM implementations for non-overlapping community detection algorithm [9, 10]. These methods have the same assumption that nodes in the network can only be assigned to one cluster, and the possibility of existence of edges between pairs of nodes depends only on the cluster to which they belong. Snijders [5] first present method of revealing such a cluster structure using posteriori information. The approach named ML-SBM [11] is to use SBM to develop a scalable non-overlapping community detection method on large graphs, which simply based on multi-stage MLE approach to learn latent parameters.

Overlapping. In their seminal work, Airoldi [12] proposes the first mixture-based model with overlapping communities and successfully applied to the real networks. This model, called the Mixed-Member Stochastic Blockmodel (MMSBM), is an adaptation of earlier mixed membership models [13] to the context of networks. Latouche et al. [14] propose another extension of the SBM to overlapping classes, called Overlapping Stochastic Blockmodel (OSBM). The main difference between OSBM and MMSB is that the latent classes are no longer drawn from the multinomial distributions but from a product of the Bernoulli distribution.

In general, comparing to many non-attribute community detection methods, ML_SBM [11] method is based on SBM to effectively infer and learn model parameters for community detection tasks, and this algorithm performs well on most networks compared to most existing methods. It is worth noting that our work is a significant extension of ML_SBM. Yet, we consider not only learning and inferring the model latent parameters, but also introducing the importance of intuitive attributes and instinct consistent with real-world network features in overlapping community detection tasks.

In this paper, an overlapping community detection approach based on SBM, i.e. adapting the Stochastic Blockmodels to Overlapping Community Detection (OCD-SBM), is proposed to conquer the limitation of high time complexity and poor scalability of SBM. Our model explicitly encodes the importance of overlapping nodes characteristic, and thus is capable to correct the bias caused by statistical inference in the traditional SBM. In summary, the contributions of this paper are as follows:

(1) We develop a fast algorithm that uses an SBM to adjust overlapping community detection in the undirected graph to address the limitations of existing algorithms of high-time complexity and scalability of large-scale networks. Contrary to other community detection methods, we use the SBM generation model to mine better clustering results in the network to preserve the characteristics of the real network.

(2) Different from the rules of establishing edge between two nodes using simple SBM, we not only consider the strength of the connection between the communities, but also the importance of nodes-to-communities. To this end, we model a method of detecting large-scale overlapping community structures in the real

world via introducing the importance of intuitive attributes and instincts consistent with real-world network features in overlapping community detection tasks.

(3) Various verification experiments performed on synthetic datasets and real-world datasets with ground-truth show that this is a new possibility to combine the advances in overlapping community detection and SBMs to broaden the understanding of organizing principles of complex networks.

The rest of this paper is organized as follows. Section 2 introduces the motivation and framework of our proposed model. Section 3 describes the inference algorithms in OCD-SBM. We describe the experimental results of simulations in Sect. 4. Section 5 concludes this paper.

2   Preliminaries

2.1   Motivation

Notation. Consider an undirected graph $G = (V, E)$, where V is the node set of size $N = |V|$, and E is the edge list of size $M = |E|$. The corresponding $N \times N$ adjacency matrix is denoted by $\mathbf{A}$, where $A_{ij} = 1$ when there is an undirected and unweighted edge for the dyad (i, j), $A_{ij} = 0$ otherwise. Let matrix $\mathbf{Z} \in [0,1]^{N \times K}$. the importance of a node is different to K blocks, where Z_{ij} represents the importance of node i for j block. And each node must subject to $\sum_{j=1}^{K} Z_{ij} = 1$. Let matrix $\mathbf{B} \in [0,1]^{K \times K}$, suggesting the probability of connection between the parameterized blocks, i.e., a node from cluster r is connected to a node from cluster s. If $r = s$, B_{rs} represents the probability of a connection within the block. The stochastic blockmodel is a special type of probability distribution over the space of adjacency arrays.

We then define the probability matrix $\theta = \mathbf{ZBZ}^T$ using matrices $\mathbf{B}$ and $\mathbf{Z}$. From the following model, the adjacency matrix $\mathbf{A}$ of a sample network can then be generated:

$$P(A_{ij}) = \begin{cases} \theta_{ij}, & if\ A_{ij} = 1 \\ 1 - \theta_{ij}, & if\ A_{ij} = 0 \end{cases} \tag{1}$$

for $i, j \in \{1, 2,...,N\}$ and $i \neq j$, indicating that A_{ij} is a sample from the Bernoulli distribution with success rate θ_{ij}.

Usually in practice, the adjacency matrix $\mathbf{A}$ can be observed from the network data set. The main purpose is to ultimately estimate $\mathbf{Z}$, i.e. the block labels.

Motivation. Our motivation for proposing the overlapping version of SBM, i.e. OCD-SBM, comes from following intuitive properties:

(1) If a node is important to a community, there are edges with most nodes in the community.

(2) The connection between node i and j is affected by the connection between the community that i and j belongs to respectively, in addition to their own importance of the community they exist.

(3) Communities can overlap, as individual nodes may belong to multiple communities.
(4) If two nodes are important to multiple public communities, they are more likely to belong to the same community. (i.e., overlapping communities are more intensive).

Our ultimate goal is to capture the following three instincts that conform to the assumptions of real-world network characteristics:

(1) the possibility that a node community membership affects whether a pair of nodes are linked,
(2) the extent of the impact (probability of node connections belonging to the same community) depends on community that node belongs to, and
(3) the connection probability is independently influencing each community.

For special probability statistical models, the maximum likelihood estimation (MLE) is a setting that maximizes the parameters of likelihood function.

As defining in Eq. (1), if only $\mathbf{A}$ is given, the log-likelihood function is

$$H_1(B, Z|A) = \sum_{i \neq j} \log P(A_{ij}) = \sum_{i \neq j} \log[(1 - A_{ij}) + (2A_{ij} - 1)\theta_{ij}] \tag{2}$$

For large graphs, directly maximizing this likelihood function with traditional optimization methods takes too much time since there are at least N^2K unknown variables to estimate.

2.2   Framework

Figure 1 clarifies the proposed generative model. Rectangle (A_{ij}) is an entry of the observed network adjacency matrix $\mathbf{A}$. Circles denote two latent variables: node importance strength $\mathbf{Z}$ and probability of connection $\mathbf{B}$. In the following section, we will reveal how to estimate community memberships from node connections of the network structure (i.e., how to infer $\mathbf{W}$ from $\mathbf{Z}$ and $\mathbf{B}$).

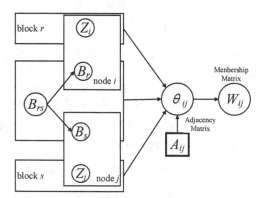

Fig. 1. Plate representation of OCD-SBM. θ_{ij}: Probability that $A_{ij} = 1$; Z_i: Importance strength of node i to block r; Z_j: Importance strength of node j to block s; B_{rs}: the probability of connections to block r and s; W_{ij}: the project of overlapping membership node matrix.

Note that the above probability model generative process satisfies our three aforementioned requests. The network edges are created due to the importance of node-to-block (Request (1)). Furthermore, each membership W_{ij} of a node i is regarded as an independent variable to allow a node to belong to multiple blocks simultaneously (Request (2)). This is in stark contrast to 'soft-membership' models, setting constraints $\sum_{j=1}^{K} W_{ij} = 1$ so that W_{ij} is a probability that a node i belongs to a particular block. Finally, because each block r generates connections between its members independently, nodes belonging to multiple common blocks have a higher probability of connection than that they share just a single community (Request (3)).

3   Method

3.1   Algorithm and Complexity Analysis

Our method is summarized in Algorithm 1. Our algorithm has the following advantages:

(1) **Interpretable Method.** Adapting the SBMs to overlapping community detection, we conquer the limitation of non-interpretable community detection.
(2) **Membership Strength.** In particular, this enables inference of not just the node's membership into communities, but also the strength of the membership in each of the communities the node belongs to.
(3) **More realistic.** Intuitive observations consistent with real network characteristics are proposed to quantify the importance of nodes to the community, which make sense actually.

Algorithm 1.Inference for OCD-SBM

Input: Initialization for model parameters matrixes **B**, $\mathbf{Z}^{(t)}$ into many tiny communities, $\mathbf{Z}^{(t-1)}$ = $\mathbf{Z}^{(t)}$, membership matrix **W**, membership threshold ε, the number of communities K, stop criterion δ.

Output: Learned model parameters **Z**, **B**, cluster structure **W**.

1. Compute variational likelihood H_{new} by (5)
2. **repeat**
3. $H_{old} = H_{new}$
4.   **inference Z, B**
5.   randomly set community number to K
6. **repeat**
7.   **for** $i = 1: N$ do
8.   compute $N^{(d)}$ for node i
9.   update Z_{ij} by block coordinate descent method via (7)
10. $Z_{ij}^{(t-1)} = Z_{ij}^{(t)}$
11.   **update** $N^{(c)}$
12. **end for**
13. **update B** via (6)
14. **determine overlapping community membership**
15. update **W** via (8)
16. Compute variational likelihood H_{new} with updated parameters by (5)
17. **until** $| H_{new} - H_{old} | < \delta$

The time complexity for each updating is $O(NK^2)$. However, if we only consider the pairs of communities that have at least one edge between them, time complexity becomes $O(M)$. Community updating runs at the end of each stage after updating $\mathbf{Z}$ and $\mathbf{B}$. The overall time cost of the algorithm is $O(tNK^2 + M)$.

3.2   Parameter Inference

The ultimate aim is to maximize the model posterior given the observations. To speed up the inferring process, a fast algorithm is proposed, which updates $\mathbf{B}$ and $\mathbf{Z}$ in turn in order to maximize the objective function $H_1(\mathbf{B},\mathbf{Z}|\mathbf{W})$, and uses a two-stage updating framework to deal with the global optimum solution approach. Given $\mathbf{A}$, MLE for $(\mathbf{B}; \mathbf{Z})$ can be defined as

$$\underset{0 \le B, Z \le 1}{\arg\max} \; \{ H_1(B,Z|A) = \sum_{i \ne j} \log[(1 - A_{ij}) + (2A_{ij} - 1)\theta_{ij}]$$

$$= \sum_{i \ne j} \log[(1 - A_{ij}) + (2A_{ij} - 1) \frac{\sum_{m=1}^{K} \sum_{n=1}^{K} Z_{in} B_{nm} Z_{jm}^T}{\sum_{j=1}^{N} (\sum_{m=1}^{K} \sum_{n=1}^{K} Z_{in} B_{nm} Z_{jm}^T)} \} \tag{3}$$

subject to $\sum_{j=1}^{K} Z_{ij} = 1$. We solve the above optimization problem by alternatively updating $\mathbf{B}$ and $\mathbf{Z}$.

As we can see that the form of θ_{ij} is too complicated for the process of maximization. In addition, maximizing the objective function is to solve a relatively apposite value not an exact value. Therefore, we rewrite Eq. (3) as the truly function of maximum likelihood:

$$\underset{0 \le B, Z \le 1}{\arg\max} \; \{ H_1(B,Z|A) = \sum_{i \ne j} \log[(1 - A_{ij}) + (2A_{ij} - 1)\theta'_{ij}]$$

$$= \sum_{i \ne j} \log[(1 - A_{ij}) + (2A_{ij} - 1) \sum_{m=1}^{K} \sum_{n=1}^{K} Z_{in} B_{nm} Z_{jm}^T] \} \tag{4}$$

Such,

$$H(B,Z|A) = \sum_{i \ne j} \log[(1 - A_{ij}) + (2A_{ij} - 1)\theta'_{ij}] \tag{5}$$

where $\theta'_{ij} = \sum_{m=1}^{K} \sum_{n=1}^{K} Z_{in} B_{nm} Z_{jm}^T$. Next we use the Optimization Strategy to update matrices $\mathbf{Z}$ and $\mathbf{B}$ in turn. When $\mathbf{Z}$ is fixed and $\mathbf{B}$ is considered as unknown, $\mathbf{B}$ is updated Gradient descent method, we have the updating strategy for elements in matrix $\mathbf{B}$

$$B_{rs} = \frac{E}{(E + \hat{E}) \sum_{m=1}^{K} \sum_{n=1}^{K} Z_{nr} Z_{ms}^T} \tag{6}$$

When $\mathbf{B}$ is fixed, $\mathbf{Z}$ is updated row by row utilizing the block coordinate descent method. The updating strategy for elements in matrix $\mathbf{Z}$ can be written as Eq. (7) to reduce time complexity, Z_{ij} is defined as:

$$Z_{ij} = \sum\nolimits_{j=1}^{K} [B_{ij}^{N_k^{(d)}} (1 - B_{ij})^{N_k^{(c)} - N_k^{(d)}}] \tag{7}$$

where $N^{(c)} \in R^K$, the entries are the number of nodes in each community, and $N^{(d)}$ is defined as the vector with the number of nodes connected to node i in each community.

Due to space limitations, we have omitted relevant proof.

3.3 Determine Community Membership

After learning $\mathbf{Z}$, the ultimate goal is to determine whether node i belongs to block j. To achieve this, if Z_{ij} is below a threshold β, it can be considered that node i does not belong to block j. Otherwise $(Z_{ij} > \beta)$, it can be regard i as belonging j. Specifically, let community membership matrix $W \in \{0,1\}^{N \times K}$, where W_{ij} indicates that node i belongs to j block.

$$P(Z_{ir}) = \begin{cases} W_{ij} = 1, & \text{if } Z_{ij} \geq \beta \\ W_{ij} = 0, & \text{if } Z_{ij} < \beta \end{cases} \tag{8}$$

Solving this inequality, let $\beta = \sqrt{-\log(1 - \varepsilon)}$. For all our experiments we set $\varepsilon \approx 10^{-8}$. It is worth noting that other values of β are also tested in practice, but the above-mentioned β setting provides overall good performance.

4 Empirical Study

In this section, we empirically evaluate our method with the aim of answering the following research questions:

- RQ1: How does OCD-SBM perform as compared with state-of-the-art community detection methods?
- RQ2: How does the overlapping community detection benefit from the importance of node-to-block assignment?

4.1 Experiments Settings

Datasets. Experiments are conducted on synthetic networks and several well-studied real-world datasets[1] (Table 1) with ground-truth community information to verify the effectiveness and efficiency. To be more objective and fairer, the results on the synthetic networks are omitted in experimental part.

---

[1] Networks are available at http://snap.stanford.edu and http://www.voidcn.com/article/p-plritjbe-rv.html.

Evaluation Metrics. For evaluation purposes, we use the metrics, Avg F1 [7] and Avg NMI [14], to quantify the degree of correspondence between the detected community and the ground truth community. In view of an agreement between the ground-truth community $C*$ and the detected community C, we adopt two evaluation procedures previously used in [7, 14] to quantify performance.

Baselines for Comparison. Experiments are conducted on various networks to demonstrate the effectiveness, and we compare OCD-SBM with following community detection algorithms:

MMSBM [13]: This is a dynamic model-based approach and it is a state-of-the-art overlapping community detection method using SBM.

BIGCLAM [7]: The method is an optimization-based method for overlapping community detection approach that scales to large networks of millions of nodes and edges.

ML_SBM [11]: This is a multi-stage maximum likelihood approach to recover the latent parameters based SBM for non-overlapping community detection.

CD-SBM: In order to further explore the benefit of node-to-community assignment to overlapping community detection methods, we denote CD-SBM as the variant method of CD-SBM as we do not perform step 15 in algorithm 1 thus each row of $\mathbf{Z}$ contains only one nonzero entry.

Table 1. Real-world network datasets statistics. N: number of nodes, E: number of edges, C: number of communities, S: average community size, A: community memberships per node. On average 95% of all communities overlap with at least one other community.

Datasets	Description	N	E	C	S	A
Youtube	Youtube online social network	1,134,890	2,987,624	8,385	26.72	0.33
Friendster	Friendster online social network	65,608,366	1,806,067,135	957,154	9.75	0.26
DBLP	DBLP collaboration network	317,080	1,049,866	13,477	429.79	2.57
Amazon	Amazon product network	334,863	925,872	75,149	99.86	14.83
Polblogs	political blog network	1,490	19,090	2	745	1

4.2 Performance Comparison (RQ1)

To answer (RQ1), we start by comparing the performance of all the methods, and then explore how the modeling of community membership improves on synthetic datasets and real-world networks.

Results of Real-Word Networks. We conduct experiment on each dataset 500 times, comparing the average NMI with three different community detection methods. Jointly analyzing Fig. 2, we have the following observations:

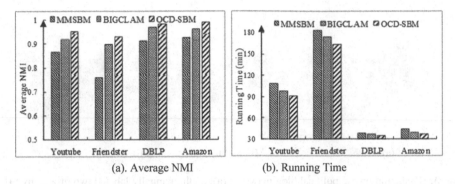

(a). Average NMI   (b). Running Time

Fig. 2. Performance evaluation for networks on Avg NMI and running time.

MMSBM: Although MMSBM can detect overlapping communities, the performance of this method is the worst among comparison methods in large networks. It may be that MMSBM is not suitable for large-scale community structures when dynamically updating community assignments.

BIGCLAM: BIGCLAM and OCD-SBM maintain high average NMI value on four datasets. However, BIGCLAM cannot correctly extract overlapping communities in the network because the BIGCLAM method implicitly assumes overlapping sparse connections between communities.

OCD-SBM: OCD-SBM performs best on four real-world networks. The reason for this may be to adopt a multi-stage maximum likelihood estimation method, which uses an important definition of nodes-to-community to accurately detect overlapping communities that are highly similar to the benchmark. OCD-SBM nearly perfectly reveals the hidden structure of the overlapping network.

4.3 Study of OCD-SBM (RQ2)

In this section, we attempt to understand how the overlapping community detection benefit from the importance of node-to-block assignment (RQ3). We observe how their representations are influenced w.r.t. the depth of OCD-SBM on political blog network. The performance evaluation of ML_SBM and CD-SBM is shown in Table 2. We have the following findings:

(a) Although the ML_SBM method can reveal the community structure, our method shows outstanding performance results in terms of NMI value and running time.

(b) Comparing the performance and clustering structure of ML_SBM and CD-SBM methods. This is consistent with the intuition that two parties have a few significant overlapping blogs of over a hundred links and the rest of the blogs with clearly connections membership. Obviously, the CD-SBM method outperforms the ML_SBM method for nonoverlapping community detection. This is verified via their clustering accuracies reported in Fig. 3.

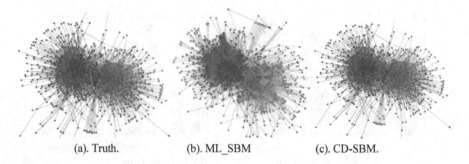

(a). Truth.   (b). ML_SBM   (c). CD-SBM.

Fig. 3. Prediction on the political blog network: (a) Truth, manually labeled two groups by [4]. (b) ML_SBM. (c) CD-SBM. Red represents the Liberal Party cluster; green represents the Democratic Party and yellow represents the overlap. (Color figure online)

Table 2. Performance evaluation of political blog networks: ML_SBM and CD-SBM.

Grade	ML_SBM		CD-SBM	
	0	1	0	1
Cluster result	727	743	754	736
Running time (min)	43.5		36.6	
Avg NMI	0. 9432		0.9855	

In short, even though both methods use the MLE to update community assignment parameters, the OCD-SBM approach integrates node-to-community importance into the optimization process of maximal community assignment parameters, which makes the detection community more accurate and meets real-world networks characteristics.

5   Conclusions

In this paper, we propose a fast overlapping community detection algorithm, OCD-SBM, to uses an SBM to perform on undirected graph. Intuitive observations consistent with real network characteristics are proposed to quantify the importance of nodes to the community. Combining the overlapping intuitions, we adapt SBM to overlapping community detection tasks. Our model explicitly encodes the importance of overlapping node features and is therefore able to correct for deviations caused by statistical inference in traditional SBM. OCD-SBM broadens our understanding of the organization of complex social networks and opens up new possibilities to combine community detection with advances in SBMs.

Acknowledgement. This work is supported by the National Natural Science Foundation of China (61762078, 61363058, 61966004), Ningbo Municipal Natural Science Foundation of China (No. 2018A610057), Major project of young teachers' scientific research ability promotion plan (NWNU-LKQN2019-2) and Research Fund of Guangxi Key Lab of Multi-source Information Mining and Security (MIMS18-08).

References

1. Chang, H., Feng, Z., Ren, Z.: Community detection using dual representation chemical reaction optimization. IEEE Trans. Cybern. **47**(12), 4328–4341 (2017)
2. Yang, L., Cao, X.: A unified semi supervised community detection framework using latent space graph regularization. IEEE Trans. Cybern. **45**(11), 2585–2598 (2015)
3. Qiao, M., Yu, J., Bian, W., et al.: Adapting stochastic block models to power-law degree distributions. IEEE Trans. Cybern. **49**(2), 1–12 (2018)
4. Goldenberg, A., Zheng, A.X., Fienberg, S.E., et al.: A survey of statistical network models. Found. Trends® Mach. Learn. **2**(2), 129–233 (2010)
5. Chen, J., Xu, G., Wang, Y., et al.: Community detection in networks based on modified pagerank and stochastic block model. IEEE Access **6**, 77133–77144 (2018)
6. Lee, Clement, Wilkinson, Darren J.: A review of stochastic block models and extensions for graph clustering. Appl. Netw. Sci. **4**(1), 1–50 (2019). https://doi.org/10.1007/s41109-019-0232-2
7. Yang, J., Leskovec, J.: Overlapping community detection at scale: a nonnegative matrix factorization approach. In: Proceedings of the sixth ACM International Conference on Web Search and Data Mining. ACM (2013)
8. Ahn, Y.Y., Bagrow, J.P., Lehmann, S.: Link communities reveal multi-scale complexity in networks. Nature **466**, 761–764 (2010)
9. Cherifi, H.: Non-overlapping community detection (2018). arXiv:1805.11584
10. Boccaletti, S., Latora, V., Moreno, Y., Chavez, M.: Complex networks: structure and dynamics. Phys. Rev. **424**, 175–308 (2006)
11. Peng, C., Zhang, Z., et al.: A scalable community detection algorithm for large graphs using stochastic block models. Intell. Data Anal. **21**(6), 1463–1485 (2017)
12. Airoldi, E.M., Blei, D.M., Fienberg, S.E., Xing, E.P.: Mixed membership stochastic blockmodels. J. Mach. Learn. Res. **9**, 1981–2014 (2005)
13. Griffiths, T., Ghahramani, Z.: Infinite latent feature models and the Indian buffet process. Neural Inf. Process. Syst. **18**, 475–482 (2005)
14. Latouche, P., Birmele, E., Ambroise, C.: Overlapping stochastic block models with application to the French political blogosphere. Ann. Appl. Stat. **5**(1), 309–336 (2011)

Overlapping Community Detection Combining Topological Potential and Trust Value of Nodes

Xiaohong Li[1(✉)], Weiying Kong[1], Weiyi Wei[1], Enli Fu[2], and Huifang Ma[1]

[1] College of Computer Science and Engineering, Northwest Normal University, Lanzhou, China
xiaohongli@nwnu.edu.cn
[2] School of Information Science and Engineering, Lanzhou University, Lanzhou, China
2384371518@qq.com

Abstract. Aiming at the problems of existing algorithms, such as instability, neglecting interaction between nodes and neglecting attributes of node, an overlapping community discovery algorithm combining topological potential and trust value of nodes was proposed. Firstly, the importance of nodes is calculated according to topological potential and the trust value of the node, and then K core nodes are selected. In final, the final division of communities are finished by using the extended modularity and core nodes. Experimental results on LFR network datasets and three real network datasets, verify the efficiency of the proposed *OCDTT* algorithm.

Keywords: Overlapping community detection · Importance of node · Topological potential · Trust value

1 Introduction

A complex network is an abstraction of a complex system. Most real-world networks, such as transportation, social or gene-regulatory networks, are complex networks. The "community" refers to the set of nodes with the same or similar characteristics in a complex network [1], there are overlapping and non-overlapping communities in complex network, which reflects the different agglomeration of nodes.

So far, there have been many research algorithms for the study of overlapping community research. Li [2] detect overlapping communities in the unweighted and weighted networks with considerable accuracy. Gregory [3] propose overlapping community detection algorithm based on nodes splitting, according to betweenness and edge-betweenness. Zhang [4] is inspired by label propagation and modular optimization, they introduce a community detection algorithm based on fuzzy membership propagation. In each iteration, candidate seed of potential communities are selected using topological features, and then the membership of the selected seeds is propagated to non-seed vertices, thus multiple communities could be obtained. Ahn [5] propose LINK algorithm performing hierarchical clustering on links based on idea of transforming in overlapping and non-overlapping communities in link networks. Although,

© IFIP International Federation for Information Processing 2020
Published by Springer Nature Switzerland AG 2020
Z. Shi et al. (Eds.): IIP 2020, IFIP AICT 581, pp. 160–166, 2020.
https://doi.org/10.1007/978-3-030-46931-3_15

researchers achieve great achievements in the research of community detection [6, 7]. Finding communities is a very challenging and promising research field. How to distinguish stable overlapping communities and propose efficient algorithms is still one of hot problems for many researchers.

We propose an overlapping community discover algorithm combining the topological potential and the trust value of nodes (Abbreviated as *OCDTT*) against problems appeared in existing algorithms. Firstly, the importance of nodes $I(v_i)$ in the network is computed combining the topological potential of nodes and the trust value of the node, and then K core nodes are selected according to $I(v_i)$. Based on the core nodes, communities are extended using the extended modularity.

2 Preliminary Study

We review the existing concepts, and define basic concepts and the problem of community detection. Table 1 gives a list of symbols used in this paper.

Table 1. Symbols

Symbols	Definition
$\Gamma(v_i)$	*The set of p-order neighbor nodes of v_i*
$s(v_i, v_j)$	*The similarity between node v_i and v_j*
c	*The size of the set $\Gamma(v_i)$*
α	*The balance factor*
$\varphi(v_i)$	*The topological potential of node v_i*
$t(v_i)$	*The trust value of node v_i*
$I(v_i)$	*The importance of node v_i*
λ	*Regulation parameter $(0 < \lambda < 1)$*

2.1   Trust Value of Nodes

Definition 1. If $path_{\min}(v_i, v_j) = p$, the node v_j is called as the *p*-order neighbor node of node v_i.

For example, when $path_{\min}(v_i, v_j) = 1$, v_j is 1-order neighbor node of v_i. The trust value of the node v_i is defined as the sum of the similarity $s(v_i, v_j)$ between v_i and all its *p*-order neighbors [8]. $v_i^A = (a_i^1 \cdots, a_i^d)$ is attribute vector of node v_i in formula (1).

$$t(v_i) = \sum_{v_j \in \Gamma(v_i)} s(v_i, v_j) \qquad and \qquad s(v_i, v_j) = \frac{v_i^A \cdot v_j^A}{\left\| v_i^A \right\| \times \left\| v_j^A \right\|} \qquad (1)$$

2.2   Topological Potential of Nodes

Potential refers the work generated by a particle moving from one point to another point in the field, and the work may depend only on the position of the particle and not depend on the path along which the particle moved in the physics science. If each node in a complex network is regarded as a particle in the field, and the edge between the nodes is used as a link between the particles to generate work [9]. Then the concept of potential field is applied to complex networks, which makes the connections between nodes have fine physical features and stability. Considering that the work will decrease with the increase of the shortest path length between nodes, So the topological potential of node v_i in the complex network G can be improved as formula (1). Impact factor $\delta \in (0, +\infty)$ is used to control impact scope of each node.

$$\varphi(v_i) = \sum_{k=1}^{p} count(k) * e^{-(\frac{path_{min}(v_i,v_j)}{\delta})^2} \tag{2}$$

Here, $count(k)$ is the number of the k-th order neighbors of node v_i. Keeping k constant, $\varphi(v_i)$ get larger as $count(k)$ gets larger, the network is densely. Therefore, the topological potential in Eq. (2) reflects the intensity of the network.

3   Implementation on Our Framework

In this research, we aim to solve community detection problem and describes how they work under this framework, the overall procedure our algorithm is shown in Fig. 1.

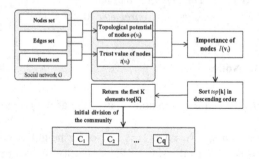

Fig. 1. Framework of OCDTT algorithm

3.1   Select Core Nodes

Due to the different positions of nodes and the difference of the interaction between nodes in complex networks, which make each node has different importance, their contributions to the network are also different [10]. Thus we can estimate the importance of nodes $I(v_i)$ from the structure of network and attributes of node.

$$I(v_i) = \alpha\varphi(v_i) + (1 - \alpha)t(v_i) \tag{3}$$

Next, top-k nodes are selected as core nodes according to the value of $I(v_i)$.

```
Input: Network G =(V, E, A),σ,α,K
Output: Core node set top[]
1. initialize top[]={0}, k=1;
2. for each vᵢ∈V do
   2.1 for each vⱼ∈V and j≠i do
       if 1< pathₘᵢₙ(vᵢ, vⱼ) <p  then
           2.1.1 compute topological field of node vᵢ;
           2.1.2 compute trust value of the node vᵢ;
   2.2 get the value of I(vᵢ)by formula (5)
   2.3 top[k]= I(vᵢ);
3. Sort the array top[k]in descending order, and select
   the first K elements to output;
4. return top[K];
```

3.2 Division of the Communities

We selects adjacent node of the core nodes in turn, and tries to add it to a community and calculate the value of EQ [11].

$$EQ = \frac{1}{2m}\sum_k \sum_{v_i \in C_k, v_j \in C_k} \frac{1}{O_{v_i}O_{v_j}}[M_{ij} - \frac{d_{v_i}d_{v_j}}{2m}] \tag{4}$$

If adding of the adjacent node makes EQ increases, then add the node into the community. Otherwise, select other adjacent node and repeat such operations until all adjacent nodes of core nodes is retrieved. Procedure is as follows:

```
Input: G=(V,E,A), core nodes set top[K]
Output: Initial community C = {C₁,C₂,…,Cₖ}
1. C = Φ;
2. Select nodes from core nodes to expand communities:
for each vᵢ∈top[K], i=1,2, …K do
2.1 Cᵢ ={vᵢ}
2.2 if(EQ(Cᵢ∪vⱼ)>EQ(ICᵢ))   then   Cᵢ = Cᵢ∪vⱼ
2.3   C = C∪ICᵢ
3. return C;
```

4 Experimental Results and Analysis

To compare and contrast the performance of the *OCDTT* method, we apply it to a variety of two datasets. We use Normalized Mutual Information (*NMI*) to evaluate performance of communities finding.

4.1 Experimental Results and Analysis

Complex simulation LFR network which internal structure and sizes of communities are scalable to demonstrate effectiveness of our method. Table 2 illustrates four groups parameter information of simulation LFR network.

Table 2. Two groups of *LFR* network parameter information

Name	N	K_{avg}	K_{max}	C_{min}	C_{max}	μ	O_m	O_n
S_1	1000	15	50	10	25	0.1	2	0–20
S_2	1000	10	50	10	50	0.1	2	0–10

For LFM algorithm, range of parameter α is [0.8, 1.6] and step is 0.1. In CFinder, k is integer in [3, 8]. Range of threshold in *LINK* is [0.1, 0.9] and step is 0.1. Impact factor of *OCDTT* $\sigma = 1.034$. Considering that structure and attributes have equal impact, set balance factor $\sigma = 0.5$.

We can study by observing Fig. 2 that *OCDTT* is more outstanding to partition communities in most conditions. It indicates that more communities a node belongs to, more complex the network is, lead to poorer performance of algorithms. It can be observed through comparing results of S_1 and S_2 that *OCDTT* is more stable than others when the number of communities increases.

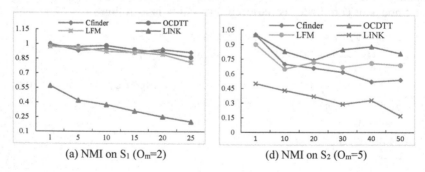

(a) NMI on S_1 (O_m=2)   (d) NMI on S_2 (O_m=5)

Fig. 2. Results of four algorithms on different subsets

4.2 Results and Analysis on Real Datasets

Three real networks consist of Karate, Dolphins and Football. Karate is friend network of 34 members in a Karate club. The network has 78 edges representing relations among 34 members. Dolphins dataset is about dolphin groups in New Zealand. The network represents biological family relations of 62 dolphins having 159 edges. Football data represent groups of match teams in a university including 115 members and 613 relations. It can be seen from Table 3 that EQ is not less than 0.5000 after partition in $OCDTT$. The partition performance is remarkable. $LINK$ algorithm produces linking communities of small sizes when implementing. It hampers form of communities, so corresponding result is the worst.

Table 3. EQ value on real network

Name	LFM	CFinder	LINK	OCDTT
Karate	0.3740	0.1860	0.0270	0.3720
Dolphins	0.4360	0.3610	0.1490	0.5000
Football	0.5260	0.4880	0.0830	0.5650

5 Conclusion

We combine the topological potential of nodes and the trust value of nodes to compute importance of nodes in the network. Start from those selected core nodes, utilize expanding module function to generate final community partition. Experimental results demonstrate that $OCDTT$ could achieve better results comparing to algorithms of the same kind. In further work, we will continue partitioning communities in aspects of structure and attributes. Based on this, optimize $OCDTT$. Strengthen efficiency of the implement. Attempt to apply the algorithm to real network analysis and web recommendations.

Acknowledgments. This work was supported in part by National Natural Science Foundation of China (No. 61762078, 61862058, 61967013), Youth Teacher Scientific Capability Promoting Project of NWNU (No. NWNU-LKQN-16-20).

References

1. Duch, J., Arenas, A.: Community detection in complex networks using extremal optimization. J. Phys. Rev. E **72**(2), 027104 (2005)
2. Li, J., Wang, X., Cui, Y.: Uncovering the overlapping community structure of complex networks by maximal cliques. J. Phys. A: Stat. Mech. Appl. **415**, 398–406 (2014)
3. Gregory, S.: An algorithm to find overlapping community structure in networks. In: Kok, J. N., Koronacki, J., Lopez de Mantaras, R., Matwin, S., Mladenič, D., Skowron, A. (eds.) PKDD 2007. LNCS (LNAI), vol. 4702, pp. 91–102. Springer, Heidelberg (2007). https://doi.org/10.1007/978-3-540-74976-9_12

4. Zhang, H., Chen, X., Li, J., et al.: Fuzzy community detection via modularity guided membership-degree propagation. J. Pattern Recogn. Lett. **70**, 66–72 (2016)
5. Ahn, Y.Y., Bagrow, J.P., Lehmann, S.: Link communities reveal multiscale complexity in networks. J. Nat. **466**(7307), 761–764 (2010)
6. Gui, Q., Deng, R., Cheng, X., et al.: A new method for overlapping community detection based on complete subgraph and label propagation. In: 3rd International Conference on Intelligent Information Processing, pp. 127–134 (2018)
7. ZhiXiao, W., Zechao, L., Xiaofang, D., et al.: Overlapping community detection based on node location analysis. J. Knowl.-Based Syst. **105**, 225–235 (2016)
8. Wang, Z., Zhao, Y., Chen, Z., et al.: An improved topology-potential-based community detection algorithm for complex network. J. Sci. World J. (2014)
9. Shen, H., Cheng, X., Cai, K., et al.: Detect overlapping and hierarchical community structure in networks. J. Phys. A **388**(8), 1706–1712 (2009)
10. Bin, W., Yayun, W., Jinfang, S., Zejun, S.: Identifying influential nodes of complex networks based on trust value. J. Chinese Comput. Syst. **40**(11), 2337–2342 (2019)
11. Moayedikia, A.: Multi-objective community detection algorithm with node importance analysis in attributed networks. J. Appl. Soft Comput. **67**, 434–451 (2018)

Brain Computer Integration

Coarse-to-Fine Classification with Phase Synchronization and Common Spatial Pattern for Motor Imagery-Based BCI

Wenfen Ling[1,2], Feipeng Xu[1,2], Qiaonan Fan[1,2], Yong Peng[1,2], and Wanzeng Kong[1,2(✉)]

[1] College of Computer Science, Hangzhou Dianzi University, Hangzhou 310008, Zhejiang, China
kongwanzeng@hdu.edu.cn
[2] Key Laboratory of Brain Machine Collaborative Intelligence of Zhejiang Province, Hangzhou, China

Abstract. How to improve the classification accuracy is a key issue in four-class motor imagery-based brain-computer interface (MI-BCI) systems. In this paper, a method based on phase synchronization analysis and common spatial pattern (CSP) algorithm is proposed. The proposed method embodies the idea of the inverted binary tree, which transforms the multi-class problem into several binary problems. First, the phase locking value (PLV) is calculated as a feature of phase synchronization, then the calculated correlation coefficients of the phase synchronization features are used to construct two pairs of class. Subsequently, we use CSP to extract the features of each class pair and use the linear discriminant analysis (LDA) to classify the test samples and obtain coarse classification results. Finally, the two classes obtained from the coarse classification form a new class pair. We use CSP and LDA to classify the test samples and get the fine classification results. The performance of method is evaluated on BCI Competition IV dataset IIa. The average kappa coefficient of our method is ranked third among the experimental results of the first five contestants. In addition, the classification performance of several subjects is significantly improved. These results show this method is effective for multi-class motor imagery classification.

Keywords: Electroencephalography · Motor imagery · Phase synchronization · Common spatial pattern · Linear discriminant analysis

1 Introduction

Brain-computer interface (BCI) is a direct communication and control channel between the human brain and a computer or other electronic device, through which people can express ideas or manipulate devices directly through the brain without using language or action [1]. It can effectively improve the ability of

© IFIP International Federation for Information Processing 2020
Published by Springer Nature Switzerland AG 2020
Z. Shi et al. (Eds.): IIP 2020, IFIP AICT 581, pp. 169–179, 2020.
https://doi.org/10.1007/978-3-030-46931-3_16

patients with severe disabilities to communicate with the outside or control external environment [2]. The BCI research team often use EEG to measure the biological brain signal [3]. Brain wave is a method of recording brain activity using the electrophysiological index [4]. It records the wave changes during brain activity and is the overall reflection of the electrophysiological activity of the brain cells in the cerebral cortex or scalp surface [5]. When a certain region of the cerebral cortex is activated by the senses, action instructions or motion imagination and other stimuli, the region's metabolism and blood stream increase, at the same time, the information is processing. These can lead to the amplitude reduction or block of the corresponding band of the EEG signal. This kind of electrophysiological phenomenon is called 'event-related desynchronization' or ERD. The brain exhibits a significant increase in electrical activity at quiescent conditions, which is called 'event-related synchronization' or ERS [3]. The theoretical basis of motion imagination lies in ERS and ERD.

Motor imagery (MI) refers to a psychological process that there are individual rehearsal and simulation of the given actions but no obvious physical activity [6]. Relevant studies have shown that the neuronal activity of the primary sensorimotor areas generated by motor imagery is similar to the neuron activities of primary sensorimotor areas generated by actual motion [7,8]. The biggest advantage of the motor imagery-based brain-computer interface (MI-BCI) system is that the EEG signal is generated by imagination without relying on any sensory stimulation. Therefore, many BCI teams based on motion imagination are devoted to the study of EEG feature extraction and classification algorithms, especially for the classification of the four-class motor imagery. Peng et al. [9] proposed a discriminative extremum learning machine with a supervised sparse preservation (SPELM) model, which is effective in multi-class classification tasks and regression tasks. Gouy-Pailler et al. [10] proposed maximum likelihood framework to improve the classification recognition rate of multi-class BCI paradigms, bridging the gap between the common spatial model (CSP) and blind source separation (BSS) of non-stationary sources. The average kappa value is 0.50. Nicolas-Alonso et al. [11] used a method for classifying four-level motion imaging tasks by combining adaptive processing and semi-supervised learning. The kappa coefficient is 0.70. He et al. [12] constructed a common Bayesian network by selecting relevant channels using nodes with common and different edges, and then classified them with SVM. The average kappa coefficient reaches 0.66.

The main purpose of this paper is to propose an inverted binary tree classification method which combines phase synchronization analysis and common spatial pattern (CSP). This method can improve the classification accuracy of multi-class motor imagery EEG. We assess this method on the data set IIa which contains four different motor imagery tasks. First, the phase locking value (PLV) is calculated as a feature of phase synchronization, then the calculated correlation coefficients of the phase synchronization features are used to construct two pairs of class. Then, we use CSP to extract the features of each class pair and use the linear discriminant analysis (LDA) to classify the test samples and obtain coarse classification results. Finally, the two classes obtained from the coarse classification form a new class pair. CSP and LDA are still used to classify the test samples and get the fine classification results.

This paper is organized as follows. Section 2 describes the BCI Competition IV dataset IIa. In Sect. 3, processing methods and all steps of the proposed method are described in detail. Experimental results are presented in Sect. 4. Finally, Sect. 5 concludes the paper.

2   Data Acquisition

Our experiment uses the dataset IIa, which is available from the 4th International BCI Competition (BCI-IV) and is provided by the Graz Technical University. Detailed description about dataset IIa can be downloaded from the website (http://www.bbci.de/competition/iv/#datasets). It consists of EEG data from nine subjects (named as A01, A02, A03, A04, A05, A06, A07, A08, A09, respectively). The cue-based BCI paradigm comprises four classes of motor imagery EEG measurements, namely left hand (class 1), right hand (class 2), feet (class 3), and tongue (class 4). Two sessions are recorded for each subject on different days, one for training and the other for evaluation. Each session is composed of 6 runs separated by short breaks. Each run consists of 48 trials (each class appears 12 times), yielding 288 trials per session. The timing scheme of one trial is illustrated in Fig. 1.

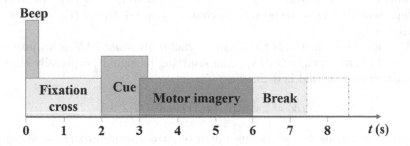

Fig. 1. Timing scheme of the paradigm for recording dataset IIa.

The subjects sit in the comfortable armchair in front of the computer screen. A cue arrow indicates to perform the desired motor imagery task. The experimental data are recorded with 22 Ag/AgCl electrodes (3.5 cm inter-electrode distance) and 3 monopolar EOG channels. The signals are sampled with 250 Hz and bandpass-filtered between 0.5 Hz and 100 Hz.

The competition requires participants to provide a continuous classification output for each sample in the form of class labels that could be '1', '2', '3' or '4'. The winner is the algorithm with the largest kappa value.

3   Methods

3.1   Data Preprocessing

In this work, the original signals derived from the BCI-IV are intercepted into single-trial data. The above-described data is then filtered between 8 Hz and 30 Hz with a third-order Butterworth bandpass filter. This band-pass frequency range is used because it covers both mu (8–12Hz) and beta (18–25Hz) rhythms. It can be seen from the timing scheme of one trial that the real motor imagery is starting at 3 s. Therefore, for the following feature extraction and classification, the 3 s data from 3 s to 6 s are intercepted from the filter data. The length of data for each sample is 750 data points.

3.2   Phase Synchronization Analysis

Phase synchronization analysis is based on the interrelation of the phase and the EEG with synchronization angle [13]. It can retain the phase components of EEG signals and inhibit the impact of amplitude.

For a continuous time signal $x(t)$ recoded from channel x, its complex analysis signal by Hilbert transform can be defined as:

$$Z_x(t) = x(t) + i\tilde{x}(t) = A_x(t)e^{i\Phi_x(t)} \tag{1}$$

where $A_x(t)$ and $\Phi_x(t)$ are the instantaneous amplitude and instantaneous phases of signals $x(t)$, respectively. $\tilde{x}(t)$ is the Hilbert transform of $\Phi_x(t)$. Analogously, $y(t)$ represent the signal recoded from channel y, we define $Z_y(t) = A_y(t)e^{i\Phi_y(t)}$ for signal $y(t)$.

There are many methods to measure synchronization. PLV is an important measure of phase synchronization when studying biosignals, especially electrical brain activities [14], and is defined as:

$$PLV = |<\exp(i\{\Phi_x(t) - \Phi_y(t)\}) > | \tag{2}$$

where $< . >$ means the averaging operator of a continues time t. $\Phi_x(t)$ and $\Phi_y(t)$ are the instantaneous phases of the analytical signals $Z_x(t)$ and $Z_y(t)$, respectively.

Every two channels can be used to build different channel pairs. Dataset IIa has 22 channels. We calculate PLV of all channel pairs. And a symmetric matrix $\mathbf{K}$ with dimension $c \times c$ can be obtained. The matrix $\mathbf{K}$ is given as:

$$\mathbf{K} = \begin{bmatrix} 1 & k_{12} & \cdots & k_{1c} \\ k_{21} & 1 & \cdots & k_{2c} \\ \vdots & \vdots & \vdots & \vdots \\ k_{(c-1)1} & k_{(c-1)2} & \cdots & k_{(c-1)c} \\ k_{c1} & k_{c2} & \cdots & 1 \end{bmatrix} \tag{3}$$

The average PLV is defined as:

$$PLV_{avg_i} = \frac{1}{N_i} \left| \sum_{n=1}^{N_i} \langle \exp(j\{\Phi_x(t) - \Phi_y(t)\}) \rangle \right| \tag{4}$$

where N_i is the number of samples belonging to class i. i denotes either class 1, 2, 3 or 4.

3.3 Correlation Coefficients of Phase Synchronization Features

The correlation coefficient calculation formula is defined as:

$$r_i = \frac{\sum_m \sum_n (\mathbf{A}_{mn} - \overline{\mathbf{A}})(\mathbf{B}_{mn} - \overline{\mathbf{B}})}{\sqrt{\sum_m \sum_n (\mathbf{A}_{mn} - \overline{\mathbf{A}})^2 (\mathbf{B}_{mn} - \overline{\mathbf{B}})^2}} \tag{5}$$

where $\mathbf{A}$ represents a symmetric matrix composed of the PLV value of a test sample, and $\mathbf{B}$ represents a symmetric matrix composed of the average PLV values of the training samples of each class. $\overline{\mathbf{A}}$ is equal to $mean(\mathbf{A})$ and $\overline{\mathbf{B}}$ is equal to $mean(\mathbf{B})$. m and n denote the row and column of the matrix $\mathbf{A}$ and $\mathbf{B}$, respectively. In this paper, as introduced in the Sect. 3.2, m and n are the same, which are equal to the number of EEG signal channels. The dataset IIa contains four classes of motor imagery EEG data, so each test sample will form four correlation coefficients. Thereby, a column vector R can be obtained:

$$\mathbf{R} = \begin{bmatrix} r_1 r_2 r_3 r_4 \end{bmatrix}^T \tag{6}$$

where r_1, r_2, r_3 and r_4 denote the correlation coefficient.

Then we can get a new column vector $\mathbf{c}$ from $\mathbf{r}$, and $\mathbf{c}$ can be expressed as:

$$\mathbf{c} = \begin{bmatrix} r'_a r'_b r'_c r'_d \end{bmatrix}^T, r'_a > r'_b > r'_c > r'_d \tag{7}$$

$r'_a = abs(r_i - mean(R))$. Analogously, r'_b, r'_c and r'_d have the same meaning.

3.4 Coarse Classification and Fine Classification

The proposed method mainly consists of two aspects: coarse classification of test samples based on phase synchronization feature correlation coefficients and fine classification of test samples based on coarse classification.

For coarse classification, we use the two classes of EEG data set corresponding to the first two correlation coefficients in $\mathbf{c}$ as the training samples for CSP feature extraction, and use LDA to classify the test samples. The test samples are classified into one of the two classes. The same operation on the last two correlation coefficients and the result are classified into the other classes.

For fine classification, with the result of coarse classification, we can get a new pair of class and then make fine classification of the test sample with the CSP and LDA to acquire final classification result.

3.5   Summary of the Proposed Method

Figure 2 shows a detailed flow chart of the proposed method. The method includes several stages: signal preprocessing with a third-order Butterworth bandpass filter, use phase synchronization analysis to measure the relationship between two different channels, calculate the correlation coefficients of phase synchronization features, coarse classification and fine classification (CSP is used to extract features and LDA is employed to classify a test sample).

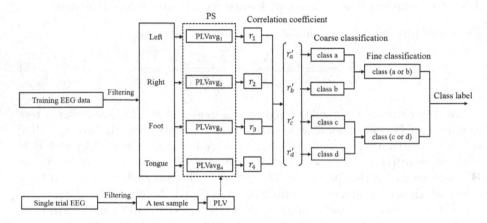

Fig. 2. Flow chart of the proposed method.

4   Experiments

4.1   Phase Synchronization Features

Dataset IIa uses 22 electrodes for data acquisition, including four-class motor imagery tasks. For training data sets, we calculate the PLV of all channel pairs and get the average PLV of each class. Each class includes 72 samples. Taking the subject A03 as an example, the average PLV matrices of each class is shown in Fig. 3. The matrix contains the interaction between the channel pairs and the instantaneous phase between the channels. The closer the chroma to 1, the more synchronized the EEG signals of the two channels. It can be seen from the figure that the average PLV feature obtained from various classes of EEG training sample is different, which can be used to classify the EEG signal.

4.2   Topography of Optimal Spatial Filter

The proposed algorithm utilizes one versus one CSP algorithm to find the appropriate spatial filter which can maximize the difference between the two classes. That is, the variance of one class is maximized while the variance of the other

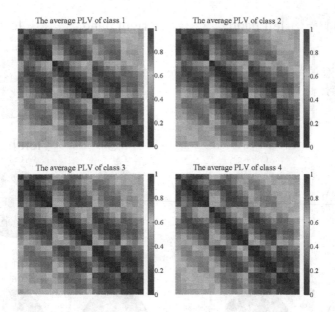

Fig. 3. The average PLV matrices of each class on training dataset.

class is minimized. In this paper, the optimal spatial filter is constructed by selecting 8 optimal projection directions (the first 4 rows and the last 4 rows). The projection direction of the spatial filter can be visualized by brain topography. Figure 4 shows the first and the last columns of the CSP filter, which corresponds to the maximum and the minimum eigenvalues of subject A03. The brain topography reflects the neural activity of the brain intuitively. After optimizing the pairing, there are significant differences in the EEG data of the two classes of motor imagery in each class pair. From the figure, we can also see the features of ERD/ERS produced by four kinds of motor imagery, which are effective for the classification of EEG data.

4.3   CSP Features Subspace Mapping

The CSP algorithm is used to calculate the eigenvector, and each sample produces an 8-dimensional eigenvector, i.e. $f = [f_1, f_2, \cdots, f_8]$. Take the subject A03 as an example, we select two spatial features from the optimized CSP features as the research object. The final result can carry out by optimizing group for three times only and constructing three spatial filters. Figure 5 shows the feature subspace mapping between the optimized combinatorial classes. The optimized combination is as follows: first, Fig. 5(a) and (b) make coarse classification of the combination of class 2 and class 4, and the combination of class 3 and class 1. Then, Fig. 5(c) obtain new optimization group and make fine classification of class 2 and class 1, which is eventually divided into class 2.

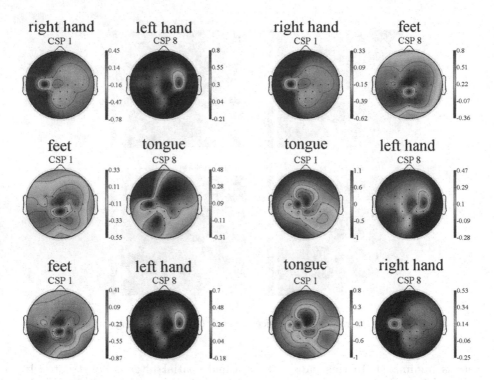

Fig. 4. Topographic map of the first and last eigenvector of CSP filters for classifying different single-trial test samples, and 22 electrode locations. The results for subject A03 are shown.

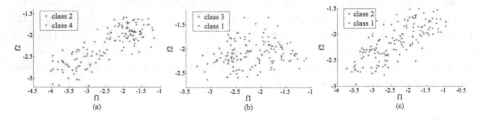

Fig. 5. (**a**) Feature subspace mapping of class 4 and class 2, coarse classification. (**b**) Feature subspace mapping of class 3 and class 1, coarse classification. (**c**) Feature subspace mapping of class 2 and class 3, fine classification.

4.4   Classification Results

After coarse classification and fine classification, the predicted label by experiment and the real label are compared to determine the coarse classification and fine classification accuracy. Table 1 shows the classification accuracy of method proposed in this paper in handling the dataset IIa.

Table 1 shows that the nine subjects have a coarse classification whose accuracy range from 62.2% (A05) to 96.9% (A01) with an average of 81.75%. The

Table 1. Coarse classification accuracy and fine classification accuracy of BCI Competition IV Dataset IIa.

	Mean	A01	A02	A03	A04	A05	A06	A07	A08	A09
Coarse(middle acc) %	81.75	96.9	72.6	91.7	74.0	62.2	65.3	93.4	87.2	92.7
Fine(final acc) %	62.66	78.8	52.8	73.6	50.4	37.2	40.3	74.0	77.8	79.2

fine classification accuracy range from 37.2% (A05) to 79.2% (A09) with an average of 62.66%. Obviously, the accuracy of coarse classification will affect the fine classification accuracy to a certain extent. The coarse classification accuracy of some subjects is about 90%, such as A01, A03, A07, A08, A09, and the corresponding fine classification accuracy is higher than other subjects.

We also calculate the confusion matrix of the four subjects, as shown in Fig. 6. It can be seen from the figure that the accuracy rate of right-hand motor imagery of subjects A03 is 100%, which is higher than all the other subjects. However, the accuracy of his feet motor imagery is the lowest. It can be inferred that the subject may be more concentrated during the right-hand motor imagery. In addition, the diagonal elements of the confusion matrix are always the largest, which indicates that the proposed method is applicable to the classification of multi-class motor imagery tasks.

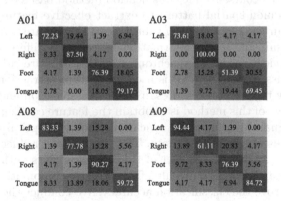

Fig. 6. Confusion matrices of four different subjects.

In the dataset IIa BCI competition IV, the winner is the method with the largest kappa coefficient. In order to make a fair comparison with the outcome of the competition, we use the same standard, that is, the kappa value obtained according to [15]. Table 2 presents the kappa values obtained from the proposed method in this paper and the best five competitors. A description of the results and the methods are provided on the website (http://www.bbci.de/competition/iv/results/index.html).

Table 2 shows that our approach produces quite good results in multi-class and multi-channel EEG identification, with the average kappa coefficient

Table 2. Kappa values of the performance of the proposed method and five best competitors in dataset IIa BCI competition IV.

	Mean	A01	A02	A03	A04	A05	A06	A07	A08	A09	Rank
Kai Keng Ang	0.57	0.68	0.42	0.75	0.48	0.40	0.27	0.77	0.75	0.61	1st
Liu Guangquan	0.52	0.69	0.34	0.71	0.44	0.16	0.21	0.66	0.73	0.69	2nd
Our method	**0.50**	**0.72**	**0.37**	**0.65**	**0.34**	**0.16**	**0.20**	**0.65**	**0.70**	**0.72**	
Wei Song	0.31	0.38	0.18	0.48	0.33	0.07	0.14	0.29	0.49	0.44	3rd
Damien Coyle	0.30	0.46	0.25	0.65	0.31	0.12	0.07	0.00	0.46	0.42	4th
Jin Wu	0.29	0.41	0.17	0.39	0.25	0.06	0.16	0.34	0.45	0.37	5th

accounting for the third of the six different approaches, slightly below the first contestant (down 0.07) [16] and the second contestant (down 0.02) [17]. However, our algorithm has a significant advantage (up to 0.19) compared to the original third of the contestants. In addition, we can also see the kappa coefficient of subject A01 and subject A09 is the highest among the six methods.

5   Conclusion

We have proposed a coarse-to-fine classification method based on phase synchronization and common spatial pattern to extract effective features and improve classification accuracy. Phase-locking value is used to measure the phase synchronization relationship and spatial information between two different channels. The correlation coefficients of phase synchronization features are calculated to construct several class pairs. The CSP is used for feature extraction and the LDA is used to classify the selected features in coarse classification and fine classification. The core idea of this method is to obtain the feature coefficient relationship between EEG signals by using phase synchronization and optimize the pair combination of various classes of EEG data. This method can reduce the number of spatial filters and weaken the impact of the two-class pairs with higher feature coincidence on the classification results. The effective combination of features is only used to improve the classification accuracy. We conduct the experiment on the dataset IIa to evaluate the performance of the proposed method. The experimental results show that the average classification accuracy can reach 62.66%. The algorithm has good feature extraction ability and increases the classification accuracy of multi-class EEG signals.

Acknowledgment. This work was supported by National Key R&D Program of China for Intergovernmental International Science and Technology Innovation Cooperation Project (2017YFE0116800), National Natural Science Foundation of China (61671193, U1909202), Science and Technology Program of Zhejiang Province (2018C04012), Key Laboratory of Brain Machine Collaborative Intelligence of Zhejiang Province (2020E10010) and the Graduate Scientific Research Foundation of Hangzhou Dianzi University (CXJJ2019121).

References

1. Pfurtscheller, G., et al.: Current trends in GRAZ brain-computer interface (BCI) research. IEEE Trans. Rehabil. Eng. **8**(2), 216–219 (2000)
2. Chen, Y.-L., Tang, F.-T., Chang, W.H., Wong, M.-K., Shih, Y.-Y., Kuo, T.-S.: The new design of an infrared-controlled human-computer interface for the disabled. IEEE Trans. Rehabil. Eng. **7**(4), 474–481 (1999)
3. Vaughan, T.M., Wolpaw, J.R., Donchin, E.: EEG-based communication: prospects and problems. IEEE Trans. Rehabil. Eng. **4**(4), 425–430 (1996)
4. Crowley, K.E., Colrain, I.M.: A review of the evidence for P2 being an independent component process: age, sleep and modality. Clin. Neurophysiol. **115**(4), 732–744 (2004)
5. Peng, Y., Zheng, W.-L., Bao-Liang, L.: An unsupervised discriminative extreme learning machine and its applications to data clustering. Neurocomputing **174**, 250–264 (2016)
6. Lotze, M., Halsband, U.: Motor imagery. J. Physiol.-paris **99**(4–6), 386–395 (2006)
7. Pfurtscheller, G., Neuper, C.: Motor imagery and direct brain-computer communication. Proc. IEEE **89**(7), 1123–1134 (2001)
8. Neuper, C., Pfurtscheller, G.: Event-related dynamics of cortical rhythms: frequency-specific features and functional correlates. Int. J. Psychophysiol. **43**(1), 41–58 (2001)
9. Peng, Y., Bao-Liang, L.: Discriminative extreme learning machine with supervised sparsity preserving for image classification. Neurocomputing **261**, 242–252 (2017)
10. Gouy-Pailler, C., Congedo, M., Brunner, C., Jutten, C., Pfurtscheller, G.: Nonstationary brain source separation for multiclass motor imagery. IEEE Trans. Biomed. Eng. **57**(2), 469–478 (2009)
11. Nicolas-Alonso, L.F., Corralejo, R., Gomez-Pilar, J., Álvarez, D., Hornero, R.: Adaptive semi-supervised classification to reduce intersession non-stationarity in multiclass motor imagery-based brain-computer interfaces. Neurocomputing **159**, 186–196 (2015)
12. He, L., Hu, D., Wan, M., Wen, Y., von Deneen, K.M., Zhou, M.C.: Common Bayesian network for classification of EEG-based multiclass motor imagery BCI. IEEE Trans. Syst. Man Cybern. Syst. **46**(6), 843–854 (2015)
13. Kong, W., Zhou, Z., Jiang, B., Babiloni, F., Borghini, G.: Assessment of driving fatigue based on intra/inter-region phase synchronization. Neurocomputing **219**, 474–482 (2017)
14. Hu, J., Mu, Z., Wang, J.: Phase locking analysis of motor imagery in brain-computer interface. In: 2008 International Conference on Biomedical Engineering and Informatics, vol. 2, pp. 478–481. IEEE (2008)
15. Cohen, J.: A coefficient of agreement for nominal scales. Educ. Psychol. Measur. **20**(1), 37–46 (1960)
16. Ang, K.K., Chin, Z.Y., Wang, C., Guan, C., Zhang, H.: Filter bank common spatial pattern algorithm on BCI competition IV datasets 2a and 2b. Front. Neurosci. **6**, 39 (2012)
17. Liu, G.-Q., Huang, G., Zhu, X.-Y.: Application of CSP method in multiclass classification. Chin. J. Biomed. Eng. **28**, 935–940 (2009)

Ballistocardiogram Artifact Removal for Concurrent EEG-fMRI Recordings Using Blind Source Separation Based on Dictionary Learning

Yuxi Liu[1], Jianhai Zhang[1,2], Bohui Zhang[3(✉)], and Wanzeng Kong[1,2]

[1] School of Computer Science, Hangzhou Dianzi University,
Hangzhou 310018, China
[2] Key Laboratory of Brain Machine Collaborative Intelligence
of Zhejiang Province, Hangzhou 310018, China
[3] University of Southern California, Los Angeles, CA 90007, USA
bohuizha@usc.edu

Abstract. Simultaneous recording of electroencephalography (EEG) and functional magnetic resonance imaging (fMRI) have attracted extensive attention and research owing to their high spatial and temporal resolution. However, EEG data are easily influenced by physiological causes, gradient artifact (GA) and ballistocardiogram (BCG) artifact. In this paper, a new blind source separation technique based on dictionary learning is proposed to remove BCG artifact. The dictionary is learned from original data which represents the features of clean EEG signals and BCG artifact. Then, the dictionary atoms are classified according to a list of standards. Finally, clean EEG signals are obtained from the linear combination of the modified dictionary. The proposed method, ICA, AAS, and OBS are tested and compared using simulated data and real simultaneous EEG–fMRI data. The results suggest the efficacy and advantages of the proposed method in the removal of BCG artifacts.

Keywords: Eelectroencephalography (EEG) · functional Magnetic Resonance Imaging (fMRI) · Ballistocardiogram · Dictionary learning · Signal processing

1 Introduction

With the development of brain science, the simultaneous acquisition of electroencephalography (EEG) and functional magnetic resonance imaging (fMRI) has attracted extensive attention and research. EEG signal has the characteristics of low spatial resolution and high temporal resolution, while fMRI has the characteristics of low temporal resolution and high spatial resolution. Therefore, the combination of EEG signal and fMRI is very important for the study of brain function, pathogenesis and cognition of mental diseases [1, 2].

However, we face a serious problem: during recording data in an MRI scanner, EEG signals are easy to be affected by the gradient artifact (GA) and ballistocardiogram (BCG) artifact [7]. Fortunately, the gradient artifacts have time-shift invariance and

© IFIP International Federation for Information Processing 2020
Published by Springer Nature Switzerland AG 2020
Z. Shi et al. (Eds.): IIP 2020, IFIP AICT 581, pp. 180–191, 2020.
https://doi.org/10.1007/978-3-030-46931-3_17

their amplitude is more than 100 times higher than that of an EEG signal [3]. Thus, gradient artifacts are easily discernable, and they can be removed from the EEG signal by average artifact subtraction (AAS) [4]. However, the original EEG signals still contain another serious artifact, the most difficult one to remove: the ballistocardiogram artifact (BCG). The BCG artifact is caused by the hall effect induced by blood flow and the scalp twitch caused by blood pulsation, which mainly covers the frequency of EEG signal at alpha (8–13 Hz) and below [12]. Therefore, BCG artifacts are a major bottleneck to the wide application of simultaneous EEG-fMRI, and it is also a problem we need to solve urgently.

To ensure the quality of EEG signals in EEG-fMRI, many methods have been used to remove BCG artifact. (1) Averaged artifact subtraction (AAS), in which a BCG artifact template is estimated by averaging over the intervals of EEG signal that are corrupted by the artifact and subsequent subtraction of the template from the corrupted segments to obtain clean signal [4]. (2) Independent Component Analysis (ICA) [5] and (3) Principal Component Analysis (PCA) [6] are used to separate the original EEG signal into different components, identify the artifact components and then remove them. The primary challenge with these two methods is the definition of a consistent standard for artificial component selection. There is always a trade-off in selecting the number of components: removing a small number of components may still leave traces in the EEG signal, on the contrary, removing a large number of components may lead to the loss of important information in the EEG signal [11].

In recent years, dictionary learning has been widely used in multiple denoising study areas concerning images and medical signals. Abolghasemi et al. [8] firstly used dictionary learning to removal BCG artifact. The method first learns a sparse dictionary from the given data. Then, the dictionary is used to model the existing BCG contribution in the original signals. The obtained BCG model is then subtracted from the original EEG to achieve clean EEG. The results show that dictionary learning is better than AAS, OBS and DHT. However, their methods lack the study of learned dictionary. Their work proved the reliability from the evaluation index while not from the dictionary itself. The features of atoms is not fully explained and the amount of useful EEG features in the dictionary on real-time data has not been proved.

In this paper, based on the previous approach, we propose a new blind source separation technique for removing BCG artifacts EEG data based on dictionary learning. The original EEG signal is firstly studied through dictionary learning, while the dictionary contains all of the features of the dictionary, which can ensure that all BCG features are fitted. Then, the atoms contain only EEG features are sorted according to a list of standards. Finally, the clean EEG signal is obtained by the linear combination of the sorted atoms. The proposed method is tested on synthetic data and real data, and compared with ICA, AAS and OBS, which proves that the method has better performance.

2   Method

2.1   Dictionary Learning

Dictionary learning is a machine learning algorithm that has been widely used in image denoising and classification, medical signals analyzing and so on. The learning method aims at inferring a dictionary matrix which can give a sparse representation of the input image or signal. Each column of the dictionary is called an atom which describes the features of the input data. The method is also called sparse dictionary learning which means the signal is represented as a sparse linear combination of atoms [13]. Assume a dictionary matrix $\mathbf{D} = [d_1, \cdots, d_K] \in R^{n \times K}$, $n < K$, has been found from the input dataset $\mathbf{X} = [x_1, \cdots, x_m]$, $x_i \in R^n$. Each column of the dataset matrix which usually represents a signal x_i can be represented as the linear combination of the atoms of dictionary, i.e. $x_i = \mathbf{D} \cdot s_i$. Representations s_i, the elements of sparse matrix $\mathbf{S} = [s_1, \cdots, s_m]$ need to achieve enough sparsity. Thus, the learning process can be formulated as:

$$\min_{\mathbf{D}, s_i} \sum_{i=1}^{m} \|x_i - \mathbf{D}s_i\|_2^2 + \lambda \|s_i\|_0, \quad \lambda > 0 \tag{1}$$

The l_0-norm in the minimization problem (1) is commonly substituted by l_1-norm for measurement of sparsity since the previous is NP-hard [17]. A usual procedure to solve the problem is iteratively updating dictionary and sparse coding, i.e. solve dictionary $\mathbf{D}$ while sparse coding $\mathbf{S}$ is fixed then solve $\mathbf{S}$ when $\mathbf{D}$ is fixed, until convergence. K-SVD [19] is a powerful algorithm that based on Singular Value Decomposition (SVD) and K-means implements the alternating minimization process well. And the paper uses K-SVD as the core algorithm to complete the dictionary learning.

2.2   The Proposed Technique

The input data for the proposed method which is the original signal added by all 32 EEG channels with length L is segmented into m pieces of data of length n. Each segment is a piece of continues EEG signal. The segments would increase the amount of the input which means there would be a certain amount of duplication between each other. This strategy, which is quite similar to the one between decision tree and random forest, has the advantage that it can capture most of the local features in the giving sample [8]. Each segment can be formulated as:

$$x_i = P_i \mathbf{X}, \quad P_i \in R^{n \times L} \tag{2}$$

P_i is a binary matrix. Hence the proposed method can be formulated as:

$$\min_{D,s_i} \sum_{i=1}^{m} \|P_i X - D s_i\|_2^2 + \lambda \|s_i\|_0, \quad \lambda > 0 \tag{3}$$

After solving the above problem, a dictionary D with atoms contain all of the features will be obtained.

Since the dictionary matrix contains the features of signals, it has similar mathematical forms with Independent Component Analysis (ICA), which the signals can be represented by the linear combination of independent components. Compared with ICA, dictionary learning has allows the dimensionality of atoms to be higher than the number of EEG channels. This property leads to adding redundant information to the dictionary, in this case, which mainly is the clean EEG but also provides an improvement in sparsity and precision of the signal features representation. To improve the result of dictionary learning, we modify the dimension of the dictionary and sort the atoms we learned through atoms classification and rearrangement. For the learned redundant dictionary matrix D, principal component analysis (PCA) is first applied to reduce the dimensionality and figure out the number k of the first principal components (Fig. 1).

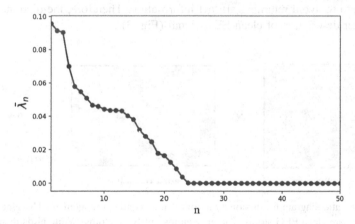

Fig. 1. The single values of PCA. In this situation, the first 3 single values mainly describe the features of dictionary.

The space spanned by the first k principal components is considered to capture the most important characteristics of the original signal that mainly depend on BCG artifacts. For the reduced dictionary atoms, k-means clustering algorithm is applied to classified BCG atoms and EEG atoms. The clustering result can be plotted to 3D-space spanned by the first 3 principal components, as shown on Fig. 2.

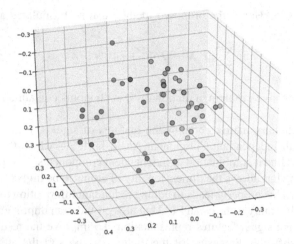

Fig. 2. Atom clustering of dictionary atoms learned from synthetic data. Red dots are BCG artifacts atoms; gray dots are EEG atoms. (Color figure online)

After identifying the atoms which describe the features of the BCG, we return BCG atoms to zero to avoid returning artifact information. Therefore, the dictionary would have a better description of clean EEG signal (Fig. 3).

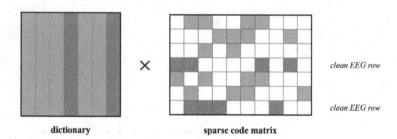

Fig. 3. Schematic diagram for dictionary atom selection and rearrangement. The green atoms in the dictionary are clean EEG atoms. The grey atoms are BCG atoms. White girds in sparse code matrix are 0. (Color figure online)

3 Experiment

In this section, we divide the experimental results into two parts: synthetic and real data. The performance of AAS, OBS, ICA and dictionary learning was evaluated by experiments on these two data types, which proved the superiority of the proposed method.

3.1 Data Acquisition

(1) Synthetic Data

The synthetic EEG data used in this paper was proposed by Abolghasemi et al. in 2015 [8]. The synthesized signal consists of two parts: 1/f noise (also known as pink noise) and BCG artifact. For the non-uniform characteristics of EEG signal, 1/f noise is selected as EEG signal [14], while the synthesized BCG artifact is overlapped by cosine waves of different frequencies and amplitudes. For the final synthesized signal, 10 dB white Gaussian noise is added, and these signals and their synthesized signals are shown in Fig. 4.

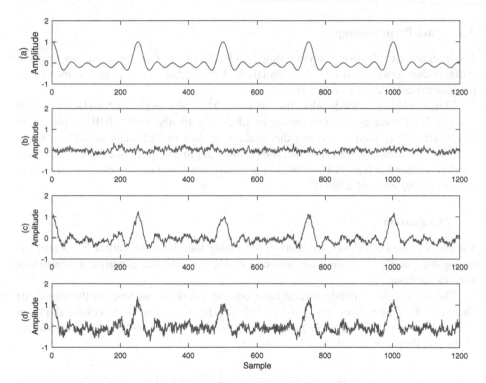

Fig. 4. Synthetic data: (a) BCG; (b) EEG (1/f noise); (c) Summation of a and b; (d) Summation of a and b. The SNR is 10 dB.

It can be seen from Fig. 4 that as the 1/f noise of EEG signal, its amplitude is significantly smaller than that of simulated BCG signal. In fact, the EEG signal of synchronous acquisition of EEG and fMRI obtained from actual acquisition is the same.

(2) Public Data

The experimental data is provided by FMRIB research center of Oxford University. The test data (FMRIB_Data.set) downloaded from the open-source EEG signal processing website includes EEG signal, BCG artifact, gradient artifact and other noises [6].

(3) Clinical Data

The experimental data were provided by the sleep neuroimaging center of Southwest University. Two healthy subjects with no history of nerve or heart disease participated in the experiment. Indicates that the object rests in the scanner with the eyes open and closed, without performing any specific tasks. Among the 32 channels recorded, 30 EEG channels used 10–20 international system. In addition, there are two bipolar channels for EMG and ECG. The data sampling rate is 5000 Hz.

3.2   Data Preprocessing

The premise of effectively suppressing BCG artifacts is that there are no gradient artifacts that seriously distort EEG signals in EEG signals, so it is necessary to pre-process the collected EEG data first.

Matlab (2017b; MathWorks, Inc., Natick, MA) and eeglab 12.0 (Delorme and makeig, 2004) were used to preprocess the EEG data. Firstly, the FMRIB 2.1 plug-in in EEGLAB [15] is used to remove the gradient artifact in EEG data of MRI scan. In order to save memory, we can down sample the data to 250 Hz. All EEG data are then bandpass filtered at 0.5–50 Hz. The data is finally converted to a 32 channel EEG with sampling frequency of 250 Hz.

3.3   Evaluation

Various evaluation indexes are used to determine the ability to inhibit BCG artifacts (more importantly, to retain brain activity), and to compare the experimental results of various methods.

The evaluation is mainly carried out from the following aspects: (a) the amplitude changes; (b) Power Spectral Density [16]; (c) Improvement in Normalized Power Spectral Density Ratio (INPS) [9]; (d) Peak-to-peak Value (PPV) [10]. In addition, INPS and PPV can be calculated as follows:

$$\text{INPS} = \frac{1}{n} \sum_{i=1}^{n} 10 \log_{10} \frac{\sum \phi_{P\text{before},i}(f)}{\sum \phi_{P\text{after},i}(f)} \tag{4}$$

$$\text{PPV} = \frac{\frac{1}{n} \sum_{i=1}^{n} V_{\text{before},i}}{\frac{1}{n} \sum_{i=1}^{n} V_{\text{after},i}} = \frac{\sum_{i=1}^{n} V_{\text{before},i}}{\sum_{i=1}^{n} V_{\text{after},i}} \tag{5}$$

4 Result

Figure 5 gives the results using AAS, OBS and ICA and dictionary learning methods to the synthetic signal.

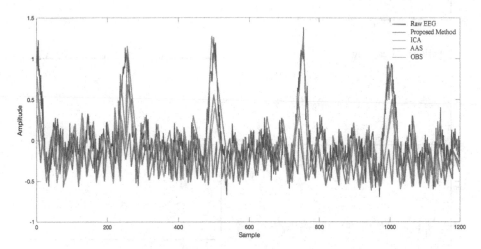

Fig. 5. Extracted BCG from synthetic data using (a) AAS, (b) OBS, (c) ICA, and (d) the proposed method.

According to the method in Sect. 3.3, the normalized power spectral density (INPS) is 13.16, the peak-to-peak value is 8.44. The values of the two performance evaluation indexes are much higher than 1, indicating that dictionary learning plays an important role in inhibiting BCG artifacts.

Figure 6 shows a segment of EEG data with a length of 10 s processed by various methods. Visualization results of EEG records before and after BCG artifact correction (AAS, OBS, ICA, proposed) of DATA 3. With the application of BCG removal method, BCG artifact contribution is attenuated, so EEG signal strongly decreases. However, it is obvious that the BCG residuals significantly decreased when using the proposed method.

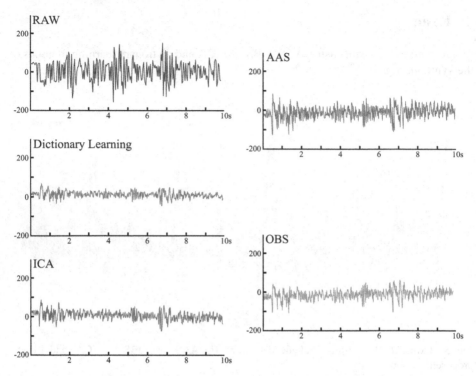

Fig. 6. Result of 10 s signal from channel Fp1 (for DATA 3) between the EEG recordings before (RAW) and after BCG artifact correction (ICA, AAS, OBS).

Figure 7 shows averaged power spectral density of EEG data using different artifact removal algorithms. It shows that our procedure can effectively reduce the artifacts in different EEG frequency bands without affecting alpha (8–13 Hz) and beta (13–15 Hz in Fig. 7) activities.

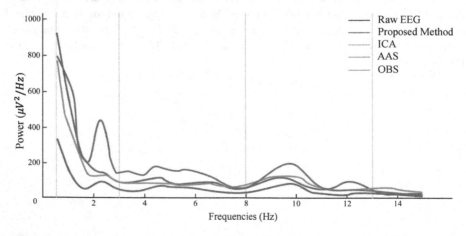

Fig. 7. Averaged power spectral density of channel Fp1 (for DATA 3) using different artifact removal algorithms.

Figure 8 and Table 1 compares the performance of AAS, OBS, ICA and the proposed method in terms of INPS ratio. It can be concluded that the proposed method is obviously superior to other methods.

Table 1. INPSs for all channels using different artifact removal methods.

	DATA 1	DATA 2	DATA 3	DATA 4	DATA 5
Dictionary Learning	8.13	6.68	12.16	5.91	4.23
ICA	7.12	6.21	9.66	5.6	4.76
AAS	3.61	−1.6	7.16	3.66	−0.77
OBS	5.78	2.77	8.6	3.83	1.33

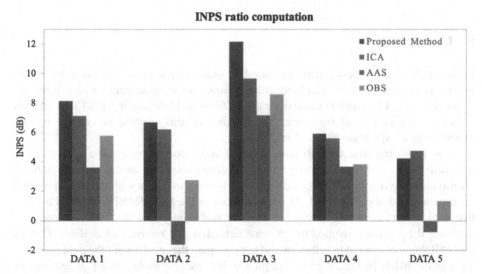

Fig. 8. INPS Reduction for all channels using different artifact correction methods versus the EEG data after removing imaging artifacts.

Table 2 compares the peak-to-peak ratio of BCG artifact suppression methods based on AAS, OBS and ICA, and the results prove the advantages of dictionary learning.

Table 2. Peak-to-peak value for all channels using different artifact removal methods.

	DATA 1	DATA 2	DATA 3	DATA 4	DATA 5
Dictionary Learning	13.40	9.18	20.03	4.22	3.71
ICA	10.74	9.03	15.44	5.57	3.11
AAS	5.57	1.52	8.72	2.08	1.30
OBS	6.15	2.63	11.16	2.69	1.52

Table 3 is the averaged INPS and peak-to-peak ratio using different method. it is obvious that the performance indexes of dictionary-based learning methods are almost higher than those of ICA, AAS and OBS methods, except DATA 3, so it can be considered that the dictionary-based learning method studied in this paper is more effective in inhibiting BCG artifacts.

Table 3. Averaged INPS and peak-to-peak ratio.

	DATA 1	DATA 2	DATA 3	DATA 4	DATA 5
Dictionary Learning	13.40	9.18	20.03	4.22	3.71
ICA	10.74	9.03	15.44	5.57	3.11
AAS	5.57	1.52	8.72	2.08	1.30
OBS	6.15	2.63	11.16	2.69	1.52

5 Conclusion

In this study, a set of new algorithms based on dictionary learning has been developed to remove BCG artifact from EEG recordings simultaneously acquired with continuous fMRI scanners. This method can reduce the BCG related artifacts in EEG fMRI records without using additional hardware. The validity of this method is verified by the experiments of synthetic data and real data.

It is gratifying that we still have a lot of room for progress. The classification standards still need further study, such as classifying the atoms through mutual information, the features of ECG are considered to sort m atoms with the largest mutual information with the ECG [18]. At present, most of the EEG-fMRI researches are on-line data artifact removal, only a few involve real-time correction. We can consider applying the proposed method to real-time detection and removal of artifacts. One of the limitations of our study is that we did not compare the results with the data recorded outside the MRI. In fact, we can design specific paradigms involving in and out of scanner experiments, so that we can how BCG was considered affecting EEG signals from these recorded data.

Acknowledgement. This work was supported by NSFC (61633010, 61671193, 61602140), National Key Research & Development Project (2017YFE0116800), Key Research & Development Project of Zhejiang Province (2020C04009, 2018C04012).

References

1. Mulert, C., Pogarell, O., Hegerl, U.: Simultaneous EEG-fMRI: perspectives in psychiatry. CEN **39**(2), 61–64 (2008). https://doi.org/10.1177/155005940803900207
2. Shams, N., Alain, C., Strother, S.: Comparison of BCG artifact removal methods for evoked responses in simultaneous EEG–fMRI. J. Neurosci. Methods **245**, 137–146 (2015)
3. Iannotti, G.R., Pittau, F., Michel, C.M., Vulliemoz, S., Grouiller, F.: Pulse artifact detection in simultaneous EEG-fMRI recording based on EEG map topography. Brain Topogr. **28**(1), 21–32 (2015)

4. Allen, P.J., Polizzi, G., Krakow, K., Fish, D.R., Lemieux, L.: Identification of EEG events in the MR scanner: the problem of pulse artifact and a method for its subtraction. Neuroimage **8**(3), 229–239 (1998)
5. Bénar, C., Aghakhani, Y., Wang, Y., et al.: Quality of EEG in simultaneous EEG–fMRI for epilepsy. Clin. Neurophysiol. **114**(3), 569–580 (2003)
6. Niazy, K., Beckmann, C.F., Iannetti, G.D., et al.: Removal of FMRI environment artifacts from EEG data using optimal basis sets. Neuroimage **28**(3), 720–737 (2005)
7. Hu, L., Zhang, Z.: EEG Signal Processing and Feature Extraction. Springer, Singapore (2019). https://doi.org/10.1007/978-981-13-9113-2
8. Abolghasemi, V., Ferdowsi, S.: EEG–fMRI: dictionary learning for removal of ballistocardiogram artifact from EEG. Biomed. Signal Process. Control **18**, 186–194 (2015)
9. Ghaderi, F., Nazarpour, K., Mcwhirter, J.G., et al.: Removal of ballistocardiogram artifacts using the cyclostationary source extraction method. IEEE Trans. Biomed. Eng. **57**(11), 2667–2676 (2010)
10. Mantini, D., Perrucci, M.G., Cugini, S., Ferretti, A., Romani, G.L., Del Gratta, C.: Complete artifact removal for EEG recorded during continuous fMRI using independent component analysis. Neuroimage **34**, 598–607 (2007)
11. Winkler, I., Haufe, S., Tangermann, M.: Automatic classification of artifactual ICA-components for artifact removal in EEG signals. BBF **7**, Article no. 30 (2011). https://doi.org/10.1186/1744-9081-7-30
12. de Munck, J.C., van Houdt, P.J., Gonçalves, S.I., van Wegen, E.E.H., Ossenblok, P.P.W.: Novel artefact removal algorithms for co-registered EEG/fMRI based on selective averaging and subtraction. NeuroImage **64**, 407–415 (2013)
13. Quan, Y., Xu, Y., Sun, Y., Huang, Y., Ji, H.: Sparse coding for classification via discrimination ensemble. In: Proceedings of the Conference on Computer Vision and Pattern Recognition (CVPR), pp. 5839–5847 (2016)
14. Demanuele, C., James, C.J., Sonuga-Barke, E.J.: Behav. Brain Funct. **3**, 62 (2007). https://doi.org/10.1186/1744-9081-3-62
15. The FMRIB Plug-in for EEGLAB. https://fsl.fmrib.ox.ac.uk/eeglab/fmribplugin/
16. Dressler, O., Schneider, G., Stockmanns, G., Kochs, E.F.: Awareness and the EEG power spectrum: analysis of frequencies. BJA **93**, 806–809 (2004). https://doi.org/10.1093/bja/aeh270
17. Mairal, J., Bach, F., Ponce, J., Sapiro, G.: Online dictionary learning for sparse coding. In: Proceedings of the 26th Annual International Conference on Machine Learning - ICML 2009 (2009)
18. Liu, Z., de Zwart, J.A., van Gelderen, P., Kuo, L.-W., Duyn, J.: Statistical feature extraction for artifact removal from concurrent fMRI-EEG recordings. Neuroimage **59**, 2073–2087 (2012)
19. Aharon, M., Elad, M., Bruckstein, A.: K-SVD: an algorithm for designing overcomplete dictionaries for sparse representation. IEEE Trans. Signal Process. **54**(11), 4311–4322 (2006)

Comparison of Machine Learning and Deep Learning Approaches for Decoding Brain Computer Interface: An fNIRS Study

Jiahao Lu[1], Hongjie Yan[2], Chunqi Chang[1(✉)],
and Nizhuan Wang[3(✉)]

[1] School of Biomedical Engineering, Health Science Center,
Shenzhen University, Shenzhen, China
cqchang@szu.edu.cn
[2] Department of Neurology, Affiliated Lianyungang Hospital
of Xuzhou Medical University, Lianyungang, China
[3] Artificial Intelligence & Neuro-Informatics Engineering (ARINE) Laboratory,
School of Computer Engineering, Jiangsu Ocean University,
Lianyungang, China
wangnizhuan1120@gmail.com

Abstract. Recently, deep learning has gained great attention in decoding the neuro-physiological signal. However, which one (classical machine learning or deep learning) has better performance for decoding the functional near-infrared spectroscopy (fNIRS) signal is still lack of full verification. Thus, in this paper, we systematically compared the performance of many classical machine learning methods and deep learning methods in fNIRS data processing for decoding the mental arithmetic task. The classical machine learning methods such as decision tree, linear discriminant analysis (LDA), support vector machine (SVM), K-Nearest Neighbor (KNN) and ensemble methods with strict feature extraction and screening, were used for performance comparison, while the long short-term memory-fully convolutional network (LSTM-FCN) method as a representative of deep leaning methods was applied. Results showed that the classification performance of SVM was the best among the classical machine learning methods, achieving that the average accuracy of the subject-related/unrelated were 91.0% and 83.0%, respectively. Furthermore, the classification accuracy of deep learning was significantly better than that of the involved classical machine learning methods, where the accuracy of deep learning could reach 95.3% with subject-related condition and 97.1% with subject-unrelated condition, respectively. Thus, this paper has totally showed the excellent performance of LSTM-FCN as a representative of deep learning in decoding brain signal from fNIRS dataset, which has outperformed many classical machine learning methods.

Keywords: Brain computer interface (BCI) · Functional near-infrared spectroscopy (fNIRS) · Brain signal decoding · Classical machine learning · Deep learning

© IFIP International Federation for Information Processing 2020
Published by Springer Nature Switzerland AG 2020
Z. Shi et al. (Eds.): IIP 2020, IFIP AICT 581, pp. 192–201, 2020.
https://doi.org/10.1007/978-3-030-46931-3_18

1   Introduction

The brain computer interface (BCI) is a technology that provides communication for the human or animal brain with the external environment [1]. When the brain performs a functional task, it activates (or suppresses) the functional brain-related regions, directly affecting the regional cerebral blood flow (rCBF) and cerebral blood volume (CBV). Changes occur and eventually manifest as rapid changes (elevation or decline) in blood oxygen levels in the corresponding regions of the brain, which is called neurovascular coupling [2]. Cerebral nerve activity causes the corresponding changes in blood oxygen levels, and the consequent changes in blood oxygen levels can impact the magnetic and optical properties of brain tissue. It is well known that the water, oxygenated hemoglobin (oxy-Hb), and deoxygenated hemoglobin (deoxy-Hb) have different absorption coefficients for near-infrared light of different wavelengths [3–5]. According to the neurovascular coupling, when the functional cognitive neural activity tasks are performed, the oxygen demand in the active area under the functional task is increased, with the perfused cerebral blood flow. In functional cognitive tasks, the activated brain region generally showed an increase in the concentration of oxy-Hb and total hemoglobin (t-Hb), a decrease in the concentration of deoxy-Hb. The well-known functional magnetic resonance imaging technique generates the blood-oxygen-level-dependent (BOLD) signals by magnetic changes caused by changes in hemoglobin concentration [6], while fNIRS measures oxy-Hb and deoxy-Hb by the absorption of near-infrared light at wavelengths around 704 nm and 887 nm [3, 7, 8].

In 2007, Coyle [9], Sitaram [10], Naito [11] has demonstrated the feasibility of controlling the output of fNIRS-BCI. Today, researchers can identify motor execution, motor imagery, metal arithmetic, music imagery with fNIRS-BCI [12]. Although deep learning has become more and more popular in signal processing, deep learning has not attracted enough attention from fNIRS-BCI researchers in recent years, which is possibly due to the limitation of relatively small samples in fNIRS-BCI experiments. For example, in 2015, Johannes Hennrich et al. has compared deep neural network with part of classical machine learning methods and they showed that deep neural network did not yield higher classification rates than the shrinkage LDA [13]. However, whether classical machine learning or deep learning has better performance for decoding the brain signal is still lack of full verification. Thus, in this paper, a public fNIRS-BCI mental arithmetic data was used to aim at completely finding out the which one (classical machine learning or deep learning) could perform better in fNIRS-BCI data processing under the brain decoding task. In order to improve the performance of machine learning, a new feature screening method is used to find out positive channels and time period of fNIRS mental arithmetic dataset.

2 Experimental Design and Dataset

In this paper, a public fNIRS-BCI dataset was involved in performance validation, which was a mental arithmetic dataset of prefrontal and temporal lobes, with a total of eight subjects, collected and published by the Neuroengineering Laboratory of Graz University [14, 15]. The designed experiment paradigm and data recording were detailed in the following sub-sections.

2.1 Experimental Paradigm

During the designed experiment, all eight subjects were firstly asked to keep an eye on the computer screen. The computer screen was black before the task was activated. Before the mental arithmetic task started, the green line appeared on the screen and lasted for two seconds. When the mental arithmetic task started, the mental arithmetic task prompt (e.g. 97−4) appeared on the screen for one second. The subject needed to follow the prompts to calculate the mental arithmetic task. Namely, the subject should calculate the 97 minus 4 task (97, 93, 89, 85…) until the green line in the middle of the screen disappeared. Specifically, the green line appeared for 14 s in each trial. The first two seconds prompt that the trial was about to start. After the green prompt line appeared for 2 s, the mental arithmetic task calculation formula appeared above the green prompt line for 1 s (e.g., 97−4). Then, the subject was asked to watch the screen and started mental arithmetic until the green line disappeared (the mental arithmetic task lasted for 12 s). After the green line disappeared, the subject continued to watch the black screen and to wait for the next trial (as a resting trial without mental arithmetic task).

2.2 Data Recording

A continuous wave system (ETG-400, Hitachi Medical Co, Japan) was used in the experimental instrument. Using 16 photo-detectors and 17 light emitters to form a 3×11 grid probe arrangement, 52 channels in total were distributed on the prefrontal and temporal lobes, and each one was capable of measuring oxy-Hb concentration, deoxy-Hb concentration and t-Hb concentration. The sampling rate was 10 Hz and the distance between the source and the probe was 3 cm. The channel closest to the nose side was arranged along the FP1-FP2 series of the International. The channel 48 in the electroencephalogram 10–20 system was located at the FP1 position (as shown in Fig. 1).

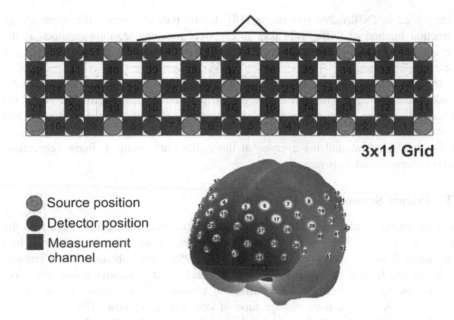

Fig. 1. Schematic illustration of the multi-channel positional layouts for 52 channels [15]

3 Classical Machine Learning for fNIRS Signal Decoding

3.1 Data Preprocessing

It well known that there is a physiological interference signal in the captured fNIRS data. In order to obtain a brain functional activation signal with high signal-to-noise ratio (SNR), it is necessary to preprocess the original data to reduce physiological noises caused by physiological activities such as heartbeat, respiration, and blood pressure fluctuations [16]. Physiological noise generated by heartbeat, respiration, blood pressure, and Mayer waves are relatively stable and statistically independent interference signal [17]. The most common method for dealing with physiological noise is to use a band-pass filter that uses a digital filter to eliminate the effects of heartbeat, respiration, Mayer wave signals, and baseline drift based on the frequency of physiological noise. In our experiment, the finite impulse response (FIR) band-pass filter is used to pass the 0.05–0.7 Hz signal, aiming at improving the SNR of the signal.

3.2 Feature Extraction

The fNIRS-BCI data refers to the time-series signal of the multi-channel scattered light intensity change collected by the fNIRS device. Statistical features directly reflect the statistical characteristics of fNIRS data and reduce the redundant information, which is widely used in fNIRS data processing [18]. In the past few years, the main feature extraction method of fNIRS-BCI data in classical machine learning methods is the average concentration of the time-intercept signal intercepted in seconds [19–22] and slope [21, 22].

In the feature extraction stage, the average and slope of the 0.5 s window and 1 s window, the average of the full data segment, the linear fitting regression value, the variance, the range, and the skewness were selected as the classification features. Each subject dataset could provide 125 features, including the average and linear regression of the time window, and the average of the entire data segment, linear regression, variance, range, and skewness.

3.3 Feature Screening and Classification

After the stages of data preprocessing and feature extraction, the feature data with the size of $36 \times 156 \times 125$ was first obtained. After the feature data was converted into two dimensions, a matrix with size of 36×19500 was obtained. The channel screening and feature screening procedure was performed to remove redundant information, and to determine the main activation channel (brain region) of the mental arithmetic task and the main change time of cerebral blood flow. The classification contribution values of each single-channel with all features data $36 \times 1 \times 125$ and the single-feature with all channels data $36 \times 156 \times 1$ were evaluated, respectively. The classification contribution values were then selected as follows: the input feature data was classified by five classifiers such as LDA, SVM, KNN, Decision Tree and Ensemble Learning classifier, and then the average value of the top three accuracy was used as a criterion.

Then, based on the channel classification contribution values and the feature classification contribution values, the optimal combination of the multiple channels and multiple features should be determined. In this paper, the channels and features combinations of multi-channel and multi-features were classified and judged by the exhaustive method with different number of optimal channels and optimal features. Although the number of channels and the number of features was simply changed in the feature screening process, the corresponding calculation time could be greatly reduced in searching optimal combinations. The approximate activation channel (in spatial domain) and approximate activation period (in temporal domain) of the mental arithmetic task were obtained by optimal combination through a large number of calculations. The detailed procedure was shown in Fig. 2.

Finally, after the procedure of feature screening, the chosen features were put into 5 classifiers (i.e., LDA, SVM, KNN, Decision Tree, and Ensemble Learning classifier) to perform the classification task.

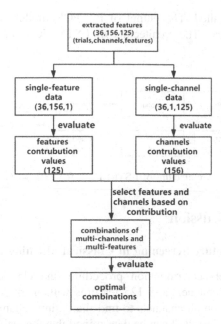

Fig. 2. Flowchart of channel and feature screening

4 Deep Learning for fNIRS Signal Decoding

In this paper, a long time-term memory (LSTM) based on a fully convolutional network (FCN) [23], namely LSTM-FCN was used. FCN replaced the last three fully connected layers of the classic convolutional neural network (CNN) [24] with three convolutional layers.

The original fNIRS data of 8 subjects were processed according to the data interception method, generating the data with dimensions of $36 \times 156 \times 200$, where 36 denoted the number of experimental trials, 156 represented the number of channels, and 200 was the length of a trial. Input data is randomly assigned in a 4 to 1 ratio to obtain the training set and test set, respectively. The followed experimental results were averaged from the results of 5 cross-validation.

The 1-D convolution has proven to be an effective learning method for time series classification problems [24]. An FCN with 1-D convolution was commonly used as a feature extractor. Global average pooling [25] was applied to reduce the number of parameters in the model before classification. In the proposed model, the FCN was enhanced by the LSTM module, and then the dropout function was involved to prevent over-fitting and to accelerate the training process [26]. The FCN module consisted of three stacked 1-D convolution blocks with filter sizes of 128, 256 and 128, respectively. Each convolution block was identical to the convolution block in the FCN architecture proposed by Wang [24]. Each block consisted of a temporal convolutional layer, each block was processed for bulk normalization [27], and then the activation function was used. The time series data was input into the LSTM block, and then the dropout function was called. The output of the FCN module and the output of the LSTM were concatenated. The architecture of LSTM-FCN for fNIRS-BCI data was showed in Fig. 3.

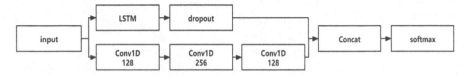

Fig. 3. Architecture of LSTM-FCN for fNIRS-BCI data

5   Results and Discussion

5.1   Channel and Feature Screening in Classical Machine Learning

In the optimal channels determination procedure, the classical machine learning methods classified 156 channels and 125 features without prior conditions, and performed exhaustive tests on all channels to find the optimal channels. After the data of several subjects was processed, it can be determined that the activated brain area of the mental arithmetic task was more significant in channel 26, 36, 37, 46, 48, which was shown in Fig. 4. Moreover, it was found in the feature screening stage that the average value of the data in the interval [6 s, 17 s] contributed more to classification performance. Each subject processing could provide a priori condition for the next data processing, which could help determine the activation brain area and activation time period.

Fig. 4. The activation channel map of mental arithmetic task

5.2   Decoding Performance: Classical Machine Learning V.S. Deep Learning

In Table 1, the highest accuracy of SVM in the classical machine learning of the subject-related classifier was 91%, and the accuracy of the deep learning method was 95.3%. Under the subject-unrelated conditions, the accuracy of classical machine learning reached 83%, and the accuracy of deep learning reached 97.1%. For the S03, S04, S07, S08, in the case of different network dropout rate, can achieve 100% accuracy. At this point, deep learning method, i.e., LSTM-FCN, has been significantly better than the classical machine learning methods have, and a 100% accuracy could make BCI system more stable.

Table 1. Accuracy of classical machine learning methods and deep learning method

		S01	S02	S03	S04	S05	S06	S07	S08	Average	All subjects
Classical machine learning	Decision tree	69.4	75	86.1	85.4	64.6	77.1	77.1	75	76.2	71
	LDA	77.8	83.3	91.7	77.1	66.7	68.8	85.4	93.8	80.5	60.1
	SVM	**91.7**	91.7	**97.2**	**93.8**	**77.1**	**83.3**	95.8	**97.9**	**91.0**	**83.0**
	KNN	77.8	83.3	88.9	89.6	66.7	77.1	**97.9**	93.8	84.3	69.8
	Ensemble	83.3	**97.2**	88.9	91.7	66.7	81.3	93.8	95.8	87.3	75.9
Deep learning: LSTM-FCN with different dropout rate	0.3	**91.7**	**91.7**	**100**	**100**	87.5	93.7	97.9	**100**	**95.3**	86.4
	0.5	86.1	83.3	97.2	**100**	**93.7**	**95.8**	**100**	**100**	94.5	**97.1**
	0.6	83.3	86.1	97.2	**100**	89.5	93.7	**100**	**100**	93.7	88.5
	0.8	**91.7**	88.8	**100**	**100**	74.9	79.2	95.8	**100**	91.3	90.8

In the subject-related classification, accuracy of S05 and S06 was lower than that of other subjects. But in deep learning method, the accuracy of S05 and S06 can reach 90%. Contritely, the deep learning method (LSTM-FCN) still got better decoding performance for the difficult subjects in the classical machine learning. In the subject-unrelated classification, the deep learning method was with significantly higher accuracy than the classical machine learning methods did. The highest accuracy of deep learning was 14.1% higher than that of the classical machine learning methods where the accuracy of deep learning is very close to 100%. Thus, according to Table 1, it was easily concluded that the LSTM-FCN method as a representative of deep learning had better performance for fNIRS-BCI decoding.

6 Conclusion

In this paper, we made a full decoding performance comparison between the classical machine learning methods and deep learning method on fNIRS-BCI data. According to the experimental results, it was found that the LSTM-FCN method as a representative of deep learning showed superior performance to all the classical machine learning methods such as decision tree, LDA, SVM, KNN and ensemble classifier. In terms of the training time in the classical machine learning methods, it took more time to do channels screening and features screening task. As the amount of data increased and the new models were developed, the deep learning methods could achieve the classification accuracy and robustness on the small fNIRS-BCI dataset. Thus, the deep learning is a promising tool for decoding fNIRS-BCI data in comparison to the classical machine learning.

Acknowledgements. This work was supported by National Natural Science Foundation of China (No. 61701318, 61971289), Natural Science Research Project of Jiangsu Higher Education Institutions (No. 18KJB416001), Project of "Six Talent Peaks" of Jiangsu Province (No. SWYY-017), Shenzhen Fundamental Research Project (No. JCYJ20170412111316339), Shenzhen Talent Peacock Plan (No. 827-000083), and Shenzhen-Hong Kong Institute of Brain Science-Shenzhen Fundamental Research Institutions.

References

1. Bauernfeind, G., et al.: Single trial classification of fNIRS-based brain-computer interface mental arithmetic data: a comparison between different classifiers. In: 2014 36th Annual International Conference of the IEEE Engineering in Medicine and Biology Society, pp. 2004–2007. IEEE (2014)
2. Pasley, B.N., Freeman, R.D.: Neurovascular coupling. Scholarpedia 3(3), 5340 (2008)
3. Scholkmann, F., Kleiser, S., Metz, A.J., et al.: A review on continuous wave functional near-infrared spectroscopy and imaging instrumentation and methodology. Neuroimage 85, 6–27 (2014)
4. Hoshi, Y.: Functional near-infrared optical imaging: utility and limitations in human brain mapping. Psychophysiology 40(4), 511–520 (2003)
5. Hoshi, Y.: Near-infrared spectroscopy for studying higher cognition. In: Kraft, E., Gulyás, B., Pöppel, E. (eds.) Neural Correlates of Thinking. On Thinking, vol. 1, pp. 83–93. Springer, Berlin (2009). https://doi.org/10.1007/978-3-540-68044-4_6
6. Kim, S.G., Ogawa, S.: Biophysical and physiological origins of blood oxygenation level-dependent fMRI signals. J. Cerebral Blood Flow Metab. 32(7), 1188–1206 (2012)
7. Leff, D.R., Orihuela-Espina, F., Elwell, C.E., et al.: Assessment of the cerebral cortex during motor task behaviours in adults: a systematic review of functional near infrared spectroscopy (fNIRS) studies. Neuroimage 54(4), 2922–2936 (2011)
8. Irani, F., Platek, S.M., Bunce, S., et al.: Functional near infrared spectroscopy (fNIRS): an emerging neuroimaging technology with important applications for the study of brain disorders. Clin. Neuropsychol. 21(1), 9–37 (2007)
9. Coyle, S.M., Ward, T.E., Markham, C.M.: Brain–computer interface using a simplified functional near-infrared spectroscopy system. J. Neural Eng. 4(3), 219 (2007)
10. Sitaram, R., Zhang, H., Guan, C., et al.: Temporal classification of multichannel near-infrared spectroscopy signals of motor imagery for developing a brain–computer interface. NeuroImage 34(4), 1416–1427 (2007)
11. Naito, M., Michioka, Y., Ozawa, K., et al.: A communication means for totally locked-in ALS patients based on changes in cerebral blood volume measured with near-infrared light. IEICE Trans. Inf. Syst. 90(7), 1028–1037 (2007)
12. Naseer, N., Hong, K.S.: fNIRS-based brain-computer interfaces: a review. Front. Hum. Neurosci. 9, 3 (2015)
13. Hennrich, J., et al.: Investigating deep learning for fNIRS based BCI. In: 2015 37th Annual International Conference of the IEEE Engineering in Medicine and Biology Society (EMBC), pp. 2844–2847. IEEE (2015)

14. Günther, B., Scherer, R., Pfurtscheller, G., et al.: Single-trial classification of antagonistic oxyhemoglobin responses during mental arithmetic. Med. Biol. Eng. Comput. **49**(9), 979–984 (2011)
15. http://bnci-horizon-2020.eu/database/data-sets
16. Kirilina, E., Jelzow, A., Heine, A., et al.: The physiological origin of task-evoked systemic artefacts in functional near infrared spectroscopy. Neuroimage **61**(1), 70–81 (2012)
17. Bauernfeind, G., et al.: Physiological noise removal from fNIRS signals. Biomed. Eng./Biomedizinische Technik, 1–2 (2013)
18. Cui, X., Bray, S., Reiss, A.L.: Speeded near infrared spectroscopy (NIRS) response detection. PLoS One **5**(11), 1–7 (2010). e15474
19. Putze, F., Hesslinger, S., Tse, C.Y., et al.: Hybrid fNIRS-EEG based classification of auditory and visual perception processes. Front. Neurosci. **8**, 1–13 (2014)
20. Yin, X., Xu, B., Jiang, C., et al: A hybrid BCI based on EEG and fNIRS signals improves the performance of decoding motor imagery of both force and speed of hand clenching. J. Neural Eng. **12**(3), 1–12 (2015). 036004
21. Buccino, A.P., Hasan, O.K., Ahmet, O.: Hybrid EEG-fNIRS asynchronous brain-computer interface for multiple motor tasks. PLoS ONE **11**, 1 (2016)
22. Raheel, B.M., Hong, M.J., Yun-Hee, K., et al.: Single-trial lie detection using a combined fNIRS-polygraph system. Front. Psychol. **6**, 709 (2015)
23. Karim, F., Majumdar, S., Darabi, H., et al.: LSTM Fully Convolutional Networks for Time Series Classification. IEEE Access **6**, 1662–1669 (2017)
24. Wang, Z., Yan, W., Oates, T.: Time series classification from scratch with deep neural networks: a strong baseline. In: 2017 International Joint Conference on Neural Networks (IJCNN), pp. 1578–1585. IEEE (2017)
25. Lin, M., Chen, Q., Yan, S.: Network in network. https://arxiv.org/abs/1312.4400 (2013)
26. Srivastava, N., Hinton, G., Krizhevsky, A., et al.: Dropout: a simple way to prevent neural networks from overfitting. J. Mach. Learn. Res. **15**(1), 1929–1958 (2014)
27. Ioffe, S., Szegedy, C.: Batch normalization: accelerating deep network training by reducing internal covariate shift. arXiv preprint arXiv:1502.03167 (2015)

Pattern Recognition

Phase Plane Analysis of Traffic Flow Evolution Based on a Macroscopic Traffic Flow Model

WenHuan Ai[1(✉)], Tao Xing[1], YuHang Su[1], DaWei Liu[2],
and Huifang Ma[1]

[1] College of Computer Science and Engineering, Northwest Normal University,
Lanzhou 730070, Gansu, China
wenhuan618@163.com, 573340970@qq.com,
463753759@qq.com, 452770064@qq.com
[2] College of Electrical Engineering, Lanzhou Institute of Technology,
Lanzhou 730070, Gansu, China
liudawei20120901@163.com

Abstract. In this paper, a new phase plane analysis method is proposed to study the nonlinear phenomena of traffic flow. Most of the papers describe only one or several traffic phenomena and do not analyze all of them from the perspective of system stability. Therefore, this paper studies the phase plane analysis of traffic flow phenomenon from the perspective of traffic system stability, and describes various complicated nonlinear traffic phenomena through phase plane analysis.

Keywords: Phase plane diagrams · Stop-and-go waves · Stability analysis · Phase plane analysis

1 Introduction

At present, traffic congestion is getting more and more serious in most cities and regions in China. In order to solve the problem of heavy traffic, we cannot simply increase the number of traffic roads and limit the driving of vehicles, which can only solve the temporary problem on the surface. Only by strengthening the research on the intrinsic nature of traffic flow can we fundamentally prevent and solve the problem of traffic congestion.

In a large number of studies on traffic flow phenomena, we find that although many scholars have studied and proposed many research methods, the results only describe one or several traffic phenomena [2, 3, 6, 7]. In this paper, from the perspective of system stability, traffic congestion and system instability are related, and a phase plane analysis method is proposed to transform the traffic flow problem into a system stability analysis problem.

The core content of phase plane analysis is variable substitution. Substitute the density and speed variables in traditional traffic models. It can be described as $\sigma = 1/v$ and $\eta = 1/(\rho_m - \rho)$. The physical meaning of variable substitution is that from $\sigma = 1/v$ it can be found that as long as traffic congestion occurs and the vehicle speed approaches zero, the state variable σ tends to infinity and the system becomes unstable.

© IFIP International Federation for Information Processing 2020
Published by Springer Nature Switzerland AG 2020
Z. Shi et al. (Eds.): IIP 2020, IFIP AICT 581, pp. 205–212, 2020.
https://doi.org/10.1007/978-3-030-46931-3_19

It can be found from $\eta = 1/(\rho_m - \rho)$ that as long as there is traffic congestion, the density of vehicles tends to saturation density, the state variable η tends to infinity, and the system becomes unstable. This means that the substitution expands the scope of the variable to infinity, so the correspondence between traffic congestion and system instability can be established on the phase plan.

2   Variable Substitution Based On a Macroscopic Traffic Flow Model

Tang et al. proposed a macroscopic traffic flow model considering the driver's prediction effect [1]. He expression is as follows:

$$
\begin{cases}
\frac{\partial \rho}{\partial t} + \frac{\partial (\rho v)}{\partial x} = 0 \\
\frac{\partial v}{\partial t} + v \frac{\partial v}{\partial x} = \frac{(1+\beta)(Ve(\rho) - v)}{T + \beta \tau} - \beta \tau c_0 \rho^2 V_e'(\rho) \frac{\partial v}{\partial x}
\end{cases}
\tag{1}
$$

Type:

ρ—Average vehicle density;
v—Average vehicle speed;
τ—Time interval;
β—Nonnegative constants;
$V_e[\rho(x,t)]$—Equilibrium speed;
c_0—Velocity of disturbance propagation;
$V_e[\rho(x,t)]$ has the following form:

$$
V_e[\rho] = v_f \left\{ \left[1 + \exp\left(\frac{\rho/\rho_m - 0.25}{0.06} \right) \right]^{-1} - 3.72 \times 10^{-6} \right\}
\tag{2}
$$

From the formula (2):

$$
V_e'(\rho) = -\frac{v_f \exp\left(\frac{\rho - 0.25\rho_m}{0.06\rho_m} \right)}{0.06\rho_m \left[1 + \exp\left(\frac{\rho - 0.25\rho_m}{0.06\rho_m} \right) \right]^2}
\tag{3}
$$

Here v_f is the free flow velocity, ρ_m is the maximum or congestion density.
In the present paper, a simple transformation is employed as follows,

$$
\begin{cases}
\sigma = \frac{1}{v} \\
\eta = \frac{1}{\rho_m - \rho}
\end{cases}
\tag{4}
$$

Substituting the variables into Eq. (1), we have a new traffic flow model as follows:

$$\begin{cases} \sigma^2 \frac{\partial \eta}{\partial t} + (\eta - \rho_m \eta^2) \frac{\partial \sigma}{\partial x} + \sigma \frac{\partial \eta}{\partial x} = 0 \\ -1/\sigma^2 \frac{\partial \sigma}{\partial t} - 1/\sigma^3 \frac{\partial \sigma}{\partial x} - \frac{(1+\beta)(v_e(\eta) - \frac{1}{\sigma})}{T + \beta\tau} - \beta\tau c_0 \left(\rho_m - \frac{1}{\eta}\right)^2 v_e'(\eta)\left(-\frac{1}{\sigma^2}\frac{\partial \sigma}{\partial x}\right) = 0 \end{cases} \quad (5)$$

Then substitute the variable into formula (2), and the expression of the equivalent velocity is as follows:

$$V_e(\eta) = v_f \left\{ \left[1 + \exp\left(\frac{0.75 - \frac{1}{\eta\rho_m}}{0.06}\right) \right]^{-1} -3.72 \times 10^{-6} \right\} \quad (6)$$

Then variable substitution $\eta = \frac{1}{\rho_m - \rho}$ is substituted into $V_e'(\rho)$, we can get:

$$V_e'(\eta) = -\frac{v_f \exp\left(12.5 - \frac{1}{0.06\rho_m\eta}\right)}{0.06\rho_m\eta^2 \left[1 + \exp\left(12.5 - \frac{1}{0.06\rho_m\eta}\right)\right]^2} \quad (7)$$

Specifically, the range of variable ρ in the original traffic flow mode is $0 - 0.25\ veh/m$ and the range of variable v is $0 - 30$ m/s, so the range of variation in density or velocity is very limited. At this time, the variable substitution in the phase plane analysis method plays a vital role, it can expand the state variables ρ and v in the original model to infinity, which means that it breaks through the limitations. It can be found that when the speed approaches zero, the state variable σ is close to infinity. Similarly, the state variable η approaches infinity when the density approaches the congestion density. The increase of state variables σ and η indicates that the average vehicle speed decreases, vehicle density increases, and the system becomes unstable. Therefore, changes in state variables can be used to judge the stability of the system. In phase plane analysis, traffic congestion can be equated with system instability.

3   Study on the Stop-and-Go Phenomenon Based on the Phase Plane Analysis

In this section, we mainly do a comparative analysis. The comparison objects are the new model with variable substitution and the traditional model without variable substitution. The method of analysis is to compare the phase plane diagram drawn by the new model with the density space-time diagram [4, 5] of the traditional model through specific numerical simulation. It turns out that the new method is consistent with the traditional method in describing the stop-and-go traffic phenomenon. But phase diagrams can more clearly describe changes in density or velocity at any time or in any part.

We can find the stop-and-go traffic phenomena in the phenomenon of small disturbance amplification. We simulate stop-and-go traffic phenomena in an enlarged local disturbance on the initial uniform traffic flow. The expression of the initial density is as follows:

$$\rho(x, 0) = \rho_0 + \Delta\rho_0\left\{\cosh^{-2}\left[\frac{160}{L}\left(x - \frac{5L}{16}\right)\right] - \frac{1}{4}\cosh^{-2}\left[\frac{40}{L}\left(x - \frac{11L}{32}\right)\right]\right\}$$

$$x \in [0, L]$$ (8)

Type:

ρ_0—Initial uniform density;
$\Delta\rho_0$—Disturbance density;
L—Section length;

Among them, $\Delta\rho_0 = 0.01$ veh/m is the amplitude of localized perturbation, the path length L investigated in this section is 32.2 km. The expression of the initial velocity is as follows:

$$v(x, 0) = V(\rho(x, 0)) \quad x \in [0, L]$$ (9)

The dynamic adjacent boundary conditions are given by the following formula:

$$\rho(1, t) = \rho(2, t), \rho(L, t) = \rho(L - 1, t), v(1, t) = v(2, t), v(L, t) = v(L - 1, t)$$

(10)

In order to facilitate the simulation, the space interval is equal to 100 m, the time interval is 1 s, and the values of other parameters in the model are as follows:

$$c_0 = 11 \, \text{m/s}, \tau = 5 \, \text{s}, v_f = 30 \, \text{m/s}, \rho_m = 0.2 \, \text{veh/m}, \beta = 0.3$$

Corresponding to the above parameters, according to the stability condition, the critical density of the prediction model is 0.037 veh/m and 0.091 veh/m, the initial density is set at 0.037 veh/m $< \rho_0 <$ 0.091 veh/m the traffic flow is linearly unstable in this range, small perturbations at this initial density will diverge and lead to stop-go phenomenon.

In this section, in order to draw the model replaced the new prediction model of the floor plan, we should first of all, for a given value, the discrete model of finite difference method, and numerical solving state variables, take $\left(\eta, \frac{\partial\eta}{\partial t}\right)$, $\left(\eta, \frac{\partial\eta}{\partial x}\right)$, $\left(\sigma, \frac{\partial\sigma}{\partial t}\right)$, $\left(\sigma, \frac{\partial\sigma}{\partial x}\right)$ as the coordinates, draw four phase plans in proper order. Through the four figures, we can study more clearly the corresponding density or velocity or displacement change at any time, thus the fluctuations of traffic flow completely into the stability of the system analysis.

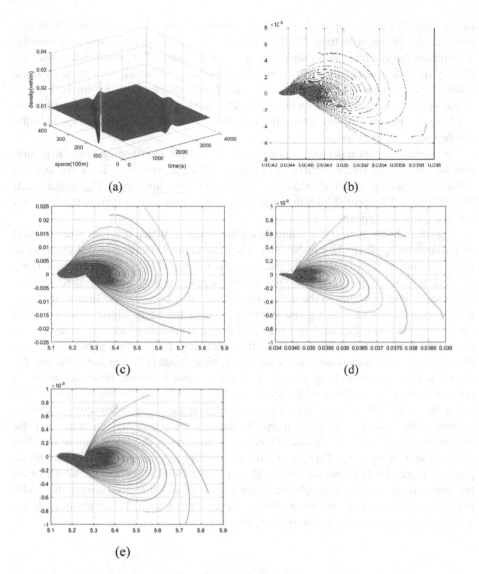

Fig. 1. $\beta = 0.2$ initial density $\rho_0 = 0.01$ veh/m (a) is the density space-time diagram, (b) is the phase plan with coordinates $\left(\sigma, \frac{\partial\sigma}{\partial t}\right)$, (c) is the phase plan with coordinates $\left(\eta, \frac{\partial\eta}{\partial t}\right)$, (d) is the phase plan with coordinates $\left(\sigma, \frac{\partial\sigma}{\partial x}\right)$, (e) is the phase plan with coordinates $\left(\eta, \frac{\partial\eta}{\partial x}\right)$.

Figures 1(b)–(e) are the phase plane diagrams of variables η and σ. We draw the stage process of the curve and find the starting point and the route of the whole run. We can see all the curve changes from outside to inside, gradually approaching the center of the ring. No curve approaches infinity, which indicates that the initial small disturbance disappears with time. On the whole, Figs. 1(b)–(c) have no curve at infinity. This means the system is stable and there are no traffic jams. This is consistent with the density space-time diagram in Fig. 1(a). The disturbance eventually disappears and the traffic flow eventually converges to the initial uniform density. Figure 1(a) is the density spatiotemporal diagram where the initial density of the model is set within the stable range. Figure 1(d)–(e) reflects the fluctuation of vehicle density and speed in the whole section at each moment.

We found that its trajectory is composed of multiple overlapping circle structure, this means that all running curve is outside-in change over time. It shows that the density fluctuations gradually reduce over time on the whole road. The initial small disturbance is disappeared with the time and the transportation system is stable. If it's unstable, it's the opposite.

Figure 2 shows an unstable traffic flow phenomenon, which diverges when a small disturbance is applied. As can be seen from the density spatiotemporal diagram in Fig. 2(a), due to the initial density taken within the unstable range of the model, the small disturbance imposed on the initial uniform density is gradually amplified with the increase of time, resulting in the instability of the traffic flow and the formation of the traffic phenomenon of walking and stopping, that is, the traffic cluster. According to curve sections, draw Fig. 2(b) and Fig. 2(d). We can find that there are many curves approaching infinity, and the further up the outer ring goes, which indicates that the density fluctuation is increasing at the top, the vehicle speed is decreasing at the top, the state variable is approaching infinity, and the system becomes unstable, which is consistent with the tendency of the system to become unstable as shown in Fig. 2(a). From the Fig. 2(d) and Fig. 2(e), we can find that there are many curves tend to infinity, which shows that the density fluctuations are enlarged with time, and the phenomenon of small disturbances diverging with time is displayed intuitively. The entire system is unstable. Compared with the density spatiotemporal map, the phase plan can more clearly reflect the density change at the current time and the next time on the entire road section. Through the phase plan, we can directly convert the traffic congestion phenomenon into the instability curve of the system. The more unstable the traffic system is, the more obvious the effect is.

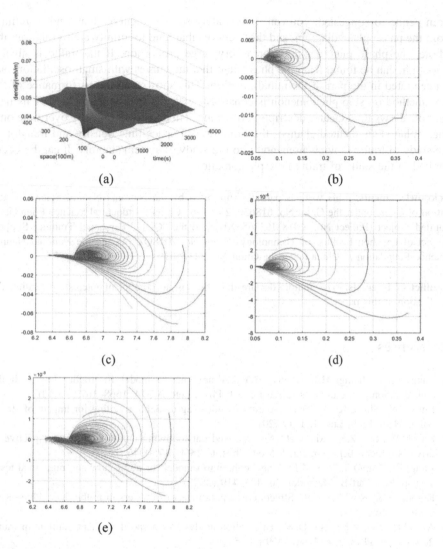

(a)   (b)

(c)   (d)

(e)

Fig. 2. $\beta = 0.3$ Initial density $\rho_0 = 0.042\,\text{veh/m}$ (a) is the density space-time diagram, (b) is the phase plan with coordinates $\left(\sigma, \frac{\partial \sigma}{\partial t}\right)$, (c) is the phase plan with coordinates $\left(\eta, \frac{\partial \eta}{\partial t}\right)$, (d) is the phase plan with coordinates $\left(\sigma, \frac{\partial \sigma}{\partial x}\right)$, (e) is the phase plan with coordinates $\left(\eta, \frac{\partial \eta}{\partial x}\right)$.

4   Conclusions

In this article, the original model is transformed into a new model by using a variable method. Using the phase plan, we can also describe the various non-linear phenomena observed in the traffic flow. We first build a new traffic flow model by replacing variables in the model. By analyzing and comparing the space-time diagrams and phase diagrams of different initial densities, it is found that when the traffic system changes from gentle to congested, you can immediately see some curves that tend to infinity from the phase plane diagram, and these curves that tend to infinity are throughout the whole The phase plan accounts for a very large proportion. If the traffic is always smooth, it can be found from the phase plan that the curves with small oscillations are concentrated in the part of the initial position. This shows that the performance of the new method on stop phenomenon is consistent with the traditional method. This new method allows for a clearer description of changes in density or velocity over time on a phase plan. This method changes the limitation of space-time density and transforms the study of traffic flow phenomenon into the study of system stability. It can be better applied to the study of traffic flow phenomenon.

Acknowledgments. This work is partially supported by the National Natural Science Foundation of China under the Grant No. 61863032 and the China Postdoctoral Science Foundation Funded Project (Project No.: 2018M633653XB) and the "Qizhi" Personnel Training Support Project of Lanzhou Institute of Technology (Grant No. 2018QZ-11) and the National Natural Science Foundation of China under the Grant No. 11965019.

Conflict of Interests. The authors declare that there is no conflict of interests regarding the publication of this paper.

References

1. Tang, T.Q., Huang, H.J., Shang, H.Y.: A new macro model for traffic flow with the consideration of the driver's forecast effect. Phys. Lett. A **374**, 1668–1672 (2010)
2. Liu, D.W., Shi, Z.K., Ai, W.H.: A new car-following model accounting for impact of strong wind. Math. Prob. Eng. **1**, 1–12 (2017)
3. Liu, D.W., Shi, Z.K., Ai, W.H.: An improved car-following model from the perspective of driver's forecast behavior. Int. J. Mod. Phys. C **28**(4), 1750046 (2017)
4. Jiang, R., Wu, Q.S., Zhu, Z.J.: A new continuum model for traffic flow and numerical tests. Transp. Res. Part B: Methodol. **36**, 405–419 (2002)
5. Kerner, B.S., Konhäuser, P.: Structure and parameters of clusters in traffic flow. Phys. Rev. E **50**, 54–86 (1994)
6. Ai, W.H., Shi, Z.K., Liu, D.W.: Bifurcation analysis of a speed gradient continuum traffic flow model. Phys. A **437**, 418–429 (2015)
7. Ai, W.H., Shi, Z.K., Liu, D.W.: Bifurcation analysis method of nonlinear traffic phenomena. Int. J. Mod. Phys. C **26**, 1550111 (2015)

Phase Plane Analysis of Traffic Phenomena with Different Input and Output Conditions

WenHuan Ai[1(✉)], YuHang Su[1], Tao Xing[1], DaWei Liu[2], and Huifang Ma[1]

[1] College of Computer Science and Engineering, Northwest Normal University, Lanzhou 730070, Gansu, China
wenhuan618@163.com, 463753759@qq.com,
573340970@qq.com, 452770064@qq.com
[2] College of Electrical Engineering, Lanzhou Institute of Technology, Lanzhou 730050, Gansu, China
liudawei20120901@163.com

Abstract. In this paper, the traffic flow problem is converted into a system stability problem through variable substitution and a phase plane analysis method is presented for analyzing the complex nonlinear traffic phenomena. This method matches traffic congestion with the unstable system. So these theories and methods of stability can be applied directly to solve the traffic problem. Based on an anisotropic continuum model developed by Gupta and Katiyar (GK model), this paper uses this new method to describe various nonlinear phenomena due to different input and output conditions on ramps which were rarely studied in the past. The results show that the traffic phenomena described by the new method is consistent with that described by traditional methods. Moreover, the phase plane diagram highlights the unstable traffic phenomena we are chiefly concerned about and describes the variation of density or velocity with time or sections more clearly.

Keywords: Phase plane diagrams · Nonlinear traffic phenomena · Stability analysis · Ramps

1 Introduction

In a real traffic flow, almost every driver meets with the phenomenon of traffic congestion. There have been several recent advances in traffic theory, notably those that treat traffic like a fluid. An important branch of the subject, with repercussions on all the other branches, is the quantitative study of traffic phenomena. More recently, there has been an increasing tendency to adopt scientific methods, and try to assess all kinds of traffic phenomena by means of controlled experiments. Paralleled with experiments, many physical models have been proposed [1–3]. Most of them are hydrodynamic models which provide a macroscopic description of traffic flow. The study of continuum traffic phenomena began with the LWR model developed independently by Lighthill and Whitham [4] and Richards [5]. In this model, vehicles have often been considered as interacting particles and traffic flow can be considered as a one-

© IFIP International Federation for Information Processing 2020
Published by Springer Nature Switzerland AG 2020
Z. Shi et al. (Eds.): IIP 2020, IFIP AICT 581, pp. 213–221, 2020.
https://doi.org/10.1007/978-3-030-46931-3_20

dimensional compressible flow of these particles. In the past decades, researchers have made many efforts to improve the LWR model, they developed many higher order models which use a dynamic equation to make speed to replace the equilibrium relationship. Subsequent studies [6–9, 11] of the models have explained many observed features of the free flow and traffic jams in highways. Gupta and Katiyar [10] develop a macroscopic continuum traffic flow model to solve the characteristic speed problem that exists in the previously developed high-order models, which is referred to as GK model.

In this paper, we use a new method to describe a variety of nonlinear traffic flow phenomena which are raised by different input and output on the ramp. We use some variable substitution to convert the traffic flow model into a functional stability model. From this model many well-known nonlinear phenomena may be analyzed. This paper studies the change of the flow at the ramp on the highway which is rarely studied by others. It includes various situations of fixed vehicle generation rate but increasing initial homogeneous density with a single ramp.

The remainder of the paper is organized as follows. In Sect. 2, we present the description of variable substitution and a functional stability model about traffic flow has been postulated. In Sect. 3, we analyze all kinds of nonlinear phenomena which are raised by different input and output on ramp by the new model. In Sect. 4, we concluded the paper.

2 Variable Substitution Based on GK Model

GK model is an anisotropic continuous traffic flow model. It has been mostly studied nowadays and has the following form:

$$
\begin{cases}
\dfrac{\partial \rho}{\partial t} + \dfrac{\partial (\rho v)}{\partial x} = 0 \\[2mm]
\dfrac{\partial v}{\partial t} + v\dfrac{\partial v}{\partial x} = a[V_e(\rho) - v] + aV_e'(\rho)\left[\dfrac{1}{2\rho}\dfrac{\partial \rho}{\partial x} + \dfrac{1}{6\rho^2}\dfrac{\partial^2 \rho}{\partial x^2} - \dfrac{1}{2\rho^3}\left(\dfrac{\partial \rho}{\partial x}\right)^2\right] - 2\beta c(\rho)\dfrac{\partial v}{\partial x}
\end{cases}
\tag{1}
$$

where ρ is the density; v is the velocity; x and t represent space and time respectively; a is the driver's sensitivity which equals the inverse of the driver's reaction time; $V_e[\rho(x, t)]$ is the optimal velocity function and has the following form:

$$
V_e[\rho] = v_f\left\{\left[1 + \exp\left(\frac{\rho/\rho_m - 0.25}{0.06}\right)\right]^{-1} - 3.72 \times 10^{-6}\right\}
\tag{2}
$$

$V_e'(\rho) = \frac{dV_e(\rho)}{d\rho}$, β is a non-negative dimensionless parameter and $c(\rho) \prec 0$ is the traffic sound speed given by:

$$c^2(\rho) = -\frac{aV_e'(\rho)}{2}, c = -\sqrt{-\frac{V_e'(\rho)}{2\tau}}.$$

(3)

Here v_f is the free-flow speed, ρ_m is the maximum or jam density.

In the present paper, a simple transformation is employed as follow:

$$\begin{cases} \sigma = \frac{1}{v} \\ \eta = \frac{1}{\rho_m - \rho} \end{cases}$$

(4)

Substituting the variables into Eq. (1), we have a new traffic flow model as follow:

$$\begin{cases} \sigma^2 \frac{\partial \eta}{\partial t} + (\eta - \rho_m \eta^2) \frac{\partial \sigma}{\partial x} + \sigma \frac{\partial \eta}{\partial x} = 0 \\ \frac{\partial \sigma}{\partial t} + \left(\frac{1}{\sigma} - 2\beta \sqrt{-\frac{v_e'(\eta)}{2\tau}} \right) \frac{\partial \sigma}{\partial x} + a\sigma^2 v_e'(\eta) \left\{ \begin{array}{c} \frac{1}{2\eta(\rho_m \eta - 1)} \cdot \frac{\partial \eta}{\partial x} + \frac{1}{6(\rho_m \eta - 1)^2} \cdot \frac{\partial^2 \eta}{\partial x^2} \\ -\left(\frac{1}{3\eta(\rho_m \eta - 1)^2} + \frac{1}{2\eta(\rho_m \eta - 1)^3} \right) \left(\frac{\partial \eta}{\partial x} \right)^2 \end{array} \right\} + a\sigma^2 v_e(\eta) - a\sigma = 0 \end{cases}$$

(5)

Similarly, substituting the variables into Eq. (2), the equilibrium velocity $v_e(\eta)$ is as follow:

$$V_e(\eta) = v_f \left\{ \left[1 + \exp \left(\frac{0.75 - \frac{1}{\eta \rho_m}}{0.06} \right) \right]^{-1} - 3.72 \times 10^{-6} \right\}$$

(6)

According to the variable substitution $\sigma = \frac{1}{v}$ and $\eta = \frac{1}{\rho_m - \rho}$, we can see that as long as the vehicles velocity goes to zero or the vehicle density becomes saturated, the state variable σ or η will approach infinity. So we can use the phase plane diagrams about the variable η or σ to describe clearly the relationship between traffic jams and system instability. When the traffic becomes congested, the state variable ρ and υ both tend to a specific value. However, through such variable substitutions, the state variable η or σ both tends to infinity. As long as there is traffic jam formation, the value of η or σ will approach infinity. So the problem of traffic flow could be converted into that of system stability. Some stability theories and mathematical tools can be applied directly to solve the traffic problems. If we use the new model by such variable substitution, we can see from the phase plane that there is a one-to-one relationship between the traffic congestion and the unstable system. The new traffic flow model can analyze various traffic phenomena directly and can also analyze the chaotic fluctuations of traffic flow.

3 The Analysis of Different Input and Output Traffic Phenomena Using the New Method

Gupta By analyzing the model, we first carried out numerical tests for the phenomena of fixed vehicle generation rate but increasing initial homogeneous density with a single ramp, which is rarely studied in the past. To study the effects of ramps, we added the source and the drain terms on the right-hand side of the continuity equation in (5) as follow:

$$\sigma^2 \frac{\partial \eta}{\partial t} + (\eta - \rho_m \eta^2) \frac{\partial \sigma}{\partial x} + \sigma \frac{\partial \eta}{\partial x} = r_{in}(t) - r_{out}(t) \tag{7}$$

where $r_{in}(t)$ and $r_{out}(t)$ represent the external flux through an on-ramp and through an off-ramp, respectively. This section uses MATLAB software to carry out numerical simulation in the Windows system environment. We have also taken the test road section as 32.2 km long and set a ramp in the middle of the road section. The vehicle generation rate was set to 0.0001 veh/m/s. That was to say, the number of vehicles through an on-ramp was 0.0001 more than that through an off-ramp every meter per second. The initial density ρ_0 was 0.037 veh/m. Other parameter values used were as follows:

$$\beta = 2.0, \ \tau = 14 \,\text{s}, \text{v}_f = 30 \,\text{m/s}, \rho_m = 0.2 \,\text{veh/m} \tag{8}$$

The results were shown in Fig. 1(a)–(e).

In Fig. 1(a), the vehicles come from the on-ramp will have an effect on the upstream traffic. Vehicles in upstream of the road need to decelerate when they move to the ramp and can't drive keeping the original speed. So the density in upstream of the road near the ramp will increase gradually. On the other hand, the initial density in downstream of the road also increases and the vehicles come from the on-ramp can't move downstream quickly, so some of them stay on the ramp, which makes the density increment on the ramp is a lot larger than that with a small initial density. The increment will decrease very fast as vehicles in downstream road sections move forward.

Figure 1(b) is the combination of variation curves of η on each road section during the first 16 min. All curves in the figure change from left to right. That is to say, the value of η which is proportional to the vehicle density keeps on increasing. So, it mainly reflects the phenomenon that the density of each road section near the ramp increased gradually with time when vehicles continually entered from the ramp. Figure 1(c) could be considered as a group of curves which describe the change of η per second on the whole road. All curves are closed curves which increase firstly then decrease again. It illustrates that the upstream density near the ramp increases gradually and the downstream density decreases as vehicles move forward. Similarly, Fig. 1(d)–(e) reflect the same phenomena based on the velocity variation with time and displacement. Moreover, both the value and the change rate of η and σ in Fig. 1(b)–(e) increase more significantly than in the Fig. 1 whose initial density is small.

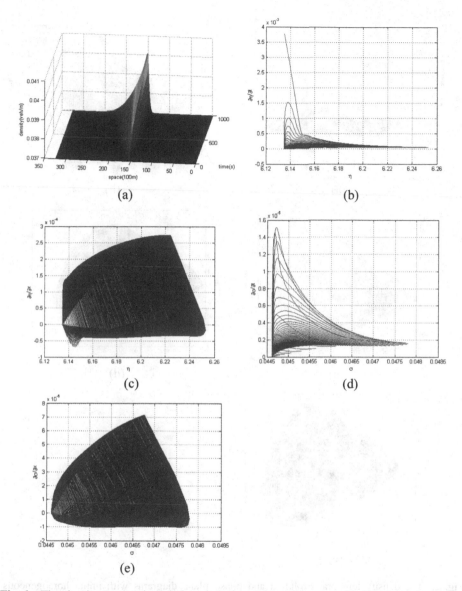

(a)

(b)

(c)

(d)

(e)

Fig. 1. The density temporal evolution and phase plane diagrams with initial homogeneous traffic of amplitude $\rho_0 = 0.037$ veh/m (a) the temporal evolution of vehicle density; (b) the phase plane diagram of $(\eta, \partial\eta/\partial t)$; (c) the phase plane diagram of $(\eta, \partial\eta/\partial x)$; (d) the phase plane diagram of $(\sigma, \partial\sigma/\partial t)$; (e) the phase plane diagram of $(\sigma, \partial\sigma/\partial x)$

If we continually increased the initial density to 0.047 veh/m and remained other conditions such as the value of vehicle generation rate unchanged, the temporal evolution of vehicle density and phase plane diagrams could be compared as follows:

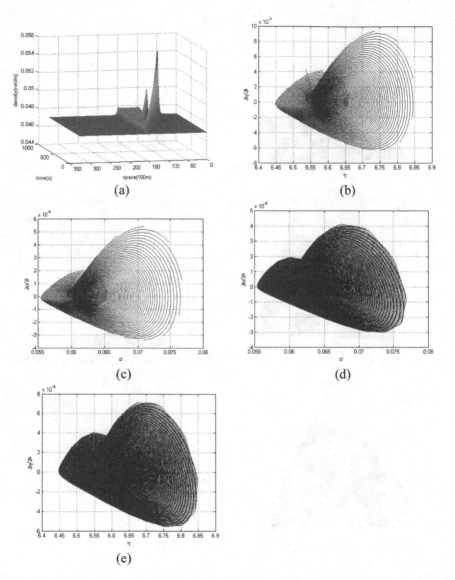

Fig. 2. The density temporal evolution and phase plane diagrams with initial homogeneous traffic of amplitude $\rho_0 = 0.047$ veh/m (a) the temporal evolution of vehicle density; (b) the phase plane diagram of $(\eta, \partial\eta/\partial t)$; (c) the phase plane diagram of $(\sigma, \partial\sigma/\partial t)$; (d) the phase plane diagram of $(\sigma, \partial\sigma/\partial x)$; (e) the phase plane diagram of $(\eta, \partial\eta/\partial x)$

Since the initial density is just above the down-critical unstable density, a small quantity of vehicles come from the ramp can be seen as a small localized perturbation on the initial homogeneous traffic flow and the amplitude of it grows in time, which eventually forms the stop-and-go traffic. The fluctuation amplitude of traffic flow is so large that the small vehicle generation rate on ramp can't make an appreciable effect on the density of the whole road. Figure 2(b)–(e) all consist of number of circles and clearly highlight the fluctuations of density and velocity with time or displacement. So they also describe the stop-and-go traffic phenomenon.

If we continually increased the initial density to 0.093 veh/m and remained other conditions unchanged, the temporal evolution of vehicle density and phase plane diagrams were shown as follows:

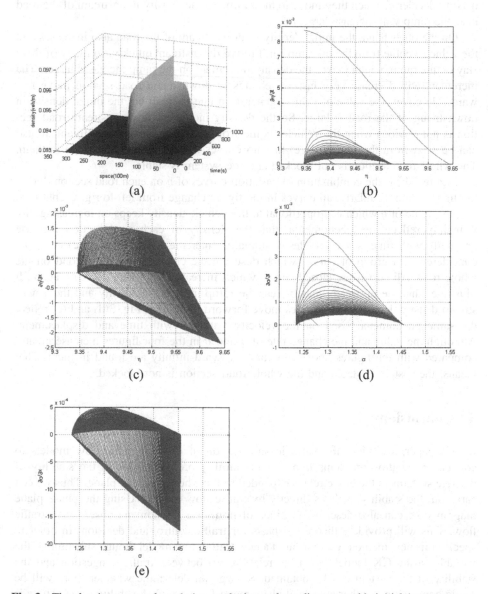

Fig. 3. The density temporal evolution and phase plane diagrams with initial homogeneous traffic of amplitude $\rho_0 = 0.093$ veh/m (a) the temporal evolution of vehicle density; (b) the phase plane diagram of $(\eta, \partial\eta/\partial t)$; (c) the phase plane diagram of $(\eta, \partial\eta/\partial x)$; (d) the phase plane diagram of $(\sigma, \partial\sigma/\partial t)$; (e) the phase plane diagram of $(\sigma, \partial\sigma/\partial x)$

Figure 3(a) shows that when the initial density becomes greater than the up-critical density, a stable regime of the model is reached again. The perturbation is dissipated and the vehicles come from the ramp will again make an appreciable effect on the whole road.

As the initial density increases even further, the vehicles come from the on-ramp will have more impact on the upstream traffic. Vehicles in upstream of the road also need to decelerate when they move to the ramp. So the density in upstream of the road near the ramp will increase largely.

On the other hand, the initial density in downstream of the road also increases and the vehicles come from the on-ramp can't move downstream quickly, so many of them stay on the ramp, which makes the density increment on the ramp increases larger. The increment will decrease very fast as vehicles in downstream road section move forward. Moreover, the value of vehicle generation rate is small but the initial density in downstream of the road is large. So the density increment in downstream road section is not obvious when the vehicles come from the ramp move downstream. It also can be seen from the Fig. 3(b)–(e) that no curves toward infinity are found in them. The whole road section is not blocked and the system is stable.

Figure 3(b) is the combination of variation curves of η on each road section during the first 16 min. Similarly, all curves in the figure change from left to right. That is to say, the value of η which is proportional to the vehicle density keeps on increasing. So, it mainly reflects the phenomenon that the density of each road section increase gradually with time when vehicles continually enter the ramp. Figure 3(c) could be considered as a group of curves which describe the change of η per second on the whole road. All curves are closed curves which increase firstly then decrease again. It illustrates that the upstream density near the ramp increases gradually and the downstream density decreases as vehicles move forward. Similarly, Fig. 3(d) and (e) reflect the same phenomena based on the velocity variation with time and displacement. Although the value and the change rate of η and σ in the four figures increase greatly compared with the figures above, no curves toward infinity are found in them. That means, the system is stable and the whole road section is not blocked.

4 Conclusions

In this paper, we adopt the variable substitution of original traffic flow models to convert traffic flow problems into system stability problems, just as the stability of discrete systems in the unit circle is expanded to the whole complex plane. Thus we can carry out the stability analysis directly by traffic flow models. Using the phase plane diagrams we can also describe all kinds of nonlinear phenomena observed in traffic flow. This will provide a theoretical basis for traffic control and decision. In order to specify this new method, we first build a new traffic flow model though substituting the variable in the GK model. Then the relationship between traffic congestion and the stability of the system can be obtained. So we can determine whether there will be traffic congestion or other abnormal phenomena from a global stability point. There is less study on the phenomena raised by different input and output on ramps. We use the new method to describe some of them with fixed vehicle generation rate but increasing initial homogeneous density with a single ramp. The results are also consistent with the diverse nonlinear dynamics phenomena observed in realistic traffic flow. Furthermore, the phase plane diagrams adopt the new model highlights the instability of the system. When the traffic became slow and congested, some curves tending to infinite can be seen from the phase plane diagrams as they account for a large proportion in the graphs while most small amplitude density fluctuations under stable traffic conditions just centered in a small area near the initial value.

In the future work, we will apply some mathematical tools such as branch and bound to analyze the nonlinear stability. It may be possible to apply some relative approaches of control theory to regulate the stability of traffic system through the equivalence relation between the traffic phenomena and system stability introduced in this paper.

Acknowledgments. The authors would like to thank of the anonymous referees and the editor for their valuable opinions. This work is partially supported by the National Natural Science Foundation of China under the Grant No. 61863032 and the China Postdoctoral Science Foundation Funded Project (Project No.: 2018M633653XB) and the "Qizhi" Personnel Training Support Project of Lanzhou Institute of Technology (Grant No. 2018QZ-11) and the National Natural Science Foundation of China under the Grant No. 11965019.

Conflict of Interests. The authors declare that there is no conflict of interests regarding the publication of this paper.

References

1. Liu, D.W., Shi, Z.K., Ai, W.H.: Enhanced stability of car-following model upon incorporation of short-term driving memory. Commun. Nonlinear Sci. Numer. Simul. **47**, 139–150 (2016)
2. Liu, D.W., Shi, Z.K., Ai, W.H.: A new car-following model accounting for impact of strong wind. Math. Probl. Eng. **1**, 1–12 (2017)
3. Liu, D.W., Shi, Z.K., Ai, W.H.: An improved car-following model from the perspective of driver's forecast behavior. Int. J. Mod. Phys. C **28**(4), 1750046 (2017)
4. Lighthill, M.J., Whitham, G.B.: On kinematic waves: II. a theory of traffic flow on long crowed roads. In: Proceedings of the Royal Society of London, vol. 229, pp. 317–345 (1955)
5. Richards, P.I.: Shock waves on the highway. Oper. Res. **4**, 42–51 (1956)
6. Ai, W.H., Shi, Z.K., Liu, D.W.: Bifurcation analysis of a speed gradient continuum traffic flow model. Phys. A: Stat. Mech. Appl. **437**, 418–429 (2015)
7. Ai, W.H., Shi, Z.K., Liu, D.W.: Bifurcation analysis method of nonlinear traffic phenomena. Int. J. Mod. Phys. C **26**, 1550111 (2015)
8. Ma, C.X., He, R.C.: Green wave traffic control system optimization based on adaptive genetic-artificial fish swarm algorithm. Neural Comput. Appl. **31**(7), 2073–2083 (2019)
9. Yang, B., Kostkova, J., Flusser, J., Suk, T., Bujack, R.: Rotation invariants of vector fields from orthogonal moments. Pattern Recogn. **74**, 110–121 (2018)
10. Gupta, A.K., Katiyar, V.K.: Analyses of shock waves and jams in traffic flow. J. Phys. A. **38**, 4069–4083 (2005)
11. Shi, Z.K., Ai, W.H., Liu, D.W.: An improved macro model of traffic flow with the consideration of ramps and numerical tests. Math. Probl. Eng. **2015**, 1–13 (2015)

Bird Detection on Transmission Lines Based on DC-YOLO Model

Cong Zou[1] and Yong-quan Liang[1,2(✉)]

[1] College of Computer Science and Engineering,
Shandong University of Science and Technology, Qingdao, China
zc17860763660@163.com
[2] Provincial Key Laboratory for Information Technology of Wisdom Mining
of Shandong Province, Shandong University of Science and Technology,
Qingdao, China

Abstract. In order to accurately detect the number of birds around the transmission line, promptly drive the birds away to ensure the normal operation of the line, a DC-YOLO model is designed. This model is based on the deep learning target detection algorithm YOLO V3 and proposes two improvements: Replacing the convolutional layer in the original network with dilated convolution to maintain a larger receptive field and higher resolution, improving the model's accuracy for small targets; The confidence score of the detection frame is updated by calculating the scale factor, and the detection frame with a score lower than the threshold is finally removed. The NMS algorithm is optimized to improve the model's ability to detect occluded birds. Experimental results show that the DC-YOLO model detection accuracy can reach 86.31%, which can effectively detect birds around transmission lines.

Keywords: Bird detection · Deep learning · YOLO V3 · Dilated convolution · NMS algorithm

1 Introduction

Transmission lines play a pivotal role in the power system, and their construction scale has increased dramatically in recent years. Bird damage is an important factor that threatens the safety of the line. Its impact on the transmission line mainly has four aspects: bird pecking, bird nesting, bird excretion, and bird flight. Aiming at the problem of bird damage, the current effective method is to install an ultrasonic bird repellent, but long-term work of the bird repellent will cause waste of energy consumption. Therefore, it is extremely important to implement accurate detection of transmission lines and timely start bird repellents when a certain number of birds are moving around the lines.

In recent years, deep learning [1–3] technology has been widely used in practical scenarios. Deep convolutional neural networks can learn autonomously when performing target detection. Target detection algorithms based on deep learning can be roughly divided into two categories: (1) two stage target detection algorithms, such as Fast R-CNN [4], Faster R-CNN [5], etc. This kind of algorithm is tested in two steps,

© IFIP International Federation for Information Processing 2020
Published by Springer Nature Switzerland AG 2020

Z. Shi et al. (Eds.): IIP 2020, IFIP AICT 581, pp. 222–231, 2020.
https://doi.org/10.1007/978-3-030-46931-3_21

first use Region Proposal Network (RPN) [6] to generate candidate areas, and then achieve target detection classification; (2) one stage target detection algorithms, such as SSD [7], YOLO V3 [8, 9], etc. Such algorithms directly predict the position of the target via the detection network and category information, which has faster detection speed and can basically achieve real-time detection.

Based on the detection algorithm YOLO V3, this paper proposes DC-YOLO model, and improves the structure of YOLO V3 in response to the problems of small targets and mutual occlusion of birds in the device acquisition pictures. In order to improve the recall rate and precision rate of small targets in the image by the network, the convolutional layer is replaced with dilated convolutional layer [10–13] to maintain a large receptive field and a higher resolution. According to the Intersection-over-Union (IOU) [14] value of the detection frame and the pre-selected detection frame, calculate the scale factor corresponding to each detection frame, thereby attenuating their confidence scores, and finally iteratively delete the detection frames whose score is lower than the set threshold. The improved network in this paper is compared with various networks on the transmission line bird data set. The experimental results show that the improved network has better detection effect.

2 YOLO V3 Algorithm

Based on YOLO V2, YOLO V3 combines the ideas of ResNet [15], FPN [16], and binary cross-entropy loss. Its backbone network is composed of 53 consecutive 1×1, 3×3 convolution layers, called Darknet-53 [17]. The structure is shown in Fig. 1. The network outputs features at three scales of 13×13, 26×26, and 52×52. The detection network performs regression analysis on the features of the three scales to generate multiple prediction frames. The NMS algorithm [18–20] removes redundant prediction frames and retains the prediction frame with a higher confidence score as the target detection frame.

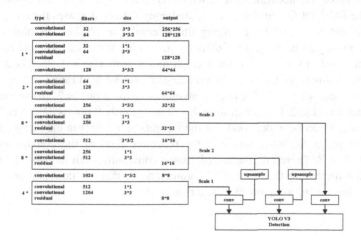

Fig. 1. YOLO V3 network structure

The YOLO V3 network first scales the input image to 416×416 and divides the image into 13×13 cells. If there is a target object in the center of a cell, the cell is responsible for detecting this object. Each cell will generate A prediction frames, the prediction frame consists of a five-dimensional prediction parameter, including the coordinates of the center point (x, y), the width and height (w, h), the confidence score s_i, the confidence score is calculated by Eq. (1).

$$s_i = P(C_i|O_{object}) \times P(O_{object}) \times IOU(truth, pred) \tag{1}$$

where $P(O_{object})$ represents the possibility of an object in the current cell detection frame, if there is an object to be detected, the value is 1, otherwise, the value is 0. $P(C_i|O_{object})$ means the conditional probability that the cell predicts the i type object when there is an object in the detection frame. $IOU(truth, pred)$ is the intersection ratio of the predicted detection frame and the real labeled frame.

Finally, the prediction frame with a higher confidence score is retained as the target detection frame by the NMS algorithm. The traditional NMS processing method is expressed in Eq. (2):

$$s_i = \begin{cases} s_i, IOU(M, b_i) < N_t \\ 0, IOU(M, b_i) \geq N_t \end{cases} \tag{2}$$

where M is the prediction frame with the largest confidence score in the current region. $IOU(M, b_i)$ is the intersection ratio of M and adjacent overlapping frame b_i. N_t is the set overlap threshold.

3   DC-YOLO Model

3.1   DC-YOLO Backbone Network Structure

In order to make the network have a wider receptive field, a dilated convolution is added to the DC-YOLO structure. The dilated convolution increases the receptive field of the convolution kernel by changing the internal rate of the convolution kernel. Figure 2 is a comparison diagram of dilated convolution kernels at different rate. (a) the figure corresponds to a 3×3 dilated convolution with rate = 1, that is a standard convolution, at this time, the convolution kernel receptive field range is 3×3. (b) the graph corresponds to a 3×3 dilated convolution with a rate = 2, the actual convolution kernel size is still 3×3, but for a 7×7 image only 9 points have a convolution operation, which can be understood that the weights of 9 points in the picture are not 0, and the rest are 0. So when rate = 2, the receptive field of the convolution kernel increases to 7×7. Therefore, the use of dilated convolution can increase the receptive field without increasing the amount of parameters, so that the convolutional network can extract feature information of a larger field of view.

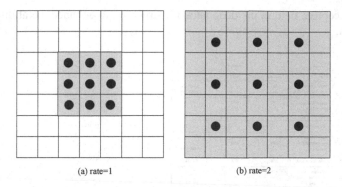

(a) rate=1   (b) rate=2

Fig. 2. Dilated convolutions.

In the YOLO V3 structure, the small target semantic features in the 13 × 13 scale feature map are seriously lost, and the 52 × 52 scale feature map has higher resolution, but it will cause larger calculation and memory overhead. In DC-YOLO, the network's last two downsampling of the input image is cancelled, so that the resolution of 26 × 26 is maintained in the last three stages. This can not only ensure moderate computing overhead, but also increase the resolution of the final output feature map, reduce the loss of semantic features of small-sized targets in deep networks, and facilitate the detection of small targets. Because reducing the number of times of image downsampling will inevitably reduce the receptive field of the deep network, the DC-YOLO structure will introduce two types of dilated convolution residual structure A and B as shown in Fig. 3.

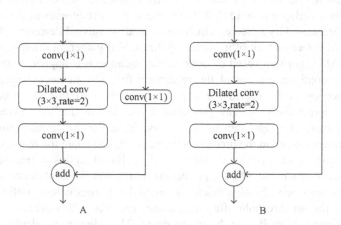

Fig. 3. Structure of dilated convolution residual

The DC-YOLO backbone network is shown in the Fig. 4. The resolution of the features directly affects the detection of small targets. The model selection has a moderate 26 × 26 resolution, which enables the model to maintain higher resolution and larger receptive field in the deep network structure, to enhance the ability to detect small targets.

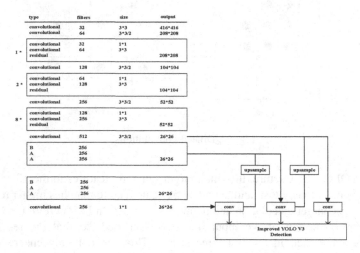

Fig. 4. Improved YOLO V3 network structure

3.2 Scale Factor NMS Algorithm

When the traditional NMS algorithm suppresses redundant prediction frames, the judgment of whether a prediction frame is redundant mainly depends on the size of the overlap threshold. The algorithm forcibly sets the confidence score of prediction frames larger than the overlap threshold to 0. When the real target appears in the overlapping area, it will be deleted by mistake, which easily leads to missed detection of the target.

In the bird detection task of transmission lines, bird gathering often occurs. In this paper, the NMS algorithm based on scale factor attenuation is applied to the detection task, and the confidence score of the prediction frame is attenuated according to a certain proportion according to the degree of overlap, so that the algorithm can effectively suppress the redundant prediction frame and reduce the missed detection rate of the target. The algorithm is as follows: b_m is the prediction frame with the highest confidence score in the prediction frame set B. Calculate the $IOU(b_m, b_i)$ value of the remaining adjacent prediction frames and b_m. Based on this value, use Eq. (3) to obtain the scaling factor w_i of each prediction frame, and the confidence score of the attenuated frames is $w_i s_i$. Finally, delete the prediction frames whose confidence scores are less than the set threshold after attenuation, and repeat this process until all the prediction frames in set B have been processed. This algorithm calculates the scale factor corresponding to the prediction frame according to the value of IOU. It is a continuous process. When the value of *IOU* is 0, the original confidence score of the prediction frame is retained.

$$w_i = 1 - lg(IOU(b_m, b_i) + 1) \tag{3}$$

4 Experimental Results and Analysis

4.1 Experimental Data Set and Preprocessing

The data used in the experiment mainly comes from the monitoring equipment near the transmission line in a certain area collected by the research team. Randomly extract the monitoring video and extract a single frame image to make a data set. Label the picture with Labbellmg tool and store it in VOC data format. There are a total of 6000 images, including 4800 in the training set and 1200 in the test set.

According to the characteristics of the research object in this article, combined with the relationship between the number of prior frames and the average Intersection-over-Union (Avg IOU), as shown in the Fig. 5. K-means clustering analysis is used to obtain the best prior frame. The distance measurement formula is:

$$d(box, centroid) = 1 - IOU(box, centroid) \tag{4}$$

where *box* is the sample; *centroid* is the cluster center; $IOU(box, centroid)$ is the intersection ratio of the cluster center and the sample frame.

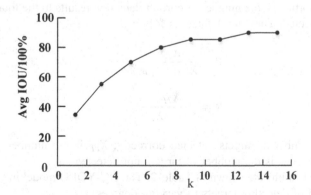

Fig. 5. K-means clustering result

When the value of k is 9, the curve gradually starts to flatten, so the number of anchor boxes is 9 and the size of the corresponding prediction frame is set to 9 cluster centers. On this training set, they are: (10,13), (16,28), (30,33), (33,61), (64,50), (69,110), (115,90), (155,198), (369,342).

4.2 Network Training

Model training parameters are shown in Table 1. In the initial stage of training, the learning rate is 0.001 to stabilize the network. When the number of training iterations is 20000, the learning rate is adjusted to 0.0001, and when the number of iterations is 25000, the learning rate is adjusted to 0.00001, which further converges the loss function.

Table 1. Model parameter description

Parameter	Value
Batch size	64
Max batches	30000
Momentum	0.9
Decay	0.0005
Match threshold	0.25
NMS threshold	0.5

4.3 Results Analysis

In order to verify that the improved network can better detect small targets and birds obstructing each other, thereby improving the overall detection effect, two comparative experiments are set up in this paper.

Small Target Detection
The SSD, Faster-RCNN, YOLO V3, and the DC-YOLO model were trained and tested on the dataset respectively. Calculate the *Precision* and *Recall* of the target, the P refers to the proportion of the number of correctly detected targets in the detection result, R refers to the proportion of the number of correct detection results to the total number of targets to be detected. They are defined as follows:

$$P = \frac{X_{TP}}{X_{TP} + X_{FP}} \tag{5}$$

$$R = \frac{X_{TP}}{X_{TP} + X_{FN}} \tag{6}$$

where X_{TP} is the number of targets detected correctly; X_{FP} is the number of targets detected incorrectly; X_{FN} is the number of targets not detected.

The experimental results are shown in Table 2. The DC-YOLO model improves the accuracy and recall of detection targets to varying degrees.

Table 2. Detection results of different models

Detection model	P (%)	R (%)	AP (%)
SSD	73.35	74.52	73.93
Faster-RCNN	79.68	82.17	80.91
YOLO V3	76.23	77.85	77.03
DC-YOLO	84.57	88.12	86.31

The average precision (AP) measures the accuracy of the model from two angles of *Precision* and *Recall*. It can be used to analyze the detection effect of a single category. The AP curve of the DC-YOLO model is shown in the Fig. 6, the AP value is increased to 86.31%.

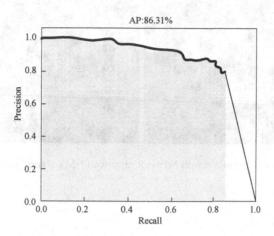

Fig. 6. AP curve of DC-YOLO

Detection of Mutual Occlusion of Birds

In the experimental data set, 100 bird images with different occlusion ratios were selected, and they were detected using the traditional NMS algorithm and the scale factor NMS algorithm improved in this paper. The detection performance is shown in Table 3. When the bird's mutual occlusion ratio is less than 30%, the detection accuracy of the two algorithms is the same; when the occlusion ratio is 30%–70%, the scale factor NMS algorithm improves the accuracy rate by 20%; When the occlusion ratio is higher, the scale factor NMS algorithm shows better performance in bird occlusion detection tasks.

Table 3. Comparison of detection performance with different occlusion ratios

Detection algorithm	Occlusion ratio (%)	AP (%)
Traditional NMS algorithm	0–30	90
	30–70	40
	≥ 70	10
Improved NMS algorithm	0–30	90
	30–70	60
	≥ 70	20

Figure 7 shows the detection results of the traditional NMS algorithm and the improved NMS algorithm at a occlusion ratio of 80%. It can be seen that the traditional algorithm cannot detect the blocked birds, and the improved NMS algorithm has a better detection effect on the blocked birds.

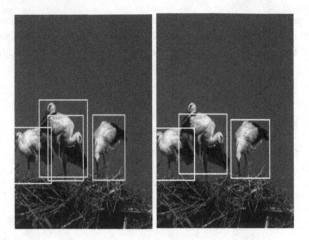

Fig. 7. Comparison of detection results between improved NMS algorithm and traditional NMS algorithm

5 Conclusion

This paper proposes a DC-YOLO model to complete real-time and effective detection of birds on transmission lines, thereby controlling the start and stop of bird repellents, and protecting the stability of transmission lines while saving energy. Aiming at the small target of the image and the problem of target occlusion, based on the YOLO V3 model, the backbone network Darknet-53 network and the NMS algorithm were improved. The experimental results show that the DC-YOLO model has a higher precision rate, and the average detection speed reaches 38 FPS, which achieves a real-time accurate detection effect.

References

1. Le Cun, Y., Bengio, Y., Hinton, G.: Deep learning. Nature **521**(7553), 436–444 (2015)
2. Goodfellow, I., Bengio, Y., Courville, A.: Deep Learning, pp. 1–33. MIT Press, Cambridge (2016)
3. Nordeng, I.E., Hasan, A., Olsen, D., Neubert, J.: DEBC detection with deep learning. In: Sharma, P., Bianchi, F.M. (eds.) SCIA 2017. LNCS, vol. 10269, pp. 248–259. Springer, Cham (2017). https://doi.org/10.1007/978-3-319-59126-1_21
4. Girshick, R.: Fast R-CNN. In: Proceedings of the IEEE International Conference on Computer Vision, pp. 1440–1448 (2015)
5. Ren, S., He, K., Girshick, R., et al.: Faster R-CNN: towards real-time object detection with region proposal networks. IEEE Trans. Pattern Anal. Mach. Intell. **39**(6), 1137–1149 (2017)
6. Girshick, R., Donahue, J., Darrell, T., et al.: Rich feature hierarchies for accurate object detection and semantic segmentation. In: IEEE Conference on Computer Vision and Pattern Recognition, pp. 580–587 (2014)

7. Liu, W., et al.: SSD: single shot multibox detector. In: Leibe, B., Matas, J., Sebe, N., Welling, M. (eds.) ECCV 2016. LNCS, vol. 9905, pp. 21–37. Springer, Cham (2016). https://doi.org/10.1007/978-3-319-46448-0_2

8. Tumas, P., Serackis, A.: Automated image annotation based on YOLOv3. In: 2018 IEEE 6th Workshop on Advances in Information, Electronic and Electrical Engineering (AIEEE), pp. 1–3. IEEE (2018)

9. Qu, H., Yuan, T., Sheng, Z., et al.: A pedestrian detection method based on YOLOv3 model and image enhanced by Retinex. In: 2018 11th International Congress on Image and Signal Processing, Bio Medical Engineering and Informatics (CISP-BMEI), pp. 1–5. IEEE (2018)

10. Yu, F., Koltun, V., Funkhouser, T.: Dilated residual networks. In: Proceedings of the IEEE Conference on Computer Vision and Pattern Recognition, pp. 472–480 (2017)

11. Wang, Y., Wang, G., Chen, C., Pan, Z.: Multi-scale dilated convolution of convolutional neural network for image denoising. Multimed. Tools Appl. **78**(14), 19945–19960 (2019)

12. Vo, D.M., Lee, S.W.: Semantic image segmentation using fully convolutional neural networks with multi-scale images and multi-scale dilated convolutions. Multimed. Tools Appl. **77**(14), 18689–18707 (2018)

13. Geng, L., Zhang, S., Tong, J., Xiao, Z.: Lung segmentation method with dilated convolution based on VGG-16 network. Comput. Assist. Surg. **24**(sup2), 27–33 (2019)

14. Bodla, N., Singh, B., Chellappa, R., et al.: Soft-NMS–improving object detection with one line of code. In: Proceedings of the IEEE International Conference on Computer Vision, pp. 5561–5569 (2017)

15. He, K., Zhang, X., Ren, S., et al.: Deep residual learning for image recognition. In: IEEE Conference on Computer Vision and Pattern Recognition, Las Vegas, pp. 770–778 (2016)

16. Lin, T.Y., Dollár, P., Girshick, R., et al.: Feature pyramid networks for object detection. In: Proceedings of the IEEE Conference on Computer Vision and Pattern Recognition, pp. 2117–2125 (2017)

17. Redmon, J., Farhadi, A.: YOLOv3: an incremental improvement. In: IEEE Conference on Computer Vision and Pattern Recognition, pp. 89–95 (2018)

18. Rosenfeld, A., Thurston, M.: Edge and curve detection for visual scene analysis. IEEE Trans. Comput. **20**(5), 562–569 (1971)

19. Hosang, J., Benenson, R., Schiele, B.: A convnet for non-maximum suppression. In: Rosenhahn, B., Andres, B. (eds.) GCPR 2016. LNCS, vol. 9796, pp. 192–204. Springer, Cham (2016). https://doi.org/10.1007/978-3-319-45886-1_16

20. Hosang, J., Benenson, R., Schiele, B.: Learning non-maximum suppression. In: Proceedings of 2017 IEEE Conference on Computer Vision and Pattern Recognition, Honolulu, HI, USA, 6469–6477. IEEE (2017)

Research on Customer Credit Scoring Model Based on Bank Credit Card

Maoguang Wang and Hang Yang[(✉)]

School of Information, Central University of Finance and Economics,
Beijing, China
Mgwangtiger@163.com, Yanghangv@163.com

Abstract. With the development of China's economy, especially the maturity of the market economy, credit is important to the society and individuals. At present, credit system is mainly divided into two parts. Enterprise credit system is an important part of social credit system. But at the same time, as the foundation of social credit system, the establishment of the personal credit system is of great significance to reduce the cost of collecting information and improve the efficiency of loan processing. At the bank level, this paper discretizes the credit card data of a bank, selects the features by calculating Weight of Evidence and Information Value, and information divergence, then uses Logistic Regression to predict. Finally, the results of the Logistic Regression are transformed into visualized credit scores to establish a credit scoring model. It is verified that this model has a good prediction effect.

Keywords: Personal credit system · Information Value · Information divergence · Logistic Regression

1 Introduction

The construction of the financial system in the 21st century is inseparable from the support of the credit system. The problems and risks reflected in the credit are followed, which shows that there are still some shortcomings in the credit system of our country: firstly, there is a lack of relevant detailed laws and regulations; secondly, the customer information data sets used by various enterprises are different, the reliability and quality of the data set used by credit agencies need to be improved.

As bank credit is the foundation of credit system, individual customer is the main part of bank customer group. The research of personal customer credit rating is of great significance. The establishment of Individual Credit Investigation System helps to predict risks in advance for commercial early warning analysis of banks. The Credit System presents the customer's credit report in the form of score, and the result is concise.

© IFIP International Federation for Information Processing 2020
Published by Springer Nature Switzerland AG 2020

Z. Shi et al. (Eds.): IIP 2020, IFIP AICT 581, pp. 232–243, 2020.
https://doi.org/10.1007/978-3-030-46931-3_22

2 Related Work

The concept of credit scoring originated from the concept of overall division put forward by Fisher (1936) in the field of statistics. Durand (1941) realized that the idea of "division" could be used in the field of economics to divide the "good" and "bad" of loans. With the emergence of credit card, Credit Scoring gradually appears and is used in banking and other fields. In short, the development of credit scoring system is mainly divided into two stages. In the initial stage of market economy, the traditional credit scoring system is also called expert scoring system. The core of credit scoring in this way is "5C" element. With the development of economy, the modern scoring method mainly uses the skills of mathematical statistics to quantify indicators. At present, there are many credit scoring systems based on data mining and big data algorithm. Among the modern scoring methods, the first one to be used is discriminant analysis. Durand (1941) first used discriminant analysis in scoring, and fair (1958) established a credit scoring system on this basis. Myers (1963) used discriminant analysis and regression analysis to establish a credit scoring system, and predicted the credit scoring. In addition to the discriminant method, the regression analysis method is widely used. Under this method, there are many branches. For example, Henley (1995) used linear regression for credit scoring, Wigington (1980) used logistic method. At the same time, this method was still the most commonly method in credit scoring, which could overcome the defects in linear regression. In addition, Nath Jackon (1992) also applied the method of mathematical programming, but it has been proved that the effect of the method of mathematical programming is equivalent to that of the method of linear programming [1]. Data mining was also used in credit scoring model, which was widely used in credit decision-making and fraud prevention. In the field of data mining, Decision Tree algorithm, Neural Network algorithm, and other methods such as Support Vector Machine (SVM) and Bayesian Network could be used [2]. According to the characteristics of the data set in this paper, and the characteristics that logistic regression could effectively screen variables, this paper used logistic regression to analyze the selected eigenvalues [3]. In the study of credit scoring card, most of the results [4] in recent years were expressed by the method of binary classification. This paper uses the calculation method for reference [5], transforms the logistic results into the form of scoring, breaks the situation of binary classification, and makes the results more intuitive by grading.

This paper obtains the credit card data of a bank customer for six months. After analyzing the obtained data, this paper will use the method of Weight of Evidence, Information Value and information divergence to select the logarithmic features, and consider the prior rules properly in the process of feature selection, so as to try to find the best feature extraction method. Through the comparison of multiple groups, the optimal feature system will be selected, and the selected features are input into the established Logistic Regression model. At the same time, the credit scoring model is built to convert the results into the credit score, and the customers are classified according to the scores. The classification result has value to the bank, and it is also convenient for customers to view their own credit rating.

3   Construction of Feature Selection System

Data and features determine the upper limit of experimental results. Therefore, feature engineering is important for a model algorithm. This paper mainly uses feature selection in feature engineering to process data.

3.1   Information Value

Information Value is a predictive ability to measure features, and the calculation of Information Value is based on the Weight of Evidence. Table 1 below lists the specific calculation method of WOE value [6].

Table 1. Weight of evidence.

Formula	Meaning
$WOE_I = \ln\left(\dfrac{P_{y_i}}{P_{n_i}}\right)$	P_{y_i}: Proportion of y = 1 samples in the current group to all y = 1 samples
$= \ln\left(\dfrac{\frac{y_i}{y_T}}{\frac{n_i}{n_T}}\right) = \ln\left(\dfrac{\frac{y_i}{n_i}}{\frac{y_T}{n_T}}\right)$	P_{n_i}: Proportion of samples with y = 0 in all samples with y = 0
	y_i: Number of samples in group y = 1
	y_T: Number of y = 1 in all samples
	n_i: Number of y = 0 in the group
	n_T: Number of y = 0 in all samples

From the formula in Table 1, it can be seen that the larger the woe value is, the better the prediction effect of this feature will be. However, it can also be seen that for each variable of each sample, the woe value contains plus and minus. If the woe value is used to measure the prediction ability of the whole feature, there may be a situation of positive and negative offsetting, which greatly reduces the overall prediction ability.

In order to make up for the deficiency of woe, it has been proposed that the calculation formula of IV based on woe is as follows [6].

$$IV_i = (py_i - pn_i) * WOE_i = (py_i - pn_i) * \ln\left(\frac{P_{y_i}}{P_{n_i}}\right) = \left(\frac{y_i}{y_T} - \frac{n_i}{n_T}\right) * \ln\left(\frac{y_i/y_T}{n_i/n_T}\right) \quad (1)$$

$$IV = \sum_i^n IV_i \quad (2)$$

Kindly According to the formula, the larger the IV is, the stronger the prediction ability of the feature is. But at the same time, in order to avoid the occurrence of extreme IV value, we need to make a reasonable discretization of the data before calculating IV.

3.2   Information Divergence

Information divergence is used to measure the contribution of a feature to the whole. It is often used for feature selection. The basis of information divergence is entropy. Entropy can be subdivided into information entropy and conditional entropy, and the calculation formula is shown in Table 2 [7].

Table 2. Calculation formula of entropy.

Information entropy	$H(S) = -\sum\limits_{i=1}^{C} p_i log_2(p_i)$
Conditional entropy	$H(C|T) = P(t)H(C|t) + P(\bar{t})H(C|\bar{t})$

The calculation of information divergence is based on conditional entropy and information entropy. The specific formula is as follows:

$$IG(T) = H(C) - H(C|T) \qquad (3)$$

By writing Python program, the entropy of the whole dataset and the information divergence of each eigenvalue can be obtained.

3.3 Data Preprocessing

This paper selects the bank credit card data of a bank in Taiwan from April to September, 2005. There are 25 fields in the data set, including 23 features, as shown in Table 3 below.

Table 3. Data feature description.

Number	Feature	Concrete meaning
x_1	LIMIT_BAL	Overdraft amount
x_2	SEX	SEX
x_3	EDUCATION	EDUCATION
x_4	MARRIAGE	MARRIAGE
x_5	AGE	AGE
x_6	PAY_0	Repayment of customers in September
x_7	PAY_2	Customer repayment in August
x_8	PAY_3	Customer repayment in July
x_9	PAY_4	Customer repayment in June
x_{10}	PAY_5	Customer repayment in May
x_{11}	PAY_6	Customer repayment in April
x_{12}	BILL_AMT1	September bill amount
x_{13}	BILL_AMT2	August bill amount
x_{14}	BILL_AMT3	July bill amount
x_{15}	BILL_AMT4	June bill amount
x_{16}	BILL_AMT5	May bill amount
x_{17}	BILL_AMT6	April bill amount
x_{18}	PAY_AMT1	Repayment amount in September
x_{19}	PAY_AMT2	Repayment amount in August
x_{20}	PAY_AMT3	Repayment amount in July
x_{21}	PAY_AMT4	Repayment amount in June
x_{22}	PAY_AMT5	Repayment amount in May
x_{23}	PAY_AMT6	Repayment amount in April

Among them, sex (=1: male, =2: female); Education (=1: postgraduate, =2: University, =3: high school, =4: other, =5 unknown, =6: unknown); marriage (=1: married, =2: single, =3 other); pay_0 (=−1: normal payment, =1: delayed payment of one month, =2: delayed payment of two months, =8: delayed payment of eight months, =9: delayed payment of nine months, and above).

It can be seen from the above table that there are many features in this data set, so it is important to select the most meaningful feature from many features. Considering that both IV and information divergence are statistics to evaluate the importance of features, this paper uses IV and information divergence to screen features respectively, and compares the results, in order to select the better feature selection method for this data set.

First, preprocessing the data, dealing with the missing and abnormal values. The following is the basic description of this data set (see Fig. 1).

	LIMIT_BAL	SEX	EDUCATION	MARRIAGE	AGE	PAY_0	PAY_2	PAY_3	PAY_4	PAY_5	PAY_6	BILL_AMT1	BILL_AMT2	BILL_AMT3	BILL_AMT4	BILL_AMT5	BILL_AMT6	PAY_AMT1	PAY_AMT2	PAY_AMT3	PAY_AMT4	PAY_AMT5	PAY_AMT6
count	30000	30000	30000	30000	30000	30000	30000	30000	30000	30000	30000	30000	30000	30000	30000	30000	30000	30000	30000	30000	30000	30000	30000
mean	167484.3	1.603733	1.853133	1.551867	35.4855	-0.0167	-0.13377	-0.1662	-0.22067	-0.2662	-0.2911	51223.331	49179.075	47013.155	43262.949	40311.401	38871.76	5663.581	5921.5815	5225.6815	4826.0769	4799.3876	5215.503
std	129747.7	0.489129	0.790349	0.52197	0.217904	1.123802	1.197186	1.196868	1.169139	1.133187	1.149088	73635.861	71173.769	69049.387	64332.856	60797.156	59554.108	16563.28	23040.87	17606.961	15666.16	15278.309	17777.47
min	10000	1	0	0	21	-2	-2	-2	-2	-2	-2	-165580	-69777	-157264	-170000	-81334	-339603	0	0	0	0	0	0
25%	50000	1	1	1	28	-1	-1	-1	-1	-1	-1	3558.75	2984.75	2666.25	2326.75	1763	1256	1000	833	390	296	252.5	117.75
50%	140000	2	2	2	34	0	0	0	0	0	0	22381.5	21200	20088.5	19052	18104.5	17071	2100	2009	1800	1500	1500	1500
75%	240000	2	2	2	41	0	0	0	0	0	0	67091	64006.25	60164.75	54506	50190.5	49198.25	5006	5000	4505	4013.25	4031.5	4000
max	1000000	2	6	3	79	8	8	8	8	8	8	964511	983931	1664089	891586	927171	961664	873552	1684259	896040	621000	426529	528666

Fig. 1. Basic data description

In order to achieve the better fitting effect, 30000 pieces of data are divided into training set and test set according to the proportion of 7:3.

At the same time, in order to calculate the IV of the feature, this paper combines the method of Optimal Binning and equal depth segmentation to discretize each feature of the sample, according to the AUC calculated by different segmentation methods as the measurement standard.

3.4 Feature Selection System Based on IV

After the data binning, the IV values of each features has been calculated (see Fig. 2).

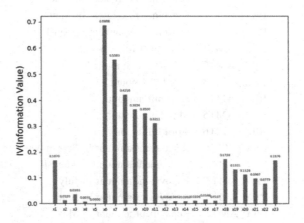

Fig. 2. Characteristic IV.

In general, the prediction ability of IV is measured according to Table 4 [8].

Table 4. IV prediction ability.

IV	Predictive power
<0.02	Unpredictability
0.02–0.1	Weak prediction ability
0.1–0.3	General prediction ability
0.3–0.5	Strong prediction ability
>0.5	Suspicious

According to the above table, the variables with no prediction ability and weak prediction ability can be eliminated in this paper: $x_2, x_3, x_5, x_{12}, x_{13}, x_{14}, x_{15}, x_{16}, x_{17}, x_{21}, x_{22}$.

Remove variables with doubtful prediction ability: x_6, x_7. A feature selection system (A_1) is obtained. A_1 contains features: $x_1, x_8, x_9, x_{10}, x_{11}, x_{18}, x_{19}, x_{20}, x_{23}$.

Considering the influence of prior rules on data sets, it is decided to further consider the contribution of x_3, x_4, x_5 to the model on the basis of A_1 feature system, and obtain the feature system (C_1). C_1 contains features: $x_1, x_3, x_4, x_5, x_8, x_9, x_{10}, x_{11}, x_{18}, x_{19}, x_{20}, x_{23}$.

As the IV of the suspicious variable is close to 0.5, based on the feature selection system A_1, considering the influence of x_6 and x_7 features on the model, the feature system (B_1) is obtained. B_1 contains features: $x_1, x_6, x_7, x_8, x_9, x_{10}, x_{11}, x_{18}, x_{19}, x_{20}, x_{23}$.

At the same time, considering the characteristics of IV and the prior rule, the feature system (D_1) is obtained. D_1 contains features: $x_1, x_3, x_4, x_5, x_6, x_7, x_8, x_9, x_{10}, x_{11}, x_{18}, x_{19}, x_{20}, x_{23}$.

3.5 Feature Selection System Based on Information Entropy

After preprocessing the original data, the data set is input into the written Python program, and the entropy of the whole data set is 0.762353. It can be seen that the data set of this paper is orderly and carries a lot of valuable information. Then calling the prepared function, calculating the conditional entropy of each feature. We can get the information divergence of each feature after sorting, shown in Table 5.

Table 5. Information divergence of 23 features.

Feature	Information divergence
x_2	0.001
x_4	0.001
x_3	0.004
x_5	0.004
x_1	0.024
x_{11}	0.038

(*continued*)

Table 5. (*continued*)

Feature	Information divergence
x_{10}	0.044
x_9	0.047
x_8	0.054
x_7	0.071
x_6	0.110
x_{22}	0.172
x_{21}	0.174
x_{23}	0.175
x_{20}	0.189
x_{19}	0.193
x_{18}	0.203
x_{17}	0.532
x_{16}	0.543
x_{15}	0.556
x_{14}	0.567
x_{13}	0.575
x_{12}	0.584

It can be seen from the table that the information divergence of the bill amount in September of x_{12} (BILL_AMT1) is the largest, which is the optimal feature. According to the number of features in A_1, B_1, C_1 and D_1 feature systems, four sets of feature systems are selected according to the information divergence. Four groups of characteristic systems are respectively recorded as A_2, B_2, C_2, D_2. A_2 selects features of the same size as A_1, and removes 14 features with small information gain. The selected feature types account for 39% of the total features. Therefore, A_2 includes features $x_{20}, x_{19}, x_{18}, x_{17}, x_{16}, x_{15}, x_{14}, x_{13}, x_{12}$. B_2 selects the number of features of the same size as B_1, removes 11 feature variables, and the selected feature types account for 52% of the total number of features. Therefore, B_2 includes $x_{21}, x_{23}, x_{20}, x_{19}, x_{18}, x_{17}, x_{16}, x_{15}, x_{14}, x_{13}, x_{12}$. C_2 selects the number of features of the same size as C_1, and removes 12 feature variables. The selected feature types account for 47% of the total number of features. C_2 includes features $x_{23}, x_{20}, x_{19}, x_{18}, x_{17}, x_{16}, x_{15}, x_{14}, x_{13}, x_{12}$. D_2 selects feature numbers of the same size as D_1, and removes 9 feature variables. The selected feature types account for 60% of the total features. D_2 includes features $x_6, x_{22}, x_{21}, x_{23}, x_{20}, x_{19}, x_{18}, x_{17}, x_{16}, x_{15}, x_{14}, x_{13}, x_{12}$.

3.6   Comparison of Feature Selection System

In the first group, the WOE/IV method is compared with information divergence in feature selection. Information divergence emphasizes the feature with the greatest contribution. IV can more intuitively observe the importance of each feature. In order to verify that the information divergence and IV are more suitable for the field studied in this paper, four groups of specific comparisons are made in this paper, A_1 & A_2, B_1 &

B_2, C_1 & C_2, D_1 & D_2. Among them, A_1, B_1, C_1 and D_1 are the feature systems obtained through IV, and A_2, B_2, C_2 and D_2 are the feature systems obtained based on entropy (see Fig. 3) for the specific comparison. It can be seen from the figure that, in the case of the same type of sample features selected, the features constructed by IV are generally better than the model based on the features selected by information divergence.

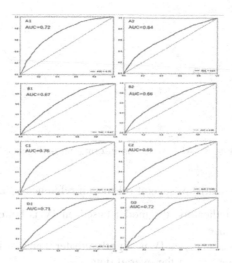

Fig. 3. Information divergence VS. IV results

In the second group, the AUC of A_1, B_1, C_1 and D_1 are shown (see Fig. 4). It can be seen from the figure that all the models built based on C_1 have better effect. Therefore, this paper selects C_1 as the feature system of this paper, inputs Logistic Regression model and finally constructs the scoring model.

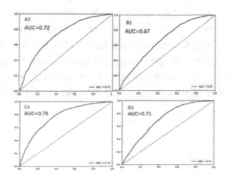

Fig. 4. AUC based on IV selection

In the third group, compare the four feature systems selected based on information divergence. The AUC calculated based on A_2, B_2, C_2 and D_2 is shown (see Fig. 5). It can be seen from the pictures that the model effect of D_2 is the best, that is, when the selected feature types account for 60% of the total features, the model will have a better effect.

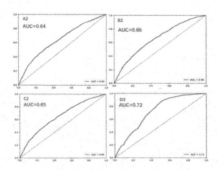

Fig. 5. AUC based on information divergence

Through the above comparison, several rules with reference value can be obtained:

1. Selecting multiple indicators, the model based on IV is better than that based on information divergence.
2. In general, when the calculated IV is slightly greater than 0.5, it is better to consider the impact of this feature on the overall data.
3. When selecting features based on information divergence, the information divergence can be sorted from large to small, and the effect of selecting 60% of the total feature types is better.

4   Construction of Feature Selection System

Logistic Regression mode can explain the dependent variables, and is often used to solve the prediction problem of data subject to Normal distribution. Moreover, Logistic Regression model overcomes the defects of linear Regression model, and has strong applicability in credit rating, which is suitable for this model. After inputting the C_1 feature system into the Logistic Regression model, and through the AUC obtained after inputting the feature into the model in the third section, it can be found that the prediction ability of this model is better. The logistic model [9] can be represented in Table 6.

Table 6. Logistic regression model.

Probability of event occurrence under the condition of characteristic x	$P(y = 1\|x)$ $= \dfrac{1}{1 + e^{-g(x)}}$	$x = (x_1, x_2, \ldots, x_n)$ $g(x) = w_0$ $+ w_1 x_1 + \ldots + w_n x_n$
Probability of event not occurring under the condition of characteristic x	$P(y = 0\|x)$ $= \dfrac{1}{1 + e^{g(x)}}$	
Event ratio odds	$\text{odds} = \dfrac{P}{1 - P}$ $\log(\dfrac{P}{1 - P}) = g(X) = w_0$ $+ w_1 + x_1 + \ldots + w_n x_n$	

The logarithm form of odds has been obtained in the above table. In this paper, the logarithm form of probability occurrence ratio is expressed as the linear combination of feature variables, and the woe of each feature is multiplied by the regression coefficient of the variable plus the regression intercept, the scale factor is multiplied by the migration amount, and the corresponding score of each feature is obtained according to formula (4) [5], Among them, odds is the ratio of good and bad customers. Based on historical experience, this paper takes the ratio of good and bad customers as 20, and in order to make the calculated score positive, this paper stipulates that the basic score is 200 at this time, and when odds doubles, the score increases by 20, so that the calculation results of factor and offset can be obtained:

$$\left(woe_i * \beta_i + \frac{w_0}{n} \right) * \text{factor} + \frac{\text{offset}}{n} \tag{4}$$

$$factors = 20/\log(2) \tag{5}$$

$$offset = 200 - \log(20) * factors \tag{6}$$

The credit score of all characteristics of a customer is obtained by sorting out:

$$score = \log(odds) * factor + offset = \left(\sum\nolimits_{i=1}^{n} woe_i * \beta_i + w_0 \right) * factor$$
$$+ offset = \sum\nolimits_{i=1}^{n} woe_i * \beta_i * factor + w_0 * factor + offect \tag{7}$$

$$Base\, score = w_0 * factor + offect \tag{8}$$

After calculation, factor = 28.85, offset = 113.56, base score = 154. The larger the score is, the higher the customer's credit rating is. According to the credit scoring model, the total score of customers in this paper is within the range of [0200]. After the study of customer scores, it is decided to divide customers into class I [0,40), class II [40,80), class III [80,120), class IV [120,160) and class V [160,200] customers by using equidistant segmentation, and the customer's trustworthiness gradually decreases. The histogram of overall customer classification is shown (see Fig. 6). It can be seen from the classification that category I has the most customers and category V has the least customers, indicating that most customers have high credit value.

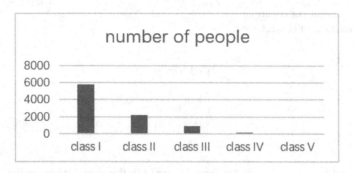

Fig. 6. Customer classification

In order to better observe the classification results, this paper makes statistics on the proportion of good and bad customers in the five categories of customers, as shown in Table 7.

Table 7. Proportion of good and bad customers in 5 types of customers.

Customer level	Proportion of good customers	Proportion of bad customers
Class I	88.81%	11.19%
Class II	68.50%	31.50%
Class III	40.02%	59.98%
Class IV	29.25%	70.75%
Class V	0%	100%

From the results of the credit scoring model in this paper, it can be seen that the two categories of customers with high credit rating, category I and II, are mostly composed of good customers, category III and IV, are mostly composed of bad customers, and category V completely untrusted customers are totally composed of bad customers. The experimental results are consistent with the actual laws, which further shows that the model in this paper has reference value.

5   Conclusion

In this paper, the bank credit card data, WOE/IV and information divergence are used for horizontal comparison. In vertical comparison, the method of feature selection considering prior rules and not considering prior rules is used. The C_1 group features of IV and prior rules are selected. 11 features are extracted from 23 features as the scoring basis, which reduces the complexity of data processing. In the process of feature selection, after many comparative tests, this paper obtains three prior rules. Then, using logistic regression model, input the calculated woe into the model, and the AUC is 0.76. The regression coefficient of each feature is obtained, so as to build a credit rating model and get customer credit rating. Users are classified according to user rating. After comparing with the actual data, it is found that the classification results in this paper are consistent with the actual. The customer credit rating model based on the bank credit card is constructed in this paper. It makes the bank refine the customer classification through the form of generating the rating, which reflects the intuitiveness of the result for the user classification and has certain warning and reference value for the bank's credit business.

References

1. Shi, Q., Jin, Y.: A summary of the main models and methods of personal credit scoring. Stat. Res. (08), 36–39 (2003)
2. He, S., Liu, Z., Ma, X.: A comparative review of credit scoring models – based on the comparison between traditional methods and data mining. Credit Reference 37(02), 63–67 (2019)
3. Ma, F.: Study on the application of logistic regression in personal credit rating in China. Shanghai University of Finance and Economics, Shanghai (2008)
4. Deng, Y.: Study on credit card risk of commercial banks in prefectural-level banks based on logistic model. Econ. Manag. J. (1), 69–80 (2018). Chinese and English version
5. Li, Y.: The establishment of credit scoring card model. Sci. Technol. Inf. (13), 48–49 (2010)
6. Gleisner, B.F.: Electronic marketplaces and intermediation: an empirical investigation of an online lending marketplace. University of Frankfurt (2007)
7. Liu, J., Jiang, X., Wu, J.: The realization of a knowledge reasoning rule induction system. Syst. Eng. 21(3), 108–110 (2003)
8. Shan, L., Mao, X.: Modeling and Application of Consumer Credit Scoring in the Internet Finance Era. Publishing House of Electronics Industry
9. Qi, L.: Distress prediction: application of the PCA in logistic regression. J. Ind. Eng. Eng. Manag. 19(1), 100–104 (2005)

Analysis of the Stability and Solitary Waves for the Car-Following Model on Two Lanes

WenHuan Ai[1(✉)], Tao Xing[1], YuHang Su[1], DaWei Liu[2], and Huifang Ma[1]

[1] College of Computer Science and Engineering, Northwest Normal University, Lanzhou 730070, Gansu, China
wenhuan618@163.com, 573340970@qq.com, 463753759@qq.com, 452770064@qq.com
[2] College of Electrical Engineering, Lanzhou Institute of Technology, Lanzhou 730050, Gansu, China
liudawei20120901@163.com

Abstract. In this paper, Analysis of the stability and solitary waves for a car-following model on two lanes is carried out. The stability condition of the model is obtained by using the linear stability theory. We study the nonlinear characteristics of the model and obtain the solutions of Burgers equation, KDV equation, and MKDV equation, which can be used to describe density waves in three regions (i.e., stable, metastable and unstable), respectively. The analytical results show that traffic flow can be stabilized further by incorporating the effects come from the leading car of the nearest car on neighbor lane into car-following model.

Keywords: Car-following model on two lanes · Traffic flow · Density waves

1 Introduction

Car-following theory is one of the most important part of modern traffic theory. Since 1953 when Pipes [1] presented the first model, an increasing number of models have been proposed [2–9]. In 2002, Jiang et al. [6] presented a car-following model called full velocity difference model (FVDM). FVDM revealed the complex dynamic characteristics of traffic flow, therefore, various developed models based FVDM were proposed.

With the development of transportation, study on two-lane traffic has been increasingly necessary. However, early car-following models like FVDM are only subject to single lane traffic, thence, many scholars have made a lot of research on two-lane traffic and proposed a series of new models, which mainly divided into lattice model and car-following model. Nagatani [10] proposed lattice model on two lane traffic in 1998. Peng [11–14] extended the two-lane lattice model, and presented a series of new models based lattice model of Nagatani. Tang et al. [15] presented a car-following model on two lanes by considering the lateral effects in traffic. They found that vehicle drivers always worry about the lane changing actions from neighbor lane and the consideration of lateral effects could stabilize the traffic flows on both lanes.

© IFIP International Federation for Information Processing 2020
Published by Springer Nature Switzerland AG 2020
Z. Shi et al. (Eds.): IIP 2020, IFIP AICT 581, pp. 244–253, 2020.
https://doi.org/10.1007/978-3-030-46931-3_23

A large of traffic accidents are caused by unreasonable lane changing. In order to avoid such accidents, drivers have to worry about the lane changing actions not only of the nearest car in neighbor lane but also of the preceding car of the nearest car on neighbor lane. In this paper, we propose an extended car-following model on two lanes though considering the effects from both the nearest car and its leading car in neighbor lane which is rarely studied by others. Then the stability condition of the new model is derived by using the stability theory. Next, we obtain the solutions of Burgers equation, KDV equation and MKDV equation, which can be used to describe density waves in three regions (i.e., stable, metastable and unstable) respectively. The analytical results show that traffic flow can be stabilized further by incorporating the effects come from the leading car of the nearest car on neighbor lane into car-following model.

2 Model

In case of two-lane traffic, it is necessary to consider the lateral effects. This is because plenty of surveys show that most drivers have to be ready to take precautions against the near vehicle on neighbor lane due to the suddenly lane changing without any alert message. The 'near vehicle' on neighbor lane is composed of the nearest vehicle and its leading car on neighbor lane. In general, the distance between one car and it's nearest car on neighbor lane is so small that drivers always judge the lane changing action of his/her nearest-lateral car by observing the distance between his/her leading car and the nearest-lateral car. Hence, the dynamic equation of the car-following model on two lanes is as follows [15]:

$$\frac{d^2 x_{l,n}(t)}{dt^2} = f_{sti}\left(v_{l,n}(t), \Delta x_{l,n}(t), \sum_l \Delta_{l,n}, \Delta v_{l,n}(t)\right) \tag{1}$$

Where $l = 0, 1$ represent the lane number, $\Delta_{l,n}$ is the distance between the n_l vehicle on lane l and the leading car of its nearest vehicle on neighbor lane.

In this paper, Eq. (1) can be rewritten as:

$$\frac{dx_{l,n}^2}{dt^2} = a_1\left[V_1\left(\Delta x_{l,n}(t), \sum_l \Delta_{l,n}\right) - \frac{dx_{l,n}(t)}{dt}\right] + \lambda_1 \Delta v_{l,n}(t) \tag{2}$$

$V_l\left(\Delta x_{l,n}(t), \sum_l \Delta_{l,n}\right)$ is the optimal velocity formulated as

$$V_l\left(\Delta x_{l,n}(t), \sum_l \Delta_{l,n}\right) = V_l\left(\overline{\Delta x_{l,n}}\right) = V_l\left(\alpha_l \Delta x_{l,n} + \beta_{1l}\Delta_{l,n} + \beta_{2l}\Delta_{1-l,n}\right) \tag{3}$$

where $\alpha_l, \beta_{1l}, \beta_{2l}$ are the weights of axial headway $\Delta x_{l,n}(t)$ and lateral distance $\sum_l \Delta_{l,n}$ respectively.

$$\alpha_l + \beta_{1l} + \beta_{2l} = 1$$

According to the optimal velocity function presented by Bando [2], the optimal velocity function on two lanes is given by

$$V_l\left(\overline{\Delta x_{l,n}}\right) = \frac{v_{l,\max}}{2}\left[\tanh\left(\overline{\Delta x_{l,n}} - h_{lc}\right) + \tanh(h_{lc})\right] \tag{4}$$

This velocity function has a turning point at $\overline{\Delta x_{l,n}} = h_{lc}$

$$V_l''\left(\overline{\Delta x_{l,n}}\right) = \frac{d^2 V_l\left(\overline{\Delta x_{l,n}}\right)}{d\overline{\Delta x_{l,n}}^2}\bigg|_{\overline{\Delta x_{l,n}}=h_{lc}} = 0 \tag{5}$$

3   Linear Stability Analysis

We apply the linear stability theory to examine the car-following model on two lanes described by Eq. (2). The uniform traffic flow is defined by such a state that all vehicles on lane l move with the optimal velocity $V_l\left(\Delta x_{l,n}(t), \sum_l \Delta_{l,n}\right)$ and the identical headway h_l and the lateral distance $\sum_l \Delta_l$; the relative velocity $\Delta v_{l,n}(t)$ is zero. The solution $x_{l,n}^{(0)}(t)$ is given by

$$x_{l,n}^{(0)}(t) = h_l n_l + V_l\left(h_l, \sum_l \Delta_l\right)t \tag{6}$$

Assuming $y_{l,n}(t)$ be a small deviation from the steady state $x_{l,n}^{(0)}(t)$, we have

$$x_{l,n}(t) = x_{l,n}^{(0)}(t) + y_{l,n}(t) \tag{7}$$

Substituting the Eq. (6) and Eq. (7) into Eq. (2), we rewrite linearized equation as

$$\frac{dy_{l,n}^2(t)}{dt^2} = a_l\left[V_l'(h_l)\left(\alpha_l \Delta y_{l,n}(t) + \beta_{1l}\Delta_{l,n} + \beta_{2l}\Delta_{1-l,n}\right) - \frac{dy_{l,n}(t)}{dt}\right] + \lambda_l \frac{d\Delta y_{l,n}(t)}{dt} \tag{8}$$

Where $V_l'\left(\overline{\Delta x_{l,n}}\right) = dV_l\left(\overline{\Delta x_{l,n}}\right)/d\overline{\Delta x_{l,n}}$, at $\overline{\Delta x_{l,n}} = h_l$, and $\Delta y_{l,n}(t) = y_{l,n+1}(t) - y_{l,n}(t)$. For a very small perturbation $y_{l,n}(t)$ at $x_{l,n}^{(0)}(t)$, we can let $\Delta_{l,n} = \Delta_{1-l,n} \cong \Delta y_{l,n+1}$.

Expanding $y_{l,n}(t)$ in the Fourier-modes, $y_{l,n}(t) \approx A_l e^{(ik_l n_l + z_l t)}$, we obtain

$$z_l^2 = a_l \left[V_l'(h_l) \times \left(\alpha_l \left(e^{ik_l} - 1\right) + (\beta_{1l} + \beta_{2l})\left(e^{ik_l} - 1\right)e^{ik_l} \right) - z_l \right] + \lambda_l z_l \left(e^{ik_l} - 1\right) \quad (9)$$

Substituting $z_l = z_{1l}(ik_l) + z_{2l}(ik_l)^2 + \ldots\ldots$ into Eq. (9), we obtain the first- and second-order terms of coefficients in the expression of z_l as follows:

$$z_{1l} = (\alpha_l + \beta_{1l} + \beta_{2l})V_l'(h_l) = V_l'(h_l)$$
$$z_{2l} = \frac{a_l V_l'(h_l)[\alpha_l + 3(\beta_{1l} + \beta_{2l})] + 2\lambda_l z_{1l} - 2z_{1l}^2}{2a_l}$$

For small disturbances with long wavelengths, the uniform steady state will become unstable when z_{2l} is negative. Thus the neutral stability curve is given by

$$a_{ls} = \frac{V_l'(h_l) - \lambda_l}{0.5\alpha_l + 1.5(\beta_{1l} + \beta_{2l})} \quad (10)$$

The uniform traffic flow will be unstable if $a_l < a_{ls}$

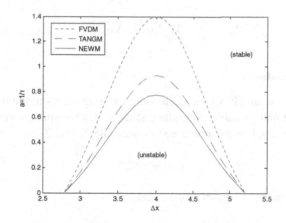

Fig. 1. Phase diagram in the headway-sensitivity space. The parameters related to the models are given in Table 1

The neutral stability curves in parameter space are shown in Fig. 1, where the sensitivity $\alpha_l = 1/\tau_l$. From Fig. 1 it can be seen that the stable region of both the new model and Tang model are larger than stable region of the FVDM. It means the uniform traffic flow has been stabilized with taking into account the lateral effects. Furthermore, relative to Tang model, the critical point and neutral stability curve of new model are lower, which shows that the uniform traffic flow has been further strengthened by adjusting the lateral effects from both nearest car and it's leader car in neighbor lane. The traffic jam is thus relieved efficiently.

Table 1. Parameters related to the models

	α_l	β_{1l}	β_{2l}	λ_l
FVDM	1	0	0	0.2
TANGM	0.75	0.25	0	0.2
NEWM	0.6	0.25	0.15	0.2

4 Nonlinear Analysis

To facilitate the study of the density wave problem in the following three regions below, we rewrite Eq. (2) as follows:

$$\frac{d^2\Delta x_{l,n}(t)}{dt^2} = a_l\left\{V_l\left(\Delta x_{l,n+1}(t), \sum_l \Delta_{l,n+1}\right) - V_l\left(\Delta x_{l,n}(t), \sum_l \Delta_{l,n}\right) - \frac{d\Delta x_{l,n}(t)}{dt}\right\}$$
$$+ \lambda_l\left(\frac{d\Delta x_{l,n+1}(t)}{dt} - \frac{d\Delta x_{l,n}(t)}{dt}\right)$$

$$(11)$$

Where $V_l\left(\Delta x_{l,n+1}(t), \sum_l \Delta_{l,n+1}\right) = V_l\left(\overline{\Delta x_{l,n}}\right)$, $\overline{\Delta x_{l,n}} = \alpha_l \Delta x_{l,n} + \beta_{1l}\Delta_{l,n} + \beta_{2l}\Delta_{1-l,n}$

4.1 Burger Equation

We now consider the slowly varying behaviors for long waves in the three regions (i.e. stable, metastable and unstable). Introduce slow scales for space variable n_l and time variable t. For $0 < \varepsilon \leq 1$, we define the slow variable X_l and T

$$X_l = \varepsilon(n_l + b_l t), T = \varepsilon^2 t \qquad (12)$$

Where b_l is a constant to be determined. Let

$$\Delta x_{l,n} = h_l + \varepsilon R_l(X_l, T) \qquad (13)$$

Substituting Eq. (12) and Eq. (13) into Eq. (11) and expanding to the third order of ε, we obtain the following nonlinear partial differential equation

$$\varepsilon^2 a_l(b_l - V'(h_l))\partial_{X_l} R_l + \varepsilon^3 \left\{a_l \partial_T R_l - a_l V''(h_l)R_l \partial_{X_l} R_l \right.$$
$$\left. - \left(\tfrac{a_l}{2}[\alpha_l + 3(\beta_{1l} + \beta_{2l})]V'(h_l) - b_l^2 + \lambda_l b_l\right)\partial_{X_l}^2 R_l\right\} = 0 \qquad (14)$$

Where $V_l'(h_l) = \frac{dV\left(\overline{\Delta x_{l,n}}\right)}{d\overline{\Delta x_{l,n}}}\bigg|_{\overline{\Delta x_{l,n}}=h_l}$, $V_l''(h_l) = \frac{d^2V\left(\overline{\Delta x_{l,n}}\right)}{d\overline{\Delta x_{l,n}}^2}\bigg|_{\overline{\Delta x_{l,n}}=h_l}$, $\partial_T = \frac{\partial}{\partial T}$, $\partial_{X_l} = \frac{\partial}{\partial X_l}$

By taking $b_l = V'(h_l)$, we eliminate the second-order term of ε from Eq. (14) and have

$$\partial_T R_l - V''(h_l)R_l\partial_{X_l}R_l = \left(\frac{1}{2}[\alpha_l + 3(\beta_{1l}+\beta_{2l})]V'(h_l) - \frac{b_l^2}{a_l} + \frac{\lambda_l b_l}{a_l}\right)\partial_{X_l}^2 R_l$$

$$= \left(\frac{1}{2}[\alpha_l + 3(\beta_{1l}+\beta_{2l})] - \frac{V'(h_l)}{a_l} + \frac{\lambda_l}{a_l}\right)V'(h_l)\partial_{X_l}^2 R_l \tag{15}$$

The coefficient $\frac{1}{2}[\alpha_l + 3(\beta_{1l}+\beta_{2l})] - \frac{V'(h_l)}{a_l} + \frac{\lambda_l}{a_l} > 0$ in the stable region satisfies the stability criterion. Thus, in the stable region Eq. (15) is the Burgers equation. The solution of the Burgers equation is as follow:

$$R(X_l, T) = \frac{1}{|V''(h_l)|T}\left[X - \frac{\eta_{n+1}-\eta_n}{2}\right] - \frac{\eta_{n+1}-\eta_n}{2|V''(h_l)|T}$$

$$\times \tanh\left[\left(\frac{1}{2}[\alpha_l + 3(\beta_{1l}+\beta_{2l})] - \frac{V'(h_l)}{a_l} + \frac{\lambda_l}{a_l}\right) \times V'(h_l)\frac{(\eta_{n+1}-\eta_n)(X_l-\xi_n)}{4|V''(h_l)|T}\right] \tag{16}$$

Where η_n are the coordinates of the intersections of the slopes with the x-axis and ξ_n are those of the shock fronts. As $T \to +\infty$, $R(X,T) \to 0$, which means in stable region all density waves eventually evolved into a uniform flow with increasing time.

4.2   KDV Equation

We consider the slowly varying behaviors for long waves near the neutral stability point. Slow variable X_l and T are defined as

$$X_l = \varepsilon(n_l + b_l t), T = \varepsilon^2 t \tag{17}$$

We set the headway as

$$\Delta x_{l,n} = h_l + \varepsilon^2 R_l(X_l, T) \tag{18}$$

Substituting Eq. (17) and Eq. (18) into Eq. (11) and expanding to the sixth order of ε, we obtain the following nonlinear partial differential equation

$$\begin{aligned}
&\varepsilon^3 a_l[b_l - V_l'(h_l)]\partial_{X_l}R_l + \varepsilon^4\left[b_l^2 - \frac{a_l}{2}(\alpha_l + 3\beta_{1l}+3\beta_{2l})V_l'(h_l) - \lambda_l b_l\right]\partial_{X_l}^2 R_l \\
&+ \varepsilon^5 a_l\left\{\partial_T R_l - \left[\frac{1}{6}(\alpha_l + 7\beta_{1l}+7\beta_{2l})V_l'(h_l) + \frac{1}{2a_l}\lambda_l b_l\right]\partial_{X_l}^3 R_l - \frac{1}{2}V_l'(h_l)\partial_{X_l}R_l^2\right\} \\
&+ \varepsilon^6\Big[(2b_l - \lambda_l)\partial_{X_l}\partial_T R_l - \frac{a_l}{24}(\alpha_l + 15\beta_{1l}+15\beta_{2l})V_l'(h_l)\partial_{X_l}^4 R_l \\
&- \frac{a_l}{4}(\alpha_l + 3\beta_{1l}+3\beta_{2l})V_l''(h_l)\partial_{X_l}^2 R_l^2\Big] = 0
\end{aligned} \tag{19}$$

where $\partial_X\partial_T = \frac{\partial^2}{\partial X\partial T}$.

Near the neutral stability point, we set $\frac{a_l}{a_{ls}} = 1+\varepsilon^2$, where $a_{ls} = \frac{V_l'(h_l)-\lambda_l}{0.5\alpha_l + 1.5(\beta_{1l}+\beta_{2l})}$

By taking $b_l = V'(h_l)$, we eliminate both the third-order and the forth-order term of ε from Eq. (19) and have

$$\partial_T R_l - f_1 \partial_{X_l}^3 R_l - f_2 R_l \partial_{X_l} R_l + \varepsilon \left[-f_3 \partial_{X_l}^2 R_l + f_4 \partial_{X_l}^4 R_l + f_5 \partial_{X_l}^2 R_l^2 \right] = 0 \qquad (20)$$

Where $f_1 = \frac{1}{6}(\alpha_l + 7\beta_{1l} + 7\beta_{2l})V_l'(h_l) + \frac{1}{2a_l}\lambda_l b_l$, $f_2 = V_l''(h_l)$, $f_3 = \frac{1}{2}(\alpha_l + 3\beta_{1l} + 3\beta_{2l})V_l'(h_l)$

$$f_4 = \left[\frac{\lambda\left(2V_l'(h_l) - \lambda\right)}{2a_s^2} + \frac{(\alpha_l + 7\beta_{1l} + 7\beta_{2l})}{6a_s}\left(2V_l'(h_l) - \lambda\right) - \frac{\alpha_l + 15\beta_{1l} + 15\beta_{2l}}{24} \right] V_l'(h_l)$$

$$f_5 = \left(\frac{2V_l'(h_l) - \lambda}{2a_s} - \frac{1}{4}(\alpha_l + 3\beta_{1l} + 3\beta_{2l}) \right) V_l''(h_l)$$

In order to drive the regularized equation, we make the transformations as follows:

$$T = \sqrt{f_1}T_{kdv}, \quad X_l = -\sqrt{f_1}X_{lkdv}, \quad R_l = \frac{1}{f_2}R_{lkdv}$$

Thus, we obtain the KDV equation with a $o(\varepsilon)$ correction term.

$$\begin{aligned}
\partial_{T_{kdv}} R_{lkdv} - f_1 \partial_{X_{lkdv}}^3 R_{lkdv} - f_2 R_{lkdv} \partial_{X_{lkdv}} R_{lkdv} \\
+ \varepsilon \left[-f_3 \partial_{X_{lkdv}}^2 R_{lkdv} + f_4 \partial_{X_{lkdv}}^4 R_{lkdv} + f_5 \partial_{X_{lkdv}}^2 R_{lkdv}^2 \right] = 0
\end{aligned} \qquad (21)$$

We ignore the $o(\varepsilon)$ term and get the KDV equation with the soliton solution

$$R_{l0}(X_{lkdv}, T_{kdv}) = A \sec h^2 \left[\sqrt{\frac{A}{12}}\left(X_{lkdv} - \frac{A}{3}T_{kdv} \right) \right] \qquad (22)$$

Where $A = \frac{21 f_1 f_2 f_3}{24 f_1 f_5 - 5 f_2 f_4}$,

Hence, we obtain the soliton solution of the KDV equation

$$\Delta x_{l,n}(t) = h_l + \frac{A}{V_l''(h_l)}\left(1 - \frac{a_{ls}}{a_l} \right) \sec h^2 \left\{ \left[n + V_l'(h_l)t + \frac{A}{3}\left(1 - \frac{a_{ls}}{a_l} \right)t \right] \right.$$
$$\left. \times \sqrt{\frac{a_{ls}A}{2a_{ls}(\alpha_l + 7\beta_{1l} + 7\beta_{2l})V_l'(h_l) + 6\lambda_l V_l'(h_l)}\left(1 - \frac{a_{ls}}{a_l} \right)} \right\} \qquad (23)$$

4.3 MKDV Equation

In unstable region we consider the slowly varying behaviors for long waves. Slow variable X_l and T are defined just as Eq. (17)

We set the headway as

$$\Delta x_{l,n} = h_{lc} + \varepsilon R_l(X_l, T) \qquad (24)$$

Substituting Eq. (17) and Eq. (24) into Eq. (11) and expanding to the fifth order of ε, we obtain the following nonlinear partial differential equation

$$\varepsilon^2 a_l \left[b_l - V_l'(h_{lc}) \right] \partial_{X_l} R_l + \varepsilon^3 \left[b_l^2 - \frac{a_l}{2}(\alpha_l + 3\beta_{1l} + 3\beta_{2l}) V_l'(h_{lc}) - \lambda_l b_l \right] \partial_{X_l}^2 R_l$$
$$+ \varepsilon^4 \left\{ a_l \partial_T R_l - \left[\frac{a_l}{6}(\alpha_l + 7\beta_{1l} + 7\beta_{2l}) V_l'(h_{lc}) + \frac{1}{2}\lambda_l b_l \right] \partial_{X_l}^3 R_l \right.$$
$$- \frac{1}{6} a_l V_l''(h_{lc}) \partial_{X_l} R_l^3 \right\} + \varepsilon^5 \left\{ (2b_l - \lambda_l) \partial_{X_l} \partial_T R_l \right. \tag{25}$$
$$- \left[\frac{a_l}{24}(\alpha_l + 15\beta_{1l} + 15\beta_{2l}) V_l'(h_{lc}) + \frac{1}{6}\lambda_l b_l \right] \partial_{X_l}^4 R_l$$
$$- \frac{1}{12} a_l (\alpha_l + 3\beta_{1l} + 3\beta_{2l}) V_l'''(h_c) \partial_{X_l}^2 R_l^3 \right\} = 0$$

Where $V_l'(h_{lc}) = \frac{dV(\overline{\Delta x_{l,n}})}{d\Delta x_{l,n}} \Big|_{\Delta x_{l,n} = h_{lc}} V_l'''(h_{lc}) = \frac{d^3 V(\overline{\Delta x_{l,n}})}{d\Delta x_{l,n}^3} \Big|_{\Delta x_{l,n} = h_{lc}}$

Near the critical point (h_{lc}, a_{lc}), taking $\frac{a_l}{a_{lc}} = (1 - \varepsilon^2)$, $b_l = V_l'(h_l)$ and eliminating both the second-order and the third-order term of ε, Eq. (25) can be simplified as

$$\partial_T R_l - g_1 \partial_{X_l}^3 R_l + g_2 R_l \partial_{X_l} R_l^3 + \varepsilon \left[g_3 \partial_{X_l}^2 R_l + g_4 \partial_{X_l}^4 R_l + g_5 \partial_{X_l}^2 R_l^3 \right] = 0 \tag{26}$$

Where

$$g_1 = \left[\frac{1}{6}(\alpha_l + 7\beta_{1l} + 7\beta_{2l}) + \frac{1}{2}\lambda_l \right] V_l'(h_{lc}), g_2 = -\frac{1}{6} V_l''(h_{lc}),$$

$$g_3 = \frac{1}{2}(\alpha_1 + 3\beta_{1l} + 3\beta_{2l}) V_l'(h_{lc})$$

$$g_4 = \left[\frac{\lambda_l (2V_l'(h_{lc}) - \lambda_l)}{2a_{lc}^2} + \frac{(2b_l - \lambda_l)}{6a_{lc}}(\alpha_l + 7\beta_{1l} + 7\beta_{2l}) - \frac{1}{24}(\alpha_l + 15\beta_{1l} + 15\beta_{2l}) - 6\lambda_l \right] V_l'(h_{lc})$$

$$g_5 = \left[\frac{(2V_l'(h_{lc}) - \lambda_l)}{6a_{lc}} - \frac{1}{12}(\alpha_l + 3\beta_{1l} + 3\beta_{2l}) \right]$$

We make such transformations as $T = \frac{1}{g_1} T_m$ $R_l = \sqrt{\frac{g_1}{g_2}} R_{lm}$

Then we obtain the modified KDV equation with a $o(\varepsilon)$ correction term.

$$\partial_T R_{lm} - \partial_{X_l}^3 R_{lm} + g_2 \partial_{X_l} R_{lm}^3 + \frac{\varepsilon}{g_1} \left[g_3 \partial_{X_l}^2 R_{lm} + g_4 \partial_{X_l}^4 R_{lm} + \frac{g_1 g_5}{g_2} \partial_{X_l}^2 R_{lm}^3 \right] = 0 \tag{27}$$

If we ignore $o(\varepsilon)$ term, this is just the modified KDV equation with a kink solution as the desired solution

$$R_l(X_l, T) = \sqrt{\frac{g_1}{g_2}} B \tanh \left[\sqrt{\frac{B}{2}}(X_l - Bg_1 T) \right] \tag{28}$$

Where $B = \frac{5g_2 g_3}{2g_2 g_4 - 3g_1 g_5}$

Thus, we obtain the kink solution of the headway

$$\Delta x_{l,n}(t) = h_{lc} + \sqrt{\frac{g_1 B}{g_2}\left(\frac{a_{lc}}{a_l} - 1\right)} \tan h \times \left\{\sqrt{\frac{B}{2}\left(\frac{a_{lc}}{a_l} - 1\right)} \times \left[n + V_l'(h_{lc})t - Bg_1\left(\frac{a_{lc}}{a_l} - 1\right)t\right]\right\}$$

$$= h_{lc} + \sqrt{\frac{(\alpha_l + 7\beta_{1l} + 7\beta_{2l})V_l'(h_{lc}) + 3\lambda_l V_l'(h_{lc})}{-V_l'''(h_{lc})}\left(\frac{a_{lc}}{a_l} - 1\right)B}$$

$$\times \tan h \left\{\sqrt{\frac{B}{2}\left(\frac{a_{lc}}{a_l} - 1\right)} \times \left[n + V_l'(h_{lc})t - B\left(\frac{1}{6}(\alpha_l + 7\beta_{1l} + 7\beta_{2l}) + \frac{1}{2}\lambda_l\right)V_l'(h_{lc})\left(\frac{a_{lc}}{a_l} - 1\right)t\right]\right\}$$

$$(29)$$

5 Conclusions

The two-lane car-following model in this paper is the extension of the FVDM in single lane. By considering the lateral effects, the model consists not only of the nearest vehicle on neighbor lane but also of its preceding vehicle. Linear analysis of the model shows that the consideration of lateral effects of the nearest vehicle on neighbor lane could stabilize the traffic flow. The solutions of Burgers equation, KDV equation, and MKDV equation have been derived to describe density waves in three regions respectively.

Acknowledgments. This work is partially supported by the National Natural Science Foundation of China under the Grant No. 61863032 and the China Postdoctoral Science Foundation Funded Project (Project No.: 2018M633653XB) and the "Qizhi" Personnel Training Support Project of Lanzhou Institute of Technology (Grant No. 2018QZ-11) and the National Natural Science Foundation of China under the Grant No. 11965019.

Conflict of Interests. The authors declare that there is no conflict of interests regarding the publication of this paper.

References

1. Pipes, L.A.: An operational analysis of traffic dynamics. J. Appl. Phys. **24**, 274–281 (1953)
2. Liu, D.W., Shi, Z.K., Ai, W.H.: Enhanced stability of car-following model upon incorporation of short-term driving memory. Commun. Nonlinear Sci. Numer. Simul. **47**, 139–150 (2016)
3. Liu, D.W., Shi, Z.K., Ai, W.H.: A new car-following model accounting for impact of strong wind. Math. Probl. Eng. **1**, 1–12 (2017)
4. Liu, D.W., Shi, Z.K., Ai, W.H.: An improved car-following model from the perspective of driver's forecast behavior. Int. J. Mod. Phys. C **28**(4), 1–12 (2017)
5. Shi, Z.K., Ai, W.H., Liu, D.W.: An improved macro model of traffic flow with the consideration of ramps and numerical tests. Math. Probl. Eng. **2015**(136451), 1–6 (2015)
6. Jiang, R., Wu, Q.S., Zhu, Z.J.: Full velocity difference model for a car-following theory. Phys. Rev. E **64**, 63–66 (2001)
7. Ge, H.X., Dai, S.Q., Dong, L.Y., Xue, Y.: Stabilization effect of traffic flow in an extended car-following model based on an intelligent transportation system application. Phys. Rev. E **70**, 066134 (2004)

8. Chen, X., Gao, Z.Y., Zhao, X.M., Jia, B.: Study on the two-lane feedback controled car-following model. Acta Phys. Sin. **56**, 2024–2029 (2007)
9. Zheng, L., Ma, S.F., Zhong, S.Q.: Influence of lane change on stability analysis for two-lane traffic flow. Chin. Phys. B **20**, 088701 (2011)
10. Nagatani, T.: Jamming transitions and the modified Korteweg-de Vries equation in a two-lane traffic flow. Phys. A **265**, 297–310 (1999)
11. Peng, G.: A new lattice model of two-lane traffic flow with the consideration of optimal current difference. Phys. Lett. A **377**, 2027–2033 (2013)
12. Peng, G.: A new lattice model of the traffic flow with the consideration of the driver anticipation effect in a two-lane system. Nonlinear Dyn. **73**, 1035–1043 (2013)
13. Guang-Han, P.: A new lattice model of two-lane traffic flow with the consideration of the honk effect. Commun. Oretical Phys. **60**, 485–490 (2013)
14. Peng, G.: A new lattice model of traffic flow with the consideration of individual difference of anticipation driving behavior. Commun. Nonlinear Sci. Numer. Simul. **18**, 2801–2806 (2013)
15. Tang, T.Q., Huang, H.J., Gao, Z.Y.: Stability of the car-following model on two lanes. Phys. Rev. E **72**, 066124 (2005)

Queue Length Estimation Based Defence Against Data Poisoning Attack for Traffic Signal Control

Xu Gao, Jiqiang Liu, Yike Li, Xiaojin Wang, YingXiao Xiang,
Endong Tong$^{(\boxtimes)}$, Wenjia Niu$^{(\boxtimes)}$, and Zhen Han

Beijing Key Laboratory of Security and Privacy in Intelligent Transportation, Beijing
Jiaotong University, 3 Shangyuan Village, Haidian District, Beijing 100044, China
{niuwj,edtong}@bjtu.edu.cn

Abstract. With the development of intelligent transportation systems,
especially in the context of the comprehensive development and popu-
larization of big data and 5G networks, intelligent transportation signal systems have been experimented and promoted in various countries
around the world. As with other big data-based systems, specific attacks
pose a threat to the security of big data-based intelligent transportation
system systems. Targeting system vulnerabilities, certain simple forms of
attack will have a huge impact on signal planning, making Actual traffic
is congested. In this article, we first show a specific attack and then add
more attack points, analyze the system's vulnerabilities, and model based
on traffic waves and Bayesian predictions, so that the attack points can
help the impact is weakened and the traffic can function normally. For
experiments, we performed traffic simulation on the VISSIM platform
to prove the impact of our attack and further verify the accuracy and
effectiveness of the model.

Keywords: I-SIG · Connected vehicle · Bayesian prediction · Traffic
wave

1 Introduction

Vehicle network technology is gradually changing the current transportation network, and not only in China but also in various countries around the world have
launched a pilot program for connected vehicles. At present, the Internet of Vehicles technology is gradually applied to online maps and some electric vehicles.
Chinese transportation departments and Internet companies are also conducting
research and experiments on intelligent traffic signal systems in recent years.

In September 2016, the U.S. Department of Transportation launched a pilot
program for intelligent traffic signal systems. In this program, the vehicle's infrastructure is connected via wireless communications, using technologies to optimize
traffic planning and prevent traffic failures and congestion. In 2018, the intelligent traffic signal system has been tested in three cities including New York.

© IFIP International Federation for Information Processing 2020
Published by Springer Nature Switzerland AG 2020
Z. Shi et al. (Eds.): IIP 2020, IFIP AICT 581, pp. 254–265, 2020.
https://doi.org/10.1007/978-3-030-46931-3_24

In order to promote deployment in the United States, USDOT [5] has proposed to authorize all new light vehicles to be equipped with connected vehicle (CV) technology [8]. No matter what technology is, as long as it is applied in the real-life field, its safety is very important to us. In order to ensure the safety of vehicle and transportation equipment infrastructure and the safety of drivers and pedestrians in the environment, understand the security loopholes in the systems we deploy are very important, which also guarantees the stability of subsequent deployments.

Intelligent traffic signal systems (I-SIG) have been widely used in various countries. Intelligent traffic signal systems carry vehicle data and traffic signal data. The Internet of Vehicles technology is the core module of the system. Its technology has gradually matured and related products have been applied to practice. The US Department of Transportation estimates that by 2020, the cost of assembling on-board units will be about $ 350, which will make the cost and benefit of car-to-vehicle deployment more beneficial to society. In this paper, we analyze the security of transportation systems based on the Internet of Vehicles technology and study the design-level security issues and challenges in the case of multi-point attacks. Finally, we use the Bayesian probability model to find the attack point for defense.

2   Related Work

2.1   Congestion Attack Based I-SIG

The first safety analysis of the emerging CV-based I-SIG was performed in [1]. Aiming at a highly realistic threat model, that is, dispersing data from an attack tool, the author conducted a vulnerability analysis and found that the current signal control algorithm design and configuration choices are extremely vulnerable to congestion attacks. The evaluation results in the real environment verify the effectiveness of the attack and show that the attack can even produce a blocking effect that prevents the entire method. Then use these insights to discuss defense direction. This work is the first step in understanding new safety issues and challenges in the next generation of CV-based transportation systems. Analysis of the internal structure and algorithms of the signal system, and the defense measures and methods we need.

2.2   Prediction Algorithm of Traffic Wave

The queue prediction is an important content in the field of transportation. The original intention of the prediction is to be able to accurately estimate the real situation of traffic when the traffic situation is uncertain. To this problem, [17] and [18] proposed two different estimation methods. Both draw on the content of physics, and from their work, we need to clean and segment the acquired data to estimate the queues for actual traffic conditions. We must connect the related parts and conduct the experiment.

Traffic wave theory [13] is contained in the field of transportation, and its original intention is to combine the changes in traffic flow with the relevant content of fluid mechanics in physics. Traffic waves are divided into evacuation waves and aggregate waves. Evacuation waves refer to the movement of the interface where traffic waves change from a high-density state to a low-density state. Decreasing the density of traffic flow will generate evacuation waves, and the opposite is the aggregate wave. This model based on physics can be easily combined with the actual traffic situation [11], and simulated and calculated by mathematical models. In this article, we have borrowed relevant knowledge in the field of transportation.

2.3   Bayesian Hieratical Model

The [19] study seeks to investigate the variations associated with lane lateral locations and days of the week in the stochastic and dynamic transition of traffic regimes (DTTR). In the proposed analysis, hierarchical regression models fitted using Bayesian frameworks were used to calibrate the transition probabilities that describe the DTTR. Datasets of two sites on a freeway facility located in Jacksonville, Florida, were selected for the analysis. The traffic speed thresholds to define traffic regimes were estimated using the Gaussian mixture model (GMM). These findings can be used in developing effective congestion countermeasures, particularly in the application of intelligent transportation systems, such as dynamic lane-management strategies.

In the field of transportation, there is also a related work to predict the length of lanes by using Bayesian and Internet of Vehicles technology [2]. Its work is based on Bayesian probability models, supplemented by vehicle data. By modeling and analyzing the data, and determining confidence degree. This Bayesian model is based on the Bayesian principle and uses the knowledge of probability statistics to classify a sample data set. Because of its solid mathematical foundation, the false positive rate of the Bayesian classification algorithm is very low [16]. The method is characterized by combining the prior probability and the posterior probability, which avoids the subjective bias of using only the prior probability and also avoids the over-fitting phenomenon using the sample information alone [12]. The Bayesian classification algorithm shows higher accuracy in the case of large data sets.

3   Defense Model

3.1   Single Point Attack

As shown in Fig. 1, the intelligent traffic signal system involves various units of actual traffic, including a road condition monitoring unit at an intersection and a vehicle-mounted unit that sends vehicle data. It was found in previous work that the security of traditional traffic infrastructure is weak, and an attacker can easily control it completely.

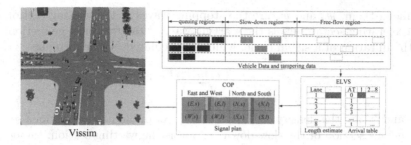

Fig. 1. The flow chart of single point attack experiment.

Therefore, in the work of this article, we focus on the safety of the on-vehicle unit, specifically by attacking the on-vehicle unit to send the wrong vehicle data to the system to affect the planning of the transportation system, and there is already a working proof. There are simple attack methods that can affect normal traffic.

In this article, we first realize the analysis of traffic congestion by sending different vehicle data while controlling the vehicle-mounted unit. Further, we add single attack points to analyze the impact of the attack points on the traffic and the interaction between the attack points. With effect the model we build is presented by the simulation software VISSIM [4] in the transportation field. It provides the Component Object Model (COM) required to build the model. This interface can input signal control into the VISSIM simulation environment, and can also obtain the corresponding intersection from vehicle data, we use code to integrate control input and vehicle output to complete the overall experimental process operation in this way. First of all, the attack process is at the stage of obtaining vehicle data. We tamper with the data obtained by the attacked vehicle to affect the subsequent traffic signal planning. The traffic planning process draws on the latest ISIG system provided by the US Department of Transportation.

3.2 Estimate Queue Length

Traffic congestion has a great impact on us. It not only increases the transit time of vehicles but also increases the probability of traffic accidents. In order to resist the impact of the attack on the traffic, we use the traffic wave model researched in the field of transportation to estimate the queue length of the current lane.

We analyzed the cause of the congestion, and we found that vehicles that were motionless in the system would have a huge impact on the I-SIG algorithm for predicting the lane queue length. In consideration of this, we observed the traffic flow at the intersection of the cycle before the attack. To predict the lane queuing length at intersections in the current cycle, we predict the current queuing length based on the traffic wave model based on the original data. The calculation formula is as follows:

$$L_p = |w_q|t_w + |w_s|t_w + |w_f|t_w \tag{1}$$

Among them, w_q and w_s are the stopping waves of the waiting section and the decelerating section, w_f is the starting wave of the free passage section, and w is the duration of a signal cycle, which is calculated by the formula:

$$w_i = \frac{k_i v_i \ln(k_i/k_j)}{k_i - k_j} \tag{2}$$

k_i and k_j are the density of the divided i section and the i previous section, the previous section of the slow-down section is the waiting section, the density of the previous section of the waiting section is equal to itself, and v_i is the average speed of the vehicles in i section.

3.3   Bayesian Defense Model

We propose a method for estimating the maximum queue length of a vehicle at a signalized intersection using high-frequency trajectory data of the vehicle. The estimated queue length is estimated from the distribution of multiple adjacent periods by the maximum posterior method. The data of these adjacent cycles are obtained through the simulation environment. We estimate the queue length at the next moment from the traffic data at the previous moment and compare it with the real value. The method of predicting the length uses the traffic wave model proposed in the previous section.

We can use the Bayesian model to predict that the current queue length meets the conditions with a certain confidence α by L_p. The specific steps are as follows:

- **Step 1:** Use the traffic wave model to predict the queue length L_w^t of the current stage t based on the data of stage $t - 1$.
- **Step 2:** Calculate the absolute valued of the predicted value L_w^t and the true value L_r^t in the current stage.
- **Step 3:** Calculate d_m.

$$d_m = \max \left\{ d \Big| \min_D \frac{\sum_i^{\{D\}} d_i}{\sum_j^N d_j} < \alpha \right\} \tag{3}$$

- **Step 4:** In the case where the confidence is, the probability P that the predicted queue length L_p is smaller than the confidence interval using the Bayesian model is

$$P(L_p < d_m | lane = l) = \sum_{d < d_m} \frac{P(L_p = d) \prod_k P(lane = k | L_p = d_m)}{\prod_k P(lane = k)} \tag{4}$$

- **Step 5:** If P = 0, there is an attacked vehicle within the predicted length, otherwise it does not.

The following is our algorithm flow for finding attack vehicles. D represents a data set constructed by collecting the difference between the predicted length of the previous cycle and the actual sample queue length in a sample of multiple traffic flows. We use the model trained by Bayesian method to compare the predicted length at the test moment. If the predicted length is within the confidence interval, we believe that there is no attack point at that moment, and it is possible that the attack did not cause system planning impact. If it is beyond the range of the confidence interval, we will find the ID of the attacked vehicle and exclude it from the calculation. This effectively prevents traffic congestion at the attack point. α is the confidence of our principle.

Algorithm 1. Defense algorithm

Require: Veh_t, Veh_{t-1}, α
Ensure: ID
 1: **initialize:** Set ID, d, $L_p = 0$, D← Veh_{t-1}
 2: **sort:** D
 3: **for** $i = 1, 2, ..., len(D)$ **do**
 4:     **if** $\sum_{j=1}^{i} D_i / \text{sum}(D) > \alpha$ **then**
 5:         $d = D_{i-1}$
 6:         **break:**
 7:     **end if**
 8: **end for**
 9: **for** $j = 1, 2, ..., len(Veh_t)$ **do**
10:     **if** $L_j > d$ **then**
11:         ID = j
12:     **end if**
13: **end for**
14: **return** ID

---

4   Experiment

4.1   Experimental Setup

Traffic Intersection Setup. By collecting data on real traffic environment, we mainly analyze the structure of the intersection and the number of lanes at each intersection. In our simulation environment, the maximum speed is limited to 40 km/h. This speed refers to the maximum speed of traffic restrictions in Chinese cities and the intersection range monitored by the system is set to be about 500 m. This range is determined based on statistical traffic flow changes. The speed that VISSIM generates vehicles is eight vehicles per ten seconds. The generated speed refers to daily life near the school counted by our students. The average traffic volume. The simulation program is integrated into Visual Studio. Each attack simulation lasts about 30 min.

The traffic light has several phases. The time and process after a straight and left turn in both directions at an intersection are called phases. The phase is

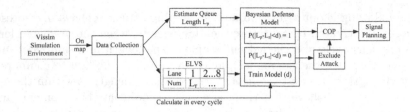

Fig. 2. The data flow of vehicle driving data in the experiment. Vehicle data comes from I-SIG based simulation environment.

determined after calculation based on the traffic volume at each intersection. The phase of each intersection is different. Start by measuring the flow, measuring various traffic flows [11] in all directions in a period, including pedestrian, non-motorized and motor vehicle traffic, and peak traffic. Then calculate the time required for them to run according to the law of traffic flow, and then determine the time of the red and green lights at each intersection, and then determine the phase. The signal lights are divided according to the diagram [9]. The odd numbers represent the left turn direction and the even numbers represent the straight direction.

Attack Data Generation. For the generation of attack data, we refer to the known work using the longest distance attack method, adding multiple attack points for the loophole length algorithm vulnerability in the system, the number of attack points is less than or equal to four, and the data structure of the attack points satisfies the basic requirements of the system. In the attack phase, we assume that the corresponding number of vehicles are controlled by us. We directly modify the corresponding number of vehicle data in the integration program and complete the modification before the signal planning. Each attack will attack the eight phases of the intersection 1000 times each time. The seeds are generated by random vehicles to ensure randomness. In the initial stage of the experiment, we used a large interval assembly rate setting for a set of experiments.

Data Collection. To prepare the data set for subsequent experiments, we integrate the system's estimation algorithm and planning algorithm with the VIS-SIM interface in VS. Each simulation will record the vehicle data at the current moment and the vehicle data for the next cycle. The evaluation file generated by VISSIM after the simulation is completed.

4.2 Simulation

The experimental work in this paper is demonstrated through the VISSIM simulation platform. The simulation experiment simulates the actual traffic situation at the intersection. Under the current development of the Internet of Vehicles, it cannot satisfy all vehicles with vehicle-mounted units. This assumption is in

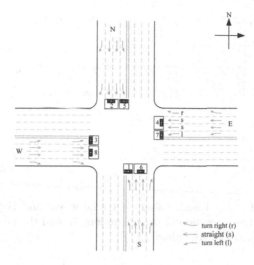

Fig. 3. This is the experimental scenario for the I-SIG system. Two phases in the four directions of the intersection are digitally marked, and each cycle calculates the time allocated for different phases in each direction. (Color figure online)

line with reality. Traffic conditions, so our experiment set the parameter of the penetration rate, the experiment with different penetration rates.

Figure 2 shows the reality used in real experiments. One of the currently known attacks is an attack on the maximum queue length. After analysis, it is determined that it is an algorithm that estimates the queue length of vehicles at the intersection. This attack in a specific traffic situation passing a single point can have a greater impact on the traffic situation of the entire intersection. This attack has the characteristics of being far from the intersection and still. We conduct follow-up research experiments through this key point. During the experiment, we first set an attack point in each direction and applied the characteristics obtained from the analysis to our attack experiments. We controlled each attack point. The speed is 0, and control its position in the intersection.

Adding attack points and feeding back the planned results to the VISSIM simulation environment is achieved through the VISSIM interface. Assuming we control the attacked vehicle through the vulnerability of the vehicle unit, we mark the ID of the attacked vehicle in the experiment. The experimental code changes its original vehicle data through using COM, delivers false data to the intelligent traffic signal system, and the system gets the plan after the attack and enters it into the VISSIM simulation environment.

5 Analysis

In Fig. 3, we describe the calculation and prediction of the average queue length of the lane. The diagonal line in the left half represents the traffic flow in different stages. For example, the green diagonal line in the lower left L_1 represents the

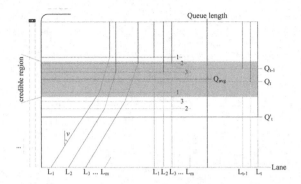

Fig. 4. Prediction of queue length based on traffic waves and Bayesian model. The right vertical axis is the projection of the queue length, and the horizontal axis marks the different lanes. (Color figure online)

traffic flow in the free passage phase of L_1. The angle between it and the vehicle's running direction is the average vehicle speed at this stage, and the vertical lines represent the corresponding distances at different stages. During the experiment, we set the distance between the intersection and the intersection to 1 km, which is also a reference. Real environment at the intersection near the school.

In the experiment, we collected the difference between the predicted value and the real value before and after the two cycles to build the Bayesian model dataset. We used the Intel i5-9400f CPU to run the program in order to collect the simulation data. The simulation results can be collected about every 30 s. We have compiled a total of 100,000 data sets to build a probability model. In Fig. 4, i in Li represents the number of lanes, the point where the horizontal axis line and the blue solid line intersect represents the queue length of the lane, and Q represents the queue length. The blue area indicates that we have obtained 95% confidence in the dataset. Q_{t-1} represents the queue length of the vehicle in the previous cycle. Q_t represents the vehicle data of the previous cycle without attacking the vehicle. The queue length, Q'_t represents the predicted queue length in the case of attacking vehicles. If the predicted queue length is outside the confidence zone, it means that there is an abnormality in the current traffic situation, that is, some vehicles maliciously send false data.

From Fig. 5 we can see that in the case of a high penetration rate, the impact on actual traffic is small. In the case of low penetration rate, because all vehicle information in the actual environment cannot be obtained, multiple attacked vehicles that send the wrong data has a greater impact on the signal planning caused by the system. Specific reasons through careful analysis of the planning part of the code and its principle, the conclusion is that the data of each vehicle is normal for the system. The data of the attacked vehicle that is far away and stationary will cause the EVLS module to incorrectly wait for the vehicle queue.

Our attack uses the longest distance strategy, which is to modify the position data of multiple attacked vehicles to the farthest distance that the system can

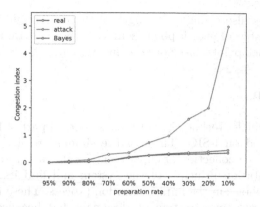

Fig. 5. Congestion index in different situations.

monitor and the vehicle speed is zero. It can be seen that our model can indeed be used at different preparation rates. Resist multi-point attacks against I-SIG. The reason is that when we find that the queue length is abnormal through the Bayesian model, the vehicle information outside the predicted area length is excluded and recorded to prevent repeated attacks in the future. It can be seen that when the preparation rate is smaller, the impact of our attack on the system is greater because the system cannot accurately obtain the queue length of the lane with less data because the calculation of the queue length needs to be more critical.

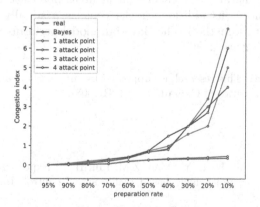

Fig. 6. The effect of adding different numbers of attack points.

Figure 6 shows the impact of adding multiple attack points on the system. Different numbers have different effects on the system. This also proves that the traffic flow between the directions of the intersection is related. Multi-point attacks make the predicted length of lanes in different directions. At the same time, their changes also change the length of the traffic lights. We found that increasing the number of attack points will affect normal traffic, but increasing the number of attack points does not necessarily enhance the effect of the attack.

6   Conclusion

The Internet of Vehicles technology is the most critical part of I-SIG. Our entire experiment is based on I-SIG. Through the simulation of the traffic simulation platform and the collection of experimental data, we gradually explore the internal implementation principle of the system and find its implementation. Problems and loopholes in the implementation process. These loopholes are not caused by inadequate consideration by designers, but because the Internet of Vehicles technology has not been widely popularized, causing the output under certain parameter settings to cause traffic congestion. In this paper, we first analyze the characteristics of single-point attacks systematically, and increase the number of attack points for experimental analysis. Finally, we propose a Bayesian model based on traffic waves to implement attacks against tampered vehicle data. The experimental results also show our model can defend well within a certain confidence range.

Although some of the multi-point attacks have no impact on the system and cannot be ruled out, this does not affect the effectiveness of the defense model. From the actual simulation results, the effect is still significant. During the experiment, we also tried to compare other models such as neural networks, decision trees, etc. From the current experimental results, these models do not have a good defense and generalization effect against multi-point attacks. Similarly, we also found that continuous addition attacks Vehicles, gradually affecting the system is a special attack method. The Bayesian model performs well, but it needs to be improved in future work.

Acknowledgement. This research is supported by the Fundamental Research Funds for the Central Universities of China (No. 2019RC008).

References

1. Chen, Q.A., Yin, Y., Feng, Y., Mao, Z.M, Liu, H.X.: Exposing congestion attack on emerging connected vehicle based traffic signal control. In: NDSS 2018, San Diego, CA (2018)
2. Mei, Y., Gu, W., Chung, E.C.S., Li, F., Tang, K.: A Bayesian approach for estimating vehicle queue lengths at signalized intersections using probe vehicle data. Transp. Res. Part C **109**, 233–249 (2019)
3. MMITSS-AZ 1.0. https://www.itsforge.net/index.php/community/explore-applica tions/for-search-results#/30/63
4. PTV Vissim. http://vision-traffic.ptvgroup.com/en-us/products/ptv-vissim
5. USDOT: Security Credential Management System (SCMS). www.its.dot.gov/factsheets/pdf/CVSCMS.pdf

6. Al-Jameel, H.A.E., Al-Jumaili, M.A.H.: Analysis of traffic stream characteristics using loop detector data. Jordan J. Civil Eng. **10**(4), 403–416 (2016)
7. Li, Z.W., Zhang, J., Gu, H.: Real-time traffic speed estimation with adaptive cruise control vehicles and manual vehicles in a mixed environment. In: Proceedings of 16th COTA International Conference of Transportation Professionals, pp. 51–62 (2016)
8. Wang, M., Daamen, W., Hoogendoorn, S.P., van Arem, B.: Connected variable speed limits control and car following control with vehicle infra structure communication to resolve stop-and-go waves. J. Intell. Transp. Syst. **20**(6), 559–572 (2016)
9. Feng, Y., Head, K.L., Khoshmagham, S., Zamanipour, M.: A real-time adaptive signal control in a connected vehicle environment. Transp. Res. Part C Emerg. Technol. **55**, 460–473 (2015)
10. Comert, G.: Effect of stop line detection in queue length estimation at traffic signals from probe vehicles data. Eur. J. Oper. Res. **226**(1), 67–76 (2013)
11. Sun, Z., Ban, X.J.: Vehicle trajectory reconstruction for signalized intersections using mobile traffic sensors. Transp. Res. Part C Emerg. Technol. **36**, 268–283 (2013)
12. An, C., Wu, Y.J., Xia, J., Huang, W.: Real-time queue length estimation using event-based advance detector data. J. Intell. Transp. Syst. **22**(4), 277–290 (2018)
13. Cai, Q., Wang, Z., Zheng, L., Wu, B., Wang, Y.: Shock wave approach for estimating queue length at signalized intersections by fusing data from point and mobile sensors. Transp. Res. Rec. J. Transp. Res. Board **2422**, 79–87 (2014)
14. Rompis, S.Y., Cetin, M., Habtemichael, F.: Probe vehicle lane identification for queue length estimation at intersections. J. Intell. Transp. Syst. **22**(1), 10–25 (2018)
15. Newson, P., Krumm, J.: Hidden Markov map matching through noise and sparseness. In: Proceedings of the 17th ACM SIGSPATIAL International Conference on Advances in Geographic Information Systems, pp. 336–343. ACM (2009)
16. Zheng, L., Sayed, T.: Bayesian hierarchical modeling traffic conflict extremes for crash estimation: a non-stationary peak over threshold approach. Anal. Methods Accid. Res. **24**, 100106 (2019)
17. Chien, J., Shen, W.: Stationary wave profiles for nonlocal particle models of traffic flow on rough roads. Nonlinear Differ. Equ. Appl. NoDEA **26**(6), 1–25 (2019). https://doi.org/10.1007/s00030-019-0601-7
18. Ma, C., He, R.: Green wave traffic control system optimization based on adaptive genetic-artificial fish swarm algorithm. Neural Comput. Appl. **31**(7), 2073–2083 (2019). https://doi.org/10.1007/s00521-015-1931-y
19. Kidando, E., Moses, R., Sando, T., Ozguven, E.E.: An application of Bayesian multilevel model to evaluate variations in stochastic and dynamic transition of traffic conditions. J. Mod. Transp. **27**(4), 235–249 (2019). https://doi.org/10.1007/s40534-019-00199-2

A Method of Style Transfer
for Chinese Painting

Cunjian Chen[✉]

Hangzhou Dianzi University, Hangzhou, China
291296924@qq.com

Abstract. This paper introduces a style transfer method for traditional Chinese painting. We improved the traditional method by adding style characteristics and constraints unique to Chinese painting. By comparing Chinese painting with Western painting and natural pictures, we find that the features such as lines and textures in Chinese painting are quite different from other images. Therefore, these features are extracted and added to the original method in a restrictive manner. Finally, experiments prove that the method has a certain improvement effect on the style transfer result of Chinese painting.

Keywords: Style transfer · Neural network · Traditional Chinese painting

1 Introduction

The earliest origin of the term neural art is in Gatys [1]. This paper is different from the traditional image style artistic method. It pioneered the use of convolutional neural networks to learn oil painting style. And Gatys also detailed the steps of image style transfer based on VGG19, which described the formation of style expressions, texture combining methods, and loss functions in more depth [1–3].

Compared to Gatys using Gram matrix to calculate the overall style effect, Li proposed to use the local texture of the style image for style transmission [4, 5]. Ulyanov, proposed a texture combining algorithm based on feedforward network. Since the network is trained in advance, their algorithm execution is faster than the Gatys algorithm [6]. Moreover, some people have designed a more Fast networks need to be trained on some large datasets such as COCO datasets, and then applied to existing images that need to be artistic, which greatly saves training time [7]. Recently, Goodfellow et al. [8] proposed a Generative Adversarial Network (GAN). Deep neural networks based on GAN ideas are gradually applied in the field of image style transfer [9–11]. For example, CycleGAN [12], DiscoGAN [13] and DualGAN [14] use the cyclic consistency loss to save the key information of the input and transformed images, and realize the image style transfer in the case of unmatched data.

Gu [15] proposed a feature reorganization style migration method based on vgg neural network. They link most parametric and non-parametric style migration methods by readjusting style loss. It has a good effect for general images. But not effective to Chinese painting, because Chinese painting is different from natural images and has

© IFIP International Federation for Information Processing 2020
Published by Springer Nature Switzerland AG 2020
Z. Shi et al. (Eds.): IIP 2020, IFIP AICT 581, pp. 266–272, 2020.
https://doi.org/10.1007/978-3-030-46931-3_25

special style characteristics. Therefore, this paper try to extract these features and use them to improve the original method to improve the effect of Chinese painting.

2 Style Description of Chinese Painting

Chinese painting is one of the oldest continuous art traditions in the world. It is derived from calligraphy, which is essentially a linear art, using strokes to evoke pictures and emotions. The painting techniques of Chinese painting are mainly expressed in four aspects: pen, ink, color and composition [16].

The use of pen is the essence of Chinese painting. Chinese painting is line-shaped and reaches its peak in the use of line technology. Thickness and thinness of the line, long and short, thick and light, light and heavy, and virtual and real are all different things. Important factors [17]. Chinese painting has many painting techniques, and lines are an important basis for these techniques.

Ink painting has always been a favorite type of painting by Chinese literati, and its ink charm has strong Chinese characteristics [18]. The key of ink painting is the harmony of water and ink. Water is the charm of ink painting. The flowing beauty of water combined with the deep ink color is like black and white dancing on paper, and light and shadow intersect. Ink is generally divided into five colors, which are burnt, thick, dark, light, and clear.

Composition generally refers to the arrangement of objects on the screen, reasonable allocation of space, and good screen management is an important basis for painting [19]. Most of the Chinese paintings refer to the structure of the article, which emphasizes the difference between the real and the false, with a clear distinction between primary and secondary. Although composition is a wild art creation process, it is not ruleless. Many long-term developments in Chinese painting have established many compositional techniques that conform to Chinese aesthetics. Such as full composition, "Zi" composition, corner composition and so on.

3 Feature Extraction

This paper improves the method in Gu [15], extracts the style features of Chinese painting. Then adds these features to the feature matrix.

In order to extract features that can effectively reflect the artistic style of images, This chapter refers to a large of art research literature and some articles on feature extraction and classification of Chinese painting [20, 21]. According to the description in the second section, the general artistic style is expressed in line drawing, frequency, and texture features. Therefore, this article chooses these three characteristics as the artistic style description of Chinese painting. The main methods are:

3.1 Line Feature Extraction

Lines are the most basic component of traditional Chinese painting. Painters use lines to extract, generalize, and abstract natural things and natural scenes. Represent a three-dimensional space with a two-dimensional plane. This experiment uses curvature to represent the fluidity F_{line} of the line, as shown in Eq. 1:

$$F_{line} = \frac{(1+f_x^2)f_{yy} + (1+f_y^2)f_{xx} - 2f_xf_yf_{xy}}{(1+f_x^2+f_y^2)^{3/2}}$$

(1)

where x and y represent the coordinates of a pixel in the image, and f(x, y) is the gray value of the pixel. $f_x, f_y, f_{xy}, f_{xx}, f_{yy}$ are the first, second, and mixed partial derivatives of f(x, y), respectively, and F_{line} is the Gaussian curvature of the pixel.

3.2   Texture Feature Extraction

Texture feature is a visual phenomenon reflected image, which reflects the surface structure of tissue having a slowly varying or periodic change of the flow properties of the surface of the object. This experiment uses LBP shown in Eq. 2:

$$LBP(x_c, y_c) = \sum_{p=1}^{8} s(I(p) - I(c)) * 2^p$$

(2)

where p represents the p-th pixel point other than the central pixel point in the 3 × 3 window; I(c) represents the gray value of the central pixel point, and I(p) represents the gray value of the p-th pixel point in the field; s(x) is shown in Eq. 3:

$$s(x) = \begin{cases} 1, & x \geq 0 \\ 0, & otherwise \end{cases}$$

(3)

3.3   Frequency Feature Extraction

The frequency of an image is an indicator of the intensity of grayscale changes in the image, and is the gradient of grayscale in plane space. Different frequency information has different functions in the image structure. The main component of the image is low-frequency information, which forms the basic gray level of the image, and has little effect on the structure of the image. The intermediate frequency information determines the basic structure of the image, which forms the main edge structure of the image. The edges and details are further enhancement of the image content on the IF information. This experiment uses Fourier transform to extract the frequency map.

3.4   Add Feature Constraint Algorithm

The three features mentioned above are combined into three channels, and a new feature with a certain width and height is added to the feature matrix extracted by the vgg19 network in the original method to form a constant width and height. New feature matrix. Can be tested in different vgg19 network layers.

4 Experiment

4.1 Build Environment

The experiment uses the caffe framework to build the network. caffe is a deep learning framework that combines expressiveness, speed, and modular thinking. Large-scale industrial applications in academic research projects, start-up prototypes and even vision, speech and multimedia. The experimental hardware platform is Intel Core i7-7800K CPU, 8G memory, NVIDIA GeForce RTX2070 GPU.

In order to verify the validity of the method, we selected some natural pictures and some Chinese paintings on the Internet as experimental materials. The subjective evaluation is used as the evaluation criterion in the experiment.

4.2 Experimental Process and Results

Experiment 1. Choose a spectacular architectural picture as the content picture and a Chinese ink painting as the style picture. Through a large number of experiments, we found that the effect of adding constraint features to the third layer of the vgg19 network is better than other layers. Therefore, this experiment only operates on the third layer of the network. Figure 1 shows the content image, style image, the composite image generated by the original method, and the composite image generated by our method. Comparing the experimental results, the results of the original method have a great impact on the content, especially the background, and the image has a serious distortion phenomenon. Ours method optimizes these defects. However, the problems existing in the original method cannot be completely eliminated. It is speculated that the style transfer based on the non-parametric method cannot effectively generate a transition for a content map with a large difference between the subject and background colors.

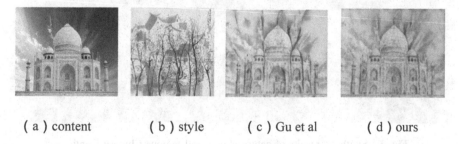

(a) content   (b) style   (c) Gu et al   (d) ours

Fig. 1. Synthesis results of architectural drawings and Chinese ink painting

Experiment 2. Choose a nature photo as the content image, and several famous Chinese paintings as the style images. After experimental analysis, it is still the best choice for the third layer operation of the network. The experimental results show that ours method also has certain improvement effects. In Fig. 2, a nature photo as content, and the style image is one of the top ten Mandarin Chinese For the Thousand Miles of Rivers and Mountains, the result generated by this method is more coordinated overall, and the details are also better.

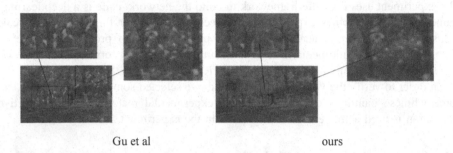

Gu et al   ours

Fig. 2. Synthetic results of nature photos and Thousand Miles of Rivers and Mountains

In addition, since the evaluation criteria of the synthesized results are subjective evaluations, 10 different people were found to conduct subjective evaluations on the result shown in Fig. 3 in this experiment. The evaluation results are shown in Table 1. It can be seen that the method in this paper has certain optimization effect on the synthesis result of Chinese painting as a style image.

Fig. 3. Synthetic results of nature photos and famous Chinese paintings

Table 1. 10 different people praise the synthesis result (Number of people who think the method in this paper is better/Total number)

Style	Landscape painting	All the Pretty Horses	Han Xizai Banquet map	Thousand Miles of Rivers and Mountains	Tang Palace Ladies	Ink painting	Han Palace spring	Five Oxen
Praie rate	0.8	0.6	1.0	0.9	0.9	0.6	0.7	0.9

5   Conclusion

This paper shows a style transfer method for traditional Chinese painting. By improving previous experimental schemes, unique style features in traditional Chinese painting were extracted and added to the feature matrix extracted by the vgg network to achieve the effect of increasing constraints. In the end, a good migration effect was obtained, but it was still unable to achieve the effect of false and real, making people feel that they should draw from the hands of celebrities, and has a certain degree of adaptability to the input image. The main reason is that the paintings in Chinese painting are extremely random and have no regular texture. At the same time, because the evaluation of artistic style images is more subjective, it cannot be objectively evaluated like photographic works. Therefore, we should focus on processing input images and classifying the input images to find the most appropriate content image and style image to match in future. And establish an objective evaluation system for Chinese painting images.

References

1. Gatys, L.A., Ecker, A.S., Bethge, M.: A neural algorithm of artistic style. Computer Science (2015)
2. Gatys, L.A., Ecker, A.S., Bethge, M.: Texture synthesis using convolutional neural networks. In: International Conference on Neural Information Processing Systems. MIT Press (2015)
3. Gatys, L.A., Ecker, A.S., Bethge, M.: Image style transfer using convolutional neural networks. In: 2016 IEEE Conference on Computer Vision and Pattern Recognition (CVPR). IEEE Computer Society (2016)
4. Li, C., Wand, M.: Combining Markov random fields and convolutional neural networks for image synthesis. In: 2016 IEEE Conference on Computer Vision and Pattern Recognition (CVPR), Las Vegas, NV, USA, 27–30 June 2016, 2479–2486 (2016)
5. Johnson, J., Alahi, A., Fei-Fei, L.: Perceptual losses for real-time style transfer and super-resolution (2016)
6. Ulyanov, D., Lebedev, V., Vedaldi, A., et al.: Texture networks: feed-forward synthesis of textures and stylized images (2016)
7. Johnson, J., Alahi, A., Fei-Fei, L.: Perceptual losses for real-time style transfer and super-resolution. In: Leibe, B., Matas, J., Sebe, N., Welling, M. (eds.) ECCV 2016. LNCS, vol. 9906, pp. 694–711. Springer, Cham (2016). https://doi.org/10.1007/978-3-319-46475-6_43

8. Goodfellow, I.J., Pouget-Abadie, J., Mirza, M., et al.: Generative adversarial nets. In: The 27th International Conference on Neural Information Processing Systems, Montreal, Canada, pp. 2672–2680 (2014)
9. Radford, A., Metz, L., Chintala, S.: Unsupervised representation learning with deep convolutional generative adversarial networks. Computer Science (2015)
10. Arjovsky, M., Chintala, S., Bottou, L.: Wasserstein GAN (2017)
11. Gulrajani, I., Ahmed, F., Arjovsky, M., et al.: Improved training of wasserstein GANs. In: The 31st International Conference on Neural Information Processing Systems, Red Hook, USA, pp. 5769–5779 (2017)
12. Zhu, J.Y., Park, T., Isola, P., et al.: Unpaired image-to-image translation using cycle-consistent adversarial networks (2017)
13. Kim, T., Cha, M., Kim, H., et al.: Learning to discover cross-domain relations with generative adversarial networks. In: The 34th International Conference on Machine Learning, Sydney, Australia, pp. 1857–1865 (2017)
14. Yi, Z., Zhang, H., Tan, P., et al.: DualGAN: unsupervised dual learning for image-to-image translation (2017)
15. Gu, S., Chen, C., Liao, J., et al.: Arbitrary style transfer with deep feature reshuffle (2018)
16. Liu, X.: Anxiety and Breakthrough—A Personal Exploration Journey of Modern Ink Figure Painting. Shandong Normal University (2004). (in Chinese)
17. Huang, Q.: On the application and emotional expression of lines in the teaching of Chinese painting. **709**(07), 100–101 (2017). (in Chinese)
18. Wu, H.: Ink Danqing, Chinese painting divine charm. Jingdezhen Ceram. **178**(06), 18–19 (2018). (in Chinese)
19. Wang, W.: Spatial Forms and Implications of Painting Compositions. Shandong Normal University (2012). (in Chinese)
20. Jiang, S., Huang, Q., Ye, Q., et al.: An effective method to detect and categorize digitized traditional Chinese paintings. Pattern Recogn. Lett. **27**(7), 734–746 (2006)
21. Jun-Jie, C., Ya-Juan, D.U.: Feature extraction and classification of Chinese painting. Comput. Eng. Appl. **74**(2), 26 (2008)

Speech Triggered Mobility Support and Privacy

Michael Zipperle[1,2](✉), Marius Becherer[1,2](✉), and Achim Karduck[1](✉)

[1] Furtwangen University, Furtwangen, Germany
michael@zipperle.de, marius.baech@gmail.com, karduck@hs-furtwangen.de
[2] University of New South Wales, Canberra, Australia

Abstract. Current voice assistants are offered by large IT companies such as Google, Amazon, Microsoft, Apple or Baidu. The voice assistants include numerous functionalities, which are usually executed centrally in the cloud by the providers. Nevertheless, the providers offer imprecise information on what happens to the input data of the users. Users cannot be sure whether their privacy and data are protected. The central research question is what is currently happening with the voice-based interaction between users and services, and what concepts for configurable data protection by users are conceivable in the future. In this article, we present the survey results obtained by speech assistant users. The results show, in particular, the willingness to pay for individually configurable privacy. The concept for a voice assistant with privacy-awareness is proposed and prototypically implemented.

Keywords: Data security · Privacy · Voice assistant · Cloud computing · Natural language processing · Mobility support

1 Introduction

Voice control is an interaction possibility where services can be controlled by human speech. Realizing voice control requires an ecosystem - the voice assistant - out of several components to deal with tasks such as converting in both ways text to speech, speech to text as well as extracting metadata from text input. Hereby, several processes can be initiated such as playing the next song, setting the alarm clock or starting an ordering process. Experts expect a growing market for voice assistants: The trade journal "PR Newswire" assumes that purchases via speech will increase twenty-fold in the next four years [5]. The magazine "Campaign" estimates that in the future the search in browsers using the keyboard will be replaced by the search via voice [15]. The voice assistants preprocess the voice in order to understand the meaning, and therefore, control several services regarding the voice input. For this reason, the voice assistant can be considered as a component between user and application that enables the interaction by the human voice.

© IFIP International Federation for Information Processing 2020
Published by Springer Nature Switzerland AG 2020
Z. Shi et al. (Eds.): IIP 2020, IFIP AICT 581, pp. 273–283, 2020.
https://doi.org/10.1007/978-3-030-46931-3_26

The applications of a voice assistant run on a platform in the cloud. Speech processing on the platform is demanding because a user's voice input runs through highly complex sub-processes of speech processing. It takes time until a suitable user response is generated. Currently, these platforms are offered by major cloud providers who have the computational resources and know-how of each sub-process. Voice assistants are offered by Amazon, Google, Microsoft or Baidu, with many functionalities and excellent performances. However, there are privacy concerns as the privacy policies of cloud providers do not clearly state what happens to users' data in the cloud. Mobile devices such as smartphones and speakers send a user's voice input to the appropriate cloud provider for analysis. The data processing is non-transparent and it opens up the opportunity to establish a side-channel between the user and its applications. In the process, data can be collected and possibly misused. Nowadays, sensitive data are shared among users and enterprises, for instance, the banking system, health care system and messaging. The use of data is specified in terms of use, but these give a limited indication of the possible usage scenarios, such as user profiling.

In this work, we conduct a survey with 110 participants to understand today's customer needs of their perspective on privacy in the domain of voice assistants. Regarding the survey, we develop a privacy-awareness concept that includes user-controlled privacy with a high level of functionality as well as performance. Besides, the concept is implemented into the privacy-awareness ecosystem consisting of three separate components: the mobile app, privacy provider, and voice assistant.

The results explained in Sect. 3 represent the motivation for the development of a privacy-awareness concept for a voice assistant. In Sect. 4.1, the privacy-awareness concept is presented to transfer full control back to the user. A full-stack architecture is shown in Sect. 4.2. Then, in Sect. 5, a prototype is presented that implements this architecture. The presented prototype allows maximum flexibility in data control and provides the user with configurable privacy. A summary of the concept, the technologies, and the developed prototype conclude this article.

2   Related Work

Voice assistants such as Amazon Alexa, Google Assistant, Apple Siri, Microsoft Cortana, and Baidu DuerOS currently dominate the market. However, they all are non-transparent in their voice assistant ecosystem and providing a minimal declaration of data usage [2,4,7,9,12]. In detail, the services in the cloud infrastructure are a hidden secret, and therefore, less privacy-awareness are provided for the users.

The conducted study on privacy risks of voice assistant apps presents diverse risks in the communication, the user identification scheme, as well as privacy-related information [13]. During their investigations, they expose that Google Assistant transfer several additional information, such as user information and user device information. Furthermore, in 50.51% of the voice assistant apps, linking customers to an identification scheme has been feasible. More significant, personal information such as birth date, name, e-mail address, blood type, gender phone number are tried to obtain from the apps. This demonstrates the high usage of data capturing data in the case of Google Assistant. Likely, the same is happening in other commercial voice assistants.

Even though the previous study exposes exploited data collection, many customers are not conscious of these hidden processes. An investigation on smart home user's indicates lacking conscious of their privacy perception of the devices, and consequently, they prioritize convenience over privacy [17]. Another study reveals the incompleteness of data activities to user perception that leads to design implications in the domain of smart home voice assistants [1]. In the security and privacy domain of voice assistant, user perception with their concerns is conducted and presents less customer disposition in discussing the costumer's voice assistants [6]. In contrast to the studies that cover users' perception and knowledge, the authors of [11] conducted a study with users and non-users of voice assistants and compared their reasons that support and criticize voice assistants. Hereby, customers did not perceive different mechanisms such as audio logs as privacy control, and additionally, other privacy controls often are not used.

Despite the forgone studies in this domain, most of them focusing on user perception and conclude lacking privacy awareness. The one weakness of those studies is the limited user feedback regarding the conducted interviews, but the main issue relies on lacking user expectations. Hereby, the studies do not understand the user needs and there willingness to overcome those privacy concerns.

Different approaches to deal mitigate privacy risk such as an access control mechanism that is used in the smart home domain by with information are delivered regarding the task context [8]. In a more abstract representation, fundamental design strategies are proposed that cover data economy, careful allocation, user ability to control, and usability of security mechanisms [16]. More specific details in terms of privacy are conceptualized in the privacy framework with a focus on privacy key risks such as system development and design and cross-organizational collaboration [14].

Overall, the previous research supports the assumption that data is collected even though not every time permission is required, such as for device ID and user ID. Consequently, users cannot control data access and monitor the data processing in clouds of global players. Although the majority of customers have a significant knowledge deficit in the privacy perception of voice assistants, the studies do not address the personal perception of specific data. Without knowing the customer's need for privacy, it is challenging for developers to understand what data violates the individuals' privacy. Furthermore, several privacy frameworks have been proposed as well as concrete implementation in access control mechanisms for task-oriented service computing. Whereas privacy frameworks are imprecisely but user-centric, concrete access control mechanisms are precisely but service-centric. Ultimately, the current research is lacking a privacy-awareness concept that considers configurable users' privacy with a large extent in functionality.

3   Motivation

In the beginning, an initial survey was carried out to determine whether more data protection is desired for voice assistants in Germany. Over one hundred participants took part in the online survey. 54.5% of the participants were male, 45.5% female, and 10% were under 18, 69% between 19 and 25, 7% between 26 and 35, and 14% over 35 years old. The participants were asked the following questions:

1. How often do you use a voice assistant?
2. Do you know what happens to your data?
3. Which particularly privacy-related information is important to you?
4. Would you pay money for high privacy?
5. How much money would you pay once for high data protection of an application?

The first question revealed that 44.5% use a voice assistant once a month or more often, whereby 90% of the participants do not know what is happening with their data. The results show that a high level of privacy is desired especially for their banking credentials, individual behavior and attitudes, communication among individuals, contacts, interests, and location.

One in four would pay for better privacy, and 56% of the participants are unsure if they would spend money on it. The group under the age of 18 years has the least willing to pay. The intersection of participants who ticked "Yes" or "Maybe" increase with age. The amount that participants would spend on better privacy varies widely. Approximately 15% of the respondents were not willing to pay for it, while the majority are. 50% of the respondents would pay up to 5€, 15% 6–10€ and 20% over 10€.

Therefore, the following conclusions can be drawn from the survey results: First, voice assistants are used to varying degrees and users do not know what happens to their data. Second, privacy for users is essential, even though the exposure level of data regards to individuals' perception and third, users would pay for the protection of their data.

4   Methodology

This section proposes a concept for high privacy-awareness, and the architecture to implement it.

4.1   Concept

Based on the survey, a concept for a voice assistant was developed. The costs for the required resources were neglected. An important requirement of the concept is the privacy-awareness considering the design principles for the multilateral privacy according to Kai Rannenberg focus on the following four points [16] and the privacy framework [14]: Data minimization, control possibilities for the user, possibilities of choice and room for negotiation, and decentralisation and distribution.

Within this concept, the focus is on the first three points. Often applications collect data from a user, which the user did not agree with, for instance, sharing device id or user information [13]. Therefore, the concept aims to ensure that an application only collects data from users who need it. Furthermore, the provided data for application should be, both physical and operational, fully-controlled by the users to enable privacy-awareness data access. By doing so, users have the opportunity to decide if they want to share no data, partially data, or the full requested data. Since some application depends on the requested data to work properly, data can be manipulated in the middle by the user to ensure privacy.

User-controlled privacy allows a user to determine what data he or she releases for specific applications. However, applications require additional data from a user to provide sufficient usability. An example is a voice assistant's question about weather forecasts. If the voice assistant knows the user's location, it can provide the weather forecast for the user's position. Otherwise, the voice assistant would first have to ask the user for which location he or she wants a weather forecast. If a user does not want to release his data for an application, he can define a fictitious context. This allows the user to use this application, but at the expense of lower user-friendliness.

4.2   Architecture

The concept for high privacy-awareness can be implemented using the architecture and technologies shown in Fig. 1. Three components are required for

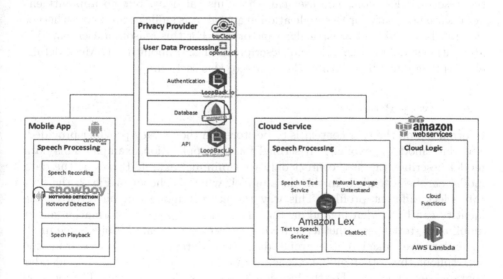

Fig. 1. Architecture overview

the implementation: First, the Mobile App serves as an interface to the user. The user can make voice entries and configure his profile and privacy via the app. Second, cloud services handle voice processing and generates output to the user. The privacy provider is accessed to generate a response. Third, the Privacy Provider is the core component, which guarantees the user more privacy. The exact structure and choice of technology are described below.

5   Prototype

In the following, the application example is described, and then the implementation of the individual components of the architecture is explained in more detail.

5.1   Application Example

The application example is intended to show how a voice assistant can be used to promote speech-based mobility support and at the same time, ensure fine-grained data protection for the user. The application example covers the following functionalities: First, the search for doctors can be carried out in a specific location. Secondly, a doctor's appointment can be negotiated, whereby a doctor's calendar is compared with the user's calendar. Finally, optional mobility support such as scala mobile, assistance to the user when leaving the house or a pick-up service, that takes the user to the doctor and back home, can be requested.

A user can define the data required for these functionalities in detail in a mobile app. For example, a user can have his location determined automatically via GPS to expose his current location, but he can also edit the location manually to preserve it location. The user can share his calendar, but no appointment details are necessary for the application example. It is sufficient to know whether the user is available at a particular time or not. For this reason, a user can hide appointment details like title and description of an appointment. More details about privacy will be shown in the course of this section.

5.2   Privacy Provider

Information on the user context is to be stored in the privacy provider provided. The data model is explicitly described for the application example. This data model describes the user context only to a minimal extent. However, the data model can be extended. In this data model, which is shown in Fig. 2, the user can select different profiles. This way the correct name can be given or the identity can be hidden behind another name. In the profile, information about mobility is stored, e.g. whether a driving service and a Scala Mobile is required. Calendars are linked to the profile data. The data is read directly from the smartphone, but other online calendars can also be added. Finally, a calendar contains several events. For the location, there is the location field. The location can be determined via the GPS sensor, or a location can be entered manually.

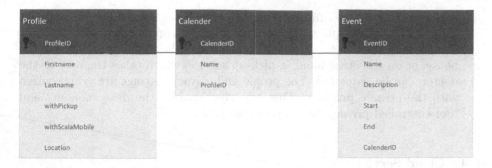

Fig. 2. Data model for the application example

5.3 Mobile App

The mobile app serves on the one hand as an interactive interface between the user and the voice assistant and on the other hand, as a privacy configurator. The app offers the following four views:

– Registration: A new user can register with the voice assistant with his e-mail and a password. The user can choose between the profile types private, doctor or mobility support. Depending on the profile type, different privacy settings are preconfigured. By default, a private profile is only accessible to the owner, whereas the profile types Physician and Mobility Support are publicly accessible.
– Login: A registered user can log in to the voice assistant with his e-mail and password.
– Voice Assistant: The voice assistant is the main view of the app, which appears as soon as a user is logged in. At the same time, the Hotword Detection is started, which was realized with Snowboy from Kitt.ai [10]. The Hotword Detection listens locally on the Smartphone until the signal word "Butler" is recognized; no data is stored and passed on to third parties. After detection of the signal word, voice processing is moved to the cloud for better performance. As soon as an interaction between user and voice assistant is finished, the hotword detection is reactivated. Also, all the output of the voice wizard on the view. The audio recording and playback were implemented with the Android SDK.
– Settings: This view allows the user to configure his profile and privacy settings. The first and last names can be set for the profile. The location can be determined either by text input or by GPS. When determining the location via GPS, the user can decide whether the location is retrieved once or whether the app can automatically update. The user can make his calendar available to the app. Besides, the automatic update of the calendar or the hiding of details such as the title and description of an appointment can be activated. This ensures that only the data relevant to the application example is accessed. Other personal data, such as the name of the calendar or the

owner, cannot be determined by the app. Next, the user can define mobility supports that are requested by default when an appointment with a doctor is made. On the one hand, Scala Mobile, which helps the user to leave the house, or on the other hand, a pick-up service, which takes the user to the doctor, can be requested. The profile and privacy settings are synchronized with the privacy provider. This app view enables the data economy and user-controlled privacy presented in the concept.

5.4   Cloud Service

As soon as the hotword detection has detected the signal word "Butler", the further processing of a user's voice input is performed in the cloud. By outsourcing resource-intensive voice processing to the cloud, users can be assured of high performance and ease of use. For the realization the following Amazon Web Services (AWS) were used:

– Amazon Lex: Amazon Lex serves as a conversation interface for speech and text. Based on the text intent, an output can be generated, which is then converted from text to speech [3]. An Amazon Lambda function is triggered to generate a response to a text intention.

Fig. 3. Mobile app

– Amazon Lambda: Based on Amazon Lambda, an application was developed that generates a dynamic response based on the text intention of the user. The application can access the privacy provider to retrieve the necessary information to generate the response by using the user's access token. Thus, the applications could realize the negotiation of a free doctor's appointment between doctors and user (Fig. 3).

5.5   Data Release

To use data from the privacy provider, the user must first be authenticated. To do this, the registration data is entered into the mobile app. When the login button is clicked, the user is authenticated by the privacy provider. During this process, the user is granted read, write and execute rights, so that data can be changed and various functions can be performed. Besides, a time-limited key is generated with which the user can grant applications access to his data. Which data can be read by an application can be released by the user in the mobile app.

6   Conclusion

Some conclusions could be drawn from the developed prototype, which offers high user security and control possibilities. It was possible to take the concept into account during implementation and aspects of multilateral security, and user-controlled privacy is also found in the prototype. The prototype consists of the voice processing environment (cloud services), the mobile app and the privacy provider.

The functionality requirements were met using Amazon's cloud services. Besides, the fulfilled General Data Protection Regulation (GDPR) guidelines of the voice services can guarantee data protection for the users. By using the speech-based cloud services, developers do not have to deal with speech processing in detail but can develop an application on an abstract level. Before a user can use the voice assistant, he or she must authenticate. This protects access from unauthorized persons. In the app, users can create different profiles with different data, the use of pseudo profiles is possible. Concerning the concept of multi-layered security, this is important to create choice and room for negotiation for the user. The user data is stored in a privacy provider. The concept of multi-level security also applies to the privacy provider. Decentralization and distribution are of great importance here. The choice of technology and provider takes data protection into account at all levels. However, there is still potential for optimization at the privacy provider, resource access should be made more configurable through authorization, duration, and filtering.

Depending on the user, the requirements for a voice assistant vary. Different applications should be able to be activated or deactivated based on the needs of a user. This functionality could extend the prototype in the future. The applications offered must inform the users about user data and thus create transparency.

A standard for data storage must be created to create an ecosystem in which every application can access the data. Otherwise, the applications will have to manage the user data themselves, and the concept of separating data and application would become obsolete.

In this article, the potential of voice assistants is referred to at various points. By the pleasant handling of the system intelligence, it offers an added value in everyday life. However, different industries must open up and offer interfaces so that bookings and reservations are not only possible by e-mail or telephone. If the infrastructure of companies is created, voice assistants will become even more attractive for users.

References

1. Abdi, N., Ramokapane, K.M., Such, J.M.: More than smart speakers: security and privacy perceptions of smart home personal assistants. In: Fifteenth Symposium on Usable Privacy and Security (SOUPS 2019), Santa Clara, CA. USENIX Association, August 2019. https://www.usenix.org/conference/soups2019/presentation/abdi
2. Amazon: Alexa internet privacy notice (2018). https://www.alexa.com/help/privacy
3. Amazon: Amazon Lex (2018). https://aws.amazon.com/de/lex/
4. Apple: Privacy policy (2018). https://www.apple.com/legal/privacy/en-ww/
5. Consultants, O.S.: Voice shopping set to jump to $40 billion by 2022, rising from $2 billion today (2018). https://www.prnewswire.com/news-releases/voice-shopping-set-to-jump-to-40-billion-by-2022-rising-from-2-billion-today-300605596.html
6. Fruchter, N., Liccardi, I.: Consumer attitudes towards privacy and security in home assistants. In: Extended Abstracts of the 2018 CHI Conference on Human Factors in Computing Systems (CHI 2018), pp. 1–6. ACM Press, New York (2018). https://doi.org/10.1145/3170427.3188448. http://dl.acm.org/citation.cfm?doid=3170427.3188448
7. Google: Privacy policies (2018). https://policies.google.com/privacy?hl=en-US
8. He, W., et al.: Rethinking access control and authentication for the home Internet of Things (IoT). In: 27th {USENIX} Security Symposium ({USENIX} Security 2018), pp. 255–272 (2018)
9. Hemple, J.: How Baidu will win China's AI race - and maybe, the world's (2017). https://www.wired.com/story/how-baidu-will-win-chinas-ai-raceand-maybe-the-worlds/
10. KITT.AI: Snowboy hotword detection (2018). https://snowboy.kitt.ai/
11. Lau, J., Zimmerman, B., Schaub, F.: Alexa, are you listening? Privacy perceptions, concerns and privacy-seeking behaviors with smart speakers. In: Proceedings of the ACM on Human-Computer Interaction 2 (CSCW) (2018). https://doi.org/10.1145/3274371
12. Mircosoft: Cortana and privacy (2018). https://support.microsoft.com/en-us/help/4468233/cortana-and-privacy-microsoft-privacy
13. Natatsuka, A., Akiyama, M., Iijima, R., Sakai, T., Watanabe, T., Mori, T.: Poster: a first look at the privacy risks of voice assistant apps. In: Proceedings of the ACM Conference on Computer and Communications Security, pp. 2633–2635 (2019). https://doi.org/10.1145/3319535.3363274

14. NIST: NIST Privacy Framework: A Tool for Improving Privacy Through Enterprise Risk Management (2020). https://www.nist.gov/system/files/documents/2020/01/16/NIST~Privacy~Framework_V1.0.pdf
15. Olson, C.: Just say it: the future of search is voice and personal digital assistant (2016). https://www.campaignlive.co.uk/article/just-say-it-future-search-voice-personal-digital-assistants/1392459
16. Rannenberg, K.: Multilateral security a concept and examples for balanced security. In: Proceedings New Security Paradigm Workshop, pp. 151–162 (2000). https://doi.org/10.1145/366173.366208
17. Zheng, S., Apthorpe, N., Chetty, M., Feamster, N.: User perceptions of smart home IoT privacy. In: Proceedings of the ACM on Human-Computer Interaction 2 (CSCW), pp. 1–20 (2018)

Computer Vision and Image Understanding

Explaining Color Evolution, Color Blindness, and Color Recognition by the Decoding Model of Color Vision

Chenguang Lu[✉]

College of Intelligence Engineering and Mathematics,
Liaoning Technical University, Fuxin 123000, Liaoning, China
lcguang@foxmail.com

Abstract. The author proposed the decoding model of color vision in 1987. International Commission on Illumination (CIE) recommended almost the same symmetric color model for color transform in 2006. For readers to understand the decoding model better, this paper first introduces the decoding model, then uses this model to explain the opponent-process, color evolution, and color blindness pictorially. Recent references on the decoding and reconstruction of colors in the visual cortex induce a new question: what is the decoding algorithm from ganglion cells to the visual cortex? This paper also explains the decoding algorithm. The decoding model is explained as a fuzzy 3–8 decoder. The fuzzy logic used is compatible with Boolean Algebra. The model first obtains the median M of three cones' outputs B, G, and R, and then obtain three opponent signals by B, G, and R minus M respectively. This model can unify Young and Helmholtz's tri-pigment theory and Hering's opponent theory more naturally than the popular zone models. It is symmetrical and compatible with the popular color transform method for computer graphics. The transform from the RGB system to HSV system according to the decoding model is introduced. Several fuzzy 3–8 or 4–16 … fuzzy decoders can be used to construct a Decoding Neural Network (DNN). The decoding algorithm from ganglion cells to the visual cortex can be explained with a two-layer DNN. The reasonability of the decoding model and the potential applications of the DNN are discussed.

Keywords: Neural computing · Color blindness · Color evolution · Color decoding · Color recognition · Neural network · Computer vision

1 Introduction

Young and Helmholtz's tri-pigment theory [1] and Hering's opponent theory [2] on color vision have been competing for a long time. A compromising viewpoint accepted widely is that color signals exist in tri-pigments at the zone of visual cones and in opponent signals at the zone of visual nerves [3]. The mathematical model with this viewpoint is called the zone model [4]. There are many improved versions of the zone model [5–8]. However, why are color signals processed in this way? and how has color vision been evolving? The answers are still unclear. To answer these questions, the author of this paper built a model of color vision named the decoding model [9], which

© IFIP International Federation for Information Processing 2020
Published by Springer Nature Switzerland AG 2020
Z. Shi et al. (Eds.): IIP 2020, IFIP AICT 581, pp. 287–298, 2020.
https://doi.org/10.1007/978-3-030-46931-3_27

is new version of the zone model, and has been verified by predicting color appearance [10]. After the author explored the information conveyed by color vision, he developed a semantic information theory [11], which can be used for machine learning [12]. Recently, the author learned that

- international Commission on Illumination (CIE) recommended almost the same symmetric color model for color transformation [13];
- the human or macaque temporal cortex can decode and reconstruct colors [14–21].

These facts impel the author to introduce his further studies on color vision. The purpose of this paper is to help readers understand opponent-process, color evolution, color blindness, color decoding and reconstruction, and color recognition better.

The decoding model should be helpful to researchers who build the color vision mechanism of robots, and it may enlighten someone to build a neural network with the fuzzy logic [22] that is compatible with Boolean algebra for applications.

To the best of the author's knowledge, no other researchers use fuzzy logic that is compatible with Boolean Algebra for color models or neural networks, not to mention explaining color evolution, color blindness, and color decoding and reconstruction.

The main contributions of this paper are

- It provides more explicit explanations of color evolution and color blindness than the popular zone models.
- It shows a simple algorithm for decoding and reconstructing colors in the human temporal cortex.
- It proposes the decoding neural network for potential applications.

The following sections first introduce the decoding model and the color transform from the RGB system to the HSV system, then use this model to explain the opponent-process, color evolution, color blindness, and color decoding and reconstruction in the visual cortex. Discussions include topics about the reasonability of the decoding model and the similarity between the decoding model and the neural network.

2   The Decoding Model of Color Vision

2.1   The Fuzzy Logic Compatible with Boolean Algebra

The 3–8 decoder is frequently used in computers or numerical circuits for selecting one register or memory from eight. If B, G, and R are binary switching variables taking values from set $\{0, 1\}$ as three inputs to a 3–8 decoder, then eight outputs will be $[\bar{B}\bar{G}\bar{R}]$, $[\bar{B}\bar{G}R]$, $[\bar{B}G\bar{R}]$, $[\bar{B}G\bar{R}]$, $[B\bar{G}\bar{R}]$, $[B\bar{G}\bar{R}]$, $[B\bar{G}\bar{R}]$, and $[BGR]$ ([...] Denotes a logical expression). For example, if $B = G = 0$ and $R = 1$, then $[\bar{B}\bar{G}\bar{R}] = 1$, otherwise $[\bar{B}\bar{G}\bar{R}] = 0$.

Now, suppose that B, G, and R are continuous switching variables, i.e. B, G, and R take continuous values from set $[0, 1]$. With the special continuous-valued logic or fuzzy logic [22], we can extend the binary 3–8 decoding into the fuzzy 3–8 decoding [9, 10]. The values of output codes are illustrated in Fig. 1.

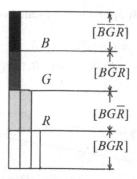

Fig. 1. Relationship between three inputs B, G, and R and eight outputs of a fuzzy 3–8 decoder. When $B > G > R$, only four outputs are not zero.

Let function $\max(a, b)$ be the maximum of a and b, $\min (a, b)$ be the minimum of a and b, and so on. Hence

$$[\bar{B}\bar{G}\bar{R}] = 1 - \max(B, G, R), \quad [\bar{B}\bar{G}R] = \max(0, R - \max(B, G))$$
$$[\bar{B}GR] = \max(0, \min(G, R) - B), \quad [BGR] = \min(B, G, R) \tag{1}$$

The others can be calculated in like manner.

2.2   Transform from the RGB System to the HSV System

Let B, G, and R be tri-stimulus valves from cones. How do we simulate the visual system to obtain H (hue), S (saturation), and V (brightness) from B, G, and R? For any given color denoted by (B, G, R), there is

$$(B, G, R) = [\bar{B}\bar{G}R](0, 0, 1) + [\bar{B}GR](0, 1, 1) + [\bar{B}G\bar{R}](0, 1, 0) + [BG\bar{R}](1, 1, 0)$$
$$+ [B\bar{G}\bar{R}](1, 0, 0) + ([\bar{B}G\bar{R}](1, 0, 1) + [BGR](1, 1, 1) \tag{2}$$

which means that any color can be decomposed into the combination of white and six unique colors in different ratios. In the above equation, $(0, 0, 1)$ stands for the most saturated red, i.e., unique red, and the coefficient $[\bar{B}\bar{G}R]$ is the redness, and so on.

It is coincident that only three items on the right of Eq. (2) may be non-zero for a given color, and the three cardinal vectors with 0 and 1 or unique colors must be at the three vertexes of one of six sectors in Fig. 2. Hence Eq. (2) can be changed into

$$(B, G, R) = m_1 e_1 + m_2 e_2 + [BGR](1, 1, 1) \tag{3}$$

where e_1 and e_2 are two cardinal vectors or unique colors, and m_1 and m_2 are corresponding coefficients or output codes' values.

Suppose the angles at which e_1 and e_2 are located (see Fig. 2) are H_1 and H_2. Let

$$H = (m_1 H_1 + m_2 H_2)/(m_1 + m_2), \quad C = m_1 + m_2,$$
$$V = m_1 + m_2 + [BGR] = \max(B, G, R), \quad S = C/V. \tag{4}$$

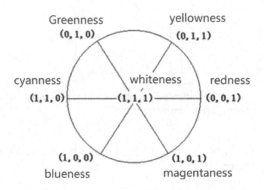

Greenness (0, 1, 0)   yellowness (0, 1, 1)

cyanness (1, 1, 0)   whiteness (1, 1, 1)   redness (0, 0, 1)

(1, 0, 0) blueness   (1, 0, 1) magentaness

Fig. 2. The decomposition of color (B, G, R).

Then H, C, V, and S will represent hue, colorfulness, brightness, and saturation of (B, G, R) properly if B, G, and R are obtained from appropriate linear and nonlinear transforms of spectral tri-stimulus values X, Y, and Z [10]. According to the decoding model, the relationship between brightness, colorfulness, whiteness, blackness, and B, G and R is shown in Fig. 3, where med(B, G, R) is the median or second one of B, G and R. For example, med$(1, 3, 5) = 3$, med$(1, 2, 5) = 2$, med$(1, 5, 5) = 5$, med$(1, 1, 5) = 1$.

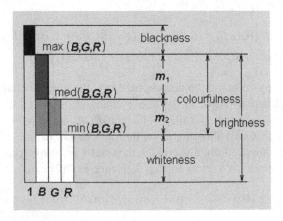

Fig. 3. Relationship between B, G, R and brightness, colorfulness, whiteness, and blackness. (Color figure online)

Later the author found the above transform is the same as that proposed by Smith earlier [23]. The differences are:

- B, G, and R in Smith's transform are the signals of three primary colors lightening a pixel of a displayer instead of the tri-stimulus values of visual cones;
- Smith uses "if-then" programming language rather than logical operations;
- The logical expressions for the opponent-process only exist in the decoding model.

2.3 Opponent-Process

We use Venn's Diagram to show the essence of the opponent-process. Let $\cap$, $\cup$, and ^{c} denote three set operations: intersection, union, and complement respectively, and let B, G, and R represent the three circular fields respectively (see Fig. 4). For convenience, we also use "‾" for complement operation and omit $\cap$. Then, the eight fields can be represented by $[\bar{B}\bar{G}\bar{R}]$, $[\bar{B}\bar{G}R]$, $[\bar{B}G\bar{R}]$, $[B\bar{G}\bar{R}]$, $[BG\bar{R}]$, $[B\bar{G}R]$, $[\bar{B}GR]$, and $[BGR]$.

From B, G, and R, we can first obtain

$$M = BG \cup BR \cup GR, \tag{5}$$

which represents the trefoil (the intersecting fields of two or three circles).

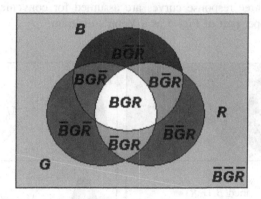

Fig. 4. Venn's diagram showing the logic operations of the opponent-process. (Color figure online)

Then, we have

$$\begin{aligned} B\bar{M} &= B\overline{(BG \cup BR \cup GR)} = B(\bar{B} \cup \bar{G})(\bar{B} \cup \bar{R})(\bar{G} \cup \bar{R}) \\ &= B(\bar{B} \cup \bar{B}\bar{G} \cup \bar{B}\bar{R} \cup \bar{G}\bar{R}) = B\bar{G}\bar{R}, \end{aligned} \tag{6}$$

where DeMorgan Law is used. Similarly, there are $\bar{B}M = \bar{B}GR$ (yellow area), $G\bar{M} = \bar{B}G\bar{R}$ (green area), $\bar{G}M = B\bar{G}R$ (magenta area), $R\bar{M} = \bar{B}\bar{G}R$ (red area), $R\bar{M} = \bar{B}\bar{G}R$ (red area), and $\bar{R}M = BG\bar{R}$ (cyan area).

Now let B, G, and R denote three cones' outputs, which take values from $[0, 1]$, and let the set operations be replaced by the fuzzy logic operations: $\vee$, $\wedge$, ‾ (‾ can be omitted). First, we obtain the median value of B, G, and R (see Fig. 5):

$$M = \text{med}(B, G, R) = [BG \vee BR \vee GR]$$
$$= \max(\min(B, G), \min(B, R), \min(G, R)). \tag{12}$$

Then we obtain three opponent signals: blueness-yellowness (M_{BY}), greenness-magentaness (M_{GM}), and redness-cyanness (M_{RC}). The calculations are surprisingly simple:

$$M_{BY} = B - M = \begin{cases} +[B\bar{G}\bar{R}], & B \geq M, \\ -[\bar{B}GR], & B < M; \end{cases} \tag{13}$$

$$M_{GM} = G - M = \begin{cases} +[\bar{B}G\bar{R}], & G \geq M, \\ -[B\bar{G}R], & G < M; \end{cases} \tag{14}$$

$$M_{RC} = R - M = \begin{cases} +[\bar{B}\bar{G}R], & R \geq M, \\ -[BG\bar{R}], & R < M. \end{cases} \tag{15}$$

The opponent-process corresponding to different monochromatic lights is shown in Fig. 5, where the three response curves are assumed for convenience. We can also consider the left-upper part of Fig. 5 as a Venn's diagram.

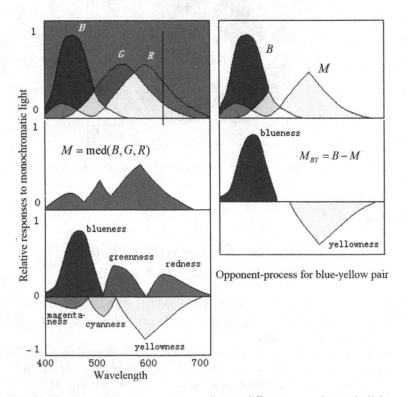

Fig. 5. The opponent-process corresponding to different monochromatic lights.

There are eight divided fields. The length of the part of a vertical line on a field is just the magnitude of the corresponding unique color signal. These fields can illustrate the changes in the color perception caused by different monochromatic lights well.

3   Further Investigations

3.1   To Explain Color Evolution

According to the decoding model, we can easily explain the evolution of color vision by splitting the sensitivity curves of visual cones (see Fig. 6). We may imagine that curves $R(\lambda)$ and $G(\lambda)$ gradually approach one another to become one curve named Y (λ). Then we would see the fields representing red, green, cyan, and magenta disappear gradually. Further, let curves $B(\lambda)$ and $Y(\lambda)$ approach one another gradually to become one curve named $W(\lambda)$. Then we would see the fields representing blue and yellow disappear gradually, and only the black and white fields remain. Now, we can imagine that color vision was evolving in the opposite procedure. First, there was only one kind of visual cones in the human retina, and only two totally different colors (black and white) could be discerned. Then, with the evolution of color vision, the cones split into two kinds that had different spectral sensitivities so that blue and yellow were also perceived. After that, the cones split into three kinds so that more colors were perceived.

We may conclude that n different kinds of cones can produce 2^n totally different color perceptions for $n = 1$, 2, 3. When $n = 4$, the conclusion seems also true. A symmetrical model of four primary colors for robots can be seen in [24]. The model has 14 "unique colors", which can be symmetrically put on the surface of a ball, besides "white" (1, 1, 1, 1) and "black" (0, 0, 0, 0). We can obtain a "color" ball that has many properties very similar to those in the Newton color wheel.

The evolution of color vision might have come in a somewhat different way. For example (see Fig. 6, deuteranopia-2), the curve $W(\lambda)$ first split into $R(\lambda)$ and $C(\lambda)$ related to cyan, instead of $B(\lambda)$ and $Y(\lambda)$, then $C(\lambda)$ split into $B(\lambda)$ and $G(\lambda)$.

3.2   To Explain Color Blindness

Color blindness has been discussed by many researchers [25, 26]. It can also be easily explained by the sensitivity curves of cones that are too close to each other (see Fig. 7). For example, monochromatism can be explained under the assumption that the sensitivity curves $B(\lambda)$, $G(\lambda)$ and $R(\lambda)$ have not yet separated from one curve; red-green blindness can be explained under the assumption that the curves $G(\lambda)$ and $R(\lambda)$ have not yet separated from one curve.

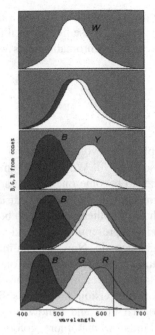

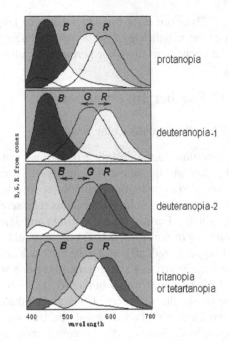

Fig. 6. The Evolution of color vision illustrated by splitting sensitivity curves. (Color figure online)

Fig. 7. Different kinds of color blindness illustrated by incomplete separations of three sensitive curves. (Color figure online)

According to the decoding model, some red-green blindness can be identified as protanopia or deuteranopia only because the peak of $Y(\lambda)$ has shorter or longer wavelength. Tritanopia and tetartanopia can be illustrated by the assumption that the $B(\lambda)$ and $G(\lambda)$ (or $B(\lambda)$ and $R(\lambda)$) have not yet separated so that each kind of color blindness can only perceive two chromatic colors: red and cyan (or green and magenta).

3.3   Decoding and Reconstructing Colors in the Human Visual Cortex

Many neurons in the visual cortex are color selective, and color-opponent responses are evident throughout the visual cortex [14, 15]. The human visual cortex can decode and reconstruct colors from the voxel responses of cones [16, 17]. Many different neurons in the visual cortex respond to many specific colors [18, 21]. However, the relation between voxel responses and decoding outputs in the visual cortex is still unclear. Reference [16] uses a matrix to represent the decoding algorithm from voxel responses to decoding outputs; reference [21] uses Poisson distributions to describe the decoding algorithm from colors to decoding outputs. However, what we need is to explain the decoding algorithm from opponent-color signals as the outputs of ganglion cells to decoding outputs in visual cortex. Using the decoding model, we can build a two-layer neural network, with which we can easily explain the decoding algorithm.

The decoding model can be regarded as a single-layer neural network with three inputs and eight outputs. If the three outputs at every sector, such as signals of white, red, and yellow, are used as the inputs of another fuzzy 3–8 decoder (see Fig. 8), then we have a two-layer neural network. We call this neural network the Decoding Neural Network (DNN). Using a two-layer DNN, we can explain how six unique colors plus white are further decoded into more specific colors that are reconstructed in the human visual cortex, as shown in Fig. 8. For example, one output represents an orange or pink color in the visual cortex.

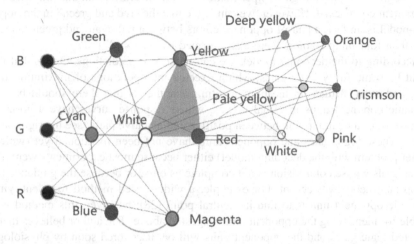

Fig. 8. A two-layer DNN can be used to explain the decoding algorithm from voxel responses in cones to decoding outputs in the visual cortex. (Color figure online)

We can also use the DNN for color recognition, not only for three primary colors, but also for four primary colors perceived by robots [24].

4 Discussions

4.1 About the Reasonability of the Decoding Model

Several reasons make the decoding model convincible:

- The model is concise, symmetrical, and without any coefficient.
- It can be used to explain the opponent-process, color evolution, color blindness more naturally than the popular zone models.
- It can be used to explain the decoding and reconstruction of colors in the visual cortex more conveniently.
- In the popular zone model, red plus green at the zone of visual cones become yellow; yet, red plus green at the zone of visual nerves become white. Therefore, the meanings of "red" and "green" in the popular zone model are easily misunderstood. However, the decoding model does not have this problem.

- The decoding model is more compatible with the laws of color mixture that are used for the color transform of computer graphics.
- We can also use the decoding model to explain the phenomenon of negative after-image conveniently. For example, when the sensitivity of the R-cone falls down, $[BG\bar{R}]$ for cyanness will be over zero when white $(1, 1, 1)$ is perceived so that white looks cyan.

There is a possible problem with the decoding model. In the popular zone model, there are only two pairs, instead of three pairs, of opponent colors. It seems that psychological and physiological experiments support the affirmation that only two pairs of opponent colors exist. However, we can argue that the "red and green" in the popular zone model is, in fact, a pair of opponent colors between red-cyan and green-magenta. More than four unique colors were also affirmed by others [27].

According to the decoding model, we can make two predictions. One is that there should be some fuzzy logic gates, which execute the operations of maximum, minimum, and even median, in the human retina. Another is that there should be some chromatic opponent units in visual nerves, whose response curves have a horizontal line, instead of a neutral point, between positive and negative parts (see the right part of Fig. 5). These logic gates and opponent units have not been mentioned yet (which is another problem with the decoding model) either because most experiments were made with animals whose color vision is not complete as ours, or because the guidance from appropriate theory was absent. For example, a widely used method for identifying a chromatic opponent unit is to find its neutral point [28]; however, this method is not suitable for identifying the opponent unit suggested above. The author believes that the predicted logic gates and the opponent units will be discovered soon by physiologists who pay attention to them.

4.2   About the Potential Applications of the Decoding Neural Network

Figure 8 indicates that we can use several or many 3–8 or $n - 2^n$ decoders to construct a two-layer or multi-layer Decoding Neural Network (DNN). Compared with the popular neural network, the DNN has different characteristics:

- It uses fuzzy logic without parameters.
- Every nerve cell in the next layer has inputs that are selected from one sector of the previous layer.
- The number of non-zero outputs is equal to the number of inputs.

Using biologic feature vectors instead of color vectors, we may use a DNN to recognize some different living things. It is possible to combine the DNN with existing neural networks to improve machine learning in some cases. We need further studies on the DNN.

5 Conclusions

This paper has introduced the decoding model of color vision, including the fuzzy logic and the opponent-process for it. This model can unify Young and Helmholtz's tri-pigment theory and Hering's opponent theory more naturally than the popular zone models. And, this model is symmetrical and compatible with the popular color transform method, and hence, is also practical. The paper has used the decoding model to explain color evolution and color blindness pictorially. It has also used the DNN, which consists of two-layer fuzzy 3–8 decoders, to explain the decoding and reconstruction of colors in the visual cortex. These explanations indicate the reasonability of the decoding model. The DNN that consists of some fuzzy $n - 2^n$ decoders has some desirable characteristics for machine learning and needs further studies.

References

1. Young, T.: Bakerian lecture: on the theory of light and colours. Phil. Trans. R. Soc. Lond. **92**, 12–48 (1802). https://doi.org/10.1098/rstl.1802.0004
2. Solomon, R.L., Corbit, J.D.: An opponent-process theory of motivation: I. Temporal dynamics of affect. Psychol. Rev. **81**(2), 119–145 (1974)
3. De Monasterio, F.M., Gouras, P., Tollhurst, D.J.: Trichromatic color opponency in ganglion cells of the rhesus monkey retina. J. Physiol. **252**, 197–216 (1975)
4. Judd, D.B.: Response functions for types of vision according to the Muller theory. J. Res. Natl. Bur. Std. **42**, 356–371 (1949)
5. Hurvich, L.M., Jameson, D.: An opponent-process theory of color vision. Psychol. Rev. **64** (6), 384–404 (1957)
6. Walraven, P.L.: On the Bezold-Brucke phenomenon. J. Opt. Soc. Am. **51**(10), 1113–1116 (1961)
7. Hunt, R.W.G.: A model of color vision for predicting color appearance. Color Res. Appl. **7** (2), 95–112 (1982)
8. De Valois, R.L., De Valois, K.K.: A multi-stage color model. Vis. Res. **33**(8), 1053–1065 (1993)
9. Lu, C.: New theory of color vision and simulation of mechanism. Dev. Psychol. (in China) **14**(2), 36–45 (1986)
10. Lu, C.: Decoding model of color vision and its verification. Acta Optica Sinica **9**(2), 158–163 (1989)
11. Lu, C.: A generalization of Shannon's information theory. Int. J. Gen. Syst. **28**(6), 453–490 (1999)
12. Lu, C.: Semantic information G theory and logical Bayesian inference for machine learning. Information **10**(8), 261 (2019)
13. CIELAB, Symmetric colour vision model, CIELAB and colour information technology (2006). http://130.149.60.45/~farbmetrik/A/FI06E.PDF
14. Kleinschmidt, A., Lee, B.B., Requardt, M., et al.: Functional mapping of color processing by magnetic resonance imaging of responses to selective P- and M-pathway stimulation. Exp. Brain Res. **110**, 279–288 (1996)
15. Engel, S., Zhang, X., Wandell, B.: Color tuning in human visual cortex measured with functional magnetic resonance imaging. Nature **388**(6637), 68–71 (1997)

16. Brouwer, G.J., Heeger, D.J.: Decoding and reconstructing color from responses in human visual cortex. J. Neurosci. **29**(44), 13992–14003 (2009)
17. Brouwer, G.J., Heeger, D.J.: Categorical clustering of the neural representation of color. J. Neurosci. **33**(39), 15454–15465 (2013)
18. Conway, B.R., Moeller, S., Tsao, D.Y.: Specialized color modules in macaque extrastriate cortex. Neuron **56**(3), 560–573 (2007)
19. Bohon, K.S., Hermann, K.L., et al.: Representation of perceptual color space in macaque posterior inferior temporal cortex (the V4 complex). eNeuro **3**(4), 1–28 (2016)
20. Zaidi, Q., Marshall, J., Thoen, H., Conway, B.R.: Evolution of neural computations: mantis shrimp and human color decoding. i-Perception **5**(6), 492–496 (2014)
21. Zaidi, Q., Conway, B.: Steps towards neural decoding of colors. Curr. Opin. Behav. Sci. **30**, 169–177 (2019)
22. Lu, C.: B-Fuzzy set algebra and generalized mutual information formula. Fuzzy Syst. Math. **5**(1), 76–80 (1991)
23. Smith, A.R.: Color Gamut transform pairs. Comput. Graph. **12**(3), 12–19 (1978)
24. Lu, C.: Models of color vision for robots. Robot (J. Chin. Soc. Autom.) **1**(6), 39–46 (1987)
25. Marmor, M.F.: Vision, eye disease, and art: 2015 Keeler Lecture. Eye **30**(2), 287–303 (2016)
26. Chan, X., Goh, S., Tan, N.: Subjects with colour vision deficiency in the community: what do primary care physicians need to know? Asia Pac. Fam. Med. **13**(1), 10 (2014). https://doi.org/10.1186/s12930-014-0010-3
27. Hardin, C.L.: The resemblances of colors. Philos. Stud. **48**(7), 35–47 (1985)
28. De Valois, R.L., Abramov, I., Jacobs, G.H.: Analysis of response patterns of LGN cells. J. Opt. Soc. Am. **56**(7), 966–977 (1966)

A Content-Based Deep Hybrid Approach
with Segmented Max-Pooling

Dapeng Zhang[1], Liu Yajun[2(⊠)], and Jiancheng Liu[1]

[1] The College of Information Science and Engineering, Yanshan University,
Qinhuangdao 066004, China
[2] Hebei Institute of Architectural Engineering Information Engineering Institute,
Zhangjiakou 075000, China
459817216@qq.com

Abstract. Convolutional matrix factorization (ConvMF), which integrates convolutional neural network (CNN) into probabilistic matrix factorization (PMF), has been recently proposed to utilize the contextual information and achieve higher rating prediction accuracy of model-based collaborative filtering (CF) recommender systems. While ConvMF uses max-pooling, which may lose the feature's location and frequency information. In order to solve this problem, a novel approach with segmented max-pooling (ConvMF-S) has been proposed in this paper. ConvMF-S can extract multiple features and keep their location and frequency information. Experiments show that the rating prediction accuracy has been improved.

Keywords: ConvMF · CNN · PMF · Max-pooling

1 Introduction

Recommender systems have drawn more and more attention in the last decade. They can help people get useful information from "the ocean of information", and can be found in many fields of our life. For example, Alibaba and Amazon use recommender systems to recommend products to their users in their e-commerce platforms. Facebook and Tencent Weibo apply recommender systems in their social networks.

Collaborative filtering (CF) is one of the main methods to build recommender systems [1]. Recently, combined with CF, there are more and more efforts to apply deep learning in recommender systems [2–8]. Due to the exploding growth of the number of users and items, the sparseness of relationships between users and items can be extremely high, which deteriorates the prediction accuracy of the CF recommender systems. In order to alleviate this problem, auxiliary information such as description documents of items, which are easily available from various sources, have been utilized to enhance the rating prediction accuracy. Especially, convolutional neural network (CNN) has been integrated into probabilistic matrix factorization (PMF) to develop convolutional matrix factorization model (ConvMF).

Convolution and pooling are of the most important stages in CNN. And max-pooling is the most common sub-sampling operation of pooling layer. It only keeps the maximum feature from each feature vector obtained from convolution layer, which has

© IFIP International Federation for Information Processing 2020
Published by Springer Nature Switzerland AG 2020
Z. Shi et al. (Eds.): IIP 2020, IFIP AICT 581, pp. 299–309, 2020.
https://doi.org/10.1007/978-3-030-46931-3_28

the following disadvantage: (1) The location information of the features is totally lost. In fact, the location information is kept in convolution layer. (2) Sometimes, certain features may appear frequently. The more frequently it appears, the stronger it is. But max-pooling also loses this frequency information.

In order to address this problem, we propose a new approach with segmented max-pooling, which is called ConvMF-S to improve the ConvMF.

2   Related Work

The great success achieved by convolutional neural network in computer vision has inspired the recent effort to apply deep learning method in NLP. Since 2014, significant work in this field have been published.

Kalchbrenner [9] has proposed a CNN model for sentence modeling, which uses dynamic k-max pooling as a global pooling operation over linear sequences. Besides, he [10] has also proposed an extended CNN for processing sequences. The resulting network has two core properties: it runs in time that is linear in the length of the sequences and it sidesteps the need for excessive memorization, which can solve the problem that the pooling layer may lose some information (whether the information is useful or useless). Chen [11] has proposed a CNN model for event extraction, which uses a dynamic multi-pooling layer according to event triggers and arguments to reserve more crucial information. Lei [12] has proposed a non-linear discontinuous CNN for text modeling, which nonlinearly transforms the convolutional layer. The multi-column CNN model introduced by Dong [13] uses multiple columns of CNN to learn the representations of different aspects of questions. Ma [14] exploits various long-distance relationships between words, and presents a dependency-based convolution framework. Johnson [15] studies CNN on text categorization, the author directly applies CNN to high-dimensional text data, which leads to directly learning embedding of small text regions for use in classification.

More recently, CNNs have also been applied in recommender systems. Several hybrid methods have been proposed for recommender systems that utilize auxiliary information, particularly, the reviews and abstracts of items. Kim [16] has presented ConvMF, a robust document context-aware hybrid method which seamlessly integrates CNN into probabilistic matrix factorization (PMF) in order to capture contextual information in description documents for the rating prediction while considering Gaussian noise differently through using the statistics of items. While its max-pooling layer extracts only the maximum contextual feature from each contextual feature vector. So the information of feature strength is lost. Meanwhile, the location that feature appears is also important, which is also ignored in ConvMF. In order to address the former limitation of ConvMF, we propose an approach with segmented max-pooling, which can keep multiple features when pooling and reflect the location information of features.

3 Improved Convolutional Matrix Factorization: ConvMF-S

3.1 Convolutional Matrix Factorization

In essence, CNN is a classifier because its object is to address classification task, such as image recognition, label predicting for words, phrases or documents. While the object of recommender is a regressive task. So traditional CNN is not suitable for recommender tasks.

Convolutional matrix factorization can address the above issue through seamlessly integrating CNN into PMF. The probabilistic model of ConvMF is shown in Fig. 1.

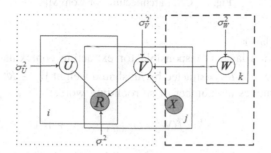

Fig. 1. Probabilistic model of ConvMF

The left dotted part is PMF and the right dashed part is CNN. Suppose we have N users and M items, and observed ratings are represented by $R \in R^{N*M}$ matrix. Then the conditional distribution over observed ratings is given by formula 1.

$$P(R|U, V, \sigma^2) = \prod_{i}^{N} \prod_{j}^{M} N(r_{ij}|u_i^T v_j, \sigma^2)^{I_{ij}} \tag{1}$$

Figure 2 illustrates the CNN architecture for ConvMF, which is composed of four layers: embedding layer, convolution layer, pooling layer and output layer.

(1) Embedding layer
The object of the embedding layer is to transform a raw document into a dense numeric matrix for the convolution layer. The document matrix $D \in R^{p*l}$ can be represented by:

$$D = [\cdots w_{i-1}, w_i, w_{i+1} \cdots] \tag{2}$$

where l is the length of the document, and p is the size of embedding dimension for each word w.

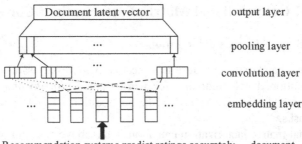

Fig. 2. CNN architecture for ConvMF

(2) Convolution layer

The convolution layer is responsible for extracting contextual features. A contextual feature $c_i^j \in R$ is extracted by jth shared weight $W_c^j \in R^{p*ws}$ whose window size ws determines the number of surrounding words:

$$c_i^j = f(W_c^j * D_{(:,i:(i+ws-1))} + b_c^j) \qquad (3)$$

where $*$ is a convolution operator, $b_c^j \in R$ is a bias for W_c^j and f is a non-linear activation function. Then, a contextual feature vector $c^j \in R^{l-ws+1}$ of a document with W_c^j is constructed by:

$$c^j = [c_1^j, c_2^j, \cdots, c_i^j, \cdots, c_{l-ws+1}^j] \qquad (4)$$

(3) Pooling layer

The pooling layer extracts representative features from the convolution layer, and also deals with variable lengths of documents via pooling operation that constructs a fixed-length feature vector. Max-pooling is utilized here to reduce the representation of a document into a fixed-length vector. The maximum contextual feature from each contextual feature vector can be expressed as:

$$d_f = [max(c^1), max(c^2), \ldots, max(c^j), \ldots, max(c^{n_c})] \qquad (5)$$

(4) Output layer

High-level features obtained from the previous layer could be converted at output layer. The produced document latent vector can be expressed as:

$$s = \tanh(W_{f2}\{\tanh(W_{f1}d_f + b_{f1})\} + b_{f2}) \qquad (6)$$

where $W_{f1} \in R^{f*n_c}$, $W_{f2} \in R^{k*f}$ are projection matrices, and $b_{f1} \in R^f$, $b_{f2} \in R^k$ are bias vectors for W_{f1}, W_{f2}

Finally, latent vectors of each document are returned as output:

$$s_j = cnn(W, X_j) \tag{7}$$

where W denotes all the weight and bias variables and X_j denotes a raw document of item j, and s_j denotes a document latent vector of item j.

3.2 Improved ConvMF with Segmented Max-Pooling (ConvMF-S)

Convolution and pooling are of the most important stages in CNN. And max-pooling is the most common sub-sampling operation of pooling layer. It only keeps the maximum feature from each feature vector obtained from convolution layer. One of the advantage of max-pooling is that it can reduce the number of the features to enhance performance and it can also keep the length of the feature vectors the same which makes it easy to construct the following layers. The architecture of max-pooling is shown in Fig. 3.

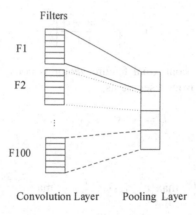

Fig. 3. Architecture of max-pooling

The disadvantage of max-pooling has been stated in Sect. 1. In order to deal with this problem, we propose a new approach with segmented max-pooling, which is called ConvMF-S to improve the ConvMF. It divides each feature vector obtained from convolution layer into segments as required and extracts the maximum value from each segments. The architecture of segmented max-pooling is shown in Fig. 4.

In ConvMF-S, the embedding layer, convolution layer and output layer are the same with ConvMF. The only improvement is in pooling layer, which is described as follows.

Suppose W_c^j is the weight matrix and c_i^j is a contextual feature extracted by the jth filter in convolution layer. The length of the document is l. Processed by the convolution layer, a document is represented as n_c contextual feature vectors, and each contextual feature vector has variable length, which is represented by $l - ws + 1$.

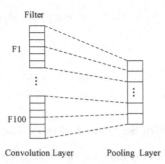

Fig. 4. Architecture of segmented max-pooling

In order to keep more information in pooling layer, we need to divide each contextual feature vector into segments, and extract the maximum contextual feature from these segments. If a contextual feature is divided into s segments, the length of each segmented contextual is represented by Eqn:

$$n = \left\lceil \frac{l - ws + 1}{s + 1} \right\rceil \tag{8}$$

Then the fixed-length contextual feature vector is converted by extracting maximum contextual features from s segments:

$$d_f = [s^1, s^2, \ldots, s^j, \ldots, s^{n_c}] \tag{9}$$

Where:

$$s^j = \left[\max(c_1^j, \cdots, c_n^j), \max(c_{n+1}^j, \cdots, c_{2n}^j) \cdots \max(c_{(s-1)*n+1}^j, \cdots, c_{sn}^j) \right] \tag{10}$$

3.3   ConvMF-S Algorithm

Integrating CNN into PMF, our ConvMF-S algorithm can be described as follows.

Table 1. ConvMF-S algorithm

Input: R: user-item rating matrix, X: description documents of items
1: Embed the one-hot encoded word vectors to generate word sequence $D \in \mathbb{R}^{p*l}$ from X
2: Process D with filters of three different window size (3, 4, 5) to extract contextual feature $c^j \in R^{l-ws+1}$
3: For each $c^j \in R^{l-ws+1}$, extracts feature values using segmented max-pooling to create the contextual feature vector d_f
4: Flatten the pooling results to make it to be one-dimensional
5: Output the document latent vectors
6: Use the document latent vectors as the mean of Gaussian noise of an item to initialize the item feature matrix
7: Initialize the user feature matrix and fit the rating matrix R with item feature matrix
8: Output the result of RSME

4   Experiments

In this section, we evaluate the performance of ConvMF-S algorithm compared with PMF and ConvMF.

4.1   Experimental Environment and Datasets

We use ml-100k dataset obtained from Movielens, which contains 100,000 ratings on 1682 movies from 943 users. And we randomly divide it into training set (80%), validation set (10%) and test set (10%).

We also obtain documents of corresponding items from IMDB. The obtained documents are preprocessed as follows: (1) Set maximum length of input documents to 300; (2) Remove stop words; (3) Calculated TF-IDF score for each word; (4) Remove corpus-specific stop words of which the document frequency are higher than 0.5; (5) Select top 8000 distinct words as a vocabulary; (6) Remove all non-vocabulary words from input documents.

4.2   Word Vectors Pre-training with Word2vec

One of the most critical issues of contextual-based deep hybrid recommender systems is how to utilize text data more efficiently to generate high-quality features. This involves text analysis tasks in NLP. Therefore, Our word embedding vectors are initialized with word2vec [17], a very popular pre-trained word embedding model. And we pre-train our word vectors on IMDB, which contains 50000 labeled comments and 50000 unlabeled comments.

Each comment in IMDB is kept as a single file. So we merge these comments as a dataset. The format of the merged dataset is shown in Table 2.

Table 2. Format of the merged dataset

Line-number	Id	Sentiment	Review
0	5814_8	1	"With all this...kay. Visually....
1	2381_9	1	"\" The Classic War of the Worlds\" by...
2	7759_3	0	"The film starts with a manager (Nichola...
3	3630_4	0	"Superbly trashy and wondrously ...

The field id in Table 1 represents the file name of the comment. Left side of the underline is the movie ID, and right side is the rating of the movie from user. The contents of review are processed by removing HTML labels, punctuations and numbers, transforming them into lowercase, splitting them into individual word and rejecting repeated words.

4.3 Experimental Results

In our experiments, RMSE (Root Mean Squared Error) is adopted as the evaluation measure, which is related to the objective functions of prediction models.

Firstly, we compare the performance of these three algorithms based on the numbers of iterations, which is illustrated in Fig. 5.

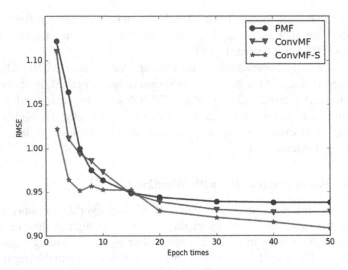

Fig. 5. Comparison of numbers of iterations

From Fig. 5, it can be seen that PMF converges quickly during the first 15 iterations, the RMSE value tends to be stable after 15th iterations. ConvMF converges quickly during the first 20 iterations. After the 20th iteration, the model is still converging, but the convergence speed is slowed down. ConvMF tends to be stable and the RMSE value does not change when the number of iterations exceeds 30. ConvMF-S is superior to PMF and ConvMF at the beginning of the model training, indicating that the segmented max-pooling effectively improves CNN's ability to analyze document data. ConvMF-S's final iterative result is also superior to the other two algorithms which further proves that the improved method can effectively improve the recommender quality.

Secondly, we compare the performance of the three algorithms on training sets with different percentages (20%, 40%, 60% and 80%). The result is shown in Fig. 6.

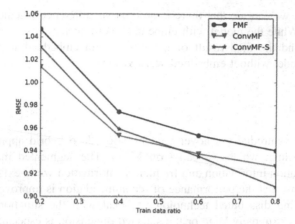

Fig. 6. Comparison on training sets with different percentages

From Fig. 6, it can be seen that the RMSE values of the three algorithms get smaller as the percentage of the training set becomes higher. The recommended results of the other two algorithms are better than the PMF algorithm, just because adding document information can improve accuracy. ConvMF is better than ConvMF-S when the percentage of the training set is beyond 40%. When the percentage of the training set rises exceed 40%, ConvMF-S surpasses ConvMF.

Finally, we compare the performance of ConvMF-S with embedded pre-trained word vectors and without embedded pre-trained word vectors. The result is shown in Fig. 7.

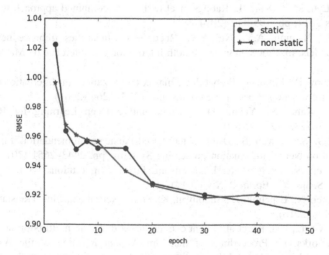

Fig. 7. Effect of the embedded word vectors

From Fig. 7, we can see that there is no obvious difference whether word vectors are embedded. While the model with embedded word vectors is still converging after 30 iterations. And the final result of the model with embedded word vectors also surpasses the model without embedded word vectors.

5 Conclusion

In this paper, we introduces a novel content-based deep hybrid approach with segmented max-pooling, which we call ConvMF-S. The segmented max-pooling can preserve the location information and frequency information while extracting features. Experiments show that the performance of recommendation is improved. Future work may include using distributed technology to deal with the situation in which the document data is extremely large or the selected dimension is especially high.

Acknowledgement. This work was supported by the Natural Science Foundation of China (No. 61303129).

References

1. Koren, Y.: Factorization meets the neighborhood: a multifaceted collaborative filtering model. In: Proceedings of the 14th ACM SIGKDD, pp. 426–434 (2008)
2. Salakhutdinov, R., Mnih, A., Hinton, G.: Restricted Boltzmann machines for collaborative filtering. In: International Conference on Machine Learning, pp. 791–798 (2007)
3. Wang, C., Blei, D.M.: Collaborative topic modeling for recommending scientific articles. In: International Conference on Knowledge Discovery and Data Mining, pp. 448–456 (2011)
4. Ling, G., Lyu, M.R., King, I.: Ratings meet reviews, a combined approach to recommend. In: RecSys 2014, pp. 105–112 (2014)
5. Maas, A.L., Hannun, A.Y., Ng, A.Y.: Rectifier nonlinearities improve neural network acoustic models. In: Proceedings of the 30th International Conference on Machine Learning (2013)
6. Salakhutdinov, R., Mnih, A.: Probabilistic matrix factorization. In: International Conference on Neural Information Processing Systems, pp. 1257–1264 (2007)
7. Wang, H., Wang, N., Yeung, D.Y.: Collaborative Deep Learning for Recommender Systems, pp. 1235–1244 (2014)
8. Dieleman, S., Schrauwen, B.: Deep content-based music recommendation. In: International Conference on Neural Information Processing Systems, pp. 2643–2651 (2013)
9. Kalchbrenner, N., Grefenstette, E., Blunsom, P.: A Convolutional Neural Network for Modelling Sentences. Eprint ArXiv (2014)
10. Kalchbrenner, N., Espeholt, L., Simonyan, K., et al.: Neural Machine Translation in Linear Time. ArXiv (2016)
11. Chen, Y., Xu, L., Liu, K., et al.: Event extraction via dynamic multi-pooling convolutional neural networks. In: Proceedings of the 53rd Annual Meeting of the Association for Computational Linguistics and the 7th International Joint Conference on Natural Language Processing, pp. 167–176 (2015)
12. Lei, T., Barzilay, R., Jaakkola, T.: Molding CNNs for text: non-linear, non-consecutive convolutions. Indiana Univ. Math. J. **58**(3), 1151–1186 (2015)

13. Dong, L., Wei, F., Zhou, M., et al.: Question answering over freebase with multi-column convolutional neural networks. In: Proceedings of the 53rd Annual Meeting of the Association for Computational Linguistics and the 7th International Joint Conference on Natural Language Processing, pp. 260–269 (2015)
14. Ma, M., Huang, L., Xiang, B., et al.: Dependency-based Convolutional Neural Networks for Sentence Embedding. ArXiv (2015)
15. Johnson, R., Zhang, T.: Effective Use of Word Order for Text Categorization with Convolutional Neural Networks. Eprint ArXiv (2014)
16. Kim, D., Park, C., Oh, J., et al.: Deep hybrid recommender systems via exploiting document context and statistics of items. Inf. Sci. **417**, 72–87 (2017)
17. Goldberg, Y., Levy, O.: Word2vec Explained: Deriving Mikolov et al.'s Negative-Sampling Word-Embedding Method. ArXiv (2014)

Image Caption Combined with GAN Training Method

Zeqin Huang[1,2(✉)] and Zhongzhi Shi[1]

[1] Key Laboratory of Intelligent Information Processing,
Institute of Computing Technology, Chinese Academy of Sciences,
Beijing 100190, China
{huangzeqin17g, shizz}@ict.ac.cn
[2] University of Chinese Academy of Sciences, Beijing 100049, China

Abstract. In today's world where the number of images is huge and people cannot quickly retrieve the information they need, we urgently need a simpler and more human-friendly way of understanding images, and image captions have emerged. Image caption, as its name suggests, is to analyze and understand image information to generate natural language descriptions of specific images. In recent years, it has been widely used in image-text crossover studies, early infant education, and assisted by disadvantaged groups. And the favor of industry, has produced many excellent research results. At present, the evaluation of image caption is basically based on objective evaluation indicators such as BLUE and CIDEr. It is easy to prevent the generated caption from approaching human language expression. The introduction of GAN idea allows us to use a new method of adversarial training. To evaluate the generated caption, the evaluation module is more natural and comprehensive. Considering the requirements for image fidelity, this topic proposes a GAN-based image description. The Attention mechanism is introduced to improve image fidelity, which makes the generated caption more accurate and more close to human language expression.

Keywords: GAN · Deep learning · Attention mechanism · Image caption · LSTM

1 Introduction

Image caption, as its name suggests, generates natural language descriptions of specific images. Due to its extensive use in image-text cross-research, early infant education, and assistance from disadvantaged groups, it has become more and more popular in academia and industry in recent years. There has produced a lot of excellent researches and results related to it [1, 2].

With the rapid development of the Internet and computer technology, we have formed a world constructed with images. Using a large number of images to automatically generate easy-to-understand knowledge has become a topic that attracts wide attention. On the one hand, the number of images is increasing, on the other hand, people cannot retrieve and find the required information from such a large number of

© IFIP International Federation for Information Processing 2020
Published by Springer Nature Switzerland AG 2020
Z. Shi et al. (Eds.): IIP 2020, IFIP AICT 581, pp. 310–316, 2020.
https://doi.org/10.1007/978-3-030-46931-3_29

images. Therefore, we urgently seek to be able to automatically analyze and understand image information, a simpler and more human-friendly way of image understanding, and image caption was born to meet this need, it can automatically build images consistent with human cognition Semantic information. At the same time, in solving such a problem of interaction between images and NLP, the traditional deep learning technology is further improved and integrated to adapt to such a difficult task.

Computer vision is an important task in the computer field, and image perception and image texting are the main problems to be solved. Studying such an image understanding technology (image caption) has very important progress significance. This is a classic artificial intelligence, brain-computer collaboration and other framework for the classic problem of image information understanding and perception, that is, how to use the computer's brain-computer collaboration, neural Understanding to simulate people's analysis, cognition, recognition and memory functions of images. What's more, this technology will be a sign that traditional artificial intelligence is moving towards true artificial intelligence. In addition, the latest research results in the field of machine learning and artificial intelligence will also be further used for this task to improve performance and theoretical supplementation. In the process, they complement each other and promote each other.

2 Related Work

In general, the current method for image caption tasks in the field of deep learning is mainly the Encoder-decoder model. That is, the basic extension of the model based on CNN + RNN. In addition, after the introduction of the attention mechanism, the performance of the universal Encoder-decoder model has been significantly improved. In 2014, Baidu's Mao Junhua and others creatively combined CNN and RNN to deal with problems such as image annotation and image sentence retrieval. At the same time, they pioneered the application of deep learning to the image caption task and achieved good results. Although the model m-RNN proposed in this paper has some disadvantages, it has achieved very good results, so far, many domain papers still use this model as a baseline [3]. Later in 2014, GOOGLE proposed the NIC model to promote the m-RNN. They replaced RNN with LSTM and AlexNet with GooLeNet, in the end the model was a great success [4].

In recent years, there have been a lot of related work and many gratifying breakthroughs in the image caption task. This has benefited from convolutional neural networks and recurrent neural networks [5], but almost all solutions have not departed from the Encoder-Decoder framework. Lu, Xiong, Parikh and Socher introduce Attention mechanism in to the CNN Part and greatly improved the efficiency of the model [6]. Anderson, He and Buehler et al. added attention-mechanism to feature extraction and caption generation to improve performance [7]. Chen, Mu et al. Tried to introduce GAN's adversarial training ideas into the image caption task to improve performance even more [8]. However, they still leave issues of feature distortion and semantic relevance.

3 Model Combined with GAN

Next, we will propose an Image Caption Model combining GAN's adversarial training ideas, based on Convolution Neural Network (CNN) and Long Short Term Memory Network Network (LSTM). And introduce with the Attention Mechanism to improve performance. When we describe an image, we need to pay attention to the content of the image as well as the language foundation. When we get the word "cat," we focus on the cat part of the image and ignore the rest. The prediction of a word requires not only the introduction of attention mechanism in the language model, but also in the image.

3.1 CNN for Feature Extraction

Bottom-up Model. In this model, we define spatial regions based on bounding boxes and use Faster R-CNN to achieve bottom-up attention model [9, 10]. Faster R-CNN is an object detection model designed to identify object instances belonging to certain classes and localize them using bounding boxes. The final output of the model includes the softmax distribution on the class labels and the class-specific bounding box optimization proposed by each box. To pre-train the bottom-up attention model, we first initialize Faster R-CNN using pre-trained ResNet-101 for classification on ImageNet. To predict the attributes of region i, we embed the average merged convolutional feature vi with the learned ground truth object classes and feed them to define the softmax distribution on each attribute class and the additional output of the "no attribute" class Layer.

3.2 LSTM for Caption Generation

Top-down Model. General RNN cannot save too much information, there is only one state in the hidden layer, if we add another state C to save long-term information, the problem will be solved. LSTM is an improved recurrent neural network, it uses gate to control long-term status C [11]. The gate can be expressed as:

$$g(x) = \sigma(Wx + b) \tag{1}$$

W is the weight vector of the gate and b is the bias term. σ is the sigmoid function and the range is (0,1), so the state of the gate is half open and half closed. The final output of the LSTM is jointly controlled by the output gate and cell state:

$$h_t = o_t \cdot \tanh(c_t) \tag{2}$$

Because of the control of oblivion gate, it can save the information of a long time ago, and because of the control of the input door, it can avoid the current inconsequential content from entering the memory.

3.3   Attention Mechanism

The AM model is one of the most important developments in the field of NLP in the past few years, and appears in most current papers with the Encoder-Decoder framework [12]. But the AM model can be used as a general idea. When the general RNN model generates a language sequence, the predicted next word is only related to its first n words.

$$y_i = f(y_{i-1}, y_{i-2}, y_{i-3}, \ldots, C) \tag{3}$$

The above formula C represents semantic encoding. Obviously, the semantic meaning of each word is unreasonable. A word will not only be related to the nearest word, so we give each word a probability distribution and express its relevance to other words. And replace C with C_i.

$$C_i = \sum_{j=1}^{T_x} a_{ij} h_j \tag{4}$$

T_x represents the number of other words related to C_i, and α_{ij} represents the probability of attention between two words. h_j is the information of the word itself. The question now is how to calculate the probability distribution. It is usually to calculate the similarity between the current input information H_i and the previous information h_j

After the multi-layer convolution structure, the image information is compressed into a vector I. When predicting each word, you need to associate some information in the vector. The image attention parameter W is a parameter that we need to train to obtain.

$$A_i = I \cdot W_i \tag{5}$$

Finally, the functional relationship of each predicted word is as follows:

$$y_i = f(A_i, C_i, y_{i-1}, y_{i-2}, y_{i-3}, \ldots) \tag{6}$$

3.4   Adversarial Training of GAN

The Generative Adversarial Network consists of a Generative Network and a Discrimination Network [13, 14]. The generating network randomly samples from the latent space as input, and its output needs to mimic real samples in the training set as much as possible. The input of the discriminating network is the real sample or the output of the generating network. The purpose is to distinguish the output of the generating network from the real samples as much as possible. The generation network should try to deceive the identification network as much as possible. The two networks oppose each other and constantly adjust the parameters. The ultimate goal is to make the judgment network unable to judge whether the output of the generated network is true. Introduced the idea of GAN's adversarial training in LSTM to make the generated caption closer to human natural language expression, that is, more authentic. In the

LSTM model discussed above, we add a discriminator $D_\emptyset$ and an evaluator E, where $D_\emptyset$ is used to determine that the caption is a machine-generated probability d and E is used to evaluate the accuracy of caption. Combine the two scores and feed them back to the network to train the network:

$$r = \alpha * d + (1 - \alpha) * e \tag{7}$$

And the whole model is shown as Fig. 1:

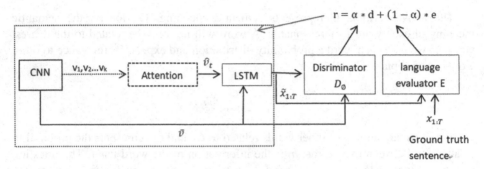

Fig. 1. Our whole model

4 Experiments

In order to compare with the prior art, we conducted a large number of experiments using the BLEU metrics [15] to evaluate the effectiveness of our model. Experiments used the MSCOCO 2014 data set, which includes 123000 images. The dataset contains 82783 images in the training set, 40504 images in the validation set and 40775 images in the test set. we use the whole 82783 training set images for training, and selects 5000 images for validation and 5000 images for testing from the official validation set.

4.1 Evaluating Indicator

A popular automatic evaluation method is the BLEU algorithm proposed by IBM. The BLEU method first calculates the number of matching n-grams in the reference sentence and the generated sentence, and then calculates the ratio of the number of n-grams in the generated sentence. As an evaluation indicator. It focuses on the accuracy of generating words or phrases in sentences. The accuracy of each order N-gram can be calculated by the following formula:

$$P_n = \frac{\sum_i \sum_k \min\left(h_k(c_i), max_{j \in m} h_k\left(s_{ij}\right)\right)}{\sum_i \sum_k \min(h_k(c_i))} \tag{8}$$

The upper limit of N is 4, which means that only the accuracy of 4-gram can be calculated.

4.2   Results and Discussion

This model is improved on the basis of the basic model and improves the performance on the basis of the baseline. By comparing with the two previous models, we get a higher accuracy rate. As we can see in the Table 1, compared with other mainstream algorithms, one and two keywords perform better, but the effect of getting more keywords is not good.

Table 1. Comparison with other methods on the MSCOCO dataset

Model	BLEU-1	BLEU-2	BLEU-3	BLEU-4
GLA	56.8	37.2	23.2	14.6
BRNN	64.2	45.1	30.4	20.3
Google NIC	66.6	46.1	**32.9**	**24.6**
OURS	**67.6**	**47.1**	31.8	22.8

5   Conclusions

Image caption is a complex task, and deep learning-based frameworks have become the current mainstream method. This paper proposes a multi-attention mechanism based on GAN training methods, which requires understanding the syntax of sentence generation and the content in images. Different words have different levels of attention to image content, and contexts have different levels of attention. Experimental results show that under the BLEU evaluation standard, the attention mechanism combined with GAN training methods can achieve better results.

References

1. Shi, Z.: Mind Computation. World Scientific Publishing, Singapore (2017)
2. Vinyals, O., et al.: Show and tell: a neural image caption generator. In: Computer Vision and Pattern Recognition, pp. 3156–3164. IEEE (2015)
3. Mao, J., Xu, W., Yang, Y., et al.: Explain images with multimodal recurrent neural networks. arXiv preprint arXiv:1410.1090 (2014)
4. Vinyals, O., Toshev, A., Bengio, S., et al.: Show and tell: lessons learned from the 2015 MSCOCO image captioning challenge. IEEE Trans. Pattern Anal. Mach. Intell. **39**(4), 652–663 (2016)
5. Hollink, L., Little, S., Hunter, J.: Evaluating the application of semantic inferencing rules to image annotation. In: International Conference on Knowledge Capture, pp. 91–98. ACM (2005)
6. Lu, J., Xiong, C., Parikh, D., et al.: Knowing when to look: adaptive attention via a visual sentinel for image captioning. In: Proceedings of the IEEE Conference on Computer Vision and Pattern Recognition, pp. 375–383 (2017)
7. Anderson, P., He, X., Buehler, C., et al.: Bottom-up and top-down attention for image captioning and visual question answering. In: Proceedings of the IEEE Conference on Computer Vision and Pattern Recognition, pp. 6077–6086 (2018)

8. Chen, C., Mu, S., Xiao, W., et al.: Improving image captioning with conditional generative adversarial nets. In: Proceedings of the AAAI Conference on Artificial Intelligence, vol. 33, pp. 8142–8150 (2019)
9. Ren, S., He, K., Girshick, R., et al.: Faster R-CNN: towards real-time object detection with region proposal networks. In: Advances in Neural Information Processing Systems, pp. 91–99 (2015)
10. Girshick, R.: Fast R-CNN. In: 2015 IEEE International Conference on Computer Vision (ICCV), pp. 1440–1448. IEEE (2015)
11. Jia, X., et al.: Guiding the long-short term memory model for image caption generation. In: IEEE International Conference on Computer Vision, pp. 2407–2415. IEEE (2016)
12. Yan, S., Xie, Y., Wu, F., et al.: Image captioning via hierarchical attention mechanism and policy gradient optimization. Sig. Process. **167**, 107329 (2020)
13. Yu, L., Zhang, W., Wang, J., et al.: SeqGAN: sequence generative adversarial nets with policy gradient. In: Thirty-First AAAI Conference on Artificial Intelligence (2017)
14. Dai, B., Fidler, S., Urtasun R., et al.: Towards diverse and natural image descriptions via a conditional GAN. In: Proceedings of the IEEE International Conference on Computer Vision, pp. 2970–2979 (2017)
15. Papineni, K., Roukos, S., Ward, T., et al.: BLEU: a method for automatic evaluation of machine translation. In: Proceedings of the 40th Annual Meeting on Association for Computational Linguistics, pp. 311–318. Association for Computational Linguistics (2002)

Author Index

Printed in the United States
by Baker & Taylor Publisher Services

Printed in the United States
by Baker & Taylor Publisher Services